8/01

MODERN ESSAYS

FRANK KERMODE

MODERN ESSAYS

fp

FONTANA PRESS

CONTENTS

ACKNOWLEDGEMENTS

Many of the pieces in this collection have already appeared in *Puzzles and Epiphanies* (London, Routledge and Kegan Paul, first published in 1962) and *Continuities* (London, Routledge and Kegan Paul, first published in 1968). For permission to reprint pieces gathered here for the first time I have to thank the *Listener* for the second half of 'Obscenity and the Public Interest', for 'The Public Image' which forms part of the essay on Muriel Spark, and for the articles on Iris Murdoch, Anthony Burgess, and John Updike; the *New York Review of Books* for the essays on Father Ong, Walter Benjamin, and Eric Bentley; the *New American Review* for the first part of 'Obscenity and the Public Interest'; and the *Atlantic Monthly* for the essay on W. H. Auden. The second half of the essay on Robert Musil has been published as the Preface to Robert Musil's *Five Women*, translated by Eithne Wilkins and Ernst Kaiser and published by Seymour Lawrence of Boston, U.S.A.

J.F.K.

August 1970

PREFACE TO THE SECOND EDITION

Almost twenty years have passed since the first publication of this book, and parts of it were written some years before that, so it might be said that the title is no longer quite appropriate. Yet it is part of the continuing interest of the modern that it dates – it does so unevenly, but nevertheless must always do so. That is why another effort of modernity, revising, extending, rejecting or professing to reject the last kind, must always be made; some perception of that truth lies behind the modern and already dated vogue of post-modernism. But there is always continuity as well as difference. Criticism is in part a defiance of the action of time, to which it is as subject as anything else, and so, like everything else, it must constantly be renewed. But the dilapidation, the unmodernizing, that time so impartially imposes on books and authors does not mean that the past is necessarily junk; it can keep its value, or, to express it quite differently, it can be incorporated into some later discourse. Even the old modern can be made modern again, and to make it so is the task of readers.

I'll take the opportunity to make a few scattered remarks about some of the pieces in this book. First, the opening chapter about poets and dancers, though thirty years old, doesn't, as I re-inspect it after many years, compel me to give up the idea that it is one of my better performances. I had been hoping to do something like it, but it was precipitated by a piece of sheer luck. I had been trying to find out more about how Loïe Fuller actually gets her outstanding effects – I needed information more technical than could be got from the poems and prose – poems and drawings of her exalted admirers. When I thought I'd exhausted the possibilities of the relevant London libraries, I made the last and least promising trip on my list, which was to the library at Cecil Sharp House. There, by the merest chance, I found not a book but a man, Mr Nicol, who knew more about Fuller and her life and her tricks than anybody else on earth, who danced in her company, and inherited her papers. Researchers need a bit of luck, and this was in my case the most conspicuous instance of it. That piece had no excuse not to be good. It might be as well to add that in writing it I wasn't much concerned with one important aspect of the dance at the turn of the century, namely its association with what John Stokes, in his recent book (*In the Nineties*, Harvester Wheatsheaf, 1989), calls 'coarse and dangerous places', such as music halls. Nowadays one would probably pay more attention to the socio-historical implications of this apparently incongruous juxtaposition – Mallarméan aesthetics and solemnly randy stage-door johnnies. But there was a conspiracy, of perhaps equal historical interest, to preserve an image of Fuller as existing in a sphere remote from all such impurity, a conspiracy in which the photographers joined the artists and the poets, and I was more concerned with the implications of that. Incidentally, this essay, when it first appeared in *Theatre Arts*, was accompanied by some splendid photographs, one of which is reproduced on the cover of this edition.

The longish piece about The Modern is, of its nature, not going to sound up-to-date a quarter of a century later; for instance, politics, said to have ceased at that time to be central to speculations about modernism, has now made an impressive comeback. But the general point, that there are broadly two kinds of modernism, here called, perhaps rather too elaborately, palaeo- and neo-modernism, is one that has to be made over and over again in various ways and new terms. The issue on which it bears has been discussed from viewpoints as distinct from mine as Paul de Man's in his celebrated essay 'Literary History and Literary Modernity' (in *Blindness and Insight*, 2nd. ed, Methuen, 1983). Moreover, as de Man well knew, being modern often involves an ignorance of history, so that another characteristic of the modern is that it often unwittingly repeats itself.

Obscenity prosecutions are no longer brought under the Obscene Publications Act; loaded though it was against liberal interpretations, it offered the police and the Crown lawyers too little assurance of convictions, especially after the pyrrhic success of John Calder's appeal against the verdict returned at the trial I here discuss. But anybody with the slightest interest in the subject is aware that obscenity prosecutions have continued – brought, by persons as ingenious as they are righteous, under other statutes or at common law. Defending oneself in these actions has – in the absence of any consideration of literary merit or public interest, or any requirement that a book should be treated as a totality rather than as an assemblage of words, some clean, some not – become even more hazardous than before. So the subject is far from dead, and memories of one notable trial, fresh at the time of writing, should still have some interest.

As to the critics discussed, it may be fair to say that although a selection more recent would contain a different set of names, these are still worth attending to. Benjamin was only just coming to notice when that chapter first appeared. The fact that it is nowadays the fashion to disparage Edmund Wilson is proof that we badly lack an Edmund

Wilson, if only to explain why it is so important to maintain high standards of intelligence and prose in reviews.

Some of the novelists and poets are snapped here at a relatively early stage in their brilliant careers (Murdoch, Spark, Burgess, Updike) and others, Tate and Auden for instance, have joined the past, though their reputations have so far survived, Auden's more confidently than Tate's, but these are early days. I have subsequently had many more afterthoughts on Wallace Stevens, and many more on Auden, but these later meditations don't involve any fundamental change of mind, or loss of affection. I should add, though, that I was wrong to suggest that 'the vogue' of Stevens might be ending. The number and weight of books devoted to keeping it going is now close to appalling, and makes you see why people complain of their being too much literary criticism.

There may indeed be too much, but anybody who has himself committed a lot of it will be happy to reflect that it must go on, even if too prodigally; and that it must sometimes even return on itself, not only because, as Stevens remarked, poetry is never 'fully disclosed', but also because, as he further remarked, 'everything is complicated; if it were not so, life and poetry and everything else would be a bore'. 'Everything else' includes criticism and also the complications, temporal and otherwise, of the critic's life, its interactions, or imbrications, of past and present: a point I can't help meditating as I turn these pages once more.

Cambridge, November, 1989.

ONE

POET AND DANCER BEFORE
DIAGHILEV

Diaghilev figures in the title simply as a terminus; he arrived in
Paris in 1909, and everybody knows what happened. *'Le rêve de
Mallarmé se réalise'*, said Ghéon. What dream of Mallarmé?
That which found a true theatrical sonority, a stage liberated
from cardboard falsities; which emerged from a confluence of
the other arts and yet remained, as Wagner did not, theatre.
The Ballets Russes demonstrated the correspondence of the arts
so wonderfully that in comparison Wagner's effort was, said
Camille Mauclair, *'une gaucherie barbare'*. Diaghilev arrived,
not a moment too soon, in response to prayers from both sides
of the Channel. One could trace the developments in taste
which prepared his reception – not only in the limited sphere
of the dance but in writings on actors (the cult of Duse, for
example), in the fashionable admiration for oriental art and
theatre, in *avant-garde* agitation for theatrical reform. In March
1908 *The Mask*, a quarterly dedicated to this end and strongly
under the influence of Gordon Craig, prayed in its opening
editorial for a religion that did not 'rest upon knowledge nor
rely upon the World' but rather brought together 'Music,
Architecture, and Movement' to heal 'the Evil ... which has
separated these three Arts and which leaves the world without
a belief'. The editor can hardly have expected his prayers to be
answered so soon – not precisely by the theatrical reforms he
had in mind, but by the Russian dancers, prophets of that Concord and Renaissance he so earnestly requested. Havelock Ellis,
with his usual wide view, put the situation thus in *The Dance
of Life* (1923): 'If it is significant that Descartes appeared a few
years after the death of Malherbe, it is equally significant that
Einstein was immediately preceded by the Russian Ballet.'

Ellis makes Diaghilev a John the Baptist of a 'classico-mathe-
matical Renaissance', and the notion that this was a renaissance of some kind or other was evidently in the air. However,
such credit as is due to its heralds should not all be awarded to
the Russian ballet. There was, obviously, Isadora Duncan; but
Isadora doesn't take us to the root of the matter. Where, for

my purposes, that lies, I can perhaps suggest in this way : what Camille Mauclair said of Diaghilev was somewhat disloyally said, for he had used almost the same words years before of the American dancer Loïe Fuller. Art, he declared, was one homogeneous essence lying at the root of the diversified arts, not a fusion of them; and Loïe Fuller was *it*, 'a spectacle ... which defies all definition ... Art, nameless, radiant ... a homogeneous and complete place ... indefinable, absolute ... a fire above all dogmas'. The language is Mallarméan; as we shall see, it was all but impossible to write of Loïe Fuller otherwise unless you were very naïve. Still, not even Mallarmé could start a renaissance single-handed, and there has to be a word or two here about whatever it was that predisposed everybody to get excited in this particular way about dancers.

The peculiar prestige of dancing over the past seventy or eighty years has, I think, much to do with the notion that it somehow represents art in an undissociated and unspecialized form – a notion made explicit by Yeats and hinted at by Valéry. The notion is essentially primitivist; it depends upon the assumption that mind and body, form and matter, image and discourse have undergone a process of dissociation, which it is the business of art momentarily to mend. Consequently dancing is credited with a sacred priority over the other arts, as by Havelock Ellis (whose essay is valuable as a summary of the theoretical development I am now discussing) and, with less rhapsody and more philosophy, by Mrs Langer in the twelfth chapter of *Feeling and Form* and (more flatly) in the opening essay of *Problems of Art*. In view of this primitivizing, it is worth remembering that the increase of prestige was contemporaneous with a major effort by anthropologists, liturgiologists, and folklorists to discover the roots of the dance in ritual of all kinds, and also with the development of a certain medical interest in dancing. We are all familiar with the interest shown by the generation of Valéry and that of Eliot in these matters; and from Eliot, at the time when he was busy with Jane Harrison and Frazer we can get some notion of how they struck the literary imagination. Here, for instance, is a passage from an uncollected *Criterion* review of two books on dancing :

Anyone who would contribute to our imagination of what the ballet may perform in future ... should begin by a close study of dancing among primitive peoples. ... He should also have studied the evolution of Christian and other liturgy. For is not the High Mass – as performed, for instance, at the Madeleine in Paris – one of the highest developments of dancing? And finally, he should track down the secrets of rhythm in the still undeveloped science of neurology.

Mr Eliot found the Noh plays exciting and praised Massine for providing in the ignorant modern theatre that rhythm regarded as essential by Aristotle. But the peculiar modern view could hardly have been developed before dancing became an accredited fine art; and the date for this seems to be 1746, when Batteux included it among the five with music, poetry, painting, and sculpture. The general and developing Romantic tendency was to give music pre-eminence as being non-discursive, 'autonomous' as the word now is, referring to nothing outside itself for meaning; poems would be like that if there were not a basic flaw in their medium, the habit that words have of meaning something in ordinary usage. But some of this prestige was undoubtedly captured by dancing; it is more 'natural' and more 'primitive' than music, more obviously expressive of what Mrs Langer calls 'patterns of sentience' and 'the mythic consciousness'. I use this late terminology because it is careful enough to avoid certain radical confusions. The dance, though expressive, is impersonal, like a Symbolist poem that comes off. Miss Deirdre Pridden[1] finds the proper word to be Ortega y Gasset's 'dehumanization'; the dancer *vide la danse, autant que faire se peut, de son humaine matière*. Something might here be said about organicist theories of expressiveness in Modern Dance, opposed not only to conventional ballet (as Fuller and Duncan and Yeats were) but sometimes even to the use of music as irrelevant to the *Gestalt* of the dance; the source of these theories is Delsarte, but they have been much refined. However, there is no disagreement from the fundamental principle that dance is the most primitive, non-discursive art, offering a pre-scientific image of life, an intuitive truth. Thus it is the emblem of the Romantic image. Dance belongs to a period before the self and the world were divided, and so achieves naturally that 'original unity' which, according to Barfield for instance, modern poetry can produce only by a great and exhausting effort of fusion.

1. *The Art of The Dance in French Literature*. London, Adam & Charles Black, 1952.

The nineties poets wrote endlessly about dancers, welcomed foreign troupes and prepared the way for the serious impact of the Japanese Noh in the next decade.² But they also enjoyed the dancers themselves, and regularly fell in love with them. Symons and his friends would meet the Alhambra girls after the show and take them along to the Crown for drink and serious talk; serious not because of what Symons called the 'learned fury' of these 'maenads of the decadence', but in a humbler way. 'This was the epoch of the Church and Stage Guild, Stewart Headlam's club for clergy and actors. Headlam believed 'in the Mass, the Ballet, and the Single Tax' and such was his balletolatry that he wrote a book on ballet technique. But he also believed that the liturgy must not continue to be deprived of dancing, and so laboured to make the stage respectable, that the stigma on dancing might be removed. Among the membership girls from the Empire and the Alhambra preponderated. Headlam was not original in his liturgical views, which may have gained currency from Anglo-Catholic propaganda for ceremonies not explicitly forbidden;³ however, he gives one a pretty good idea of what must have been a common enough belief in this passage from an article he contributed to his own *Church Reformer* (October 1884) in a series on the Catechism :

... to take an illustration from the art of dancing, which perhaps more than all other arts is an outward and visible sign of an inward and spiritual grace, ordained by the Word of God Himself, as a means whereby we receive the same and a pledge to assure us thereof; and which has suffered even more than the other arts from the utter antisacramentalism of British philistia. Your Manichean Protestant, and your superfine rationalist, reject the Dance as worldly, frivolous, sensual, and so forth; and your dull, stupid Sensualist sees legs, and grunts with some satisfaction : but your Sacramentalist knows something worth more than both of these.

2. It is quite untrue, by the way, that Fenollosa and Pound 'introduced' the Noh plays; interest in them is at least as old as this century.

3. Mr Ian Fletcher directs my attention to Sabine Baring-Gould's periodical *The Sacristy* (1871–2) where liturgical dancing is discussed with other matters such as liturgical lights and symbolic zoology, and to later ecclesiastical contributions.

He knows what perhaps the dancer herself may be partially unconscious of, that we live now by faith and not by sight, and that the poetry of dance is the expression of unseen spiritual grace. 'She all her being flings into the dance.' 'None dare interpret all her limbs express.' These are the words of a genuine sacramentalist...

The poet is T. Gordon Hake. Headlam knew Symons well, and also Yeats and many other nineties poets and painters. He seems, in his Guild and in writing of this kind, to reflect rather accurately the liturgical, poetic, and music-hall aspects of this renaissance of dancing. The liturgical ingredient developed luxuriously in the border country of Anglo-Catholicism; witness R. H. Benson's essay, 'On the Dance as a Religious Exercise', an account of the Mass as a dramatic dance:

The Catholic ... is not ashamed to take his place with the worshippers of Isis and Cybele, with King David, and with the naked Fijean, and to dance with all his might before the Lord.

The antiquarian interest culminated in G. R. S. Mead's *The Sacred Dance of Jesus* (published in *The Quest* in 1910, but long excogitated). This was Havelock Ellis's chief source, and it is a work of great and curious learning, written in a long tradition of attempts to explain Matt. xi. 1.7, 'We have piped unto you and ye have not danced.' Mead was most interested in the second-century *Hymn of Jesus*, but he deals with the Fathers and with medieval church dancing, with the liturgies of the Greek Orthodox and Armenian churches, and so forth. I doubt if Mead is taken very seriously by modern historians – he isn't cited in the large bibliography of Backman's *Religious Dances* (1952) – but for a while he mattered a lot. Yeats, for example, went to his lectures. He was by no means the only zealous dance-historian of the time. Toulouse-Lautrec, who was not interested in these matters, had an English *savant* thrown out of a dance-hall for plaguing him about antiquity; this could have been Mead, but not necessarily. At a time when it was relatively easy for a dancer to acquire a reputation for learning, Loïe Fuller was said on high authority (Anatole France) to be wise in the history of dancing; she took as her prototype

Miriam, who, according to Philo, as quoted by Mead, symbolizes perfect sense, as Moses symbolizes perfect mind.

The presence of the *savant* in the *bal* tells us something
about the seriousness with which music-hall dancing was taken
on both sides of the Channel. From Symons and Goncourt one
knows that it was so; and of course this was a period of close
relations between London and Paris. Yvette Guilbert often
appeared in London, Marie Lloyd and others in Paris; it was
fashionable to treat them both as very great artists. This cult of
the music-hall has been persistent; there is a classic statement
of it in Mr Eliot's essay on Marie Lloyd (1932), and it still goes
on in a London which has only one or two feeble surviving
halls, constantly threatened with demolition. Nothing distresses
some English intellectuals more than the closing of a music-
hall. This attitude is a weakly descendant of a positive *avant-
garde* reaction against commercial theatre in the nineties; failing dance-drama or über-marionettes, there were still Marie
Lloyd and Little Tich, defying cultural and social division,
freely satirical, speaking with the voice of the belly. You could
talk of Yvette Guilbert, who, according to André Raffalovitch,
sang 'the sufferings of those the world calls vile', in the same
breath as the Duse.

The Parisian music-halls were certainly not short of a similar
intellectual *réclame*, and had their place, as part of the metropolitan experience, with all the other pleasures devised for an
élite that took its pleasures seriously – fine clothes, Japanese
prints, neurasthenia. They are as important in the early history
of modern art as folk-music and primitive painting, with which
indeed they are obviously associated. Our received idea of this
world owes more to Toulouse-Lautrec than anybody else, and
there is no reason to think it very inaccurate. The circus, the
vaudeville, the *bal*, were serious pleasures; the primitive, the
ugly, the exotic were in demand. The brutal patter of Aristide
Bruant, La Goulue coarsely cheeking the Prince of Wales, the
emaciated and psychopathic May Belfort, the cherished ugliness of Mme Abdala; all are characteristic. The mood is that
of the violent Lautrec drawings of Guilbert and Jane Avril, of
dancers calling themselves Grille d'Egout or La Goulue, of café-
concerts with such names as Le Divan Japonais and prostitutes
with such *noms de guerre* as Outamoro. In this atmosphere all
the dancers I am concerned with did their work, and were
treated very seriously.

Of a good many of them it was enough to say, as Symons did in his excited lines on Nini Patte-en-l'air, that they possessed

> The art of knowing how to be
> Part lewd, aesthetical in part,
> And *fin-de-siècle* essentially.

Symons was one of those Englishmen whose solemn Parisian pleasures were the admiration of Lautrec – Conder, the strangest of them, he often drew, superbly drunk in his fine evening clothes. But Symons was building an aesthetic in which dancing was to have a central place – the climactic essay is called 'The World as Ballet' – and so his interest was slightly different from the painter's. Lautrec was equally absorbed by La Goulue and Jane Avril; but for Symons the former, a Messalina who wore her heart embroidered on the bottom of her knickers, was less important than the latter, who demonstrated that the female body was 'Earth's most eloquent Music, divinest human harmony'.

Some time in the thirties a French exhibition, devoted to life under the Third Republic, showed Jane Avril and Loïe Fuller as representing the Dance, and most of what follows is concerned with these dancers. Like Fuller, Avril had the reputation of literacy, and enjoyed the friendship of Lautrec, Renoir, Théodor Wyczewa, Maurice Barrès. It is clear from Lautrec's posters that what interested him was the lack of conventionality, almost the *gaucherie*, in her attitudes, her being set apart from all the other girls. She danced a good deal alone, and not only in the solo variations of the quadrille; she designed her own dresses, and got some of her effects by whirling movements possibly learned from the English dancer Kate Vaughan, also perhaps a source of inspiration to Fuller – she was well thought of in the eighties and later for bringing back long skirts for dancers. Avril, again like Fuller, lacked formal training and mechanical predictability; Pierre Charron said she was like

> une fleur balancée, troublante
> Au souffle du vent chaud qui l'endort doucement ...

Avril had special privileges at the Moulin Rouge; she alone was not required to take part in the quadrille. In the poster Toulouse-Lautrec did for her London season you see her waving a thin leg at a different angle from the other three dancers'; in other drawings she is alone, one leg seemingly twisted, the other held clumsily up, or circulating skinny and solitary in the shadow of La Goulue. Symons saw her dancing before the mirrors in the Moulin Rouge and wrote of her 'morbid, vague, ambiguous grace, in a poem called 'La Mélinite : Moulin Rouge', which Yeats in 1897 called 'one of the most perfect lyrics of our time'. The only possible explanation of this enormous over-estimate is the irresistible appeal of a poem combining the Salome of the Romantic Agony with Pater's Monna Lisa :

> Alone, apart, one dancer watches
> Her mirrored, morbid grace;
> Before the mirror face to face,
> Alone she watches
> Her morbid vague, ambiguous grace,
> And enigmatically smiling
> In the mysterious night,
> She dances for her own delight.

But she had talent. Whereas La Goulue and others gambolled, says Francis Jourdain, Avril danced. '*L'arabesque tracée dans l'espace par une jambe inspirée, n'est plus un signe vain, c'est une écriture*,' he says, echoing, perhaps unconsciously, a phrase of Mallarmé.

There is small doubt – and here lies much of her interest – that this dancer owed most to the air of morbidity of which Symons speaks, and specifically to the long time she spent in her teens as a patient of Charcot at the Salpétrière. This hospital, and particularly the ward of the *grandes hystériques*, in which Avril had been treated for her chorea, was used as a kind of alternative to music-halls; Charcot and his patients welcomed visitors, and the symptoms of hysteria[4] were well known to a large public. Charcot is celebrated for having turned Freud 'from a neurologist into a psychopathologist', but despite his discovery that he could induce hysterical symptoms by hypnotism, and his observation that certain nervous dis-

4. Still thought of as a female disorder; Freud's Vienna paper on a male hysteric brought him a reproof from a senior who said that if Freud had known any Greek he would have seen that male hysteria is an impossibility. *Sigmund Freud, Life & Work I.* By E. Jones. London, Hogarth Press, 1953, p. 254.

orders were always a question of 'la chose génitale', Charcot himself did not know as much as Freud was to learn from watching him.[5] He was greatly impressed by the resemblance between the symptoms of his patients and medieval descriptions and representations of demoniac possession and obsessive dancing. He seems not to have known the theory, now, I gather, beyond dispute, that the saltatory epidemics were caused by ergotism, a disease brought on by eating blighted rye. As early as 1877 he wrote of an hysteria patient who had hallucinations of serpents and exhibited 'in an embryonic state and sporadic form, a specimen' of medieval dancing mania, emphasizing that the symptoms appeared 'in a rudimentary state' and were arrested by compression of the left ovary. In 1887 he wrote, with Paul Richer, a book called Les Démoniaques dans l'art, in which he tries to show that the convulsions and dances of the possessed are characteristic of various stages in the hysterical seizures he had observed, and of which he shows sketches. Avril was never permanently cured of chorea, and had ample opportunity to observe her fellow-patients; whether by accident or design she seems to have reproduced some of the symptoms of hysterical dancing, doubtless in a rudimentary form, and I have no doubt that Charcot would have found Lautrec's famous poster 'Jane Avril aux serpents' characteristic of hysteria (compare, for example, the sketch from Mazza da Bologna on p. 72 of Les Démoniaques). 'Ambiguous grace', certainly; but the ambiguity was agreeable to a public much interested in 'neurasthenia' (an American discovery, but rapidly naturalized in Paris). Considered in this light, as combining certain powerful aesthetic and pathological interests of the period, it is easy to see how Avril produced a frisson nouveau and encouraged the literati to love the highest when they saw it in the Moulin Rouge.

Under these conditions it is not surprising that a good many dancers came to be associated with avant-garde movements in the other arts, and there was to be an idéiste dancer, Valentine de Saint-Point, who performed against a screen upon which

5. Jones traces the development of Freud's psychoanalysis from this point. By 1892 he knew that 'sexual disturbances constitute the sole indispensable cause of neurasthenia' (I. 282) (he gave up this word later) and by 1895, nine years after his studies with Charcot, the pattern was taking psychoanalytical shape. It was formed by 1897, (I. 294).

'geometric shadows' were cast,[6] and a Cubist and Dadaist dancer, Nina Payne, whose dancing to jazz music greatly pleased the fastidious Levinson. The Cubism, he said, must have something to do with a strange cylindrical *couvrechef* she wore. There were also vaguely Vorticist dancers in Mme Strindberg's Cave of the Golden Calf in London just before the first war; we know that cut-outs and shadows were used (see F. M. Ford's novel, *The Marsden Case*) but the memoirs of the period are hazy about what went on, and Miss Margaret Morris, who certainly knows, will not say. Isadora Duncan was a 'symbolist' dancer; but it is sometimes forgotten that she derived much that was admirable in her dancing from Loïe Fuller, and this brings me to the most important of all these names, to the woman who seemed to be doing almost single-handed what Diaghilev was later to achieve only with the help of great painters, musicians, and dancers.

Many living people must have seen Loïe Fuller, but there is no book about her, except her own autobiography, and no powerful tradition, as there is for Isadora Duncan. The standard reference books are scanty and inaccurate, and so should I have been, had I not had the good luck to encounter Mr E. J. Nicol, a nephew of the Miss Nolan who not only backed Fuller but carried out the famous experiments in textiles and dyes which were associated with the dancer's vogue. Mr Nicol also belonged to Fuller's company as a child, and knows all about a great many matters which were kept secret, mostly of a technical sort. For all correct comments on such techniques in what follows Mr Nicol is responsible, and for none that is incorrect. The rest of the material comes from diaries, newspapers, theatre programmes, publicity hand-outs, and the like; and, of course, the autobiography, *Fifteen Years of a Dancer's Life* (French edition, 1908; English, 1913).

Loïe Fuller was born in Illinois in 1862, under trying circumstances: she claimed to have caught a cold at birth which was never cured. She used this claim in much the same way as Isadora insisted that her character was predetermined from the womb ('Before I was born my mother was in great agony of spirit and in a tragic situation. She could take no food except iced oysters and iced champagne'). Throughout her life, Fuller

6. She was a friend of Marinetti and wrote on the place of women in Futurism. Like Florence Farr, she eventually retreated to the East.

made much of her congenital ill-health and demanded certain extraordinary attentions. Mr Nicol does not think she was particularly frail. A talented child, she captivated audiences with her songs at the age of five, and at the age of thirteen with her temperance lectures, during which she exhibited coloured illustrations of the liver. Later she went on the stage. Her early career was undistinguished, but she gave a hint of things to come by forming her own company and taking it on a long, but disastrous, tour of South America. In 1889 she made her first London appearance in *Caprice*, which opened on 22 October at the Gaiety and closed almost at once. She went back to New York. At this time she had played everything from Shakespeare to burlesque but she had never danced.

In the early days of what is called Modern Dance it seems to have been a convention that all the best things happened by accident, like Ruth St Denis's getting the idea of her oriental dancing from a cigarette packet. Loïe Fuller encouraged the idea that she developed from one happy accident to the next. The first radical bit of luck came when she was acting, at a small New York theatre, a part in which she was hypnotized. To get the atmosphere right the management arranged for the stage to be illuminated entirely by green footlights, while the orchestra played sad music. During this hurriedly mounted piece, Fuller found herself on stage wearing a gauzy Indian skirt that was much too long for her. She says in her book that it was a present from an heroic admirer who later fell in the Khyber Pass; and she told a French historian that she got it from another girl. Anyway, she hit upon the idea of gliding hypnotically about the stage, holding the skirt up. To her surprise there were pleased exclamations from the house: 'It's a butterfly!', 'It's an orchid!' She danced around amid applause and then dropped ecstatically at the hypnotist's feet, 'completely enveloped in a cloud of the light material'. Next day she put the skirt on again and was studying it in a looking-glass when she noticed that sunlight made it translucent. 'Golden reflections played in the folds of the sparkling silk, and in this light my body was revealed in a shadowy contour.' Thereupon 'gently, almost religiously', she waved the silk about, and saw that she had 'obtained modulations of a character before unknown ... Finally I reached a point where each movement of the body was expressed in the folds of the silk, in a play of colours and draperies that could be mathematically and systematically calculated.'[7]

Such was the basis of her original act. She whirled about with her arms aloft – later she extended them with sticks concealed in the drapery as shown in Toulouse-Lautrec's lithograph – and the resultant spiral or serpentine effect she differentiated into twelve characteristic motions or dances, each carried out with different lighting. The lighting was provided by an electric lantern with coloured glasses, another device she was later to develop to an extraordinary degree. The final dance was performed in total darkness save for a single ray of yellow light crossing the stage. From the outset she invited attention to those optical effects; she was never beautiful, and even in these days too plump for her shadowy contour to be an important part of her appeal. This was new, though she admits modestly that at this stage she was 'far from imagining that I had hold of a principle capable of revolutionizing a branch of aesthetics'. Her very ignorance of classical technique was to contribute, with the hypnotic attitudes, the resemblances to natural objects, and the optical illusions, to her establishment as a living emblem of a new aesthetic.

The act was almost immediately successful. 'Three cheers for the orchid, the cloud and the butterfly!' cried the New York audience. But the New York managers were full of greed and duplicity; she was at once plagued by imitators, some even

7. This story may not be absolutely true. In the *Magazine of Art* for 1894 there is an article by Percy Anderson, a man so anxious to harry the short skirt from the English stage that he made, for an opera called *The Nautch Girl* (Savoy, 1889), a copy of an 'eastern dancing-dress' in the 'Indian Museum'. 'The great quantity of material used, in order that the dancers might envelop themselves in billowy folds of drapery, seemed to be an obstacle, but the result was curiously graceful. A clever American dancer, who was engaged at the Gaiety Theatre, saw that the idea might be even further developed; so, with the practical instincts of her race, she sped across the ocean and appeared at the New York Casino Theatre in the now famous "Serpentine" dance which has set the impressionable Parisians frantic with delight. . . . All this was the result of one dress, which is lying hidden in the security (or obscurity) of the Indian Museum.' This seems a more likely story, though Mr Nicol doesn't accept it, and Fuller was not appearing as a dancer at the Gaiety in 1889. The truth may be that her having such a good idea owed a little more than she admitted to other dancers (like Kate Vaughan) and their dresses. But she made it her own.

using her name (a trouble she was to have for many years) and after certain vicissitudes and wanderings she found her true home in Paris, where she arrived in October 1892. She was engaged to dance at the Folies-Bergère, and with a programme of five dances including the Serpentine she achieved a fantastic success, which was augmented later in the decade when she returned with new items. All over Europe and America she was imitated, but never successfully, largely because of the care she took to keep secret the technical apparatus upon which she depended. She was not overstating her triumph when she said that the usual audience at the Folies-Bergère was every evening 'lost amid a crowd composed of scholars, painters, sculptors, writers, and ambassadors'. Outside the theatre, students pelted her with flowers and drew her carriage; the police, about to take brisk action against a procession obstructing circulation at the Madeleine, held their hands when they discovered that all was in honour of La Loïe Fuller.

At the time of her first success she was taken up by Rodin, who declared that she was 'a woman of genius, with all the resources of talent' and 'a Tanagra figurine in action'. She painted Nature, he said, in the colours of Turner; she was the woman on the famous Pompeian frieze. Anatole France, who wrote a preface for her autobiography in 1908, called her 'marvellously intelligent' but added that it was her unconscious that really counted. 'She is an artist ... the chastest and most expressive of dancers, beautifully inspired, who reanimated within herself and restores to us the lost wonders of Greek mimicry, the art of those motions, at once voluptuous and mystical, which interpret the phenomena of nature and the life history of living things.' Other admirers were the Curies, to whom she later dedicated a remarkable dance. She knew anybody she cared to know. Pretty well all the theatrical artists of Paris represented her at this time, notably perhaps Steinlen and Toulouse-Lautrec, whose lithograph is probably the best of all; but she asked neither Lautrec nor Steinlen for posters, preferring their imitators. A pretty poster drawing by Chéret hung in her dressing-room. Perhaps she supposed herself too far from the real centre of Lautrec's interests; anyway, he soon moved on to more congenial subjects.

Loïe Fuller undoubtedly enjoyed all this. In a Paris that paid her 12,000 francs a month and was full of women wearing wide Loïe Fuller skirts, she expected a lot of attention. There is a note of rare disenchantment in an entry in Renard's diary (1901) which tells how he met Fuller in an omnibus, a shapeless figure too highly painted, sausage-fingered, with only the rings to make any divisions, an intermittent smile, as if everybody on the bus was the Public; vague myopic eyes. She was turned off the bus for not having her fare; Renard wanted to say, 'Mademoiselle, I know and admire you; *voilà dix sous!*' But he did not. It is surprising to hear her using a bus; she lived extravagantly.

Her well-publicized hypochondria did not diminish. She took elaborate precautions against headache, and informed journalists that she was threatened with paralysis of the arms. Every performance ended in what looked like total collapse. Isadora Duncan, who never forgave Fuller for launching her, does nothing to spoil the picture of Fuller as agreeably mysterious, hypochondriacal and queer. She speaks of visiting her in Berlin, where Fuller sat in a magnificent apartment at the Hotel Bristol, surrounded as usual by an entourage of beautiful girls who were 'alternately stroking her hands and kissing her'. 'Here', says Isadora, 'was an atmosphere of such warmth as I had never met before'. Fuller complained of terrible pains in the spine, and the girls had to keep up a supply of icebags, which were placed between her back and the back of the chair. Judge Isadora's surprise when, after an expensive dinner, Fuller went off and danced. 'Had this luminous vision that we saw before us,' asks Isadora, 'any relation to the suffering patient of a few moments before?' Fuller was clearly one to keep separate suffering and creation. M. F. Jourdain also vouches for the ice-pack, but remembers it as wielded by the faithful Gab, a Mlle Bloch who was for many years Fuller's companion-manager, and who kept the company going after Loïe's death in 1928. (It survived, though in decline, till 1940, when the Occupation put and end to it; but something called the 'Loïe Fuller ballet' turned up in 1958 in a French film called *Femmes de Paris*.) M. Jourdain testifies that every noise made Fuller suffer, even that of conversation; 'when the level of noise increased she would hastily apply the icepack to her neck, and, begging for silence with a gesture of supplication, she would stop her ears'. Once he saw her rehearse. She did not take off her coat, but sat on the stage, placed the icepack on her neck, stuck her fingers in her ears, and signalled the conductor to begin. She then followed his gestures with her eyes, taking care to hear as little as possible of the noise she had unleashed. Then she went back to her carriage. Naturally the performances were a little more tiring, and she was carried home to bed after every one of them. Mr Nicol says she had sinus trouble and loved overheated rooms; she was capable of arranging the kind of tableau Isadora came upon simply to impress visitors. As to rehearsal, she treated her company less tenderly than herself, wearing them out with all-night sessions. Mr Nicol was suspended from the company for inattention during a long rehearsal, at the age of five.

Fuller remained for a great many years enormously popular in the music-halls of Europe. She conquered London, as they say, in 1893, appearing during the interval of George Edwardes's *In Town*, a show distinguished by May Belfort's performance of 'Daddy wouldn't buy me a bow-wow'. But this did not prevent the English intelligentsia from taking her quite as seriously as the Parisian; for instance, there is an odd poem in French, in *The Cambridge ABC* of June 11th, 1894 – it did not last long but had a cover by Beardsley – which refers to the *'Varicolore et multiforme'* Fuller, and uses such expressions as *'une volupté profonde ... inquiétant mystère'*, etc. The popular press found her both amazing and moral – her Mirror Dance showed *eight* Loïe Fullers 'dancing as if they were the fabled victims of the Tarantula, the whole forming an artistic spectacular effect that the world has never seen equalled'; yet she made no 'gesture or movement which would offend the susceptibilities of the most modest-minded of British matrons or maidens'. Her long skirts seemed to bring about a long-needed *rapprochement* of Art and Morality.

Quite early in her career she had built up a company, and her shows grew more elaborate. She had her own theatre at the Paris Exposition, and in it she introduced Sada Yacco to the European public. Yacco's success, unlike Fuller's, was not unmixed. Eventually Fuller built around Yacco her 'Japanese company' – I think Yeats had this company in mind when he spoke of her 'Chinese Dancers' in 'Nineteen Hundred and Nineteen', for she seems never to have had a Chinese troupe – and took them, with Isadora Duncan, on a tour of Germany. (Isadora left this 'troupe of beautiful but demented ladies' and struck out on her own, without ever rebutting the charges of immodesty, ingratitude, and treachery which Fuller laid against her.)

A French journal of the Exposition period describes her as
'*parfaitement double* ... *à la ville petite, à la scène grande* ... a
very pushing woman'. By this time Mr Tindall of *Pearson's
Weekly* was willing to claim that 'she had given the world
such ideas of colour as had never been conceived before; look
at the pictures in the Paris salons if you would see some of the
more striking effects of Loïe Fuller's dancing ... she ranks with
the great geniuses of the ages'. But she went on appearing at
the Coliseum, in (for example) a variety bill called 'La Miracu-
leuse Loïe Fuller in the Grand Musical Mystical Dances', which
was itemized as follows

(1) The Flight of the Butterflies (Radium)
(2) The Dance of the 1,000 Veils,

this in five tableaux : 'Storm at Sea – Wrecked, Lost'; 'The
River of Death'; 'The Fire of Life'; 'Ave Maria'; 'The Land of
Visions'. How two famous dances, 'The Butterfly' (subject of
many photographs) and 'Radium', a dance in honour of the
Curies, came to be conflated, I do not know. 'The Land of
Visions', Mr Nicol surmises, was a way of using up some
photographs she had had taken of the surface of the moon.

As time went by, she depended more and more on her company, but also upon ingenious optical effects. Before 1909 she
had founded her School, and by 1912 the best dancers were
allowed to take over her Lily, Serpentine, and Fire Dances. But
the new dances were more and more abstract. Her troupe had a
great success in London in 1923 with a shadow ballet called
Ombres Gigantesques. There are some splendid photographs in
the *Sketch* for 13 December of that year, the eve of a charity
performance to be attended by the King and Queen. An enormous shadow hand plucks at the cowering dancers; a vast foot
descends to crush them. In other performances, for example in
a ballet using Debussy's *La Mer*, the dancers were not seen at
all, but simply heaved under a huge sea of silk. One late dance
'consisted solely of silver-sequined tassels being "dabbled" in a
narrow horizontal shaft of light – the background and the performers being veiled in black' (E. J. Nicol). Other performers –
Maud Allen is a notable though forgotten Salome – came and
went; but Fuller remained in the front line till her death in
1928.

The career of Fuller is unintelligible without some reference to her technical repertory. She had, of course, her own aesthetic notions, and claimed to have brought about a revolution in the arts. At first she saw the dance as arising naturally from music, but expressing human emotion best when unimpeded by training. 'The moment you attempt to give dancing a trained element, naturalness disappears; Nature is truth, and art is artificial. For example, a child will never dance of its own accord with the toes pointing out.' Rodin expressly agreed, and Massenet was so struck with the doctrine that he gave Fuller unrestricted performing rights in his music without royalty. Debussy was also interested, and Florent Schmitt wrote Fuller's Salome music (1893). But she very often used commonplace music, and it is hard to believe that her mature doctrine was either musical or expressive, The line of the body, never, as we have seen, the principal exhibit in her performance, grew less and less important, and in the end hardly counted at all – witness those dances in which no human figure was perceptible to the audience. The story she tells of her stumbling upon a new art of illuminated drapes in motion – and this at the outset of her career – has the germ at any rate of the truth. In a theoretical chapter of her autobiography she has some reflections on Light and the Dance; she was greatly concerned with the affective qualities of colour and its relation to sounds and moods (speculations much in vogue at the time) and was once thrown out of Notre Dame for waving a handkerchief in front of a sunlit window. She maintained the opinion that 'motion and not language is truthful', a view not likely to meet much opposition among the poets of the time, but she did not mean the simple dancer's motions or even those involuntary gestures organized into art which are the basis of Modern Dance; she meant the manipulation of silk and light. With them she could penetrate the spectator's mind and 'awaken his imagination that it may be prepared to receive the image'.

Fuller used in her publicity a remark by Pierre Roche that she was unequalled as an electrician and used her coloured lights on silk with a painter's art. In fact in the earliest days of theatrical electricity she seems to have gone a remarkably long way towards realizing that dream of a Farbenkunst which had been epidemic since the eighteenth century. She was given great credit for her skill at the time, not only by aesthetes who thought of the whole thing as a transcendent success for cosmetics but by practical theatre people. Sarah Bernhardt consulted her. There was growing interest in the spectacular possibilities of electric light on cheap materials, but nobody else brought off what Mallarmé called the 'industrial achievement' of substituting coloured light for all other properties, '*instituant un lieu*'.

The means by which she did this were closely-kept secrets. She put it about that one very striking effect was discovered by accident, when an electrician 'the worse for strong drink, threw two lights of different colours on the stage together' (*Pearson's Weekly*). In fact, of course, she was intensely preoccupied, and most ingenious, with light. She used the carbon arc-lights and coloured gelatines with which the theatres of the period were equipped, but with colours of her own specification. More important, she designed large magic-lantern projectors with slides of plain or frosted glass. The slides, which she painted with liquefied gelatine, were the fundamental secret, and only Fuller and Miss Nolan had access to them. Theatre men were not allowed to work the projectors, and the Company had its own trusted electricians. It was on such slides that she printed the photographs of the moon for the 'Nuages' ballet. The bewildering 'Radium' dance was done by projecting iridescent colour on to silks using first one multi-coloured slide, then superimposing another, and then withdrawing the first. When one thinks of her influence on future stage lighting, one should remember not only the Lyceum pantomimes in which she was regularly copied, but also that, as Mr Nicol says, 'our whole modern system of projected stage lighting owes its origin to her ingenious mind'. Experiments with coloured shadows on the cyclorama, and also with mirrors, were natural developments of such interests.

Her innovations were not confined to the lighting. She also did surprising things with silk. 'The idea of dyeing and painting silk in terms of abstract colour and not of pattern seems, undoubtedly, to have been Fuller's own,' writes Mr Nicol. The work was carried out by Miss Nolan, and the dyed silks became a commercial success, still remembered as 'Liberty' silks. Mr Nicol would credit Fuller with an influence on Gordon Craig and others; certainly we have been underestimating her during all the years when her revolutionary innovations were forgotten. One has a clear picture of a performer who converted dancing into something quite other, whose scenes and machines were of a new theatrical epoch, and whose gifts lay primarily in such inventions. Writing of a performance at the Théâtre Champs-Elysées in June, 1922, Levinson said, 'Even though she has the insipid primary *plastique*, the scholarly *faux-héllenisme* of the Anglo-Saxon (which forms an apparent link between her school and Isadora's) her personality is none the less fascinating ... She is a great imaginative creator of forms. Her drapes animate and organize space, give her a dream-like *ambiance*, abolish geometrical space ... Whatever belongs to the dance is ordinary; but *tout ce qui tient de l'optique est plein d'intérêt.*' Levinson had no doubt that this was another matter entirely than '*les enfantillages caduces de Duncanisme et ces vaines danses d'expression*'.

It is a little surprising, therefore, that much of Fuller's fame derived from her ability to represent natural objects – moths, butterflies, lilies, etc. Dances of this kind were frequently photographed, and she kept them in her repertoire right into the twenties. The serpentine dance is part of the history of *art nouveau*; it would be tedious to make a list of the compliments paid her by distinguished men on her power to reveal fugitive aspects of nature. Certainly some of the photographs are impressively moth-like and lily-like. With this strain of compliment there was mingled a persistent note of praise for her Orientalism and her Hellenism too. Such contradictions, if they are so, may be reconciled in the aesthetic of a Mallarmé; he wrote that the dancer was not a woman dancing but a metaphor containing elemental aspects of our form, sword, cup, flower, etc. And Symons, in *The World as Ballet*, finds in the dance 'the evasive, winding turn of things ... the intellectual as well as sensuous appeal of a living symbol'. She was a power like one of Nature's, and her creation had the same occult meanings.

The heart of this matter is, indeed, the chorus of poetic approval, and the terms in which it was couched. Consider, for example, the 'Fire Dance', a popular item from early days. She told the credulous Mr Tindall of *Pearson's Weekly* that this dance had its origin in an accident: when she was dancing her Salome at the Athénée (1893) she danced before Herod as 'the setting sun kissed the top of Solomon's temple'. But it also kissed her garments, and the public, always vocal, cried out and called it 'the fire-dance'. In fact this was merely another attempt to offset the cold electric calculations of Fuller. The

Danse de Feu was lit from below stage, by a red lantern
directed through a glassed-in trap. The effect was striking (*Pearson's Weekly* has some lurid coloured photographs). Fuller
appeared to the music of the 'Ride of the Valkyries', shaking,
we are told, and twisting in a torrent of incandescent lava, her
long dress spouting flame and rolling around in burning spirals.
She stood, says Jean Lorrain, in blazing embers, *and did not
burn*; she exuded light, was herself a flame. Erect in her brazier
she smiled, and her smile was the rictus of a mask under the
red veil that enveloped her and which shook and waved like a
flame along her lava-nakedness. Lorrain goes on to compare her
with Herculaneum buried in cinders (it wasn't, of course), the
Styx and its banks, Vesuvius with open throat spitting fire.
Only thus, he argued, could one describe her motionless, smiling nakedness in the midst of a furnace, wearing the fires of
heaven and hell as a veil. Gustave Fréville called her a nightmare sculpted in red clay. 'The fire caresses her dress, seizes her
entirely, and, inexorable lover, is sated by nothing short of
nothingness.' Years later Yeats was pretty certainly remembering this dance as well as Dante and a Noh play when he spoke
in his 'Byzantium' of the dance as an emblem of art, caught up
out of nature into the endless artifice of his Byzantium, the
endless death-in-life of the mosaic:

> ... blood-begotten spirits come
> And all complexities of fury leave;
> > Dying into a dance,
> > An agony of trance,
> An agony of flame that cannot singe a sleeve.

The 'Fire Dance' had all the qualities Yeats asked of the art, for
not only was the dancer unconsumed, but she also wore the
obligatory enigmatic smile. 'From his flame which does not
burn,' says Ménil in his *Histoire de la Danse* (1904), 'there leaps,
between two volutes of light, the head of a woman wearing an
enigmatic smile.' Ménil, as it happens, goes on – as Jourdain
did – to question whether all this trickery of silk and electric
light was really dancing at all, and he wonders how, from the
vulgarity of the cheap glare and waving skirt, there could come
this hashish-like experience. Goncourt's reaction was similar:
'What a great inventor of ideality man is!' he moralized, contemplating this 'vision of what is strange and supernatural' yet

has its origin in common stuff and vulgar lights.

Other dances were greeted with equal rapture. Georges Rodenbach draws widely on Fuller's repertoire in his poem 'La Loïe Fuller', first published in *Figaro* in May, 1896, and warmly praised by Mallarmé. It has fifty-eight lines, and is too long to quote in full, but here are some samples:

> *Déchirant l'ombre, et brusque, elle est là: c'est l'aurore!*
> *D'un mauve de prélude enflé jusqu'au lilas,*
> *S'étant taillé des nuages en falbalas,*
> *Elle se décolore, elle se recolore.*
> *Alors c'est le miracle opéré comme un jeu:*
> *Sa robe tout à coup est un pays de brume;*
> *C'est de l'alcool qui flambe et de l'encens qui fume;*
> *Sa robe est un bûcher de lys qui sont en feu....*
>
> *Or, comme le volcan contient toutes ses laves,*
> *Il semble que ce soit d'elle qu'elle ait déduit*
> *Ces rivières de feu qui la suivent, esclaves,*
> *Onduleuses, sur elle, en forme de serpents...*
> *O tronc de la Tentation! O charmeresse!*
> *Arbre du Paradis où nos désirs rampants*
> *S'enlacent en serpents de couleurs qu'elle tresse!...*
>
> *Un repos.*
> *Elle vient, les cheveux d'un vert roux*
> *Influencés par ces nuances en démence;*
> *On dirait que le vent du large recommence;*
> *Car déjà, parmi les étoffes en remous,*
> *Son corps perd son sillage; il fond en des volutes...*
> *Propice obscurité, qu'est-ce donc que tu blutes*
> *Pour faire de sa robe un océan de feu,*
> *Toute phosphorescente avec des pierreries?..*
> *Brunehilde, c'est toi, reine des Walkyries,*
> *Dont pour être l'élu chacun se rêve un dieu....*
>
> *C'est fini.*
> *Brusquement l'air est cicatrisé*
> *De cette plaie en fleur dont il saigna. L'étreinte*
> *De l'Infini ne nous dure qu'un court moment;*
> *Et l'ombre de la scène où la fresque fut peinte*
> *Est noire comme notre âme, pensivement.*

What Mallarmé liked about this was the recognition that Rodenbach restores to dancing its ancient character – it provides its own décor (*elle s'étoffe*). For Fuller's 'imaginative weavings are poured forth like an atmosphere' in contrast with the short-skirted coryphées of the ballet, who have no *ambiance* save what the orchestra provides.

Everything conspires to bring Fuller's performance into the position of an emblem of the Image of art, 'self-begotten' in Yeats's favourite word; or like the body of a woman yet not in any natural sense alive (*prodige d'irréel*), enigmatic, having the power of election. The darkness of the stage at the end of the performance is the natural darkness of the modern soul which only the Image, hardly come by and evanescent, can illuminate: 'the embrace of eternity lasts us only a short moment'. This power of fusing body and soul, mending all our division, is celebrated even in *Pearson's Weekly*. More completely than any other dancer before her, Loïe Fuller seemed to represent in visible form the incomprehensible Image of art in the modern world,[8] as Mauclair said: 'The Symbol of Art itself, a fire above all dogmas'. And she remains the dancer of Symbolism, from Mallarmé to Yeats; a woman yet totally impersonal, 'dead, yet flesh and bone'; *poème dégagé de tout appareil du scribe*. 'Thanks to her,' said Roger Marx, 'the dance has once more become the "poem without words" of Simonides ... above all one is grateful to her for giving substance to that ideal spectacle of which Mallarmé once dreamed – a mute spectacle, which escaped the limits of space and time alike, and of which the influence, powerful over all, ravishes in one common ecstasy the proud and the humble.'

In February 1893 Mallarmé went to the Folies-Bergère to see Loïe Fuller. It was an historic evening. André Levinson, complaining in the early twenties of the exaggerated deference paid in literary circles to the music-hall, credits the Goncourts and Huysmans with beginning the vogue, but goes on: 'One day Stéphane Mallarmé, aesthetician of the absolute, was seen pencilling, in his seat at the Folies-Bergère, his luminous *aperçus* on the so-called serpentine dances of Loïe Fuller, *fontaine intarissable d'elle-même*. Since then the whole world has followed ...' What Mallarmé was writing emerges as a passage of

8. I ought to say that this passage will make more sense to anybody who has read my *Romantic Image*. London, Routledge & Kegan Paul, 1957.

prose notably difficult even for him, but the centre, indeed the source in most cases, of contemporary poetic comment on Fuller. Concerning her, he says, and the way in which she uses the fabrics in which she is dressed, the articles of contemporary enthusiasts – which may sometimes be called poems – leave little to be said. 'Her performance, *sui generis*, is at once an artistic intoxication and an industrial achievement. In that terrible bath of materials swoons the radiant, cold dancer, illustrating countless themes of gyration. From her proceeds an expanding web – giant butterflies and petals, unfoldings – everything of a pure and elemental order. She blends with the rapidly changing colours which vary their limelit phantasmagoria of twilight and grotto, their rapid emotional changes – delight, mourning, anger; and to set these off, prismatic, either violent or dilute as they are, there must be the dizziness of soul made visible by an artifice.' He goes on to suggest that in this kind of dancing, in which the dancer seems to have the power infinitely to expand the dance through her dress, there is a lesson for the theatre, in which there is always a banality that rises up between dance and spectator. Loïe Fuller makes one see how the subtleties inherent in the dance have been neglected. 'Some restored aesthetic,' says Mallarmé, 'will one day go beyond these marginal notes'; but he can at least use this insight to denounce a common error concerning staging, 'helped as I unexpectedly am by the solution unfolded for me in the mere flutter of her gown by my unconscious and unwitting inspirer'. And he speaks of the dancer's power to create on the boards of the stage her own previously unthought-of milieu. The *décor* lies latent in the orchestra, to come forth like a lightning stroke at the sight of the dancer who represents the idea. And this 'transition from sonorities to materials ... is the one and only skill of Loïe Fuller, who does it by instinct, exaggeratedly, the movements of skirt or wing instituting a place.... The enchantress makes the ambience, produces it from herself and retracts it into a silence rustling with *crêpe de Chine*. Presently there will disappear, what is in these circumstances an inanity, that traditional plantation of permanent sets which conflict with choreographic mobility. Opaque frames, intrusive cardboard, to the scrap-heap! Here, if ever, is atmosphere, that is nothingness, given back to ballet, visions no sooner known than scattered, limpid evocation. The pure result will be a liberated stage, at the will of fictions, emanating from the play of a veil with attitude or gesture.' He sees the dance of Fuller as 'multiple emanations round a nakedness' which is central, 'summed up by an act of will ecstatically stretched to the extremity of each wing, her statuesque figure strict, upright; made dead by the effort of condensing out of this virtual self-liberation delayed decorative leaps of skies and seas, evenings, scent and foam'. And he concludes, 'I thought it necessary, whatever fashion may make of this miraculous contemporary development, to extract its summary sense and its significance for the art as a whole.'

There is dispute among students of Mallarmé as to the place of dancing in his unsystematic system, and less attention than might be expected is paid to this tribute to Loïe Fuller. But there seems to be no very good reason for discounting what it says: that she represented for him at least the spirit of an unborn aesthetic; that she offered a kind of spatial equivalent of music; that she stands for the victory of what he called the Constellation over what he called Chance, 'le couronnement du labeur humain', as Bonniet describes it in his Preface to Igitur. Like the archetype of Art, the Book, Fuller eliminated hasard. Thibaudet, indeed, believed that the whole concept of the Book owed something to Mallarmé's meditations on the dance; so did Levinson, arguing that Mallarmé glimpsed in the ballet 'a revelation of the definitive Œuvre, which would sum up and transcend man'; so, more recently, does M. Guy Delfel. The fitness of the dance as an emblem of true poetry is clear. Valéry was expanding the views of Mallarmé when he made his famous comparison between them (poetry is to prose as dancing is to walking). Mallarmé's growing concern for syntax, so irrefutably demonstrated by L. J. Austin, does not militate against this view that the dance took over in his mind some of the importance of music; for syntax is the purposeful movement of language and such movement has, in either art, to be assimilated to the necessarily autonomous condition of the Image. The dance is more perfectly devoid of ideas, less hampered by its means, than poetry, since it has not the strong antipathy of language towards illogic; yet it is not absolutely pure; the dancer is not inhuman. Mallarmé deals with precisely this point in the opening article of Crayonné au Théâtre (before 1887) when he discusses the ambiguous position of the dancer, half impersonal; very like the position of the poet ('The pure work requires that the poet vanish from the utterance' in so far as he can). But Fuller was more purely emptied of personality : an apparition, a vision of eternity for Rodenbach; for Mallarmé *'l'incorporation visuelle de l'idée'*.

If it seemed necessary, as it did, for poets to reclaim their heritage from music, the dance provided something more exactly fitting as an emblem of what was aspired to; and in a sense Fuller can stand for the liberation of Symbolism from Wagner. She is much more properly the Symbolist dancer than any orthodox ballerina; and there is a clear discontinuity between the general admiration for dancers of French poets earlier than Mallarmé and his praise of Fuller. In Baudelaire the 'human and palpable element' counts for much; in Gautier also. But in the new age, the age of Mallarmé and Yeats, what matters is that the dancer 'is not a woman'; that she is 'dead, yet flesh and bone'. The difference constitutes a shift in the whole climate of poetry, represented by the shift in English poetic from Symons to Pound, from Symbolism as primarily an elaborate system of suggestion, of naming by not naming, to the dynamism of the Vortex and the Ideogram. For Fuller is a kind of Ideogram : *l'incorporation visuelle de l'idée*, a spectacle defying all definition, radiant, homogeneous.

Such, at any rate, was the way those people saw Fuller who saw her with eyes opened to dance as a *majestueuse ouverture* on a reality beyond flux. They saw in her *'la voyante de l'infini'*. When Diaghilev came, defying the *genres*, overwhelming the senses with music and colour and movement, one or two people perhaps remembered her as having been the first to do it. I am convinced that Valéry did. Again and again he returns to the dance as a satisfactory emblem of a desirable poetry. It best illustrates what he calls non-usage – 'the *not* saying "it is raining" – this is the language of poetry; and movement which is not instrumental, having no end outside itself, is the language of dancing. Poetry, like dancing, is action without an end.' As the dancer makes an image of art out of the quotidian motions of her body, so the poet must 'draw a pure, ideal Voice, capable of communicating without weakness, without apparent effort, without offence to the ear, and without breaking the ephemeral sphere of the poetic universe, an idea of some Self miraculously superior to Myself'. The Dance makes of an activity of the body – sweat, straining muscle, heaving chest – an idea, a diagram of a high reality. Valéry called his dialogue, *L'Ame et la Danse*, of 1921, 'a sort of ballet of which the Image and the Idea are Coryphaeus in turn'. The dialogue embodies in language of refined wit and gaudy elegance the essence of our post-Wagnerian aesthetic. Athiktè, the central figure, is usually thought of as a conventional ballet-dancer; and she does dance on her points. But, as Levinson said in his pamphlet on the dialogue (*Paul Valéry, poète de la danse*, 1927) the *tourbillon*, her ecstatic finale, is not merely a ballet step, it is the whirling of a mystic's dance. Though Valéry collected ballet photographs, they were of a special sort, *chronophotographies*; the plates were exposed in darkness, the dancers carrying lights; and the result was a whirl of white lines, a record of the pattern of aimless poetical acts. In any case, we need not suppose him so devoted to the ballet as to have forgotten Loïe Fuller. He was on the point of refusing the invitation to write the dance dialogue because he 'considered ... that Mallarmé had exhausted the subject' and undertook it finally with the resolve that he would make Mallarmé's prodigious writings on the subject 'a peculiar condition of my work'. So I believe that when he came to write the passage comparing the dancer with a salamander – living 'completely at ease, in an element comparable to fire' – he was remembering Fuller. The passage culminates in a long, rhapsodical speech from Socrates : 'what is a flame ... if not *the moment itself*? ... Flame is the act of that moment which is between earth and heaven ... the flame sings wildly between matter and ether ... we can no longer speak of movement ... nor distinguish any longer its acts from its limbs'. Phaedrus replies that 'she flings her gestures like scintillations ... she filches impossible attitudes, even under the very eye of Time !' Eryximachus sums it up : 'Instant engenders form, and form makes the instant visible.' And when the dancer speaks, she says she is neither dead nor alive, and ends : 'Refuge, refuge, O my refuge, O Whirlwind ! I was in thee, O movement – outside all things ...' A Bergsonian dancer almost, '*révélatrice du réel*' as Levinson says.

The propriety of yoking together Avril and Fuller as I have done here is now, perhaps, self-evident. Avril is a smaller figure altogether, but she demonstrates the strength of the link between dancing and poetry, as well as the important pathological element in the dancer's appeal. Fuller deserves, one would have thought, some of the attention that has gone to Isadora. Levinson, who repeatedly declares his faith in classical dancing as the one discipline '*féconde, complète, créatrice*', respected Fuller, but despised Duncan as having no technique, no beauty, no suppleness, her feet flattened and enlarged by years of barefoot prancing, her music primitive. The fact is that Duncan was much more the Tanagra figurine, the dancer from the Pompeian fresco, than Fuller, who earned these descriptions in her early days. And Duncan certainly did not submerge her personality in strange disguises and unnatural lights. The Modern Dance has developed theories sufficiently impersonal to make it intensely interesting to Mrs Langer, creating a symbolic reality independent of nature. But it depends always upon the body – upon the power of the body not to express emotion but to objectify a pattern of sentience. Fuller with her long sticks, her strange optical devices, her burying the human figure in masses of silk, achieved impersonality at a stroke. Her world was discontinuous from nature; and this discontinuity Valéry, speaking of his Symbolist ancestry, described as 'an almost inhuman state'. She withdrew from the work; if to do otherwise is human, said Valéry, 'I must declare myself essentially inhuman.'

This is the doctrine of impersonality in art with which T. E. Hulme and T. S. Eliot among many others have made everybody familiar. 'The progress of an artist is a continual self-sacrifice, a continual extinction of personality ... the more perfect the artist the more completely separate in him will be the man who suffers and the mind which creates.' Thomas Parkinson, commenting on Ortega y Gasset's 'dehumanization' – 'a point can be reached in which the human content has grown so thin that it is negligible' – remarks acutely that the confused reception accorded to Pound's *Pisan Cantos* was due to critical shock at their identification of the sufferer and the creator. Pound, in leaving off his 'ironic covering', simply broke with a rule of poetic that he himself had done much to enforce. Mr Parkinson is glad; he wants to let 'the Reek of Humanity' back into poetry, where he thinks it belongs, and he seems to regard the impersonality doctrine as a lengthy but temporary deviation from some true 'romantic aesthetic'. I am not sure that he is right, or how far he misunderstands the human relevance of what the impersonal artist attempts. Mrs Langer could answer him, and I am quite sure that there Pound does not show the way back to reeking humanity. In Mr Eliot, in Valéry, we surely are aware of what Stevens called 'the thing that is incessantly overlooked: the artist, the presence of the determining personality'.

However this may be, Fuller's progressive extinction of the dancing body was a necessary component of her success as an emblem of the Image, out of nature. The imagination of the spectator fed upon her, independently of what she intended (she once caught sight of herself in a glass when dancing, and was surprised that what she saw bore no relation to her intention). She is abstract, clear of the human mess, dead and yet perfect being, as on some Byzantine dancing floor; entirely independent of normal action, out of time. It is a highflown way of talking about an affected music-hall dancer with an interest in stage-lighting; and, but for the example of Mallarmé, we should hardly venture it. Yet she was not a mere freak; dancers are always striving to become, like poems, machines for producing poetic states; 'they labour daily', as Levinson says, 'to prevent a relapse into their pristine humanity'. Only when the body is objectified in this way does it function, in the words of Whitehead, as 'the great central ground underlying all symbolic reference'. Also, it dies; and in so far as it is permitted to appear like something that does, it cannot represent victory over *hasard*, perfect being, the truth behind the deceptive veil of intellect. How is this to be overcome? 'Slash it with sharp instruments, rub ashes into a wound to make a keloid, daub it with clay, paint it with berry juices. This thing that terrifies us, this face upon which we lay so much stress, is something they have always wanted to deform, by hair, shading, by every possible means. Why? To remove from it the terror of death, by making it a work of art.' So William Carlos Williams on primitive ways into the artifice of eternity. Fuller's dehumanization was another way; it is very closely related to a critical moment in the history of modern poetic, but it is also, and this is as we ought to expect, rooted in the terror and joy of the obscure primitive ground from which modern poets draw strength for their archaic art.

(1958–61)

TWO

THE MODERN

Discrimination of Modernisms

Recently an advertisement for an 'ardent novel available only by mail' described the work as 'the story of a *modern* American marriage'. A favourable review was then cited, explaining that 'the painfully significant enigma' of modern marriage is the ambition and aggressiveness of woman. The husband in Meredith's sequence, lying there in tragic parody of a knight on a tomb, thought it was her infidelity. To both novelist and poet, 'modern' seems to mean something not altogether agreeable and disturbingly at odds with the way things used to be. If pressed, they might talk about radical changes in sensibility, as they affect love. Pressed harder, they might have to admit that ambition, aggression, infidelity, are no newer in women than refined or perverse sensibility in men.

The fact is that we all use the word in this unexamined way, and nobody notices how nearly meaningless it is until called to order by some pronouncement about The Modern. The context will usually be aesthetic, but even this limitation is not enough to ensure accurate definition. In 1894 John Lane announced that his *Yellow Book* 'would seek always to preserve a delicate, decorous and reticent mien and conduct' but 'at the same time have the courage of its modernness'; that it would be 'charming', 'daring', and 'distinguished'. The first number included a poem by Gosse, Saintsbury on wine, and a very good story by James, but only Beerbohm's 'Defence of Cosmetics' could be called 'daring' or, in its fashion, courageously modern. Later this might be said of the realism of Crackanthorpe; for modernism was not only the dangerous line of Beardsley, the clever excess of Wilde and Beerbohm; it was also the French cult of things as they now are. These two modernist strains were well distinguished by Arthur Waugh, in his attack on the magazine; he found on the one hand 'a want of restraint which starts from enervated sensations', and on the other an 'excess which results from a certain brutal virility', itself the consequence of 'coarse familiarity with indulgence'. Or you might say, exquisite sensibility and realism. The new sensibility required formal experiment, which was therefore associated with 'deca-

´dence'; squatness and ugliness of presentation, a prudent lack of enterprise in content, could now confer upon publishers who declined the financial and social risks of modernity a certain adventitious virtue. 'Modernness', in its Flaubertian alliance of formal experiment and realism, took over the old role of shock and protest, and its practitioners dissociated themselves from many concerns that seemed characteristically bourgeois, such as politics.

Politics returned in a later phase of modernism, and has now gone away again; on the whole one would want to say that politics has no essential part in the Movement. If there is a persistent world-view it is one we should have to call apocalyptic; the modernism of the nineties has a recognizable touch of this, if decadence, hope of renovation, the sense of transition, the sense of an ending or the trembling of the veil, are accepted as its signs. At such times there is a notable urgency in the proclamation of a break with the immediate past, a stimulating sense of crisis, of an historical licence for the New. And there appears to be a genuine continuity here, for all modernist art and literature between the nineties and now is associated with similar assumptions in some form or other. Naturally the contents of *The Yellow Book* have long ceased to look modernist; its cosmetic avant-gardism is archaic, as neurasthenia is archaic; its artists were not only Beardsley and Conder but Puvis de Chavannes and Moreau. The radical changes that were *implied*, somehow, by what they were doing – revolutions in architecture, music, painting, and poetry – were of a kind that shocked such a survivor as Beerbohm and forced Yeats to accept the necessity to 'remake' himself. The difference be-tween *The Yellow Book* and, say, *Blast*, indicates that however persistent the apocalyptic background may have been, some pretty radical changes of manner had occurred. The nineties were certainly precursors, but anybody who thinks about what modernism now means will rightly look more closely at the period between 1907 and, say, 1925; this is true despite the fact that the 'aestheticist' element in later modernism is often underplayed, and still accounts for that disregard of politics in relation to literature characteristic of so much modern criticism, so that Conor Cruise O'Brien justly but hopelessly complains that even intelligent critics are 'acute on small matters and absent-minded on very large ones'.[1]

1. *Writers and Politics*. London, Chatto & Windus, 1965.

There is at present much interest in this question of the modern. Last year Professors Ellmann and Feidelson published a huge 'casebook' on the subject;[2] it was a work of which Professor O'Brien might well complain in the same terms, but it was also a serious attempt to get into one volume most of the radical documents of modernism, and to explain the parts of Kant and Blake, Nietzsche and Darwin, Wilde and Pater, as well as Apollinaire and Tzara, Werner Heisenberg and Karl Jaspers. Now Mr Cyril Connolly, by way of choosing and describing its '100 Key Books', has undertaken to characterize what he calls The Modern Movement.[3] He limits himself to the years between 1880 and 1950, and to works in English and French. The American book is vast, solemn, and not easy to get on with; Mr Connolly's is light, bright, superficially stylish; but the Americans offer much useful and reliable information, and Mr Connolly's book does not. It is careless as to detail; the date of Spender's Struggle of the Modern is wrong, the Skeleton Key to Finnegans Wake is put thirteen years too late, the publication dates of Four Quartets are not accurate; you will search the Inferno in vain for a passage on Arnaut Daniel. Mr Connolly likes Yeats and quotes him, apparently, from memory; but what he actually wrote about the first night of Ubu Roi was 'After us the Savage God'. Perhaps one can take the misprint Little Gitting as an unconscious tribute to a contemporary poet and biographer of Keats; but whoever suggests that the opening line of The Winding Stair is 'The calm of evening, Lissadell' may be called upon to prove that he can be trusted with a great poem.

It seems a pity that Mr Connolly, so well equipped by temperament and experience, should have settled for sprezzatura and forsworn accuracy and sometimes thought itself. He sneers at professional students not for their real faults but because they get things right, and at 'theses' because they begin when 'the Titans depart'; yet after all he is a professional student, and this is a thesis, written, on the author's view, when the Titans have departed, arguing a view of a literary period, and complete with a bibliography (admittedly by another professional hand, and not in any case very useful). Whether we call it a thesis or not, it too often lapses into its own kind of nonsense

2. See below.
3. The Movement, 100 Key Books from England, France and America, 1880–1950. London, Deutsch & Hamish Hamilton, 1965.

and bad writing: 'As all objectives were gained and the complacent hypocrisy of the nineteenth century punctured, its materialism exposed, the Movement ground to a halt.' It is hard to say whether a good supervisor would be more depressed by the historical generalization or by the prose.

However, Mr Connolly is not wholly serious. That books are written in German or Russian will not prevent some of them from being 'Key Books', and he also omits all books he does not like (Claudel, Stein); all books that are not both good and rebellious, as well as historically important; and all books that are simply think-books (Bergson, Freud, Russell, Wittgenstein, etc.). With what is left he is pleasantly dogmatic. The Modernists inherited 'critical intelligence' from the Enlightenment, and 'exploring sensibility' from the Romantics. As near as it can be dated, the union of these qualities occurred around 1880; the Journals of Baudelaire and the *Bouvard et Pécuchet* of Flaubert ('our two fallen fathers') appeared posthumously in the following year. Mr Connolly's comment on Baudelaire can only reinforce the strong sense we may already have of slapdash unexamined history; he claims that this poet, 'after being for many years the private literary property of Arthur Symons ... has emerged to be re-interpreted by Sartre and magnificently translated by Robert Lowell'. After 1880 modernism came on in waves: the generation of James, Mallarmé, Villiers de l'Isle Adam, Huysmans, is followed by that of Debussy, Yeats, Proust, Jarry, Valéry, and that by the generation of Eliot, Pound, Lawrence, and Joyce; and so on. Admittedly such lists don't lend themselves to fine distinctions and discriminations, but this one makes the subject sound unintelligibly weird.

It is true that there was a sort of *translatio studii moderni* from France to England and America, and that the peak period of the Movement must be placed somewhere around 1910–1925, as Connolly says. But it is begging many questions to argue that after the death of Virginia Woolf and Yeats the Movement became 'degenerate'. He avoids some difficulties by saying that Beckett, together with Robbe-Grillet and Butor, 'falls just outside my dateline' (*whoroscope*, 1930, *Proust*, 1931, *More Pricks than Kicks*, 1934, above all *Murphy*, 1938). The 'frustrated forties' saw the end of the Movement. Burroughs and the Beats represent a continuing rebelliousness here attributed merely to the prevalence in America of 'unrevised attitudes to drug-addiction and homosexuality'. The best Mr Connolly can say about the future is that the Movement's 'twin features', described arbitrarily as 'faith in the intellect' and 'belief in the validity of the imagination', together with 'the enlargement of sensibility', will again 'inspire a masterpiece'.

It all sounds much too simple, and it is – labels are doing the work, announced as a labour of historical inquiry; words such as 'imagination' and 'sensibility' are being left to get on with it while the author chats brightly. Why did the Movement peter out? Because there were so many defectors from Humanism : 'some followed Huysmans into the religious fold (Eliot, Edith Sitwell, Waugh, Auden), some became fascists (Pound, Lewis) etc.' Subsequently modernism flourishes best in the theatre, where there is more to rebel against (Artaud, Ionesco, Pinter). If anybody would have been more surprised than Wyndham Lewis to be called a humanist or a defector from humanism, it might perhaps have been Artaud. Malraux defected from humanism by becoming a politician. What can 'humanism' mean in this discussion where 'dehumanization' is more commonly regarded as a symptom of the modern? Well, Gide and Forster perhaps; but when one speaks of their humanism one is simply in a different context from that appropriate to a discussion of modernism. By his abuse of this word, and in an entirely different way, of 'sensibility', Mr Connolly simply obscures this interesting issue; his book will add confusion where there is enough already.

I have so far said nothing of the books chosen. They are listed in chronological order, each with a chatty paragraph; *Bel Ami*, for example :

> Born in 1850, Maupassant died insane from syphilis in 1893. 'Another man for the scrap-heap,' he cried to his valet. ... Patron saint of best sellers, he has profoundly influenced Maugham. ...

Number 1 is *Portrait of a Lady*, Number 100 is *Paterson*. Among the books mentioned which seem to be there not for their 'modernness' but because the compiler likes them are *Siren Land* (hard by Apollinaire and Proust), *The Casuarina Tree*, *Sanctuary* ('Critics enthuse on *The Sound and the Fury*. ... *Sanctuary*, however ... is Faulkner for the non-Faulknerites'), *Animal Farm*, and the *Selected Poems* of John Betjeman. *Lady*

Chatterley's Lover and *Sea and Sardinia* get in, but not *Women in Love*. On the whole, however, the list, within its limits, is not unreasonable; only the comments are deplorable. The twenties, Mr Connolly's favourite decade, are celebrated by comment on *Ulysses* equally jejune in praise and condemnation, on Radiguet mere gossip, without the slightest justification for the choice, and on Wallace Stevens hasty and meaningless patter. *The Great Gatsby* is a 'light-hearted masterpiece of the boom years', but its contemporary, *The Sun Also Rises*, unites 'post-war disillusion and the post-war liberation ... in the physical enjoyment of living and the pains of love. Perhaps that is what expatriation was about.' It is hard even to see what this means.

The thirties – the 'disastrous decade' – were devoted to 'lost causes like anti-fascism'; nevertheless, this was 'a good period to be young in' since the world was 'still open for the traveller (Bali, Afghanistan, etc.)'. The forties account for twelve books, including *Darkness at Noon*, *Another Time* (though *Poems*, 1930, did not make it), the two Orwells, Betjeman, *Paterson*, however, makes a good modernist noise at the close, and Williams' 'Nothing is good save the new' neatly echoes Baudelaire at the outset: '*Au fond de l'Inconnu pour trouver du nouveau*'.

It should now be clear that if you want to know what Baudelaire and Williams are talking about, this poor little book, so unworthy of its author, will not help you to find out. What will? Since there is so much talk about these and related matters at the moment, it might be useful to look about for recent writing that has something to say. With this in mind, and perhaps somewhat naïvely, I turn to a very large new *Encyclopedia of Poetry and Poetics*[4] and look up 'modernism'. This volume is the work of very learned contributors and editors. If you want to look up *meiosis* or *meiurus*, *payada* or *penthemimer*; if you need a quick run through Albanian, Byelorussian, Danish, Persian, Romansh, or Yiddish poetry; if you are disturbed by the problems of belief, meaning, intention, or by the relationship of poetry with science or religion; if more modern critical terms baffle you, and you are interested in *tenor and vehicle*, *symbol*, *pseudo-statement*, *tension*, *ambiguity*, *aesthetic distance*; or in the vexed problems associated with *baroque*, *mannerist*, *conceit*, then on all this and more

4. Edited by Alex Preminger. London, Oxford University Press, 1965.

you will as a rule be amply supplied. But if you look up 'modernism' you will be told that it was 'the movement in Hispanic letters which began in the 1880s in Sp. America, blending Sp., Fr., and other foreign influences. . . .' Hard by, however, there is a long entry on *Modern Poetics*; it begins at 1750, which is justifiable, and begins to cater for our present interest when it reaches, after much scholarly explanation, our fallen father Baudelaire and his accursed sons the Symbolists. They were in favour of music and against logic (of course; and for all Mr Connolly says anti-intellectualism is a characteristic of the modern) – and they gave rise to a newly orientated poetry, arcane even when colloquial, interested in mental states below consciousness ('extended sensibility') and prolific of very difficult notions, such as Rilke's *Dinge* and Imagism and the vorticized or classicized Symbolism of Hulme, Pound, and Eliot. Hence 'the theoretical banishment from poetry (we might add the visual arts) of much that has been generally thought to give it seriousness'; and hence also a number of baffling ambiguities in the terminology, still troublesome; for it is hard to say what, for example, 'imagist' means, and even harder to be clear about 'abstraction' (good in, say, Worringer and Stevens, bad, generally, in the literary critics)[5] or even 'intellect', an anti-poetic instrument which poets are always blamed for not using.

There is some use in the *Encyclopedia* article; it ends with a very cautious statement of one of the major issues in later modernism, warning us that if we think poetry 'the completest mode of utterance' we should not be too anxious to separate it from other forms of discourse. Can 'art' and 'life' really be as discontinuous as the early modernists implied? More of that later, when it will emerge, I think, that poetry is not the best point of departure here. The theory behind very modern poems (like, for example, the enchanting 'Message Clear' of Edwin Morgan, in the *T.L.S.*, 13 January 1966) seems to derive from the thinking of artists and musicians, and finally we shall have to turn to them. The poetry encyclopaedia has, not surprisingly, no entry under *avant-garde* or New, though there are the Neoterici of Cicero to prove how old the New really is, as well as the New Criticism, now worn out, and the New Humanism,

5. The *Encyclopedia*, I have just confirmed, provides a good brief account, under *Concrete and Abstract*, of the way they use such words.

another historical description. It does not help us much with the modern Modern, the new New.

Professors Ellman and Feidelson find the concept of the modern 'intimate and elusive' but are quite sure it does not refer, as some now argue, only to what was happening almost half a century back; according to them, it 'designates a distinctive kind of imagination, themes and forms, conditions and modes of creation, that are interrelated, and comprise an imaginative whole'. This suggests a sort of imaginative mutation, ways of looking and making virtually unrelated to older ones; and that is another frequent claim one should look into. But it also suggests, and rightly, that we will agree to call a great many different things modern – not only the novel I mentioned at the start, or *Who's Afraid of Virginia Woolf?* ('strange love talk, is it not?' as Meredith remarked) but all manner of superficially incompatible things: *Howl* and *The Waste Land*, Cubism and Pop Art, Stravinsky and Stockhausen, Gaudier-Brzeska and Tinguely. Other things we shall most of us agree not to call modern: Meredith, for instance, Verlaine; and some we're not sure about: Freud, for example. We might even agree, at any rate so far as the arts are concerned, to a useful rough distinction between two phases of modernism, and call them palaeo- and neo-modernism; they are equally devoted to the theme of crisis, equally apocalyptic; but although they have this and other things in common, they have differences which might, with some research, be defined, and found not to be of a degree that prevents our calling both 'modernist'.

Before these or any other phenomena are called 'modern' there must, presumably, be a general sense of escaping from an older state of affairs, an *ancient* state of affairs. *Devotio moderna* was not only a movement for a new morality and a new piety, but also a movement against pilgrimages and excessive ornament. The Moderns of the seventeenth century had a programme with a similar double aspect. Their enemies would call it a preference for grubs and darkness over sweetness and light, but in its positive aspect it was a programme calling for new knowledge and assuming such knowledge could be made relevant to human concerns; while in its negative aspect it contested the view that the culture of their time necessarily imitated and must always be a derivative of ancient culture. This was perhaps the decisive confrontation, involving as it did the overthrow of ideologies both ecclesiastical and secular : the revision of the theologian's *curiositas*, which limited the bounds of intellectual inquiry in one way, and of the secular ideologies, imperial or sentimental-republican, which insisted upon classical norms and tended to equate change with decay. This was the Modernism that created a climate in which hypothesis and fiction replace myth, in which the nature of ideologies is to undergo rapid alteration and fragmentation, as ours do. Imperialism, republicanism, and classicism survive, of course, but much fragmented and modified, and usually in a posture of resistance. In short, the great seventeenth-century Modernism involved getting out from under something, and modernist programmes have the habit of claiming that this is what they always have to undertake.

What we got out from under is one of those questions that set up, it seems, an infinite recession. Certainly it wasn't Victorian complacency, as Mr Connolly is satisfied to say; and the reason why the American scholars find themselves reprinting Goethe and Kant is quite simply that the historical study of modernism will certainly take you back there, and beyond, to the seventeenth century obviously, and less obviously beyond that. This was long ago recognized, but stated in a distorted way, by those who sought parallels between the two periods as each exhibiting the catastrophes that come from too much brain and too 'abstract' sensibility. It is now much more fashionable to regard our plight as without parallel, and the past as irrelevant – an equally misleading error, and one which is responsible for further ideological muddle, as well as for certain false oppositions between palaeo- and neo-modernisms.

Nothing can so muddle argument as the claim that there exist no standards by which an argument can be judged, or even no language in which it can be opposed; this claim is now supported by several influential epoch-makers, notably Marshall McLuhan, an admirable and fertile inquirer who has brought science fiction to history and sociology. There are other theorists who overdevelop the metaphor of a cultural *mutation* and say that this renders the old 'humanism' powerless to judge or communicate, since the mutants speak an anti-language and aim at anti-art, anti-ethics, anti-sex; and instead of merely revising the concept of form – as the Romantics and the palaeo-modernists did – have abolished it. Indeed, if we want to understand the similarities and differences between the modernisms we shall have to look at this question of form more closely.

Objects, Jokes, and Art

Do we have a 'rage for order'? It has long been thought so, and the arts have long been thought ways of appeasing it. But there is a difference between 'order' and 'an order'; and what looked like the first can become simply the second: the conventional literary epic, or pastoral poetry, or the heroic couplet, or history-painting, or sonata form. In the older modernism, order grew mysterious. Following the organicist view of the Romantics, and the sophisticated gloss put on it by the Symbolists, poets treated it as the property of works purged of personality and emotion, new shapes out there and independent, perceptible by an *élite* which had transcended bourgeois literacy and could operate a logic of imagination divinely void of intellect. Thus the highly original forms of Mallarmé and, later, Eliot, have only a tenuous relation to more vulgar notions of form; and in the novel, for instance, the kind of extreme deviation from prevailing norms which had formerly occurred only now and again became a regular feature. The great experimental novels of early modernism – Kafka, Proust, Joyce, Musil, for instance – are all characterized by a kind of formal desperation.

Yet such forms continue to assume that there was an inescapable relationship between art and order. Admittedly when the forms of the past grew 'rigid and a bit absurd' you undertook a new research and produced modern forms. They might indeed be extremely researched, as Wallace Stevens suggests when he says we can't have the old 'romantic tenements' and that what will now suffice may be much less palpable: merely, perhaps

<blockquote>
a woman dancing, a woman
Combing. The poem of the act of the mind —
</blockquote>

but the act of the mind is still a form-creating act, and the form it creates provides satisfactions of the rage for order that cannot be had in life not so organized, so that art is different from life at least in this respect. And this view of the matter is still in many ways standard. Its various implications – 'autonomy', antididacticism, everything that attracts, both for the

arts and the criticism that attends them, the epithet 'formalist' –
are, whether we like it or not, still in the minds of most of us
when we consider a work of art. The first thing we can think
about is that this is a poem or a painting, and if it were not we
should find another way of speaking than the one we choose.
'*Art is not life and cannot be/A midwife to society*', as Mr
Auden pedagogically explained. It may be somewhat illiberal,
even untruthful, and reactionary by its very nature, as Mr
Trilling thinks; he is supported in his opinion by the theorist of
the formal *nouveau roman*,[6] and also, as we will see, by the
Apollinaire of the New York renaissance, Harold Rosenberg.

The fact that we have inherited the set of aesthetic assumptions I have very roughly sketched above makes it all the more
difficult for most of us to understand the new men, who claim
to be destroying the barrier between life and art, asserting their
indifference to the question 'Is this a picture?' and professing
contempt for ideas of order, especially when they can be associated with the art of the past. Nevertheless we shall certainly
understand the older modernism better if we come to terms
with the newer.

There seems to be much agreement that the new rejection of
order and the past is not quite the same thing as older rejections

6. Robbe-Grillet's collection of essays, *Pour un nouveau roman*,
published in 1963, has now been translated, together with the short
pieces called *Instantaneés* of the same year, by Barbara Wright
(*Snapshots & Towards a New Novel*, Calder).
Robbe-Grillet comes out strongly for the view that art is gratuitous, and from the revolutionary point of view 'useless, if not frankly
reactionary'; the fact that it will be on the good side at the bar-
ricades must not be allowed to interfere with our freedom to pursue
'art for art's sake'. This book, obviously one of the really important
contributions to the theory of the novel, deserves much more discussion than it has yet had in England or the U.S., and the translation is welcome. Incidentally, there is some justice in his claim
that it is other people who have *theories* of the novel; his is an anti-
theory, so to speak, and for all his 'formalism' that is modern
enough.
I should also mention here Anthony Cronin's *A Question of
Modernity* (London, Secker and Warburg, 1966) which is somewhat
commonplace in the title essay and often simply bad-tempered, but
as to the matter of art and life there are some fine things, including
a brilliant long essay on *Ulysses* and one about the novel which is
full of original ideas.

of one's elders and their assumptions. It is also agreed that this neo-modernist anti-traditionalism and anti-formalism, though anticipated by Apollinaire, begins with Dada. Whether for the reason that its programme was literally impossible, or because their nihilism lacked ruthlessness, it is undoubtedly true, as Harold Rosenberg has observed, that Dada had many of the characteristics of a new art movement, and that its devotees treated it as such, so in some measure defeating its theoretical anti-art programme. Raoul Haussmann only recently attacked the 'Neo-Dadaists' because what they were doing was ignorantly imitative, but also because it wasn't 'art'. If what we want is to understand anti-art I suppose our best plan is to follow the signs back to Duchamp, whose importance in this context is that he expressly and intelligently sought ways of 'no longer thinking the thing in question is a picture'.

The point is simply this : whereas such a poem as *The Waste Land* draws upon a tradition which imposes the necessity of form, though it may have none that can be apprehended without a disciplined act of faith, a new modernism prefers and professes to do without the tradition and the illusion. At this point there begin to proliferate those manifold theoretical difficulties associated with neo-modernist art. They are usually discussed in terms of the visual arts and music, probably because they are palpably even greater in the case of literature. Duchamp could pick something up and sign it, as he did with his 'ready-mades', and this raises problems, but at least it does not move from 'the plane of the feasible'.[7] In poetry one can of course use chunks of economic history and the collage of allusion, but usually for some formal irony, or to get a special effect by juxtaposition; simply to sign a passage ready-made by somebody else is not to change it but to plagiarize it. It would not matter if the borrowed passage were in most ways as commonplace as a mass-produced artefact; it would only be a more obvious case of plagiarism. A legal argument about a Duchamp ready-made might be interesting, but one would not expect a plausible defence in a case of literary ready-mades. The closest poetry can get is to cultivate impersonality and objectivity –

7. The phrase is Beckett's. His 'Three Dialogues with George Duthuit' (on Tal Coat, Masson, and Bram von Velde) have just been published, together with the early Proust essay, by John Calder. They are excellent examples of Beckett's philosophico-farcical manner in the discussion of the arts.

Williams' wheel-barrow and Robbe-Grillet's out-there coffee-pot. The things made are not wheel-barrows and coffee-pots; but similar theoretical assumptions are involved.

Duchamp used to speak of 'Dada blankness' – a way of making or naming things which has no relation to humanity or nature, no 'responsibility'; 'alien objects of the outer world', as Lawrence D. Steefel puts it, 'are reduced to instruments of the artist's transcendence of them.'[8] Blankness and indifference, like the 'impersonality' of Eliot, become, from one angle, a kind of egoism, indeed dehumanization has always been, from this angle, the apotheosis of the *culte du moi*. Dada, at its most apocalyptic, had it both ways, and proclaimed that after the present phase of quasi-Oriental 'indifference' there was to follow an era of purged personality, 'the cleanliness of the individual' (according to Tzara). The extreme and, on the face of it, paradoxical individualism of, say, Eliot, Lewis, and Pound, is the parallel case.

There is, in short, a family resemblance between the modernisms. 'Indifference' and the abrogation of 'responsibility' are the wilder cousins of the more literary 'impersonality' and 'objectivity'. The palaeo-modernist conspiracy which made a cult of occult forms is not unrelated to the extremist denial that there are any. These are the self-reconciling opposites of modernism.

Duchamp, like some of the older poets, is a man whose intelligence has been dedicated to anti-intellectualist ends. The paradoxical pursuit of randomness in the arts – a consequence of doctrinaire anti-formalism – is now carried on with every resource of ingenuity by very intelligent men. To early modernists the subjection of personality and the attack on false orders were one and the same process; the logicians of neo-modernism have not only accepted the position but developed it into an attack on order, perhaps not successfully, but with energy. Viewed in this light, the new theory bristles with paradoxes as, for instance, in Rauschenberg's remark : 'I consider myself successful only when I do something that resembles the lack of order I sense.'

The theoretical situation is in detail puzzling, but it must be admitted that in its practical and personal manifestations it is often pleasing, and indeed funny. For this reason Calvin Tom-

8. 'The Art of Marcel Duchamp,' *Art Journal*, XXII (Winter 1962–3).

kins' book, which is not only a set of 'profiles' but an intelligent presentation of ideas, is as amusing as it is informative.[9] His four subjects are Duchamp, Cage, Tinguely, and Rauschenberg. They are all, as he says, very different – Duchamp more detached, Tinguely more destructive, Cage more programmatic, and Rauschenberg more anti-art than the others – but they have many interests in common. For instance, all of them say that *art is much less interesting than life*, and not generically different from it. *All* seek impersonality (though strong personalities are vividly present in their work) and therefore *experiment with chance. All accept that art is characteristically impermanent*, being made up of things without transcendence. And *all* rejoice to *work on the borders of farce*. They make random and unpredictable things in a world consisting of random and unpredictable things, an activity that is anyway absurd; the purposeless is pursued with fanatic purpose, and this is farcical in itself. One difference between a Tinguely machine and a Heath Robinson is that Tinguely takes it past the drawing-board stage, but another is that Robinson aimed to amuse, whereas Tinguely, though he doesn't mind amusing, has no affective purpose at all; and there is a somewhat similar distinction to be drawn between a Hoffnung concert and a Cage recital.

These propositions and attitudes are characteristic of neo-modernism, and the literary man should learn what he can from them. The view that art is not distinct from life, to which (in Cage's words) it is 'inferior in complexity and unpredictability', is of course 'anti-formalist'. In the past we have simply been wrong in supposing that order is a differentia of art; hence the new doctrine, propounded by Cage and given an elaborate philosophical defence in Morse Peckham's recent book, *Man's Rage for Chaos*, that 'a work of art is what the perceiver observes in what has been culturally established as a perceiver's space. This can be anything. . . .' In Cage's 4' 33" the pianist sits before a closed piano for four minutes and thirty-three seconds, and the only sound is what floats in randomly from outside – bird song, buses – or what the spectators make themselves. So long as there is a concert-situation there is a concert, although the content of the concert is random and minimal. This is a logical step forward from Satie's musical

9. *The Bride and the Bachelors.* London, Weidenfeld & Nicolson, 1965.

collage, and is perhaps more like Kurt Schwitters simply plant-
ing bits of things before the observer in a 'perceiver's space'. It
pushes the protest against 'retinal' art, and its musical equivalent, to the point where it is a protest against the seriousness of
palaeo-modernist protest, and where the difference between art
and joke is as obscure as that between art and non-art. A point
to remember, though, is that the development can be seen as
following from palaeo-modernist premises without any violent
revolutionary stage.

I myself believe that there is a difference between art and
joke, while admitting that it has sometimes been a difficult one
to establish; and I would want to call 4' 33" and Tinguely's
famous self-destroying machine ('Homage to New York') jokes,
if only because however satisfying they may be, they do not
seem sufficient in respect of the needs which what is called art
has usually sufficed. But this is to use very inadequate criteria;
and having supposed vaguely that neo-modernism was heavily
dependent on the extension of modernist *theory*, I was glad to
find a philosopher, Arthur Danto,[10] saying this very thing in a
sharper way. Danto says the difficulties begin when one for-
sakes the old mimetic assumptions and says, for example, that
a painting of a table is as real as a table. If this seems hard to
take when the painting is Post-Impressionist, it becomes easier
when the objects painted are strictly inimitable – the numeral 3,
for example. Any copy of that simply *is* the numeral 3. What
kind of mistake would you be making if you tried to sleep in
Rauschenberg's famous *Bed*, which is a bed? You cannot mistake reality for reality. Danto suggests that we use *is* in two
distinct senses. We say a spot of white paint 'is' Icarus, and
also that 'this is a bed'. These two usages are presumably both
present when we say that *Bed* is a bed; but if it has paint on it
and is in a 'perceiver's space' then the Icarus *is* is dominant.

Actually for Danto the physical location is less important
than a sort of intellectual or theoretical space – call it the
atmosphere of intellectual assumptions breathed alike by the
artist and the game spectator.

To see something as art requires something the eye cannot
descry – an atmosphere of artistic theory, a knowledge of
art : an artworld.

10. 'The Artworld', *Journal of Philosophy*, LXI, p. 571 (1964).

But it all comes to the same thing. If Brillo made their boxes out of plywood they would still not be Warhols, and if Andy Warhol made his out of cardboard they would not be Brillo boxes. Provided the 'space' and the aesthetic convention were right he could simply sign a real Brillo box ready-made.[10a] We know what it is by where it is, and by our being induced to make the necessary theoretical dispositions (or not, as the case may be). As Jasper Johns puts it, 'What makes an object into art is its introduction into the art context.' Examination question : what is a signed Warhol Brillo box, found among a stack of Brillo boxes in a supermarket? Assuming, of course, that the customer knows the name, and what Mr Warhol does for a living. Another related question is, 'What makes an object into a joke?'

The theory so far is, then, that art is whatever you provide when the place in which you provide it is associated with the idea, and contains people who are prepared to accept this and perhaps other assumptions. Mr Peckham would argue that our failure to have noticed this earlier resulted from persistent brain-washing of the kind that stuck us with the notion that we have a 'rage for order' – that we seek the consolations of form amid natural chaos inhospitable to humans. This in his view is entirely false. We have, on the contrary, a natural rage for *chaos*, and that is why, truth prevailing, the concept of form is dead. With it, of course, dies the notion that the artist has to do with establishing and controlling a formal order in his work (what Keats in ignorance called 'information') and, also, the notion that this order has a high degree of permanence. Of course these notions have at one time or another been challenged before, though perhaps not in their totality. Artists have always known that there was an element of luck in good work ('grace', if you like) and that they rarely knew what they meant till they'd seen what they said; and there are milder traces of a doctrine of impermanence in palaeo-modernism, even in poetry, where Stevens articulates it clearly. But once again neo-modernism presses the point, and gives it practical application.

The most notable instance of this seems to be the neo-modernist *interest in chance*, a long way on from what Pope called 'a grace beyond the reach of art'. Although 'indetermi-

10a. Mr Warhol later took to doing precisely this.

nacy' has affected literature, it has had more importance so far in music and painting, and these are the areas of theoretical inquiry. There is obviously room for teleological differences between artists who employ random methods. Duchamp argued that 'your chance is not the same as my chance', and when he wrote random music insisted on regarding it as personal to himself and also funny. His dislike of order (perhaps as betraying him) emerges in his publishing the notes on *La Mariée mise à nu par ses célibataires, même* in random order, so anticipating the cut-up-fold-in Burroughs techniques as he had anticipated the methods of aleatory music. Duchamp, incidentally for all that he anticipated so many innovations, was always aware of a tradition, which he saw himself at the end of; he is a very sophisticated figure, and his critical superiority over some of his imitators is demonstrated by his immediate dismissal of the idea that there could be any relation at all between indeterminacy in the arts and indeterminacy in physics – this covert bid for prestige promotes nothing but confusion, of which (*pace* Peckham) there is quite enough already.

The layman who wants to know what Cage is up to has to confront the whole problem of chance. Without being at all solemn, Cage employs his considerable intellectual resources on constantly changing experiments of which the object is to ensure that his art shall be 'purposeless play'. Not for the first time in musical history, harmony (ideologically associated with ideas of order) had to go; it is replaced by 'duration', as percussion replaces melody. Music now deals in every kind of natural sound (the extreme naturalism of Cage is attributed by Tomkins to the influence of Coomaraswamy) but every other kind of sound too, except what might be made by conventional instruments. The piano has bolts between the strings to make it simply percussive. As to indeterminacy, Cage achieves it by many methods, including the use of the Chinese I Ching, coin-tossing, and yarrow-sticks. In one piece every note required 18 tosses of the coin.[11] He has now found speedier methods, using computers and, like Rossini before him, the imperfections in paper as a suggestion for notes.

On this view of the matter there can be no question of judg-

11. The process is described at length in Cage's *Silence* (Wesleyan University Press, 1961) pp. 60–1. This beautiful and very pleasant book contains material of great interest to anybody concerned with avant-gardism.

ing a particular work. 'There are no catastrophes,' he says. But audiences can of course be affected in different ways, and Cage has experienced wildly various reactions from his auditors. Certainly he sometimes makes it seem that aleatory art is, in a manner as yet unexplored, close to humour, as in the view of some tragedy is close to farce. Tomkins quotes Virgil Thomson's account of a concert given in New York's Town Hall in 1958, which was

> a jolly good row and a good show. What with the same man playing two tubas at once, a trombone player using only his instrument's mouthpiece, a violinist sawing away across his knees, and the soloist David Tudor crawling around on the floor and thumping the piano from below, for all the world like a 1905 motorist, the Town Hall spectacle, as you can imagine, was one of cartoon comedy ... it is doubtful whether any orchestra ever before had so much fun or gave such joyful hilarity to its listeners.

This is very sympathetic, but Cage believes that 'everything is music', and if, out of all the possibilities, he often chooses what makes for hilarity, this is evidence that such an assumption tends to confuse art and joke. There is a current of apocalyptism in all neo-modernism, and it is no bad thing that the Last Days should occasionally be good for a giggle, as they are in Beckett and in Tinguely. 'When seeing a Tinguely mechanism for the first time,' says Mr Tomkins, 'most people burst out laughing.' Peter Selz, the Curator of Painting and Sculpture at the Museum of Modern Art, was delighted with the famous *Homage*, which destroyed itself successfully, though not quite in the manner planned by the artist, before a distinguished audience. 'Art hasn't been fun for a long time,' he said. Duchamp congratulated Tinguely on being funny, and said that humour was a thing of great dignity.

It is, no doubt, part of the picture that all this would have been less funny had it gone according to plan. The humour is a matter of chance, of 'aleation'. Aleation in the arts, I suggested, pushes into absurdity a theory based on observation, that chance or grace plays a role in composition. In so far as palaeo-modernism pretended to be classical, it played this down; but between it and neo-modernism stands surrealism, and other manifestations of irrationalism. On the new theory, which has a wild logic, you leave everything to chance, and the result will make its mark either as very natural or as providing the material from which the spectators in the right place will make whatever they need for their own satisfaction. Anything random has some kind of an order, for example a bag of marbles emptied on to a table. Or, as Monroe Beardsley puts it in that interesting section of his *Aesthetics* from which I have already borrowed, 'they are in an order but not in order'. The difference between aleatory art and the art which appealed to 'the logic of imagination' (if for a moment we imagine them both as doctrinally pure) is simply this: the first in theory seeks only to produce an order (and in this it cannot fail) whereas the palaeo-modernists had not reduced grace to chance, and sought to make order.

So far as I can see this would be disastrous to aleatory art were it absolutely true, because the reason why we speak of 'an order' as against 'order' is that we drop the article as a sign of our wish to dignify what interests us more. We have discovered, in the process of getting by amid what Cage thinks of as the wonderful complexities of life, that order is more *useful* than an order: for example, the telephone book would be harder to use if the names were printed haphazardly. In a way, the alphabetical arrangement is perfectly arbitrary, but it happens to be something that the people who compose it and the people who use it agree upon. It might, of course, be said to give a very imperfect impression of the chaos and absurdity of metropolitan life, or life at large, and the consolation of knowing you can find your way about in it is in some ways on some very strict view perhaps somewhat fraudulent. It is not quite 'order', anyway, though it is not merely *an* order. And this in-between order is what most of us mean when we talk about 'order' in aesthetic contexts. One can avoid a divorce between art and life without going to the extremes recommended by Cage. When Cage grew interested in mushrooms he quickly discovered that some knowledge of their botanical classifications was a necessary modification to the practice of eating them at random.[12] Also, that when somebody arranged a happening in his honour, which required that he should be physically assaulted, he had to say that whereas his view was still that 'anything goes', this was so only on condition that one could manage to be free without being foolish. The implied criteria can only derive from the sort of education which dis-

12. See *Silence*, pp. 261-2 for a gastronomic misadventure.

tinguishes between an order and order. Order turns out to be more comfortable and useful. If our orientation towards it is not biological, then it is cultural or educational; and the reason why an order posing as order sometimes seems funny is that it is always presupposing orderly criteria by which its randomness can be measured; so, having reduced tradition to absurdity, one makes allusions to tradition by which the absurdity can be enjoyed as such. Thus silent music and Void or all-black painting presuppose music which employs conventional sounds and paintings with colour and shapes. They are piquant allusions to what fundamentally interests us more than they do, and they could not exist without it.[13]

Aleatory art is accordingly, for all its novelty, an extension of past art, indeed the hypertrophy of one aspect of that art. Virgil Thomson, who has been very sympathetic to Cage, allows that his random music is not really a matter of pure chance but a game of which the rules are established by Cage himself. No matter how much he tries to eliminate his own choices, it is always a Cage-game, and it involves calculation and personal choice. Admirers of William Burroughs' *Nova Express* admit that the randomness of the composition pays off only when the text looks as if it had been composed straightforwardly, with calculated inspiration. The argument is too obvious to labour. Even Duchamp didn't pick up *anything* and sign it. What seems clear is that a gross overdevelopment of the aleatory element in art tends to make it approximate to humour; thus the seventeenth-century conceit, over-extended, became a joke, and Jan Kott can turn *King Lear* into an absurd farce. The transformation would be impossible without the theory and practice of predecessors. Its nihilism is meaningless without an assumption of the plenitude of the past. Thus neo-modernists tend to make the mistake they often scold other people for, which is to attribute too much importance to the art of the period between the Renaissance and Modernism. By constantly alluding to this as a norm they despise, they are

13. The *ought* concealed in Cage's *is* is just that this should not be so, because such an interest is a vestige of the false fictions of order that should die with old technologies. Thus: 'let sounds be themselves rather than vehicles for man-made theories in expressions of human sentiments' (*Silence*, p. 10). And the interest of an all-white painting lies in its shadows, the random change of light upon it.

stealthy classicists, as the palaeo-modernists, who constantly alluded to Byzantine and archaic art, were stealthy romantics.

The point that in theory there is nothing very new about the New, that it is in this respect little more than a reverie concerning the more important and self-conscious theoretical developments of an earlier modernism, was made by Harold Rosenberg himself, when he observed that an Oldenburg plastic pie is not so much art, and not so much a pie, as 'a demonstration model in an unspoken lecture on the history of illusionism', adding that this kind of thing represents the union of many different tendencies in the art of the past half-century. As to why modernism should tend in this way towards pure farce, he cites Marx's observation that farce is the final form of action in a situation which has become untenable. Like Beckett's hero we can't and must go on, so that going on is bound to look absurd, a very old-fashioned thing to be doing in a situation you have shown to be absolutely new. On rather similar grounds he attacks the fashionable 'aesthetics of impermanence', saying that the time-philosophy involved is evidently wrong, and that 'art cannot transform the conditions of its existence'.

Such comment amounts to a radical criticism of the theoretical bases of extreme neo-modernism, and it prepares one for the impact of one of Rosenberg's best essays, so far uncollected, which appeared five years ago in *Partisan Review* under the title 'Literary Form and Social Hallucination'. When the subject is literary, this critic seems to see with great clarity truths which become obscure when the topic is painting. He argues that the form of a literary work militates against its ability to 'tell the truth'; that part of its function is in fact to 'tease us out of thought' (an argument employed, though with differences, by Iris Murdoch). From the political point of view this makes form suspect, anti-liberal; for by inducing us to descend into 'outlived areas of the psyche' it takes our eye off the actual demands and complexities of the world, arms us against the fact. It could perhaps be said that here the criticism is of Form when it ought to be of forms; that the constant researches of the arts into form have as a principal motive the fear that obsolescent *fictions of form* will cause them to be untruthful, or at any rate less truthful than they might be. Thus it is in the popular arts, where the question of fidelity to the world as the clerisy understands it does not arise, that conventions have the longest life. While the highbrows are pondering the *nouveau roman*, the great mass of fiction, which satisfies readers who would never dream of asking that it do more than a token amount of truth-telling, continues to use the old stereotypes.[14] It would probably not occur to the readers of such fiction that truth required the abolition of form, and if it did they might think the point too obvious to mention. Fiction, they know, is different from fact because it is made up. Yet it is precisely this point that, as Rosenberg sees, we need to be reminded of. Theoretical contempt for form in the arts is a fraud.

> Formlessness is simply another look and a temporary one at that. In time, organization begins to show through the most chaotic surface ... the subversion of literary form cannot be established except by literary means, that is, through an effort essentially formal.

This must be true, despite all the recent anti-formalist researches, aleatory, schismatic, and destructive. In neo-, as in palaeo-modernism, research into form is the true means of discovery, even when form is denied existence. So it becomes a real question whether it helps to introduce indeterminacy into the research, even if it is agreed that this is possible to any significant degree (and it is not). With Danto's remarks in mind we can at least ask ourselves whether dependence on an erroneous or distorted theory cannot be in some measure incapacitating. We need not expect a simple answer, since a great deal that is done in the arts is founded on theoretical positions which are later found to be leaky. We should need to reflect that there is a certain prestige to be had in minorities by professing to concur with what appear to be revolutionary advances in thinking about the arts, so that to find an audience claiming proficiency in a 'new' language is at present by no means difficult.

This is not a problem one can discuss now. What one can do is to say of the theoretical bases of neo-modernism, in so far as they show themselves in relation to form, chance, humour,

14. It is obviously in order to meet this situation head-on that Robbe-Grillet makes his fantastic claim to have at last found a novel-form acceptable to the man-in-the-street.

that they are not 'revolutionary'. They are marginal developments of older modernism. It can be added that disparagement and nihilist rejection of the past are founded partly on ignorance and partly on a development of the earlier modernist doctrine which spoke of retrieving rather than of abolishing tradition, just as the abolition of form is a programme founded on the palaeo-modernist programme to give form a new researched look. A certain extremism is characteristic of both phases. Early modernism tended towards fascism, later modernism towards anarchism. What Cyril Connolly calls the evolution of sensibility is a matter of changing theory. Romantic egotism becoming 'impersonality' and this later turning into 'indifference'. In the same way chance replaces the quasi-fortuitous collocation of images characteristic of earlier modernism. The anti-humanism – if Mr Connolly will allow the expression – the anti-humanism of early modernism (anti-intellectualist, authoritarian, eugenicist) gives way to the anti-humanism (hipsterish, free-sexed, anti-intellectualist) of later modernism. As to the past, history continues to be the means by which we recognize what is new as well as what is not. What subverts form is 'an effort essentially formal'; and the sense of standing at an end of time, which is so often invoked as an explanation of difference, is in fact evidence of similarity. The earlier humanism went in a good deal for the capitalization of what Mr Rosenberg calls 'outlived areas of the psyche', and so does the new modernism. For a 'movement' united by a detestation of logic, Modernism has generated an immense amount of theory; this was admittedly much more coherently expressed in the earlier phase. Later it has been scrambled by the babble of smaller voices, and in some aspects has been heavily overdeveloped, as I have tried to show. In both periods there was a natural tendency (inescapable from the Modern at any period and easier to justify half a century back) to exaggerate the differences between what one was doing and what had been done by the old guard, and this has helped to conceal the truth that there has been only one Modernist Revolution, and that it happened a long time ago. So far as I can see there has been little radical change in modernist thinking since then. More muddle, certainly, and almost certainly more jokes, but no revolution, and much less talent.

That is why, on the one hand, one cannot accept Cyril Connolly's assurance that it is virtually all over, and on the other

Leslie Fiedler's claim that we have a new art which reflects a social revolution so radical that he can call it a 'mutation' and its proponents 'The New Mutants' (*Partisan Review*, Fall 1965). Henceforth, he thinks, literature and criticism will forget their traditional observance of the past, and observe the future instead. Pop fiction demonstrates 'a growing sense of the irrelevance of the past' and Pop writers ('post-Modernists') are catching on. The new subject will be 'the end of man' and the transformation of the human life into something else (curious echoes of Mr Connolly, who also thinks of modern writers as post-Modernist in sensibility, and anti-humanist). Mr Fiedler explains that he means by humanism the cult of reason, from Socrates to Freud. This is what is being annihilated, and the Berkeley students were protesting against universities as the transmitters and continuators of the unwanted rationalist tradition. The protest systematically *anti*-s everything: a Teach-in is an *anti*-class banners inscribed FUCK are *anti*-language, and so on. Actually, a teach-in is only an especially interesting class, because the teachers are volunteers and just as engaged with the subject as you are. There is the oddity that this class really works as a 'dialogue' and goes on and on. The banners are no more anti-language than collage is anti-painting; and the absolutely blank banners which succeeded the 'dirty' ones were certainly a very good joke in the new manner, like Rauschenberg erasing a De Kooning, or a Klein Void.

Fiedler's observations on the new life-style of his 'mutants' are more interesting. He stesses a post-Humanist contempt for ideology; a post-Humanist sexuality which has discounted masculinity and developed characteristic patterns of homosexuality, usurpation of female attitudes, polymorphous perversity; and a new range of post-Humanist stimulants (*LSD*, airplane glue, etc.). This amounts, he argues, to 'a radical metamorphosis of the Western male', a real revolt, unlike our ritual contentions with father. These young people have made the breakthrough into new psychic possibilities, and recognize in Burroughs the laureate of their conquest.[15]

15. It may be worth pointing out that Burroughs himself is far from thinking that drugs will bring this about. His *Paris Review* interviewer (Fall '65) asked: 'The visions of drugs and the visions of art don't mix?' and he said, 'Never.... They are absolutely contraindicated for creative work, and I include in the lot alcohol, morphine, barbiturates, tranquilisers....'

Whether this is nonsense, and whether it is dangerous, is not in my brief. I will only say that the whole argument about 'mutation' is supererogatory; the phenomena should be explained more economically. If the prole has replaced the shepherd, the savage, and the child as pastoral hero, it isn't surprising that those who seek to imitate him should imitate his indifference to ideology and history and sexual orthodoxies. This is not the first recorded instance of libertinage among the well-heeled. Drugs and four-letter words are not new, even among poets, even among the young. The display may seem unusually ostentatious, but it is worth remembering that Fiedler's prime example derives from that highly abnormal institution, the University of California, the unbelievably well-endowed organ of the educational aspirations of a state which is not only very rich but is famous for the unique predominance of the young in its population. In so far as the protest was 'pure' protest, protesting against nothing whatever, it was surely luxurious attitudinizing on a familiar undergraduate model but hypertrophied by sociological causes well within the purview of old-style analysis. A thirst for the unique and unprecedented can lead to the exaggeration of triviality or to claims which the record refutes. Thus Fiedler finds in Ken Kesey's (very good) novel *One Flew Over the Cuckoo's Nest* evidence that for the mutants the schizophrenic has replaced the sage as culture hero, whereas by narrating this madhouse fiction from the point of view of an inmate of limited and varying perceptiveness Kesey is using a now time-honoured technique. So with his sociological observations. Even the male behaviour to be observed after midnight on 32nd and 43rd Streets hardly needs to be explained in terms of 'mutation'. To treat such symptoms as unique, as signs that the Last Days are at hand, is to fall headlong into a very naïve – and historically very well-known – apocalyptism.

It is the constant presence of more or less subtle varieties of apocalyptism that makes possible the repetitive claims for uniqueness and privilege in modernist theorizing about the arts. So far as I can see these claims are unjustified. The price to be paid for old-style talk about 'evolving sensibility' is new-style talk about 'mutation'. It is only rarely that one can say there is nothing to worry about, but in this limited respect there appears not to be. Mr Fiedler professes alarm at the prospect of being a stranded humanist, wandering among unreadable books in a totally new world. But when sensibility has evolved that far there will be no language and no concept of form, so no books. Its possessors will be idiots. However, it will take more than jokes, dice, random shuffling, and smoking pot to achieve this, and in fact very few people seem to be trying. Neo-modernists have examined, in many different ways (many more than I have talked about), various implications in traditional modernism. As a consequence we have, not unusually, some good things, many trivial things, many jokes, much nonsense. Among other things they enable us to see more clearly that certain aspects of earlier moderism really were so revolutionary that we ought not to expect – even with everything so speeded up – to have the pains and pleasures of another comparable movement quite so soon. And by exaggerating the drawing, the neo-modernist does help us to understand rather better what the Modern now is, and has been during this century.

On the whole one has to say that the older modernists understood all this better. Eliot in his last book, tired and unadventurous as it is, said it once again, and said it right:[16]

A new kind of writing appears, to be greeted at first with disdain and derision; we hear that the tradition has been flouted, and that chaos has come. After a time it appears that the new way of writing is not destructive but re-creative. It is not that we have repudiated the past, as the obstinate enemies – and also the stupidest supporters – of any new movement like to believe; but that we have enlarged our conception of the past; and that in the light of what is new we see the past in a new pattern.

This does not allow for the possibility that chaos and destruction could be introduced into the programme, except by its 'stupidest supporters'; but it does seem to make sense in terms of a quest for 'what will suffice'. In the end what Simone Weil called 'decreation' (easy to confuse with destruction) is the true modernist process in respect of form and the past. Or if it is not we really shall destroy ourselves at some farcical apocalypse.

16. *To Criticise the Critics*. London, Faber & Faber, 1965.

Definitions and Variations

Somebody should write the history of the word 'modern'. The OED isn't very helpful, though most of the senses the word now has have been in the air since the 16th century and are actually older than Shakespeare's way of using it to mean 'commonplace'. The international row about Moderns in the seventeenth century is terribly well-documented but the historian might find that it only muddied the waters. An earlier usage in the fifteenth-century *devotio moderna* seems more significant, because it connotes a sharp sense of epoch, and of a reaction against the style of life and thought of immediate predecessors, something rather more than the technical operations indicated by the word 'new' – in the 'new' poetry or the 'new' music. That the Modern is a larger and more portentous category than the New our own usage confirms, or at any rate did so until very lately. The New is to be judged by the criterion of novelty, the Modern implies or at any rate permits a serious relationship with a past, a relationship that requires criticism and indeed radical re-imagining. This sense of 'modern' is the one Mr Spender explored in his book *The Struggle of the Modern*. His is a traditionalist modernism. There is another kind, which Spender wanted to call the 'contemporary', and which Mr Trilling characterizes as anti-cultural. This is the schismatic modernism associated with Barzun's 'clean break' and 'new start', or, less academically, with the doctrine of The New.

One of the things the historian will have to decide is whether the concept of the Modern, even in its traditionalist phase, isn't open to the kind of attack that is mounted, as a matter of intellectual hygiene, by Ernst Gombrich against any method or set of assumptions that seems to him tainted by Hegelianism, whether of the 'Right', as in Malraux, or of the 'Left', as in Arnold Hauser. Another problem is the degree to which the 'traditionalist' sense is merely a specialization of the academics, related only obscurely to the ordinary-language usage; this, however, seems to reflect nowadays the sense that 'modern' doesn't quite have the up-to-date flavour wanted. The shops call their furniture and curtains 'contemporary', a word intellectuals dislike, partly because it is uselessly ambiguous, and partly because it is used in this ignorant way mostly of nasty things. However, the historian of the word must be left to sort all this out. On the whole, everybody knows what is meant by

modern literature, modern art, modern music. The words suggest Joyce, Picasso, Schoenberg, or Stravinsky – the experiments
of two or more generations back.

The fact that defining the modern is a task that now imposes
itself on many distinguished scholars may be a sign that the
modern period is over. We need a language to argue about it, as
we argue about Renaissance. The formulae devised will, in the
same way, vary with time. A documentary history of the
modern would have been different 20 years ago, and will be
different 20 years hence, from the one now presented us by
Ellmann and Feidelson.[17] They try, in a book of about half a
million words, to crystallize the modern sense of the modern –
the traditional modern, as their title suggests, for they print not
only the twentieth-century documents but also what are now
regarded as the sources of the modern, as far back as the
eighteenth century. It is fair to say that the book contains a
high proportion of material that would have been in any good
book of this kind, as well as some things that have only a
doubtful right to be there; and of course one can think of
omissions, some which may be considered rather damaging.

The editors don't try to define 'modern', saying that it is
'intimate and elusive' and that it is 'not like the reassuring
landscape of the past, open and invadable everywhere'. Of
course their purpose is to make it reassuring and invadable, to
confirm it as part of the past. But they argue that it is more
than a merely chronological description because it 'designates a
distinctive kind of imagination, themes and forms, conditions
and modes of creation, that are interrelated, and comprise an
imaginative whole'. These arguments, assuming the discontinuity of the modern mind, are themselves modern, and indi-
cate a degree of sympathy with the material of the book which
explains why so few of the passages included are from writers
critical of the conspiratorial element in modernism – the
agreement, which can be too easy, that our problems are
unique, our world uniquely chaotic, so that we are entitled to
mistrust formal arrangements acceptable in the past. They do
mention that the modern view of the world – as presenting
unheard-of difficulties in the matter of relating imagination to
reality, as providing no trustworthy fictions – tempts artists
who suffer under it into a familiar historical game, that of de-

17. *The Modern Tradition.* Edited by Richard Ellman and Charles
Feidelson. Oxford University Press, 1965.

ciding when the rot set in: was in with Giotto or with Shakespeare, with Napoleon or the Great War? 'The paradoxical task
of the modern imagination', they say somewhat obscurely, 'has
been to stand both inside and outside itself, to articulate its
own formlessness, to encompass its own extravagant possibilities'. They allow the modern its cherished formulae, and get
one of its favourite paradoxes into the title.

The editors are well-known literary critics, and their book is
quite properly centred in literature. 'He makes literature include philosophy?' someone asks Boon in Wells's novel.
'Everything,' replies Boon. 'It's all the central things.' The
editors agree, but to document the modern you need to consider purely discursive statements about it, and topics which
are not quite literature, though related to it. They have nine
topics: Symbolism, Realism, Nature, Cultural History, The Unconscious, Myth, Self-Consciousness, Existence, and Faith. The
first has bits of Kant and Coleridge, Blake and Goethe, Baudelaire and Flaubert, Nietzsche and Wagner, Pater and Wilde
(who most certainly would not have got in had the book been
written even 10 years ago). The central documents are from
Rimbaud, Mallarmé, Valéry, Yeats, Eliot, Rilke, Pound, Joyce;
but Picasso, Arp, Ernst, Duchamp, Klee, Dubuffet, and Malraux
are also present. The passages may be famous, as with those of
Apollinaire, Pound, and Klee, or merely useful to make a point,
as with Forster's lecture 'Art for Art's Sake'.

This first section, itself the size of a normal book, is very
useful. The introduction to it briskly outlines the current doctrine: 'the symbolist is a kind of romantic, one who singles out
and develops the romantic doctrine of the creative imagination
... the image possesses absolute autonomy ... its maker, the
artist, is the truly heroic man.' The history of this group of
notions is rapidly traced from Kant and Blake through Flaubert
and Wilde and Nietzsche on fictional affirmations, to 'pseudo-
statements' and Wallace Stevens, with Cubists, Vorticists and
Surrealists chiming in. That the first piece in the book is
Wilde's 'Decay of Lying' tells one something about the new
modern and about the topicality of this book. But students
(basically this is a gigantic textbook) and others will find this
way of handling the subject illuminating. There is a point in
being rushed from Kant to Arp, from Blake to the Bauhaus –
where they also tried, in their way, to prepare a rest for the
people of God. In the section on autonomy Baudelaire helps to

prepare them for Duchamp, and Apollinaire, announcing that artists are men who above all want to be inhuman, sounds the theme of dehumanization. Ortega, surprisingly, is left out, although he spent so much time on the concept of the modern, and on dehumanization. There are such gaps – no Wyndham Lewis, no Worringer, no Kandinsky in this section; but Pound on Vortex – juxtaposed with Dubuffet on zinc oxide – perhaps takes care of that. There is almost nothing about music, either here or anywhere else. Yet this opening section will give many people a clearer notion of the history of the modern literature than they had.

The remaining topics must have been harder to select. 'Realism' is obvious enough, a very modern problem; the editors begin, badly, with George Eliot (the excrescent chapter in *Adam Bede*) but end well with Lukàcs (late, unfortunately) and Robbe-Grillet, the prophet of a fully dehumanized realism. One of the great omissions of the book – the relation of art and artists to the modern city and the modern worker – is partly repaired by bits of the Communist Manifesto and Trotsky. No Carlyle, no Ruskin. 'Nature' runs from Darwin and Schopenhauer to Dewey and Heisenberg; the introduction tells us, what I do not believe, that there is 'some analogy' between instrumentalism and the indeterminacy principle, and 'the linguistic experimentalism of the symbolists'. Here axes begin to grind. Heisenberg would not, I think, regard himself as providing material for a waste-land myth of meaninglessness, or confirming Existentialist anxiety; but the editors want to end with Tillich on 'the courage to be ... when God has disappeared', and they shape the whole thing accordingly. One sees this in the central position given to Spengler in the 'Cultural History' section. The critics of historicism are not represented, except by Berdyaev.

The section on the 'Unconscious' opens with Goethe, Blake, and Nietzsche, has Freud in the middle, and goes on to Lawrence, Tzara, and Breton. There is no Diderot, amazingly little sex (which might have had a section on its own) and no neo-Freudians. Dada and Surrealism are here because of their flight to unreason; but Dada is one kind of modernism, capitalizing alienation, schism, destruction – the shout into the Marabar Caves – and Surrealism, in spite of the acknowledged links, is another, with implications of social revolution as a reasonable goal. However, as the section of 'Myth' confirms, the interesting aspect of modernism at present is the unreasonable one. I don't know why the quest for a mythology, here represented by Jung, should not equally well have been represented by Madame Blavatsky and Eliphas Lévi. 'Self-consciousness', one of the odder topics, runs from Rousseau through Kierkegaard and Dostoievsky's Underground to Proust, Gide, Kandinsky, and Yeats. 'Existence', strangely marred by confining the Sartre selections to *Existentialism and Humanism*, has Kierkegaard, Nietzsche at one end and Heidegger and Jaspers at the other. The last section starts with Blake, and arrives, by way of the Grand Inquisitor, at Barth and Tillich.

This list of names is meant to give a notion of what may be found in a rich, inexpensive, and useful, if somewhat tendentious book. It tells you what very well-equipped American scholars take the Modern Movement to be; and if the ideas represented are not criticized, and the map a little out of date, that may be because the reader is expected to do some of the work. While I was reading the book I came across Mr Trilling's essay 'The Two Environments', which quotes Saul Bellow's attack on the complicity of critics in the creation of a dangerous modern waste-land myth 'on which literature has lived uncritically'. Bellow says such critics have helped to 'enfeeble literature'. The editors of this in most ways admirable compilation might, on the severest view, be held not to escape Bellow's condemnation.

Meanwhile, the word 'modern' can still mean something like 'written in the past 10 years', and this is the way it's used in Mr LeRoi Jones's title.[18] He calls his contributors 'the restorers of American prose'. Their tone is 'non-urban', belonging to the West of the United States. They are separate men, with an affinity for the 'non-civilized', remaining 'outside the mainstream of the American organism'. They study the 'fellaheen', in Spengler's word – hoodlums, homosexuals, Negroes. Theirs, says the editor, is a 'populist modernism'. The result is grey enough, rather like some *Yellow Book* stories. There is a lot about cities – John Rechy on Los Angeles and Chicago ('savage city'), Kerouac on Seattle and New York. Strip shows are a favourite topic. There is a brisk bit of urban reporting by Hubert Selby Jr, which seemed the best writing in the book. Kerouac describes a Negro cat asleep in the tube. 'I love him,'

18. *The Moderns*. London, MacGibbon & Kee, 1965.

he confesses. There is some Burroughs. The appendix consists of theoretical pieces, banal for the most part and badly written; one is Kerouac's 'Essentials of Spontaneous Prose', which ought to be read by anybody who cares about the American future, for it has been recommended to undergraduates as a style-sheet. Burroughs has a piece explaining the cut-up-fold-in technique. Tzara began it, but now, 50 years late, the writer can copy collage and the cinema. 'The best writing seems to be done almost by accident but writers until the cut-up method was made explicit had no way to produce the accident of spontaneity.' Now a pair of scissors will do it.

But this takes us out of the Modern into the avant-garde; and pat comes a book of examples.[19] Burroughs again, a long stretch of Butor, Cocteau (how did he get in here?), and others less famous. There is an editorial introduction of the kind Americans call sophomoric, a display of unmastered terminology, produced with inexplicable heat. 'We have the right to convey the fictive of any reality at all – and there is nothing that is not real – by any method we wish,' Mr Orlovitz boldly pronounces. The whole point is to set forth a demonstration in the fictive that will generate tension even in a reader mystified by the significs, he adds. 'The notion of value belongs to *ad hominen* (*sic*) pleaders,' the man says. Those who suppose that to be avant-garde all you need is to abandon the mind to it, together with the language and the compositor, would doubtless like to think so. Anyway, it shows that there is a difference between 'modern' and 'avant-garde'. But somebody should write a history of that word, too.[20]

(1965–6)

19. *The Award Avant-Garde Reader*. Edited by Gil Orlovitz. New York, Award Books.

20. The late Renato Poggioli did so in *The Theory of the Avant-Garde*. Trans. Gerald Fitzgerald, Oxford University Press, 1968.

THREE

OBSCENITY AND THE PUBLIC INTEREST

The London trial of the publishers of *Last Exist to Brooklyn* crystallized, I thought, some of the issues arising from the extreme variety of attitudes that may be held within one society in the matter of obscenity. In the United States, I am told, the literate now feel that total permissiveness rules; the enemies of candour have run out of legal resources. I should not like to say that this belief in a liberal victory is premature, though it might be held to underestimate the forces of reaction. But even if it is true that a book can no longer be tested in the courts with any reasonable chance of success for the prosecution, it is unlikely that opposition of other kinds has permanently ended. It may therefore be of interest to American readers to consider for a moment whether there is anything to be learnt from the conviction of John Calder and Marion Boyars, the English publishers of Selby's novel. Their trial lasted ten days, one of which was almost wholly devoted to my testimony, so I have naturally given a good deal of thought to what the court was supposed to be doing, and what I was supposed to be doing; and I conclude that although the whole thing was in many ways bewildering to the point of incomprehensibility, it did provide a kind of allegory of the situation in which authors and publishers find themselves when they must take account of the opinions of the general rather than of the literary public.

First a necessary word on the local legal position. Until 1959 any book could be prosecuted at any time for obscene libel. Under this law, well within living memory, a country magistrate condemned Boccaccio. Under a similar law, in 1944, an Australian court condemned a book which contained the word 'incest', certified to be obscene by a police inspector who confessed in cross-examination that he did not know what it meant. In 1954 there was a series of prosecutions, which worried the Society of Authors. They set up a committee to draft a parliamentary Bill. Thanks in large part to the determination of Roy Jenkins, later Home Secretary and later Chancellor of the Exchequer in the Labour Government, the administration was forced to take notice of this private measure, which it did by substituting its own much less liberal draft. Contested with great pertinacity through committee, this Government measure underwent a good many liberalizing amendments, and by the time it became law as the Obscene Publications Act of 1959 it was much less reactionary than had at times been feared, though it was not quite the Act its sponsors had originally hoped for.

The Act of 1959 provided, among other things, that in any proceedings a book must be considered as a whole – it would not be enough to establish the obscenity of isolated passages. The prosecution would have to show that the whole book was obscene. But even if it were found to be so it could still be held that its publication were 'for the public good on the ground that it is in the interests of science, literature, art or learning, or other objects of general concern'. In other words, the prosecution has to prove obscenity; if the jury thinks it has done so it passes to the second question, the question of 'literary merit'. There, of course, the onus is on the defence, which will depend upon its expert witnesses. Since obscenity is defined by the Act as, and only as, that which has a tendency to deprave or corrupt, and since the expert witnesses are expressly forbidden to comment on that aspect of the proceedings, it will be evident already that 'literary merit' under the law is abstracted from the affective qualities of the work, and the handicaps this placed upon the 'expert witnesses' are, I am sure, relevant to the outcome of the 1967 trial. There have been two major trials under the Act, and in neither of them would the Judge allow evidence to be called as to the tendency of the book to deprave or corrupt; this, it was said, the jury must decide for themselves without such help, presumably by examining themselves spiritually for stains incurred during their reading of the books. The witnesses on either side had to deal with one question only, that of literary merit so abstracted. They were of course unable to do so.

One other provision of the Act is relevant. It provided for more summary proceedings, intended to be used against 'pulp' pornography. For such any member of the public could seek a 'destruction order' – ask a magistrate to have a publication destroyed. But it allowed that publishers and authors might appear in the magistrate's court to defend their property, which had not formerly been the case.

To the great surprise of its drafters, the Act first came into use at the trial of a book which they thought to be the kind to which it would afford protection. The famous case of the Crown *vs.* Penguin Books, the *Lady Chatterley* trial, occupied six days in the Fall of 1960. The Act got its first work-out, and precedents were established, but it was in many ways a somewhat misleading case. The defence insisted that the jury read the whole book before having their attention drawn to particular passages. It also insisted that, in terms of the Act, a book was not obscene unless it led the reader 'to do something wrong that he would not otherwise have done'. The judge explained clearly to the jury what they must do : first they were to make up their minds as to whether the book was obscene, and if they decided it was proceed to the next question : was it nevertheless of such merit that its publication was in the public interest? On this second question, if they got to it, they should consider the evidence of the thirty-odd expert witnesses; but they should not be over-impressed by the large number of them, and they should remember that the witnesses were specialists; the book might present a different picture to 'a person with no literary background, or little knowledge of Lawrence'. The possible implication, that the very expertness of the defence witnesses made it possible for the jury to disregard them if they chose, was to be of importance at the *Last Exit* trial; the defence can defend only by means of these witnesses, who must be 'expert', yet their professional qualifications make their testimony only ambiguously relevant to the deliberations of the non-expert jury.

What tended to make the *Lady Chatterley* case a dubious precedent were the following considerations. First, the book was in various ways already famous, and by a famous writer. Secondly, so far as the court was informed,[1] the sexual behaviour described in it was not perverse. Thirdly, the prosecution called no witness as to literary merit. Fourthly, a great part of the trial was taken up in the discussion not of situations but of words, the famous four-letter words which were really all that distinguished *Lady Chatterley's Lover*, so far as the

1. It was after the trial that critics, especially Mr John Sparrow, maintained that the seventh act of intercourse between Connie and Mellors was an act of buggery.

charge of obscenity goes, from a great many other books dealing with adultery; and it was possible for the defence to argue that these words were used with extremely serious and even puritanical intent. As C. H. Rolph remarks at the end of his invaluable book on the trial, 'It was the words which caused all the trouble, putting her Ladyship on trial as an adultress where a more conventionally spoken gamekeeper might have lent her the impunity of Emma Bovary or Anna Karenina.'

In the years between the trials of *Lady Chatterley* and *Last Exit* there were some changes in the law, and some evidence that the intention of its drafters could be further frustrated. Thus *Fanny Hill* was prosecuted under the forfeiture procedure described above, which by-passes jury trial altogether. In the same year, 1964, the Conservative Government enacted an amending measure by which it became an offence to have an obscene book for sale; and a book could be deemed to have been published for sale even if it were still a manuscript in the hands of the publisher. In 1967 Mr Jenkins, true to the intention of the 1959 Act, inserted a clause in a Criminal Justice act to prevent proceedings of the kind taken against *Fanny Hill*, but this became law too late to save *Last Exit*. Sir Cyril Black, MP, a man very certain of his own judgement in matters of public morality, had asked in the House of Commons whether the Crown would proceed against *Last Exit*. On being assured by the Director of Public Prosecutions that no such proceedings were contemplated, he took copies of the book to a magistrate and asked for their destruction. After a long trial the magistrate ordered them destroyed. This prevented the further sale of the book, which had, as a matter of fact, greatly increased while these proceedings were pending. The Director of Public Prosecutions thereupon changed his mind and announced that Calder and Boyars must stand trial in the Central Criminal Court under the 1959 Act. Thus it was possible for a watchdog of public morality to cause the law officers of the Crown to change their minds in a matter which involved publishers in a criminal trial, and, at worst, in imprisonment and an unlimited fine. Because of the recent change in the law this can no longer be done in quite the same way, but that it can still be done nobody doubts. And even if he is acquitted the publisher may face enormous legal costs. Such is the price of disagreement between the literary public and the general public as to what measure of literary merit excuses the publication of any book of unusual sexual candour.

Literary people probably overestimate their ability to judge the state of the public mind on this, as on other questions, but if the *Last Exit* trial is an indication of any value the English mood is at present one of a certain revulsion against 'dirty books'. In this, as in other matters, a marked tendency to repressiveness on the part of police and judiciary meets with surprisingly little disinterested public comment. Thus the fans, but so far as I can see only a few of their elders, were disturbed by the Rolling Stones drug trials. A couple of days ago someone got 18 months for possessing LSD. One of my own students is serving a prison sentence of *twelve months* for a peaceful demonstration at the Greek Embassy[2]; there was admittedly some public and newspaper comment on the severity of the sentence, which was upheld by the Appeal Court, but it seems to be taken as a reflection of the tough mood we have got into during the Home Secretaryship of the very Roy Jenkins whose name was so strongly associated with liberalizing measures. Of course these symptoms are very difficult to read, very mixed, as they are in the U.S. also. Thus 1967, the year of these drug and demonstration cases, the year of the *Last Exit* case, was also the year in which the British Parliament reformed the law on homesexuality and abortion, and a Bill further liberalizing the divorce law made good progress in Parliament.

Lady Chatterley was acquitted; *Last Exit* was not. Yet the rules of the game had changed very little between the two cases. These rules have a most curious effect upon what may be said in defence of a book; when you take literary criticism into a law court strange things happen to it. For obvious reasons I shall describe my own experience, rather than that of the twenty-nine other defence witnesses. Having read the sixty-five pages of the transcript which record my performance, I can swear that I am not motivated by vanity.

Defence witnesses were instructed that testimony as to the literary merit of the work (we were required to have ready definitions of literary merit) could, under the rules of evidence, make reference to 'honesty of purpose, moral tone, and the extent to which the book increases its readers' understanding

2. This was of course before the exemplary sentences on the Cambridge students tried for their part in the Garden House affair.

of society', but must not include the expression of any opinion as to whether the book had 'a tendency to corrupt and deprave, evidence on this last point being for expert psychiatric witnesses (if this is allowed at all)' (it was not). I got an inkling of what I was in for during a three-hour discussion with defence counsel, a few days before the trial; we went through the book commenting on one passage after another, obviously with the purpose of finding some common ground between what could be said critically and what should be said legally. There are relevant differences between the criticism game and the law game.

The trial began on 13 November with brief opening submissions, and then the jury was sent out to read the book. The *Lady Chatterley* jury took two and a half days to read that book; this jury returned after about one hour and a half and announced that they were ready. This was surprising, since *Last Exit* is not exactly an easy work, even for American readers; it dispenses with typographical conventions helpful to the ordinary reader and cannot be read fast. For Englishmen there is the additional difficulty that it is written in an unfamiliar demotic. After protest from the defence they were sent out to read it more fully, and on the third day witnesses were called, defence witnesses first. There were to be thirty of them, against six for the prosecution. The strange critico-legal seminar began.

Much the greater part of my testimony related to particular passages, but near the beginning I was asked for an overall impression, and said that I was greatly moved by the book, and by its originality and 'moral power'. What did I mean by 'moral power'?

It seems to me that one of the purposes of serious novelists has always been to deal with what some of the earliest proposers of realism called 'contemporary moral reality', and it seems to me that this book does therefore stand, with all its differences of manner and language, in a tradition which is a very honourable one – the tradition which uses novels not as forms of entertainment so much as ways of examining – not for propaganda purposes – but simply examining and laying before the reader a picture of contemporary moral reality. I thought that this book, dealing as it does with the lower depths of a great city, was very much in the tradition of

Dickens, who spoke of the shame, misery and desertion of a great capital.

This isn't very well put, though literary people will take the point easily enough; what became very evident when one read the newspapers next day was that only the comparison with Dickens, a very limited one, made any impact. *The Guardian* headlined its story 'As From the Pen of Dickens'; a satirical journal ran a piece on the trial of *Pickwick Papers*. Nobody went into the question of what might be meant by 'contemporary moral reality'. This kind of misunderstanding is absolutely unavoidable, I now see, when literary 'experts' are used for such purposes.

When we passed to individual passages it was soon evident that what the 'expert' felt like saying and what the defence lawyer wanted him to say were by no means the same thing. There is a note of impatience in the questioning; I am told not to say so much, or to say more; not to go forward so quickly or to move on. Here and there I miss the point of some line of questioning. It is the lawyer's reading of the book – undertaken with the 1959 Act open before him – that matters, not mine, except in so far as mine corroborates his. We spend a good deal of time on the biblical epigraphs to each section, touch on the four-letter words, the absence of quotes. We are trying to show that the violence of Vinnie's group, inhuman, motiveless in the stories, is necessary to the fulfilment of the author's honourable intention. We quote from the text: words like *shiteatinbastards*, pronounced in English accents, quietly, hang in the air of the court. Counsel introduces *King Lear* and asks me if there are passages in it that some people might find distasteful. After forty-five minutes we have got to page 12 of the novel.

The second section of the novel, which is mostly about an orgy in the apartment of Georgette and his queer friends, required us to deal at some length with the cultural aspirations of the central figure. We elucidated, with the help of the judge, her references to well-known Italian operas. The judge also made some jokes, at which everybody laughed. We agreed that Georgette's mother was fond of him, so that it would be untrue to state that there was no affection in the book. We explained that to register characters like these you have to use their kind of language, and use it a lot. We maintained that the rough treatment of the pregnant girl is so described as to show that

77

the author is in no sense endorsing such conduct. We identified *The Raven* as a poem by Edgar Allen Poe, characterized the fine writing that occurs in that passage as falsely glamorous, noted that the subway was what we call the underground, and conjectured that Georgette, at the end of the story, was distressed by the fact that she tastes faeces on Vinnie's penis. This, and other disagreeable experiences, we averred, were not recommendations from Mr Selby. He did not appear to be proposing Tralala's career as a model for other girls, or suggesting, in 'Strike', that men who feel sick when they make love to their wives should make free with union funds and consort with male prostitutes.

We talk of violence, lovelessness, disorder. We say that Satan finds work for idle hands to do. We explain to the court what is meant by a *dragball*, and what is meant by a *fruit*. We admire the construction of the last section of the book, comment on the history of stream-of-consciousness techniques, claim originality for Selby – 'I don't know that these lower social depths have ever been recorded in such concrete detail' – deny that Selby has to date shown the intellectual grasp and power of Bellow and Mailer, but conclude that he presents 'a hard clear image, with all the implications we might ourselves attach to it, of a society in desperate danger'. We attribute to Selby 'great integrity of purpose, and above all ... a passion and sympathy for these ... deprived and depraved people which communicates itself very strongly to the reader'.

In cross-examination I was asked about 'contemporary modern reality'. 'Moral reality was the expression I used.' 'Moral reality', the prosecution counsel patiently amended. What does it matter? Everybody admits you have the *highest* qualifications; but why, with the greatest respect, does it require someone like you to come along and explain to us what the book is about, and how it shows contemporary *moral* reality? In short, the object of the prosecution was to show that the need for 'expert witnesses' is in itself an indication that there's something wrong with the book. Against this one struggled as one could. 'If you mean that one has to be a professor of literature in order to do it, I don't say that. I think ... any person whom I would regard as a literate person could do as well as I've done.' But would I say 'the normal average reader' would be able to analyse the book in this way? 'Possibly he would lack the same degree of explicitness, which has been forced on me by the situation in which I find myself ... a good deal of the skill which people who read novels develop almost without knowing it is to take points without actually spelling them out.' In saying that this book in no way invites imitation or participation on the part of its readers, I am speaking only for myself, surely? No, as a member of a literate public. Would I claim that every normal person would see the *literary* purpose of the beating-up in the first story? But this question I was not allowed to answer; it was against the rules. It was exactly what the jury had to decide; my business was with literary merit only, and my answer to this important question was of no relevance.

This was much the most entertaining part of my testimony, since it involved the attempt to sail in the right direction with the legal wind, as it were, against me. This will do as an instance: counsel asks whether the feelings of homosexuals, under the influence of huge doses of benzedrine, are not described as pleasurable.

KERMODE: I think you must distinguish between a passage which says that homosexuals are sometimes happy and a passage which says: come and be a homosexual. There seems to me to be no implication here whatsoever that this is a good idea....

PROSEC: ...You're answering the question now which I'm not allowed to ask you ... I'm sorry – it's not your fault – but those are the rules.

KERMODE: May I ask a question, my lord? I'm not clear what I did wrong there —

JUDGE: You didn't do anything wrong.

Counsel ignored this exchange, and proceeded to 'Tralala'. I said the story asked you to attend to a situation in which people can become so dehumanized. 'But what am I meant to do about it?' asked counsel. 'Works of art aren't meant to make you *do* something,' replied the expert witness. 'They're meant to make you contemplate something.' 'I'm not quite following you,' said counsel. Nor did he follow when I said that Tralala – a child totally degraded – aroused one's pity. At whatever level of sophistication, the expert witness is hard to follow. In his re-examination defence counsel made much of the point that works of art did not make you want to go and do something.

So ended the third day. There were seven more, but in a

sense the issue – or so it seems by hindsight – was settled. The jury took five and a half hours to decide, and what they decided was that the book was obscene, but that its literary merit was not such that its publication was in the public interest. They followed the advice of the prosecuting counsel, who had insisted that since anybody with thirty shillings could buy the book, it was hardly sensible to apply to it the sophisticated distinctions between art and propaganda, action and contemplation, proposed by the expert witnesses. They believed instead Mr Robert Pitman[3], of the Beaverbrook Press, who said that 'young people at universities who might read about orgies in this book are precisely those who would feel the printed word gives them almost a kind of authority for imitating them'. They believed the one witness they would certainly have heard of, the Rev. David Sheppard[4], who was an international cricket hero before he took over a slum settlement in East London: he testified that although he had come across behaviour of the kind described, a reading of Selby's book had *marked* him. As when Sir Basil Blackwell said that a reading of *Last Exit* had darkened his life, the jury may have supposed that these expert witnesses were claiming to have experienced something like the corruption or perversion which, legally, make a book obscene. And then, presumably, they decided they had felt it themselves.

So the jury, representing one public, took the advice of the judge and refused to be impressed by the great mass of testimony offered by members of that other, the literary public. Almost certainly they would have in the back of their minds the memory of the Moors murders, which were committed by people who read the Marquis de Sade and tortured children to death, recording their cries. Here was highbrow literature used in a spirit of action rather than contemplation; no complex stasis of patterned responses in Brady and Hindley, but an unspeakable devotion to do-it-yourself. This would foster the plain man's easy contempt for the highfalutin 'expert', who emerges blinking from his library to tell the world to have complicated thoughts about simple matters. Who doesn't know a dirty book when he sees one? The prosecution encouraged this line of thought.

It must henceforth be recognized that 'literary merit' is,

3. Now deceased.   4. Now Bishop of Woolwich.

under the Act, a very unreliable defence, and that it must always be so, and not only in Britain, so long as the general public is made the judge of it. I suppose it was a sort of triumph to have made the Act so sophisticated as to allow such a defence – certainly our earlier censors and licensers would not have dreamed of admitting it – but no one foresaw that the law's interpreters would tell the jury to pay attention to expert witnesses only if they chose to. 'You must be the judges,' not only of obscenity but of literary merit. Yet one can qualify for jury service without ever having read through a book in one's life, and certainly without the slightest inkling of the place of passion, and of perversity, in the literature of the world.

The trial was, therefore, a sad parable. Imagine having to persuade such a jury of the merit of *any* book, let alone one charged with obscenity; imagine trying to persuade it that literature itself is in the public interest. And of course the difficulty is much intensified in cases of obscenity. Either you believe that literature, by means of invented forms, deepens your apprehension of human problems, subverts your moral stupidity, and, by intensifying your sense of what it means to be alive, justifies its destruction of your easier comforts; or you don't. When Horatio told Hamlet, as he speculated on our posthumous state, that he was considering too curiously, he was saying what men who content themselves with the stale fictions of an unconsidering society will always say about men who won't do that, men who examine death, for instance, in tragedies. And if you accept the comfortable myths of whatever decency rules at the moment, you will certainly have little patience with those who believe that to disturb it, to let reality break in on it, is not merely good in itself but indispensable to a proper humanity. In what W. H. Auden called 'the expansive moments of constricted lives/In the lighted inn' the enemies of the comfortable myth are allowed to make a sterile appearance in jokes; the four-letter words are for the bar, not the bedroom. A man who uses prostitutes can still think *Bubu of Montparnasse* a dirty book; a man who buys hardcore pornography may nonetheless, in his most impressive civic moment, as a juror in an important trial, put away these childish things and take what seems an adult view of the matter. The impressive game in which he finds himself seems to require it.

For the law, which is not an ass, is a game, and calls for

ritualized behaviour. English lawyers justify the formalities of their proceedings, their wigs and robes and ritual cries, by saying that these things may have survived their historical causes but continue to serve, by a providential arrangement, as a kind of cooling system. The heat of litigation is reduced by ceremony. In fact an obscenity trial, which is, as I have maintained, a struggle between the culture and one of its subcultures, is transformed by the rules of law into something that resembles the real social issue about as much as chess resembles war. There is one difference, which is that the expert witness is not strictly comparable with a chess knight; to get the idea of how he is compelled to behave you would have to imagine a knight whose first step must always be sideways. He cannot, faced with such a jury, behave according to the rules of his own game. He cannot speak his own language. His task is to prevent the jury from saying, on its retirement, that it knows a dirty book when it sees one; and this is not his métier. Also he has to defend his evaluations, and the jury has not. Theirs, not his, is the public interest. The criteria by which lawyers decide what is and what is not relevant are in the public interest and not his.

Possibly the democrat should find some grim consolation here. The form taken by the 1959 Act, hammered out in a contest between a popularly elected government and a progressive lobby, reflects an authentic democratic process. The legal interpretation of the act – the discrediting of the progressive witnesses by the prosecution and by the judges' summing up in both trials – enacts the inertia of a genuine majority. No doubt many books owe their unpersecuted existence to this inertia – they have escaped the notice of what is after all a non-reading public. But when its attention is called to a particular work it is likely to confound literary merit with a concept of purity which excludes sexual candour, and to proceed on the assumption that sex ought not to achieve verbal expression at all, except perhaps in the ritualized and licensed media of instruction manuals and oral jokes. It will be of small use to tell this public that Last Exit was no more intended to make people experiment in perversion than a joke about little Alphonse; that the tensions which are released by the laughter at the end of a joke are a little model of the tensions, equally without immediate practical issue, induced by a literary work of art.

The difference is simply between a public which reads and a

much larger one which does not. Whether you think *Last Exit*
will influence conduct for good or ill depends entirely upon
that. The literary public is a large club, held together by
adherence to certain rules. These rules slowly evolve. We have
not always believed that poems, plays, and novels should carry
the label 'no road through to action', but we have believed it
for a long time. Of course they may deal with matters upon
which action is necessary; but one reason why we think
Middlemarch a better novel than, say, *Uncle Tom's Cabin* is
precisely that although *Middlemarch* deals with a great historical crisis it never says, we shall get over this only if we improve the condition of women, or whatever. So it is easy for
readers who have joined the club to see that *Last Exit* is neither
a plea for drugs and homosexual behaviour nor a warning that
we must improve our low-cost housing projects. It says : this is
your kind of hell; in the city where you live this is what
becomes of natural instinct; this is what you leave out of view
when you benevolently contemplate your society. Even that
makes it sound too much like a pamphlet, too little like an
image; but it is already as far beyond the scope of the non-
literary as it would be if one spoke of 'patterns of sentience' or
'organization of stimuli'.

A case of this kind ought to make the literary public consider how far it has detached itself from the culture as a whole.
The evidence suggests that the lack of any common language
in matters of aesthetic is a measure also of enormous ethical
differences. In the eyes of the literate, the world of the jury
will seem as obsolete as the conventional structure of some
dead novel, the world, say, of some average Gothic novel before *Northanger Abbey*. The sexual reticence of the average
person, except in privileged situations, is as meaningless as the
design of a well-made play. Of course the conventions of non-
literate behaviour change too, but they change at a different
rate, and certainly not fast enough for us to expect that a man,
summoned to the Old Bailey, will not put on his Sunday best
and vote down highbrow dirt. After all, in swinging London we
still groan under eighteenth-century Sunday Observance laws
which only a few people actively endorse, but which remain
unaltered because the people who don't like them would continue, in their role as serious citizens, to withhold their votes
from politicians who tried to abolish them. All liberalizing
legislation would come to an end if tested by plebiscite; re-

forms relating to capital punishment, homosexuality, and abortion are brought about in part by the skill and persistence of their supporters, in part by that same inattentiveness on the part of the general public which has allowed certain books to be published which would never have survived the ordeal of the courts.

In a period of inattentiveness, such as American literati are at present enjoying, the gap between the publics widens very rapidly. Unrestrained sexual explicitness is easy enough, and has no necessary relation to aesthetic merit. Occasionally this gives rise to concern on the part of the literate; not long ago George Steiner was saying that he thought the flood of such writing invades our erotic privacy and devalues our sexuality; that it is no real gain to the reader to have his sexual imagining done for him. This implies that the tabus of the non-literate have their value. The argument is cogent, but neglects, I think, to consider that the literary subculture has its own tabus. The ordinary man protects himself against dangerous or unwelcome stimuli by laughter; that is why his jokes are often on such serious subjects as adultery, homosexuality, disease. The literate protect their privacy by criticism. Detailed and repetitive accounts of sex and fantasy tend to comply with certain conventions. These conventions, like all others, are bound to grow rigid and be seen as intolerable insults to truth, as fossilized as Gothic; and some *nouvelle vague* will consign them to the past. Thus do the literate keep a balance between imagination and reality; they have always known how to cope with the exploitation, by inferior talents, of the imaginative values established by better ones.

This will not, of course, be a puritan counter-revolution though it may resemble that in some ways. Nor will it solve the general problem of whether sexual explicitness, in truly imaginative works, can be shown to be to the general good. The literate, who change rapidly under the pressure of an observed discrepancy between art and reality, will already have turned their attention and their sophisticated procedures to new problems.

In short, little can be expected from a dialogue between the two publics on the subject of 'the public interest'. The trial of *Last Exit* has shown that, if it has shown nothing else. The literary public is, in such a situation, always the defendant, and it must defend itself not in its own tongue but in a language improvised for the occasion and unequal to it. Such a trial is acutely representative of a communications problem that is by no means merely a matter of what is or is not obscene; but obscenity is more than other literary deviationism a source of interest to the larger public. It is hard to see how this conflict of interest could be resolved. The present American truce may be temporary. In Germany, I am told, one can get disputed books by signing a sort of poison register at the bookseller's. In Ireland there is a state censorship.[5] In these or other ways the general public will, at times, intervene to disturb the dialectic of saturation and rejection which is characteristic of literary history. We, the literate or literary, would no doubt prefer to be without this clumsy intervention, and the unfortunate publisher whose livelihood may be at stake is unlikely to feel philosophical about it. We should prefer to work out our own salvation; but *they* insist, at irregular intervals, on our behaving as if we belonged to a larger society which includes them. If our privacy is in danger, we should prefer our own way of safeguarding it; but from time to time we must consider theirs. In this larger social context we can only be as liberal as we are allowed to be (just as we can only be as socialist as we are allowed to be) and this will sometimes seem to be not liberal (or socialist) at all. But we may find some consolation (I do not find much) in reflecting that it is only when we quarrel with it that we are conscious at all of our inescapable involvement with the other and larger society.

(1968)

The report of the working party convened by the Arts Council to consider the laws relating to obscene publications has attracted so much attention that it seems we are again about to ram what C. H. Rolph calls 'a thought-barrier at least as old as the Great Rebellion'. This is the instant assumption of many Englishmen that whatever they dislike ought to be put a stop to, on self-evident moral grounds, and that if it is a book its publisher should be hanged, have his ears cut off, be sent to prison or fined, whichever is the going revenge. To help us see what we are up against historically we now have Mr Donald Thomas's history of literary censorship in England, which is

5. Since this was written Denmark has tried the experiment of abolishing all censorship.

concerned with prosecutions for blasphemy and sedition as well as obscenity, and which carries, in its extremely scholarly wake, an appendix consisting of vivid instances of the insupportable. That the treatment of such publishers as A. S. Frere, F. J. Warburg, and John Calder as potential felons is not the only or indeed the best way to protect the national morality is suggested by the example of Denmark, but also by that of the U.S.A., where, as he testifies in a witty and interesting book, Mr Charles Rembar, by advocacy more astute than we are used to in *our* obscenity trials, has got his country's nose, at least, through a barrier as old as the foundation of the Commonwealth of Massachusetts.[6]

As to books, I am – though I hope aware of the complexities of a situation – in favour of abolishing the obscenity laws. May we rival the happiness of Denmark! As to theatre, I support the working party's recommendation (in its draft Bill) that the Theatres Act of 1968 be 'brought into line', assuming that the expression has legal precision sufficient to the purpose. But I do so with less assurance that I have seen all the angles. For the case seems to be very different from that of books. There has not been a qualitative change in the nature of books : we know fairly exactly what we are talking about there. But the theatre seems to be in a revolutionary phase, trying to turn into something else. Unprecedented erotic manifestations are an important sign of this, and we are much less well prepared to understand them and foresee their outcome than we are to take the point, and guess the future, of written erotica.

Nobody pretends that the obscenity law works well. Lawyers find it confusing, judges misread it, defendants cannot know in advance of the verdict whether they are criminals. It enforces an arbitrary, obsolete, and largely irrelevant definition of obscenity, formulated in a wholly different connection 102 years ago. It allows a modern judge to restate the archaic and appalling doctrine that the court is *custos morum*. The defence of merit outweighing obscenity, which was formally introduced in 1959, is appraised by a jury which, randomly chosen, may know nothing of books. When Lord Campbell introduced his Obscenity Bill in 1857, Mr Thomas informs us, he brandished a

6. *Books in the Dock*. By C. H. Rolph. London, Deutsch, 1969. *A Long Time Burning*. By Donald Thomas. London, Routledge & Kegan Paul, 1969. *The End of Obscenity*. By Charles Rembar. London, Deutsch, 1969.

copy of *La Dame aux Camélias* as an instance of a book he disliked but which would not be the target of his legislation, the purpose of which was to stop works written 'with the intention of corrupting morals'. But not so long afterwards Vizetelly was in prison for publishing Zola. Compare the dismay felt in 1960 by the sponsors of the 1959 Act, who never dreamt it could be used against such a book as *Lady Chatterley's Lover*.

Such laws are a great menace to literature, and not very effective against lucrative 'filth'. Furthermore, in differences of opinion as to what is currently acceptable to our society, they add to the repressive side of the argument that shadow of archaic rigour which lies over the criminal courts. Mr Rolph quotes a letter from A. S. Frere about the near-panic he felt in the dock at the Old Bailey; and even witnesses can testify to the unease bred by the unfamiliar setting, the manners of counsel, and the unreality of an argument which will be settled by a group of people quite possibly unable to follow it, and conscious of a hopeless discrepancy between the world as they know it and 'the standards of what is acceptable' which they are, for once in their lives, expected to establish. Those who fear abolition ought at least to keep one eye on Denmark, and another on the U.S.A., where, says Mr Rembar, no book can now be proscribed unless it is found to be 'utterly without redeeming social value'.

I was a member of the working party and of the sub-committee which examined the possibilities of amendment rather than abolition; we even produced a draft Bill for this purpose. But what one really discovered was the hopelessness of the present law, so deep in that tinkering with definitions could hardly help it; and since our brief was to recommend what seemed right rather than what Parliament might be expected to act upon, I happily capitulated to the abolitionists. Much more impressively, Mr Rolph and Mr Montgomerie, vastly more learned and experienced in the law, capitulated with equal readiness. The case in respect of literature is, I think, made.

What about the Theatres Act, which is to be 'brought in line'? Well, it must be so brought. But about the effect of this one is less happy. The theatre is considering a return from drama to ritual, from Apollonian to Dionysian; or so we are told. But the only theatre we know as theatre is Apollonian in its texts, its sociology, its architecture. That things are not done on the stage as they are in life is not arbitrary formalism but in the nature of the institution. Sēami, lawgiver of the Japanese Noh plays, tells of a nobleman who reproved an actor for not holding a scythe as a labourer does : he got a lecture on the elements of the *vraisemblable*. Stage-scything is not like scything. Until recently stage-kissing, and stage-whispers, were distinguishable from kissing and whispers. And stage-killing continues to be simulated. Why, then, should truth cry out that coitus, fellatio and cunnilingus should at this time be performed without dissimulation on the stage?

It is useless to say that, in a precious etymological sense, this would be obscene, since the whole idea is to overthrow former notions of what may be represented, and how. We have seen the disappearance of the proscenium arch, the involvement of previously passive spectators, the decay of plot : all are moves against old formalities, but none is so violent as to constitute, of itself, a new theatrical *discours*. But surely stage coitus does. There are, as I see it, two objections to it : it is ideologically suspect, and it is destructive of *theatre*.

The ideology of sex on stage is not an ideology of sex but of protest. As the title of *Che* implies, a play of revolutionary sexual explicitness is an urban guerrilla operation. You have to know the ideological set-up before you get the point that fellatio, normally a private act, stands for public revolution. It certainly does not stand for itself, since in itself it needs no audience, and is arguably better without one. Indeed, an audience might well be disgusted by an elementary failure to estimate its presence. For what goes on in the true theatre is something meant to be exhibited before an audience, so that if certain events are enacted which are socially private in character, such as murder or copulation, they are simulated. Not to see this is to risk confusing the theatre with the brothel, failing to observe that one goes to each with a different purpose. This confusion will seem the more confounded if one reflects that no stage scenario or script can require spontaneous sexual performances by artists; the best it can expect is an un-Dionysian routine by paid performers, disagreeable even to the voyeur.

This suggests that the real-sex movement is theatrically wrong. But there is another point to be made. Whether the object of the experiment is Dionysian-primitivist or more directly revolutionary, it is unwise of theatrical people to forget what the theatre can be and do. It has never, since it ceased to be ritual, gone in for orgy. Striptease serves an audience unified in advance by a single need, but theatre unifies a disparate assembly, each beginning in, and in a measure remaining in, his privacy.

Privacy, perhaps, is the key to it all, educated privacy. The new draft Bill is devoted to it. It would allow everybody to read what he wanted, without interference by other persons, while preventing the public display of possibly offensive material, and its transmission by post to unwilling recipients. The difficulty is that privacy is a much more difficult concept in the theatre than in one's own room, or indeed in the cinema.

Sex exhibited before an audience, if it fails (as under normal conditions it presumably will) to make them part of the show, can either homogenise them into a simple *exhibition* group or freeze them into attitudes of lonely discomfort. Probably the latter : men of good will have elevated notions of sex and deplore whoredom. The evidence is that they think the theatre a place of complex simulation, not simple. Those whose business it is to cherish the theatre should, given their total freedom, consider this respectable point of view. Cherishing the theatre is, after all, the whole point of the present operation.

(1969)

Note : Much has happened since I wrote the earlier part of this chapter. The appeal of Calder & Boyars was upheld on a technicality : the judge was held to have misdirected the jury in explaining the provisions of the Act, which have by now proved virtually incapable of explanation. Nothing that was said towards the clarification of the law was reassuring to publishers; on the contrary, the assertion that it is criminal to 'induce erotic desires of a heterosexual kind' means that one can be tried for having, with or without intent, induced somebody to do something perfectly legal. Furthermore the instances of increasing repressiveness (p. 75) are now sadly out of date.

FOUR

ANTON EHRENZWEIG

The Hidden Order of Art[1] though a very challenging book is probably less original than it seems. But it does raise many questions, and it is a great misfortune that the author has not survived to answer them. It is not only that the material of the book is difficult but that Ehrenzweig employs unusual methods of presenting it. Without his prefatory warnings, the reader might suppose the book to be somewhat repetitious; actually, he says, it's stereoscopic, and the same line of argument is treated in a variety of contexts. The reader can either see it in stereoscopic depth or follow one thread and ignore all the others. Anyway, he can understand the whole without understanding all the parts. This formal innovation is itself of some interest, but like other aspects of the book it will have to yield precedence to the more urgent issue, which is really to decide what Ehrenzweig is talking about and whether it makes sense. What does he mean by 'the hidden order of art'? Is the notion new, or correct?

The short answers are these. It is new only in accidentals, not in essentials. You can't even consider the possibility of its being right until you come to terms with the author's apparently unexamined muddles about the relations of modern and older forms of art. As to its being useful, it is so in much the same way as other pedagogic fictions are useful – primarily to teachers of the more prophetic and doctrinaire variety.

Since so much of the argument turns on the specific virtues of the modern and involves the notion that newness is the greatest asset – though it's obviously a rapidly wasting asset – of art, I'd better say a word first about the kind of art Ehrenzweig is talking about. Very crudely, the book is a psychoanalytic manifesto for Abstract Expressionism. One has a picture of a blank surface and a man marking it in one way or another, thereby creating 'pictorial space' and bringing some internal conflict to equilibrium. To describe the conflict and equilibrium, Ehrenzweig uses a psychological theory adapted or de-

1. By Anton Ehrenzweig. London, Weidenfeld & Nicolson, 1967.

veloped from Freud, and alluding to, but controverting, *Gestalt* theory. But he never – I think – makes it quite clear whether this approach can be applied, except destructively, to pre-twentieth-century art, unless you think of mythology as a form of art.

On the whole he seems to be involved in the assumption that, for two reasons, only very modern art works. The first is that true communication between artist and consumer depends heavily on surprise – on the discontinuity of what one is looking at from anything recognizable as a pre-existing scheme. Related to this is the view that any valuable response must be to a form which is not only novel but indeterminate, leaving the observer to do his own work of selection among a theoretical infinity of possible responses. The second is that only modern art has intuitively understood that it is concerned with the recording of tensions existing in our psychic processes, so that it alone has any chance of objectifying the valuable 'order' of art, which is a hidden order.

What is the hidden order? One way of describing it is this. Think of psychosis, of a patient paralysed by tensions between unconscious and conscious, caught in a mental stasis. Then think of an artist: he is not sick, but unprecedentedly healthy. Instead of being paralysed, he is animated by the same conflicts. In his mental process there are three stages. The first is schizoid, and it produces a violent chaos, the chaos of un-differentiation as Ehrenzweig calls it. This highly destructive movement of the psyche is followed by a manic stage. This is integrative: it is a scanning of the apparent primary chaos for a hidden order. After this confrontation in the lower reaches of the ego there is a third stage, labelled depressive, and in this the mental material – a chaos of potential forms – is fed back, reintrojected, into the surface ego. This is the painting or the music finished, and made available to the observer or listener. There is an evident analogy with some modern studies of dreaming, since art in this view is like the dream in that it is not a function of wish-fulfilment but of ego-synthesis.

However, it is different from dreaming in so far as it has a social aspect: it is not only offered as a set of symbolic meanings, to the observer, but actively requires his collaboration. He has to *scan* it: in doing so he discovers the hidden form. He is involved in the work to a degree which Ehrenzweig thinks impossible in traditional art, because this better kind of art involves a schizoid assault on pre-existing schemata which the observer is required to carry out in his turn, whereas traditional art tends to comply with the very schemata that have to be assaulted. There is one limiting factor : in so far as we scan and select from the work of art to make it available to our consciousness, we interfere with it : nobody can apprehend it in its nuclear integrity, just as the physicist cannot study his particles without changing the situation he would like to contemplate.

It will be clear, I hope, even from this potted account, that this is a modernist theory, emphasizing anti-traditional novelty and a complicated expressionist aesthetic and psychology. I suppose the most striking innovation introduced by Ehrenzweig is the idea of unconscious scanning. E. H. Gombrich has made us familiar with the theory that one scans a picture and relates it to schemata which are culturally or even biologically predetermined;[2] but Ehrenzweig, though he refers to Gombrich, is saying something entirely different. He is saying that unconscious syncretistic scanning – which happens below the level of what Gombrich calls the educated eye – is the basic act of the fit observer. The observer thus repeats what the artist achieved in the second manic stage : he detects the potentiality of form in the chaos of undifferentiation. Gombrich says 'the ignorant eye sees nothing'. For Ehrenzweig ignorance is not a relevant term : it is at a lower level of consciousness that the decontaminated eye sees everything. It takes in the scattered profile and the irrational 'handwriting' of the artist, just as the decontaminated ear takes in the simultaneous possibilities of serial music. For only now, in our time, have we acquired arts which recognize and collaborate with our powers of unconscious scanning, and defeat the undesirable possibility of simple, conscious 'following'.

Of course the orders scanned by the uncontaminated eye are hidden orders. To be authentic they must reflect the whole process of the ego scattering and reforming; if they don't they are mere ornamental imitations, like a lot of modern abstract art. This requirement extends to the performing arts : a great musician's use of, say, rubato, or portamento, or vibrato, at this but not at that point, has a rightness we sense and marvel at, for it proceeds from a total unconscious scanning of the whole

2. *Art and Illusion*. London, Phaidon Press, 1960.

score and could never be achieved by conscious study. This is something we have known about in general, but which art only recently caught on to. We recognize the phenomenon in games. There are 'born' card-players – people who sense how the cards lie at bridge.

It does seem strange that Ehrenzweig should have got so close, in this part of his argument, to Michael Polanyi's theories of tacit knowing; perhaps the strong psychoanalytical basis of his thought prevents him from seeing the affinities. And when he talks of Wittgenstein, and how useful the philosopher would have found the notion of unconscious scanning in the *Philosophical Investigations*, he omits to mention that there are well-known works, for example those of Barfield and Empson, which do, in their own way, scan words for hidden orders. But Ehrenzweig passes on to a full psychoanalytical account of his theory, and then to the part that seems to have interested him most, an elaborate proof that the myth of the Dying God is a 'poemagogic' image of the creative process described earlier : the fragmenting, the manic reintegration, the reintrojection. All tragic images are, for Ehrenzweig, images of this creative process, and the Dying God is their archetype.

Now although this *tour de force* of argument will be for some readers the heart of his book, I shall say no more about it. Ehrenzweig is here, I think, writing fiction, and the connections between his Dying God and art are less useful even than such ideas as the 'displacement' of some modern Freudian literary critics, or the 'symbolic action' of Kenneth Burke. All he does is provide a mythic dress for his own psychoanalytical theory.

This, incidentally, is also, in a way, fictive. We can translate the theory into much more familiar modern terms. In fact, if we drop Freud as well as Frazer we are left with a much more manageable set of ideas. For instance, unconscious scanning : Ehrenzweig makes a good deal out of its importance in the choice of motives, as much in literature and music as in painting. As to literature, there is a classic treatment of the subject in Valéry's meditations on the *donnée*, but Valéry shows that it is possible to despise the *donnée* precisely for its unconscious origin : what matters is the sequel, the *calculée*, which engages the whole mind. He spoke of the conversion by intelligence, of 'confused arbitrariness' into 'explicit and well-defined arbitrariness' and despite great differences of emphasis and vocabulary, this new account of the basic creative process is not so different from Valéry's. You can see that they both descend from the same ancestors, nineteenth-century traditions of romanticism and symbolism.

The same point can be made about his interest in the happy accident, the unplanned felicity that crops up in the course of composition. This is something artists have always known about. The neo-classical artist, according to Ehrenzweig the one most indissolubly wedded to conscious schemata, most defiant of the unconscious, knew about it, and called it the 'grace beyond the reach of art'. He knew, though the knowledge may have seemed less important to him, that you don't know what you meant till you've seen what you say. The tension between this luck, or, as I prefer to call it, grace, and one's elaborate conscious preliminary design, is familiar to anybody who has ever written a book. It wouldn't be worth doing if one could not hope for grace. Thus the whole idea of the tension between what Ehrenzweig calls the schizoid and manic aspects of creativity is quite humbly familiar.

Why, then, do I call this book distinctively modern? Because it is in this century that these and other such insights have been most challengingly formulated, and have become part of the programme of many artists. I've just been talking about grace or luck: only in our time has this been exploited by people who make a cult of randomness. You might even say that Ehrenzweig's creative process is itself an image or allegory of modern art: the schizoid is Dada, the manic Surrealism. Unconscious scanning is a Cubist technique. The whole theory certainly fits twentieth-century art best. This is obviously so in the matter of novelty. Ehrenzweig argues that art can achieve its fullest impact only when new – the swing between schizoid and manic, focused *gestalt* and oceanic undifferentiation, is fully available only for a brief moment. We can never fully scan even the greatest past art: Beethoven, in his last years, may have seen that one had to enact the destructive processes of the schizoid stage, but we can no longer truly experience the fragmentations of the Ninth Symphony. Time and familiarity erode the power of art to induce the right tension in us.

Obviously this is part of the truth, but a misleading part. It's misleading even if taken to apply only to twentieth-century art, which is not all violent. It seems to be true that we identify great art by its power to destroy or extend conscious schemata of perception, but not that this always requires traumatic shock and total historical discontinuity. Ehrenzweig is what I call a schismatic modernist. He does believe in the great early moderns, but seems to think that their traditionalism was merely vestigial. He overvalues the shock of novelty because his theory requires art to be destructive. Measuring art by standards which belong to psychotherapy, he takes the violence of novelty as essential to success. Thus he never asks why, or in what manner, art survives its particular moment, and seems to think that the built-in impermanence and obsolescence of some modern art is equally a characteristic of all the art of the past.

This is a thought familiar from the writings of Harold Rosenberg. Late modernism is a highly theoretical affair – it is heavily dependent on systematized versions of older insights, of the kind I have referred to, concerning randomness, seriality, and so forth. It is this, I think, that creates the impression of a total break with the past; but Ehrenzweig, who accepts that break, explains it otherwise. He says artists and spectators now *understand* the need for aggressive fragmentation, now regard form as 'a conscious signal of a vast unconscious structure', and because they know this art simply works better now. The very sharp oppositions he makes between the art of the past and modern art are always, naturally, to the credit of the new. Thus Renaissance painting was in error when it simulated space behind the frame; modern art uses pictorial space which bulges out and, as it were, envelops the spectator; and this is what painting *should* do.

These notions are, as I said, in the air. Ehrenzweig idiosyncratically echoes not only Rosenberg but John Cage, and the aesthetician, or anti-aesthetician, Morse Peckham, author of *Man's Rage for Chaos*. Peckham regards the function of arts as being to strengthen our capacity to endure disorientation, and the function of the artist as being to achieve a maximum degree of discontinuity with the past. To associate art with any apprehensible idea of order is, for Peckham, to neutralize it by mixing it with some irrelevant, unshocking, pre-existing schema : art serves not a human need for order but a human need for chaos. E. H. Gombrich, reviewing Peckham's book, noticed that this escalation of a familiar requirement into an absolute demand for shock and discontinuity supports absurd conclusions – for instance, that Cage's silent composition 4′ 33″

is the greatest of all music. Here, as sometimes in Ehrenzweig, a few familiar insights have been rigidly systematized and offered as a total programme for modern art.

So there are questions to be asked. For example, is violence so important as a criterion of value in art? Believing that art must communicate directly a maximum of violence and un-reason, Ehrenzweig is faced with the conclusion, which he seems ready to accept, that the art of today is healthier than, and superior to, that of any time in the past. He also accepts the consequence that it very rapidly becomes obsolete : after all, it is that from which the healthy art of the future will have to be discontinuous. This is a timebound theory indeed, as if Wyndham Lewis's exaggerated fears were being proved true by history. It is simply untrue that the work of the past has no power to survive. How it survives is an interesting and difficult question, but that it does so is beyond argument. And this alone calls into question the notion that the hidden orders of works of art impinge upon us by novelty and shock alone. For a work that still affects us after a long time – we can leave aside the element of pure ceremoniousness in our response to it – will presumably be very rich in precisely those 'signals' which indi-cate some humanly valuable order. They can do the business which, on Ehrenzweig's view, only modern art can carry out.

I admit I've left a lot out, and reduced the book to a set of simple, and, as I think, erroneous propositions about modern-ism. He takes the modern to be, ideally, schismatic and violent, a triumph of unreason, wholly Dionysian. In fact the un-named hero of the book is Nietzsche. But to categorize Ehrenz-weig's book isn't the same as to tame it. Teachers and painters will very likely read it with some excitement, if only the excitement of recognition. Even in its fantasies it has its own shock value. For Ehrenzweig, at any rate in part, manages to make his book in the image of the art he advocates.

(1967)

CRITICS

FIVE

FATHER ONG

Now that the other eminent Catholic-electronic prophet, Marshall McLuhan, seems to have gone into orbit with his fantasy-probes, we shall all no doubt need to attend more closely to Fr Ong, who says so many of the same things but appears to say them more judiciously.[1] He is a good typographical man – encyclopaedic, repetitive, and committed to the past, not only as scholar but as theologian. He makes an occasional bow to his cool colleague, whose account of the new oral culture he echoes, but he appears to be of the opinion that if you have a theory you should be willing to defend it and produce evidence; he too says very extraordinary things but assumes that he has to vouch for them, and allow you to agree or disagree. I don't know what McLuhan would say about the more theological formulations of Ong, but in so far as he spells out the argument about the periodic modifications of the sensory apparatus from oral to visual etc., it seems clear that any critique of Ong is substantially one of McLuhan also, a momentous consequence that will be in everybody's mind as he toils through these pages.

The book began life as the Terry Lectures at Yale, a series founded 'to the end that the Christian spirit may be nurtured in the fullest light of the world's knowledge', and one presumes that the lectures lacked something of the sheer density of the book. Certainly it doesn't suggest oral performance; in fact it is a monument to those methods of information-storing, such as handwriting and printing, which – alas, as some say – replaced the early oral techniques of rhetoric and memonic. If one calls the style of the lectures highly typographic, it is only a way of saying that they have no style at all. Like many other aspects of our culture which tend in these discussions to be overlooked, prose style is in some respects an oral fossil; whether you are speaking of the splendid Ciceronian balances of Dr Johnson or the smart Tacitean curtness of J. F. Kennedy, you always appeal to early oral modes when you talk about prose

1. *The Presence of the Word.* By Walter J. Ong, S.J. Yale University Press, 1968.

style; or, in the appropriate language, you refer inevitably to the inveterate orality of learned Latin, and measure a deviation from the informative sequential native jogtrot of printed English. This book has no more style than a printbound Utilitarian tract of the last century, or a print-oriented Ph.D. thesis in this :

> Undoubtedly, if we consider in these perspectives[2] the work of an earlier Terry Lecturer, John Dewey, we will find that one facet of his many-faceted significance is that he climaxed the large-scale movement away from polemic in favour of an irenic approach to learning.

Fr Ong throws down hundreds of sentences like this one – coils of lecturer's demotic bruised with learning. They lie on the page like apple parings carelessly dropped, taking what shape chance or grace will give them. Perhaps this is not a matter for complaint; to have everything spelled out with neutral typographical explicitness is to have the chance of replying, in a familiar language, to proposals which appear to be conquering the world without much hindrance from criticism.

What one is criticizing is a theory of history. Characteristically Fr Ong's initial insight into its structures derived from a study of transmutation of Aristotelian logic in the sixteenth century. The innovations of Petrus Ramus, a Huguenot scholar and teacher who lost his life in the Massacre of St Bartholomew, have often been regarded as of revolutionary influence in poetry as well as in education, and they certainly affected the character of theological argument at a time when this seemed important. Ramism is not a philosophy in itself, only a modernization of the old logic; its inventor has been called 'the great master of the short cut'. Reducing logic to dialectic, Ramus concentrated on its practical use as a way of finding things out, and as an instrument for the logical correction of one's adversaries; thus he became the master of Protestant controversy. Since he was a teacher and greatly valued visual aids in the form of charts, Ong found in his work the critical point of change from oral disputation to the print-oriented cult of 'the

2. Ong uses this distressingly visual word more than once, and even apologizes for doing so, but somehow it turned out to be indispensable.

clear and distinct'. In other words, Ramus stands for the super-session of scholastic disputation, which is oral and temporally successive, by a dialectical method which prefers to set out argument spatially, and so destroys its temporal aspect, as print does. And if you meditate on the *kind* of change this represents, extending your meditation backward from the oral-script writing culture to the more purely oral (preliterate or pre-alphabetic) cultures of the past, and forward from the purely typographical to the typographical-electronic cultures of the future we now inhabit, you can easily observe that the kind of revolution typified by Ramism is to be found at other critical moments of history. Thus, as the oral yields to script, type, in our time, yields to oral-electric, and with the necessary qualifications and sophistications you can make yourself an inclusive theory.

If this is a fair account of how Ong's theory developed, it seems that any analysis of it will necessarily concern itself with two questions. First a critique of the evidence: do the historical documents genuinely comply with this theory, and not with any theory that contradicts it? Secondly a critique of satisfaction: what is the theory *for* (is it a means of finding out what is inevitably happening to our sensoria and our history, or is it in any sense apologetic or activist – say, in the sense that Marxism was intended to shorten the birthpangs of history)?

First it must be said that, although he shares with McLuhan a basic typology of explanation, Ong differs considerably in detail, largely because he is more interested in detail, but also because he wants a question-proof system, not merely a suggestive diagram. He can't, therefore, beg questions, as McLuhan does when he makes a script culture much closer to oral than to typographical. McLuhan wants a clear revolutionary situation, the sharpest possible demarcation between pre- and post-Gutenberg, a collapse into the limitations of a vision-dominated sensory system, a dissociation of sensibility. Ong, though he too thinks of the end of oralism as a kind of Fall, cannot so crudely over-dramatize history. He is always insisting on the overlap of oral and manuscript, oral and manuscript and print, all three of them and electronic-oral. At times the prophets seem to contradict one another; for McLuhan one of the curses of print is that it reduces everything to the visual and successive; for Ong that it destroys oral successiveness and encourages simultaneity and spatial interpretations ('operations with the alphabet imply that words ... can somehow be present all at once'). Perhaps this disagreement is caused by radical differences of temperament. Ong, a learned primitivist, looks back to a purely oral society with nostalgia, but sees that such a society must have lacked the relative instantaneity of print; whereas McLuhan, in love with the ideogram, the 'inclusive image', and the much greater instantaneity of electronic communication, sees print as relatively time-bound and defective in instantaneity. Broadly one could say that his criteria derive from a future, Ong's from a past.

Anyway, this disagreement may be a sign that the documents can be used to support apparently contradictory theories of sensorial revolution. However, Ong on the whole feels he has to attend to aspects of history that roughen up the theory; only very occasionally does he use the space-probe method in a McLuhanish way, and even then he builds in so many precautions that the probe never leaves the ground. Why then construct it? Perhaps we have here the hint of an answer to our question, what needs does the theory satisfy? What is it for? One such probe, for which the countdown never reaches zero, is a discussion of the analogies between development of communications media and the psychosexual stages of Freud. The oral in one, we are told, parallels the oral in the other, and print is anal, just as oral-electric is genital. Oral-aural cultures even if, like the Greek and Latin, they had writing, enjoy *copia*, the free flow of words; writing and print retain them, squeeze them in like a trained sphincter, though print moves on into a transitional phallic intrusiveness. The later electric-oral corresponds to 'mature genitality', social, oriented towards child-rearing. Ong is very uneasy about all this 'there appears no particular reason why the psychological development of an individual human being should provide an exact model for describing the development of the communications media'), and he hedges it about with disabling qualifications: 'this kind of selectivity is often more stultifying than illuminating'. McLuhan would not have said that; if the space probe doesn't work, send up another. That Ong should have said it is illuminating. Against his historian's judgement he had to get in something that proved the good primitivist position that the new reflective Eden of modern orality is somehow better than the old unreflective one we lost when we began our long exile in the alphabetic wilderness. He wants that to be true, but is rightly unhappy about the proof. Nevertheless he leaves it in.

Let us look at another space probe, this time one that does leave the launching pad, in what is, to me, both the most astonishing and revealing passage in the book. Indeed, I suspect that readers will find the book pregnant or vacuous in accordance with their reaction to it. It concerns the Incarnation, and the careful divine timing of it. The question is, why did God 'enter human history' when he did? The answer is that he did so 'at the precise time when psychological structures assured that his entrance would have the greatest opportunity to endure and flower', that is, when the oral was still dominant but the alphabet existed to give the Word endurance and stability. Moreover the obfuscation of the real (oral) nature of the Word by print was still remote. This makes God sounds like J. Walter Thompson, the Incarnation a well-researched Madison Avenue operation. I have very great respect for Fr Ong, but no idea how he came to write this passage. What it *tells* us, however, is clear: that historical explanations according to media development, which already have a strongly primitivist tone, are now to be thoroughly reconciled with Christian historiography, partly by a huge pun on the word Logos, which is at once the oral-aural word and the incarnated God. Ong's habit of interpreting words as carrying primarily the sense of their root etymology is indeed a way of arguing by pun. *Logos,* no matter what else it means, means primarily the spoken Word; so Christ is oral, adapted to a primarily oral-aural sensory system ('Light of Light' in the Nicene Creed is an early visualist deviation).

This oral primitivism, reinforced by selective semantics, underlies the whole argument about the effects of successive technologies. So does the other kind of selectivity Ong says he feels dubious about. For example: the eighteenth century, standing between feudalism and democracy, neither of which cares much about individual taste, is naturally the period when taste achieved some dominance in the sensory system. The synaesthesia of the *symbolistes* fits neatly the beginnings of modernism. Yet *taste* in eighteenth-century aesthetics carries very complex analogical meanings, as anybody familiar with Gombrich's study of it can see. Furthermore, modern gastronomy, where taste is truly exalted, is a nineteenth-century invention. Again, it is a fact that the synaesthetic interests of the late nineteenth century were anticipated in the eighteenth. If you wanted to, you could make what is virtually the opposite point to Ong's, without changing his system: you would simply be satisfying different needs. In fact the question as to what one wants to prove, and the question whether the facts as adduced really do fit the proof, can't be separated. They combine to form another: whether this historical system – early-aural-manuscript-print-late-oral – is not of the kind that can simply swallow anything it selects, including contradictions, like Hegel's Primitive-Classic-Romantic, denaturing fact as it does so.

So as we attend to the question of how the visual succeeds the oral, imposing visual models and perspective, creating private sight-readers and upsetting the Catholic Church. We are increasingly compelled to ask questions about the facts; indeed Fr Ong very often has to ask them himself. Why was the age after the invention of print so oral? It revived classical rhetoric, studied and distributed the commonplaces, worked on memory systems, cherished the sermon, reinvented tragedy. 'Oral-aural cultural institutions have been surprisingly tenacious,' concedes Fr Ong. Why 'surprisingly'? Because the tenacity doesn't really fit the theory. No wonder the Renaissance, in its welter of oral, script, and print, is called 'complex and confused': it tends to make the argument complex and confused. One needs epicyclical theories to explain such power in merely vestigial elements. Latin, for example, was for centuries a sight-bound scholarly *lingua franca*; why did the Renaissance want to revive the oral Latin of Cicero and his tricks of oral performance? Why did Protestants preach as well as meditate and polemicize? Whatever the reasons, these facts have to be explained; for the theory insists, for example, that the Catholic Church preserved the old oral wisdom against visualist Protestant innovation, just as it preserved the oral 'magic' in the sacraments and the oral authoritarianism. Protestantism has to be print-bound, rationalist, anarchic. Visualism, according to Ong, not only narrows the sensorium but does violence to the oral Logos.

The Logos is not as audible as formerly because 'we are abject prisoners of the literate culture in which we have matured'. An instance of the change might be Addison's 'The spacious Firmament on high', which says that we can't physically hear the music of the spheres; only in 'Reason's ear' do they 'utter forth a glorious voice'. The reason, Ong argues, is that the universe, in an age of typographically motivated science, has become silent, devocalized. But Shakespeare, and everybody else who exploited this famous topic, said you couldn't hear the music of the spheres – because of the Fall, the muddy vesture of decay, or whatever; in other words, Newton isn't to be blamed, this isn't the dissociation of sensibility but a commonplace in a new context. But blaming Newton, and ultimately print, is a help towards establishing the theory that later sensorial arrangements, and superior methods of information-storage, make the Word hard to hear, so that we must make an historical effort to recreate the older situation.

I have no doubt that Ong can somehow explain away this small misinterpretation of Addison : it seems everything can be explained away. If it appears strange, for example, that the overthrow of feudalism should have had to wait for print, when script might have done it, you write : 'Though feudalism died slowly and from a variety of maladies, it was under serious threat from the time of the invention of script.' Thus he at once considers and dismisses from the argument the failure of script to kill feudalism. The argument simply can't lose. The Word had a bad time under print, and now we shall, in our new oral situation, have a chance to reflect on why this occurred, and so create conditions in which its Presence can again be felt. 'Reflection' consists of making history consistent with this hope.

It will be clear by now what the Ong theory is for. Our progress into a new age is to be the means of a return to old orality. Ong values orality because it is holy, because it places a high value on the sacred. Visuality, typography, desacralized the world. The oral Word is a Presence, the written word is not; the oral Word presents an interior, the typographical word a surface. He even complains that traditional theologies of the Trinity tend to spatialize it by speaking of distinct entities somehow not divided. Ong rather wants an oral-aural theology of the Trinity which would explicate the 'inter-subjectivity of the three Persons in terms of communication conceived of as focussed (analogously) in a world of sound'. The Christian form of worship must now be conceived as oral-aural. In other words, Christians have too long conceived of their God as visual, with much loss to the deeper, more interior sense of his Presence that should accompany an oral-aural concept of him. And this is what, aided by our enormously enhanced control of the past and history, we have now somehow to recover; the oral Word in its old purity, in our new oral world, hardly yet recovered from the decadence of print. We have to recover the oral sense of presence and compensate for typographical desacralization.

On the whole Fr Ong thinks the chances are good. Though our media have made God seem silent, we have certain advantages. The characteristic mental disorder of alphabetic societies is schizophrenia, but of analphabetic societies it is anger and polemicism. Old oral was very angry; it led to the kind of immediate personal attack that still characterized Renaissance and Reformation scholarship. This wore off, as print and science made us more objective. Hence our present irenic mood, our tolerance, our openness to argument. When we are not irenic, tolerant, understanding, it is just the oral polemicism cropping out again. But it would be 'an affectation to pretend' that 'technologized urban living' cannot provide a very suitable ground for open communication, man to man and God to man. The 'hominization' of the world goes on apace. Thanks to the development of the media we are aware as never before of the world as fully peopled, as dominated by the presence of humans we have to live with. As the human consciousness thus 'expands its purchase on the universe, enlarges itself, the ground on which grace operates and God's presence is felt is enlarged'. Oral sacrality may thus be restored. And the instrument of restoration. the continuing Presence of the Word, is the Catholic Church.

Thus, whistling apologetically in the dark, Fr Ong reaches his optimistic conclusion. We shall have our oral Word again, like the Jews and the primitive Christians, but without all the bullying, the anger, the animistic nonsense, that characterized the earlier 'verbomotor' epoch.

Much of this will strike the sceptical layman as pure fantasy, or specialism (the belief that the current irenic mood, such as it is, among Christians, means that we are growing more patient and tolerant in our cities; the quest for an oral-aural theology). Perhaps one can nevertheless make allowance for the author's *parti pris* and still admire his account of the development of the media typology, the great revolutionary movements from oral-aural to script, script to print, print to electronic-aural? But this can't really be done, if only because Fr Ong's using the historiographical system to support something so strange and so partisan shows what is wrong with the system. It is so loose that you can easily accommodate it to anything else you believe. You can be extremely general, not, for example, discriminating between different *kinds* or orality (why did the Jews care so much about their kind of history? why were they so very different from oral, pre-Platonic Greeks?) or extremely special, offering details about the vocal powers of primates. If nothing else will make the theory fit you insert transitions, overlays, etc. Whatever the Theory eats turns into the Theory.

There are further problems, akin to those raised by Marxism and other historicist doctrines. Should we, at last aware of how history works, *do* anything, or just let the grace-controlled operation go forward, confident that we are growing gentler, more receptive, in our new culture, ready to receive an early-oral God into a fully computerized society? If God were now considering the intervention he so carefully timed, how would he work out the balance between analphabetic Chinese, oral Russians, and electric-oral Americans? Would he find the atmosphere truly irenic? He would not be surprised to find that his Church has turned out to be the sole repository of the old oral-sacral, but would he be pleased that, so late as this, one of his learned historians seems to have overlooked a modern commonplace, that the method of investigation defines the field?

St Paul spoke of faith as the evidence of things unseen; and St Augustine said that in heaven *fidem succedit species quam videbimus*, what succeeds faith is something we shall be able to see. It is true that he wrote also, in the *Confessions*, one of the most beautiful accounts of the struggles of the senses, and dwelt particularly on the power of the ear; but he had the authority of the New Testament for arguing that 'the general experience of the senses ... is called *the lust of the eye*, because the office of seeing, wherein the eyes hold the prerogative, the other senses by way of similitude take to themselves, when they make any search after knowledge'. This extremely oral saint was already a visualist, a slave of the decadent alphabet. Perhaps St Paul was, too. We seem to have been a long time in the wilderness out of which Fr Ong now seeks to show us the way.

(1968)

SIX

WALTER BENJAMIN

Walter Benjamin was born in 1892. He killed himself in 1940 when he was refused permission to cross from France to Spain in order to take ship from Lisbon to the United States, where he would have joined his emigré associates Adorno and Horkheimer at the Institute of Social Research in New York. He was of that Jewish class in which it was normal for fathers who had made a success in the world of business to support their sons in the life of independent scholarship, and although his father happened not to wish to do this Benjamin nevertheless pursued such a life, intending to make himself the best German critic.[1] Miss Arendt, in her Introduction to this book, emphasizes the peculiarity of such Jewish intellectuals; they administered, as Moritz Goldstein remarked, 'the intellectual property of a people which denied them the right and the ability to do so', and because there was very little in their own lives to connect them with the religion or manners of their fathers they were often as much at odds with the Jewish as with the larger community.

Benjamin showed a characteristic wavering between the two available possibilities of affiliation: Communism and Zionism. But he remained, in spite of persistent misfortune and uncertainty, his own man, a unique and puzzling figure. He was a collector, and had a large library; he preferred to live in Paris; his extreme idiosyncracy, which Hofmannsthal at once recognized as genius, caused his closest associates, such as Adorno, to withhold his work from publication. His entire life seems, on one view, to have been, in Miss Arendt's phrase, a matter of bungling and bad luck, right down to its end, which would have been averted if he had arrived at the frontier twenty-four hours earlier.

When he died his work was known to a few; it is only in the past fifteen years or so that Benjamin's name has become well known, and that in limited circles. But they widen, and so do

1. *Illuminations, Essays and Reflections.* By Walter Benjamin. Edited by Hannah Arendt, translated by Harry Zohn. New York, Harcourt, Brace & World, 1969.

the claims made for him. He is referred to as a great critic, the greatest, perhaps, of his time.

Reviewers of this book, therefore, are likely to be oppressed by two considerations, first that they have taken on something exceptionally important, and secondly that they have taken on something unusually difficult. The first appearance in English of a writer who is the subject of such high claims amply justifies the first sentiment, and the idiosyncracy of his method as well as the complexity of his historical situation excuses the second. Hannah Arendt shows an almost Benjaminite boldness of metaphor in her attempts to characterize that idiosyncracy, but she seems more authoritative, because more intimately concerned, as the expositor of a tragic historical situation.

Robert Alter in a brilliant *Commentary* review challenges her sharply on her reading of Benjamin's political, social, and racial position, and the focusing of argument there seems to me, however sensitive the discussion of Benjamin's criticism as such, to leave room for a commentator with different priorities – and no competence to dispute with the learned on such matters as German Marxism and Zionism between the wars – to try other ways of demonstrating its greatness. If it is as a critic that Benjamin counts – and he certainly thought so – it is arguable that his precise relation to Marxism or Zionism, the extent of doctrinal deviations detected by his pupil Adorno, the question whether Brecht was good for him or not, are secondary issues.

The English reader has now a couple of hundred pages to go on. It is not much. The circumstances of Benjamin's life and also his temperament were so strange, so unlucky, that even now, nearly thirty years after his suicide, much of his extant work has not achieved publication in German; presumably the material held in Frankfurt by Adorno will now see the light. Of the works available in German Miss Arendt has, she assures us, given the most important, with two exceptions, these being essays on Goethe and Karl Kraus. One often feels in reading her Introduction, that she is speaking of aspects of the writer not represented here; but there is for all that enough to be grateful for, and to give a fair idea of Benjamin's stature.

In trying to say what that is I intend, perhaps ungratefully, to avoid the front entrance, where Miss Arendt's essay lies coiled at the gate, and slip in at the side. One might as well begin with

literary criticism. There is a longish piece on Kafka. It starts off
with a story about Potemkin, but this only sounds like a leis-
urely belletristic overture. *Stories*, as we shall see, are crucial to
Benjamin. Soon he is discoursing intelligently about the ugly
sexy women in Kafka, and about the beauty of the guilty.
Good but not amazing, it sounds like capable commentary; but
Benjamin distinguished between commentary and criticism,
the latter being the higher activity and concerned, not with the
communication to readers of *information*, here italicized as a
word with special senses to be discussed later, but with, to be
less vague than one sounds, the intuition of essences. Then,
arising out of some remarks on *Amerika*, this passage occurs :

> Kafka's entire work constitutes a code of gestures which
> surely had no definite symbolic meaning for the author at
> the outset; rather the author tried to derive such a meaning
> from them in ever-changing contexts and experimental
> groupings ... The greater Kafka's mastery became, the
> more frequently did he eschew adapting these gestures to
> common situations or explaining them.... Each gesture is an
> event – one might even say, a drama – in itself.... Like El
> Greco Kafka tears open the sky behind each gesture; but as
> with El Greco ... the gesture remains the decisive thing ...
> He divests the human gesture of its traditional supports and
> then has a subject for reflection without end.

This condensed version perforce leaves out the supporting
examples. The reader will supply them : the hunched backs, the
raised hands, all those postures and movements which, in
Kafka, import familiar behaviour into a context which alters or
strips it of usual meanings. Thus we know it is wrong to think
of the novels as if they were analogous to dreams. Benjamin is
saying why. Kafka 'took all conceivable precautions against the
interpretation of his writings', which is why explications and
allegorizings, psychoanalytic or theological, are always wrong.
He made *stories*; he dealt in primordial experience, which is
why

> His novels are set in a swamp world. In his works created
> things appear at the stage which Bachofen has termed the
> hetaeric stage. The fact that it is now forgotten does not
> mean that it does not extend into the present.... An ex-
> perience deeper than that of an average person can make
> contact with it.

But of course it cannot be interpreted in another language. Like all the literature of wisdom (wisdom being truth in its epic aspect) it expresses itself as story, a lost art. Kafka's world is not ours, if only because 'his gestures of terror are given scope by the marvellous *margin* which the catastrophe will not grant us'. Hence his wisdom, traditional though in decay; hence also his 'radiant serenity', his acceptance of a world without hope for us, who have no source of serenity.

Benjamin, as one sees from this, is not a critic who goes in for 'close analysis'. He isn't even, on this evidence, the master of any great range of critical strategies. He is not noisily prophetic or apocalyptic; certainly he sees Kafka as providing a relevant wisdom, but he does not pretend that Kafka was needed to show the world what was already obvious, that it was on the brink of a disaster. On the other hand it must be said that he chooses his illustrations with extraordinary skill and insight. The code of gestures is a brilliant notion; the analogy with El Greco – one of many such rapid allusions to painting and sculpture – has terrific assurance and point. But it is doubtful whether these advantages alone would guarantee Benjamin the now widely endorsed opinion that he is pre-eminent among twentieth-century critics. And if we try to describe the quality which does vindicate that opinion I doubt if, at this stage, we shall come up with anything much more illuminating than *certainty*.

The centrality of Kafka is a public concept, but most ways of stating it simply seem intolerably vulgar and imprecise after Benjamin, who knows the author in his essence, and has exactly the means, nothing beyond or short of necessity, to show it forth. You hardly feel that you have been reading criticism; this is not because the method is eclectic or 'impressionist', but because it requires the kind of response we are accustomed to give to works of art. This is the quality Miss Arendt is trying to describe when she talks about the poetic nature of his thought. Benjamin's is, however, a poetic of accuracy, not of vague suggestion. And this is why he really is a great critic. The fact that his primary critical operations had methodological by-products which he employed, with great ingenuity and taste, in the construction of literary and cultural theories, is interesting but less important; what counts here is the art of criticism.

Before I go on to those secondary matters I had better give a further example of the primary. On the evidence of this book, the second author of whom Benjamin speaks with unequalled authority is Proust, who figures largely not only in the essay devoted to him but also in the longest and most elaborate of the studies, the one on Baudelaire, who, for Benjamin, was Proust's evangelist.

Baudelaire, as we all know, invented for art the modern city – *l'immonde cité* – and its crowds. Benjamin subjects this commonplace to extraordinary processes of elaboration and refinement. For him the city is not only the locus of our complex modern isolation, it is also the source of modern *shock*. Its gestures are all productive of, or protective against, shock : switching, inserting, pressing, snapping; the exchange and avoidance of glances; the barrage of incomplete and discontinuous impressions. (This aspect of metropolitan life, incidentally, fascinated Conrad. Benjamin would have been very good on Conrad, but he lived in Paris and chose Poe.)

What is destroyed by this continuous discontinuity is a quality Benjamin calls *aura*. This is variously described and apprehended. It is, for example, the quality of the unique work of art, handed down by a tradition, a quality lost in mechanical reproduction.

That which withers in the age of mechanical reproduction is the aura of the work of art. This is a symptomatic process whose significance points beyond the realm of art. . . . The technique of reproduction detaches the reproduced object from the domain of tradition. By making many reproductions it substitutes a plurality of copies for a unique existence. And in permitting the reproduction to meet the beholder or listener in his own particular situation, it reactivates the object reproduced. These two processes lead to a tremendous shattering of tradition which is the obverse of the contemporary crisis and renewal of mankind.

Another great enemy of aura is the movie camera; the film, assaulting the senses in an almost tactile way by violent and discontinuous cutting, is the great agent of shock. Benjamin does not fail to relate these effects to those of the assembly line on unskilled workers.

In a film, perception in the form of shocks was established as a formal principle. That which determines the rhythm of production on a conveyor belt is the basis of the rhythm of reception in the film.

And he goes on to cite Marx. But primarily he is concerned to say something about the essential Baudelaire and the essential Proust.

How, then, do aura and shock concern Proust? Proust, like Kafka, discovered, though at great cost, a way of preserving wisdom and telling stories (stories, the receptacles of wisdom, of experience with its auras) in the modern city. Fantastically devoted to 'information' (the enemy of wisdom and story) he lived in the world of conscious memory but nevertheless retained access to the *mémoire involuntaire*, where everything has aura. 'To perceive the aura of an object we look at (? for) means to invest it with the ability to look at us in return.' Thus Proust was able to find what was lost in the midst of things that had 'lost their ability to look'. And for Benjamin all that is left of 'tradition' in our world is a store of discrete, fragmentary deposits like those attained by the Proustian involuntary memory.

No summary can convey much of the richness of these insights, nor of the high skill with which the controlling ideas are manipulated. Writing of Proust alone, Benjamin is content with simpler brilliance; but he adds greatly to our knowledge of Proustian essences. He chooses an anecdote, matches it with one of his own,[2] speaks aphoristically of Proust's defining the structure of the society by a 'physiology of chatter'; asks whether it is not 'the quintessence of experience to learn many things which apparently could be told in a very few words' but actually require an enormous mimicry of the society and its language. 'Proust's most accurate, most convincing insights fasten on their objects as insects fasten on leaves, blossoms, branches, betraying nothing of their existence until a leap, a beating of wings, a vault, show the startled observer that some incalculable individual life has imperceptibly crept into an

2. I mention this in passing, though lacking space to illustrate it, or to explain that Benjamin's arguments are nearly always supported by instances, anecdotes, allusions, of dazzling appropriateness. This is why one thinks of his methods as characterized by a sort of metropolitan *certainty*.

alien world.' So keen is Proust's sense of concealment that he even mimics the concealment practised by the class he is describing, its silence as to its economic foundation. A consequence is that the greatness of Proust's work 'will remain inaccessible until this class has revealed its most pronounced features in the final struggle.'

That last doctrinally adhesive observation is of a sort that occasionally occurs in Benjamin's work, but has to take its place with quite other kinds. The essay ends astonishingly with a meditation on Proust's psychogenic asthma as source and condition of his art: 'Proust's syntax rhythmically and step by step reproduces his fear of suffocating.' Thus begins the concluding passage, as accurate, as original, and as free from critical or ideological vulgarity, as the essay on Kafka.

Now it must be already clear that Benjamin uses some terms – 'aura', 'shock', 'experience', 'story', for instance – in a special sense; and they do indeed form a substructure which lies as it were between the criticism itself and the Marxist foundation on which his thinking, officially but as all admit precariously, rests. This is to be inferred from the criticism, but is also the material of some extracritical speculation. I put it this way because it is so important to see the 'poetry' of the criticism as primary, and because it will help us to see why Benjamin is a finer critic than Lukács, who is for the most part a critic last not first.

Yet it is precisely this extremely characteristic and independent layer of doctrine that has made it difficult for critics who know Benjamin's cultural milieu to convey their sense of his greatness. Miss Arendt calls him a kind of poet, but her superb essay is coloured, I think, by a sense that Benjamin is somehow, considered as an intellectual, a little irresponsible. Mr Alter rightly observes that Benjamin's mind normally operates 'quite outside the prefabricated structures of Marxist theory', and properly regards this as distinguishing his work from that of Lukács or Goldmann. But even so there is always a feeling that Benjamin's individuality must be expressed by showing how he deviates from one to another philosophical norm. Thus Miss Arendt, for all her resourcefulness, seems secretly puzzled that he can be so good: in linking the Marxist 'superstructure' to Baudelaire's *correspondances* he is showing himself the most peculiar Marxist who ever lived; his central image of the *flâneur* – the nineteenth-century gentleman-stroller, connoisseur of metropolitan curiosities – is very un-Marxist, etc. Just so Adorno criticized him for using the relation of sub- and super-structure as metaphor rather than as fact. Instead of system there is, to everybody's surprise, poetry : they ask for a stone and are given bread.

Benjamin, we remind ourselves, aspired to literary criticism; he wanted to be the chief German literary critic. Like good poets, good literary critics need to have a lot in their heads, but it need not be systematic; and there is no need to be surprised that Benjamin at his best uses Marxist as well as Hasidic knowledge as elements of a system imposed by the criticism more or less *ad hoc*. (Thus, although Mr Alter ingeniously and usefully compares him with Trilling, the best American comparison would be with Blackmur.) And in between the criticism and the big system falls his own body of systematic inference.

A knowledge of Benjamin's secondary preoccupations will prevent the objection that he is too often merely paradoxical. For example, in his essay on translation he proposes a doctrine of inutility. Translation is not a means of conveying information; all good translations of a particular text, taken together, constitute an attempt to reveal some hypothetical ur-language underlying that in which the original was written; every translation is in a sense a contribution to the restoration of an ideal never wholly knowable. He even says that a translation is linguistically more definite than an original, since it can no longer be displaced by a secondary rendering; but that is a flourish, and the basic insight (founded on no more than the observation that we really always assume a text *can* be translated) is a Mallarméan sense that the imperfection of languages, as revealed in the plurality, implies an ideal, *l'immortelle parole*, to the discovery of which each translation contributes.

It follows that the translator ought not to try for a version that sounds original in his own language, but rather that he should let the original taint his version deeply. This, in its expression, sounds rather dandyish, rather *épatant*. Its implications are, however, serious; Benjamin would have approved of 'Homage to Sextus Propertius' and, perhaps, of Zukofsky's Catullus. And its rationale is also serious. 'Information' is the enemy of art, inutility the necessary condition of the essential act of criticism, as Benjamin conceives it, which is at the farthest possible remove from reviewing or textbook writing, being more like the action of the involuntary memory, a *recherche* of the only possible kind into *le temps perdu*. Benjamin speaks thus of translation for the same reason that he abjures the close examination of the existential flurry of the 'words on the page'. He is interested in what does not render itself visible, whether it is language, a poem, or a Proustian memory.

In the great essay on Leskov he adumbrates a theory of story consistent with these assumptions. The art of story ends in modern times, ends, in fact, with the invention of the novel. Story belongs to a time before the machine devalued human experience; being the communication of experience as authenticated counsel; it belongs to wisdom, which is truth in its epic aspect. The decay of story and of wisdom is a 'concomitant symptom of the secular productive forces of history'. The novel has nothing to do with wisdom. It belongs to print, to a world in which the teller is not impressing his aura on the tale, is 'himself uncounselled', and offers not a guide to the perplexed but mere perplexity. Information, which is absent from story, is critical to the novel; and the greatest novelists, Kafka and Proust, as we saw, achieve that greatness by finding ways to convert the novel into story, information into wisdom.

There follows a passage which might serve as a crucial instance of Benjamin's genius. Story, he says, belongs to a world in which death is familiar, a part of daily life. Now we have tidied death out of our houses and the novel is obliged, in conveying something of the 'meaning of life', to provide it. Hence the extreme importance of the ends of novels, and the manner in which we regard characters as people in whose experience of death we intend to share; for if they do not actually die they suffer a figurative death at the end of the book. 'This stranger's fate, by virtue of the flame which consumes it, yields us the warmth which we never draw from our own fate.'

'Incomparable' is a word that as attached to Benjamin; it may be coolly applied to these few paragraphs on the eschatology of the novel. And it must not be forgotten that all such speculations are solidly supported by work on *novels*. So too with the 'probes' about technology and aura; so with almost all the more speculative material. It may have elements borrowed from more formal thinkers (the theory of the novel owes something to Lukàcs's early book on the subject) but the force is generated by contact with texts. Thus the most McLuhॱnish piece in the book, 'The Work of Art in the Age of Mechanical Reproduction', is ostensibly an independent study of how certain superstructural changes had become visible 'only to-day', half a century after the corresponding changes in the economic base. These changes alter the whole character and political bearing of art. The great single difference is repro-ducibility, with the attendant loss of aura. The old notion of art is now Fascist, because concepts such as creativity, genius, eternal value, mystery 'lead to a processing of data in the Fascist sense'. So Benjamin, in this essay, wishes to replace them with others that are more concordant with revolutionary de-mands.

Yet for all this half-willing radicalism, the concept of aura still belong to his study of pre-revolutionary art, an art that seeks to recover wisdom, an art associated with the sacred ritual from which mechanical reproduction will deliver it into the realm of politics.

Whenever Benjamin develops his ideas beyond their heuristic utility he arrives, naturally enough, at some such political posi-tion, so that his pronouncements can on occasion be rather remote from his critical practice. One such is the famous observation, made with Marinetti in mind, that Fascism aestheticizes politics while Communism politicizes art. We reach ideological base here, and also in some of the 'Theses on the Philosophy of History', in which he emerges, under the duress of a mode of thought that must often have been uncongenial, as an abolitionist. The art of the past is a set of trophies celebrating the victory of the few over the many. 'There is no document of civilization which is not at the same time a document of barbarism,' he wrote shortly before his death in 1940. 'Barbarism taints also the manner in which it was transmitted from one owner to another (though this transmission he earlier associates with aura). A historical materialist therefore dissociates himself from it as far as pos-sible.' Yet the Theses also associate this materialism with a kind of muted Messianism. We are thus reminded that the Jews, forbidden to investigate the future, were instructed in remem-brance of things past. Instruction in remembrance (though the world is full of 'information') is his serious project : to give, without ignoring the modern intellect, without minimizing the

shocks of modern reality, a human structure, so far as it may
be had, to the 'time of now'.

The dilemma is clear enough, and in 1940 Benjamin must
have experienced it with tragic fullness. The 'politicization' of
art, which the situation required, marks the end of the historical process in which barbarism assisted at the creation of those
virtually sacral essences which it was his special gift to divine.
His major essays take cognizance of the shock as well as of the
aura. He believed both that the material of great criticism was
being destroyed, and that it ought to be destroyed. In wanting
to be a great literary critic he discovered that he could only be
the last great literary critic, and in explaining *that*, he explained certain aspects of the modern with an authority that
thirty years of unpredictable change have not vitiated. And
although some may think him unlucky, deviant, others will
regard him as one of the norms by which fortune and correctness need to be judged.

(1969)

SEVEN

EDMUND WILSON

Mr Wilson is a very productive author; I don't know if he would call *Axel's Castle* his best book, though he might agree that it is his most influential.[1] If one wanted to get a complete view of his work on the authors discussed in it, one would need to consider later essays as well; but it is more to the present purpose to see *Axel's Castle* as it stands, unrevised, a testimony to the author's flexibility and diagnostic power at a time when his subject as a whole was considerably more obscure than it is now. The first powerful impression one receives on re-reading the book is that it anticipates a whole era of literary discussion; many writers, including the present, might unworthily murmur over its pages, *pereant qui ante nos nostra dixere*. Naturally one soon rests in a more comfortable conviction that it also missed quite a lot, and left employment for Mr Wilson's successors. But his real achievement was to identify, even if he could not completely describe, the master-spirit of an age. He grasped the relation between Romantic and Symbolist, the ivory tower and the cork-lined bedroom; he understood the role of various substitutes for science, and the persistent anti-intellectualism of the whole tradition; he saw how the Romantic cult of personality was turned into its apparent opposite, a cult of impersonality; he understood why English seventeenth-century poetry took on a special import-ance in the age of Symbolism; and he perceived that the arts of post-Symbolism had a special survival problem. He was able to say new things of a period just past, and make intelligent guesses about the immediate future, becuse he was sensitively aware of the actual moment and its moods. For example, he is very shrewd about Mr Eliot's effect on the sensibility of the period: 'the sound of jazz, which formerly seemed jolly, now inspired only horror and despair'; and this quality enabled him also to see that hope for the future of verse-drama must rest, as it still does, on 'Wanna Go Home, Baby?' (*Sweeney Agonistes*).

The real *donnée* of *Axel's Castle* is the perception that the literary history of our time is 'to a great extent that of the

1. New York, C. Scribner's Sons, 1931. London, Fontana, 1961.

development of Symbolism and of its fusion or conflict with Naturalism'. In view of the close relations of Symbolist and Romantic aesthetics, this can be taken to mean that modern literature is still working out the revolutionary theses of the first Romantics. The scope of the twentieth-century revolution is thus greatly reduced, and it is possible to see it as an effort to develop, almost to the point of mania, some elements of the earlier movement. Thus Wilson, who admires nearly all the authors he discusses, is nevertheless able to say that their works are greatly and unnecessarily at odds with the world they live in, that they neglect the purposes of art as he understands them, and that they may very well be cultivating powers which will destroy art. In short, he was patient and flexible; he knew how to attach himself and then withdraw; to ascertain and subsequently to comment critically upon the master-spirit of the age. He exhibits, in his fashion, the Arnoldian qualities.

In a lecture of 1940 Wilson says what he thinks literature is, and how the historical critic ought to deal with it. He is not a critic who finds literature all-sufficient; without mistaking it for another thing he is always asking whether another thing will tell him more about it. He uses Freud and Marx and the anthropologists; if a machine can be devised to give information about that emotional stimulus from which criticism begins, he will use that, too. He has no interest in any notion of literature as autotelic.

All our intellectual activity, in whatever field it takes place, is an attempt to give a meaning to our experience – that is, to make life more practicable; for by understanding things we make it easier to survive and get around among them. The mathematician Euclid, working in a convention of abstractions, shows up relations between the unwieldy and cluttered-up environment upon which we are able to count. A drama of Sophocles also indicates relations between the various human impulses, which appear so confused and dangerous.... The kinship, from his point of view, of the purposes of science and art, appears very clearly from the case of the Greeks.... The experience of mankind on the earth is always changing as man develops and has to deal with new combinations of elements; and the writer who is to be anything more than an echo of his predecessors must always find expression for something that has never yet been expressed, must master a new set of phenomena.... With each such victory of the human intellect ... we experience a deep satisfaction; we have been cured of some ache of disorder, relieved of some oppressive burden of uncomprehended events.

This is clearly the credo of a man with a deep theoretical hostility to Symbolism. Yeats, for example, would have found it almost entirely abhorrent. It emphasizes the intellectual aspect of art, treats the intellect as an instrument of biological adaptation; it speaks of man as developing, and of art as dealing in phenomena. How, then, does he come to write so well of the heirs of Symbolism? How does he avoid treating *The Waste Land* as a mere symptom of decadence, or – in the language of a celebrated contemporary review – as a terrible warning ('the ravings of a drunken helot')? The reason is simply that he has a powerful primary, undogmatic, response to poetry; he can attach himself and then withdraw, and on withdrawal feels free to disapprove. In fact this is the whole method of *Axel's Castle* : passionate identification with the work under discussion; followed by detached appraisal; followed by historical inference, which does not neglect the primary response. Before asking whether the work is of any use to mankind, whether it will help us round the environmental obstacles, he proves that he has, in any case, responded to it. Now and again there may be an apparent split down the middle of his criticism, self-contradiction almost; but that is because he is working out in his own head the whole dialectic of Symbolist art and the world it inhabits.

Mr Wilson has one skill which may seem a very humble one, and does not occupy the attention of theorists; he is a master of summary. In this book he summarizes all the major works of his authors, sometimes at considerable length, as with *Ulysses* and *A la Recherche du Temps Perdu*. This part of his work is exemplary, for he is patient and thorough, and never 'loads' his accounts to make his later withdrawal and appraisal simpler. The chapter on Yeats, a poet whose cast of mind is antithetical to Wilson's own, is in some ways inadequate (it ends, characteristically, with a warm tribute to 'Among Schoolchildren', which he sees as a great poem without being able to say why) but it contains a very careful account of *A Vision*, a good and simple explanation of the doctrine of the Mask; in short, the critic gave his mind patiently to matters which must in themselves have seemed sadly trivial. Similarly with Valéry; without sacrificing his independence Wilson gives almost the account of a disciple, and then withdraws, complains that Valéry is often platitudinous or affected, and sometimes makes a pretence of exactitude in order 'to cover a number of ridiculously false assumptions', the chief of which is the assumption that verse is an intellectual product absolutely different in kind from prose.

This method is most clearly perceived in the chapter on Proust, where twenty-three pages go by before we turn over and find this : 'The fascination of Proust's novel is so great that, while we are reading it, we tend to accept it *in toto*.' Then comes the withdrawal, the questions, and qualifications. Throughout the remainder of the chapter the critic's admiration for Proust's novel has to contend with his disturbance at its contempt for those problems which, in his view, it is the business of art to solve. Proust, he decides at last, was the 'last great historian of the ... Heartbreak House of capitalist culture'. So with Joyce; a full admiring account of *Ulysses*, and then the reservations : with so much vitality, why does Joyce have so little movement? Being 'the great poet of a new phase of human consciousness', why should Joyce have cultivated opacity where it could have been avoided? Instead of making his book as easy as possible for the ordinary reader, he often makes it harder than it need be, 'as if he were shy and solicitous about it, and wanted to protect it from us'. Even Gertrude Stein, nearer the pole of uncommunicativeness, gets a fair showing.

For what reason, apart from his evident pleasure in the books, did Wilson think them worth his care, deplorable as their tendencies seemed to be? One answer is that he saw them as, almost in spite of themselves, closely related to modern scientific speculation, repeating the Greek pattern. Proust provides 'a sort of equivalent in fiction for the metaphysics' of Whitehead. In his world, 'as in the universe of Whitehead, the "events", which may be taken arbitrarily as infinitely small or infinitely comprehensive, make up an organic structure'. Joyce's world resembles those of Proust, Whitehead, and Einstein, in that it is 'always changing as it is perceived by different observers and by them at different times. It is an organism made up of "events".' Wilson likes these authors, and would be happy to think they collaborated with the scientists and philosophers in developing a new and more useful world-view; in optimistic mood he dares to hope that Valéry was wrong in his prediction that the arts and sciences would become infinitely specialized; perhaps, on the contrary, they will 'finally fall all into one system'. This indeed is the note upon which he ends, emphasizing the great gifts these authors have made to mankind: new flexibility, new freedom of movement in a better-understood world,

> the hope and exaltation of the untried, unsuspected possibilities of human thought and art.

But the question remains, how is this hope compatible with what has been said of the antisocial assumptions of these writers? They belong to the cork-lined cell; they shun all experience except that which can be 'savoured in solitude'. When we read them, says Wilson,

> we are oppressed by a sullenness, a lethargy, a sense of energies ingrown and sometimes festering. Even the poetry of the noble Yeats, still repining through middle age over the emotional miscarriages of youth, is dully weighted, for all its purity and candour, by a leaden acquiescence in defeat.

They saw the future as dark; art surviving only as a game, the ceremony of innocence drowned. They lived on the past and the primitive; on their own despair and isolation, and the poverty of the new world. They make Wilson wonder whether poetry is not destined soon to fall into complete disuse.... What I am pointing out in *Axel's Castle* is not a contradiction but a tension; the book contains in little whatever can be said for and against the kind of art we now have. In some ways the whole issue is now clearer, not because we are shrewder than Wilson, but because we have watched it develop. He saw it, and accurately described it, thirty years ago; and he did more, he put the tension into his book instead of merely talking about it. This is to ascertain the master-spirit of the age. For all that we need to supplement it with other and lesser books, *Axel's Castle* is very much alive, and everybody's business.

(1961)

And this bwings us to liquorary quiddicism. What a wonderful is liquorary quiddicism! What fastiddily! what intellectual breath! what unreproachable stammards and cry-
tearia! what inside and painentralia! *The Three Limperary
Cripples* (1930)

And it raises the question why Edmund Wilson should be
thought to be, as in my view he is, so pre-eminently the
greatest periodical critic of his time, at any rate in English. The
younger Americans have of late been showing some disappointment with him, finding him cranky and unwilling to deal
with *their* new things as he had dealt with his own. We have no
special reason to like him, as the English are a source of
annoyance and disappointment to him and he has often said so.
He once began a review thus: 'Mr E. H. Carr is an odd phenomenon – perhaps a symptom of the decay of Great Britain.'
Nor does this remark, which – leaving aside the justice of the
diagnosis – could only have been made by a very difficult and
occasionally somewhat ludicrous critic, stand alone. Needing to
make it clear that despite his admiration for Marx and Engels
he loathes the Dialectic, he tosses off the proposal that the
Hegelian triad, like the triangle of Pythagoras, the Christian
Trinity and the Wotan–Brunnhilde–Siegfried set, were symbols
of the male sexual organs (*To the Finland Station*, II, 11). This is
an emotional way of saying that he finds the Dialectic and the
Trinity extremely unreasonable, and lest argument should fail
to establish this he throws in a tremendous symbol of irra-
tionality. Much too often, I think, he uses Freudian explanations in a similar way: *The Wound and the Bow* is on re-
reading his least interesting book (though it is still a good one)
partly because the theory ends the argument prematurely, and
the essay on Ben Jonson in *The Triple Thinkers*, for all its
richness of reference and structural power, is so busy with the
thesis of Jonson's anal eroticism that it neglects to examine his
works. *Texture* is important in Jonson, and its examination is
not one of Wilson's strong points. I am not saying the thesis is
wrong or even that it is irrelevant, but only that it obtrudes
itself, as E. M. Forster once said mysticism might, 'at the wrong
stage of the affair'.

This only begins the tale of Edmund Wilson's deficiencies,
and we might as well mention one more which has a bearing on
his view of the English: this is simply that he is so *echt* Ameri-

can that it shows in some ways which may strike us as inappropriate. Red Bank, Princeton, houses, friends, heroes such as H. L. Mencken and John Jay Chapman, they all become part of a patrician mythology rather like Yeats's, and sometimes Wilson seems to feel a need to Americanize before he can offer sympathetic understanding. An essay on Dostoevsky makes the point that when the Russian is writing on Russian exiles 'a good deal of what he says applies equally to expatriate Americans in Europe'. Fair enough; but two pages later we read this: 'Dostoevsky's instinct was sound: the fact that the American problem seems a particularly formidable one is no cause for fleeing or evading it.' In the same way we feel an unexpected sympathy with Lenin's red hair and Marx's boils and certain Russian country houses. The Jews are translated into New Englanders. Going to America made Auden a good poet; leaving it made Eliot a sort of cultured Uriah Heep. Finally, *Patriotic Gore*, for all its virtues, obviously indulges a nostalgic, bitter Americanism; so does *The Cold War and the Income Tax*.

Good reviewing in the weeklies and monthlies is, as Wilson himself very well knows, an essential element in the hygiene of a literary culture; yet he has done it more or less under protest over a long period of his life; and this from vanity rather than laziness, for he is apparently a tireless reader and writes (judging from the bulk of his work, and the ease with which it is articulated) with as much facility as any one, though this is a quality that casual readers are very apt to exaggerate. It is not surprising, therefore, that his critics notice a decline in the interest and penetration of his journalism between the work of the twenties and thirties collected in *The Shores of Light* and that of the forties collected in *Classics and Commercials*.[2] No doubt a further decline may be found in the new collection from later years, which is called – as if to emphasize a certain inconsiderate isolation, a galloping off in directions that interest only him – *The Bit Between my Teeth*.[3] If the best journalism belongs to the twenties and the best criticism of the more formal kind is in *Axel's Castle* (1931), there is some justification for the view of various commentators that this formidable figure has – for reasons only to be guessed at,

2. Both collections, London, W. H. Allen, 1952 and 1951 respectively.

3. London, W. H. Allen, 1965.

though often related to the politics of the thirties – grown less and less useful over the last thirty-five years. And we can at least be sure that Wilson himself unreservedly accepts the criterion of utility in matters of criticism, as in literature itself. Broadly speaking, this is the way Norman Podhoretz talks about Wilson in what is probably the best essay about him. 'From now on,' Podhoretz says at the end of his piece, 'we shall have to look elsewhere for the kind of guidance that it was his particular glory to give.'

It is not difficult to understand Podhoretz's disappointment. A man who had clearly seen, and tirelessly propagated, the right programme for American letters – who had, with serious optimism, insisted upon their relevance to the health of American society – seems to have contracted out, calling himself an alien in his own country, constructing a misanthrope's *Vision*. All that patrician generosity, all that subtle meditation on social justice, were converted into the gloomy execrations of un-American self-exile; like Shakespeare's Poet visiting Timon in the woods, the dependent critic is rewarded with curses and gold thrown in his face. This is how it must seem to the leaderless.

This is of course primarily an American problem, and it is interesting to notice that a new book on Wilson tackles it quite differently. Mr Sherman Paul[4] has, in fact, written a very elaborate study of the large and varied *œuvre* with the intention not of demonstrating Wilson's cultural usefulness but of tracing in it the lines of an important writer's personal development. This strategy has its drawbacks, the worst of which is that it gets Wilson's public achievement out of focus; Paul attends just as closely to writings of small public importance as to the major works, and even the criticism is treated as if it were *à clef*. There are other disadvantages. Nobody can write about Wilson without inviting hostile comparisons between his prose and that of his subject. It would have been tactful of Mr Paul to avoid usages formally condemned by his hero, such as *demean* in the sense of 'disparage' or 'abase', which occurs twice in the book.

All the same, this is a valuable study. From the opening chapter on the critic's youth one gets a perfectly valid slogan :

4. *Edmund Wilson: A Study of Literary Vocation in Our Time.* University of Illinois Press.

Wilson is finely Puritan, if the word can mean 'concerned with moral precision'. The dominant virtue of the intellectual is a demythologized charity, and if Wilson has often lapsed from this, both by mythologizing and by uncharitable behaviour, who among critics working under such pressures has been more faithful? Certainly not Taine, his earliest model, who 'shrank ... into professional superiority' when progress came to be associated with vulgar revolution: 'a remote disapproval chills his tone, all the bright colours of his fancy go dead'. Again and again Wilson finds in the career of distinguished writers a similar shrinking: in Eliot, for example, and all the neo-Christains (as Mr Empson calls them), in Anatole France and Bernard Shaw. But even in the days when the rightness of the Marxist diagnosis seemed most dreadfully confirmed by the condition of America. Wilson wanted Marxism without the mythology, wanted people to prove their charitable faith by good works rather than by an abdication of the reason. Whatever the mistakes, he did seek to carry out the Jamesian programme of 'striving to understand everything' about human relations in a world not in itself organized for humanity, and discovering what might be for humanity 'indubitable values'. Even now it is not the values that have changed, but society that has turned out to be less corrigible than he hoped.

In the early days of his career, at Princeton and in Greenwich Village, the constant pursuit of abstract civil virtue and *il ben del intelletto* seem to have set him a little apart even from his brilliant contemporaries. Part of the difficulty was doubtless that for all his excitement at an American renaissance, his superior understanding of the modern, Wilson was always a man for continuity. He remained devoted to his Princeton teacher Christian Gauss, who believed that to adapt to his environment man must master it intellectually. Criticism would ideally be an aid to this; it should try to be 'a history of man's ideas and imaginings in the setting of conditions which have shaped them'. *Axel's Castle*, which acts upon this belief, is dedicated to Gauss; and it is not merely an exceptionally intelligent and original piece of literary history but an attempt to improve the possibility of literature becoming an agent of human mastery over the modern environment. For Wilson literature is always a way of knowing the world, and however much one may say of it as a giver of pleasure it is measured finally by its utility. It will not be useful unless it is fully informed, and neither the writing nor the exposition of imaginative works can, in his view, be worth much unless the author or the expositor has a deep familiarity with his subject and the knowledge to provide broad contexts. That is why his own programme had involved the mastery of many languages and literatures, and why he despises monolingual and one-subject professors. It is also the reason for his commitment to the past – not only the American past, but to the best in Greek, Latin, Italian, French, and Russian literature as well as English and American, and for his guilt about Latin-American writing. His 'adventure on reality', as Mr Paul calls it, required also an education in politics and economics. Later Hebrew demanded attention. The artist – and Wilson thought of all his work as an artist's – is committed to the past, to the present, and to the community.

Wilson's plays and his fiction, with the important exception of *Memoirs of Hecate County,* belong mostly to his earlier years. In respect of the need of discipline he did not discriminate between criticism and fiction, and there is a sense in which it is plausible to say, with Mr Paul, that *Axel's Castle* and *I Thought of Daisy* belong together; they were worked on at the same time, and deal with the same problem, 'the writer's allegiance to society'. But even Mr Paul, who devotes many pages to the novel, cannot deny that there is in it a programmatic stiffness, a lack of easy invention, which throws into high relief the ease and authority of the critical work; and Wilson's later memoir of Edna St Vincent Millay tells us more and more movingly about the personal element than the story can, however teased out by interpreters. She fits, as Wilson's heroes do, into a system not so much autobiographical as symbolizing the structure of the world as he finds it: with Scott Fitzgerald and Paul Rosenfeld and Mr Justice Holmes and Whitehead and Gauss and Mario Praz.

This personal mythology is important and valuable to a writer, but Wilson speaks best when he speaks out. His prose style is designed for speaking out: his language is in his own terms, 'the language of responsibility', as men engaged upon decisive action speak it; he is with Lincoln and Grant, not with the non-participants, Henry James and Henry Adams. If his prose has often an antique balance and his diction an etymological exactitude, this is proper enough, for his action is the action of structural thought; and if it sometimes seems pedantic in its cultivation this is because solecism and vulgarism enfeeble the activity of language. Wilson's prose, whether one speaks of it in quite this way or not, is certainly a powerful instrument; despite his own fears it has remained supple and strong over a long and arduous career. One consequence is that schooled to correctness, one is shocked in Wilson by what would pass almost unnoticed in another writer; when he uses *attainted* for *tainted* a bell rings violently in the mind ('Mr Krutch ... gives some evidence of being attainted with this tendency').[5] Anyway, there is a small doubt that Wilson's style is better adapted to the exposition of literature and ideas than to fiction.

'Participation in public life through literature' is the programme of *Axel's Castle*; for Mr Paul it is related to the same needs expressed in the novel, which is the author's need to extinguish in himself any symptoms of Axel-Symbolist withdrawal and leaving living to the servants. Having written these books, he was ready for the labours of the thirties; Mr Paul quotes with approval a contemporary opinion that 'one could plot a graph of Mr Wilson from Proust to Karl Marx', and this is what he does, having chosen to make the inward movement of Wilson's mind the theme of his book. Consequently one needs, if one is to seize Wilson's real importance, which is a matter of creative criticism rather than of literary personality, to get some view of the outward as well as the inward aspects of this as of other periods of his work; and this one can do by reading such books as Daniel Aaron's *Writers on the Left*, Malcolm Cowley's *Exile's Return*, Alfred Kazin's *Starting Out in the Thirties*, anything that, however obliquely, gives one the feeling of that decisive New York decade. Throughout this time Wilson, Trotskyist at least in this respect, maintained the values of bourgeois culture in the classless society, and saw in Marx and Engels poets of the political vision, as Michelet had been, and as he was now trying to be himself.

To the Finland Station was the result of the arduous reading of the thirties. Alfred Kazin reminds us of Wilson's invaluable self-discipline, a 'habit of willed attention, of strained concentration', essential to work of this kind; and we can also remember his power to organize large bodies of material, to make self-

5. Mr. Wilson has in a letter defended this usage, but – so far as I can see – without avail.

consistent structures, and establish large relevances. It is perhaps the noblest of Wilson's books. It appeared, as Paul remarks, too late, when Stalin had put an end to the dream of the
'first truly human culture'; but in so far as it is about intellectual heroism and the role of honest imaginative thinking in the
creation of a good society it is a work of permanent value. It is
true that the tone is of biography rather than ideology; but
this, like the author's tendency to identify his own mind and
methods with those of the subjects, gives it an exceptional
resonance, and makes it, like *Axel's Castle*, a book of use even
to those who can no longer be instructed by it. One notes that
the praise of Marx's expository method represents admiration
for an ideal the author himself aims at ('the exposition of the
theory – the dance of commodities, the cross-stitch of logic – is
always followed by a documented picture of the capitalist laws
at work ... we feel that we have been taken for the first time
through the real structure of our civilisation, and that it is the
ugliest that has ever existed.'). Here I have had to leave out the
long and powerful sentence in which the working of the
capitalist laws is described; long, but lucid and forceful, as
Wilson thinks expository sentences should sometimes be. And I
take it that even the expert will not deny the clarity and
cogency of the exposition in this book. Engels as a man is
treated with affectionate admiration, but with Lenin one senses
the author's detachment : just as Marx was 'incapable of
imagining a democracy', Lenin shunned 'gratuitous intellectual
activity'. If Marx was psychologically crude, he was in other
ways Wilsonian, 'heavily loaded with the old paraphernalia of
culture' and making of *Das Kapital*, somewhat unexpectedly, a
work which has affinities with the *Anatomy of Melancholy*.
But Lenin was not a scholar, not a writer; his style (as Gorky
observed) was 'the cold glitter of steel shavings'. He was the
New Man, the modernist of Marxism; exponent of an un-Wil-
sonian break with the past. 'We don't need bourgeois democracy,' he said in his speech at the Finland Station. In an epi-
logue looking back over the whole story in 1940, Wilson is
finely himself; he cannot allow that the failure of Marxist
dogma means the failure of all hope for a society without class
exploitation. Doing without the Dialectic is only a small part
of the challenge, which will 'require of us', as he very characteristically concludes, 'an unsleeping adaptive exercise of
reason and instinct combined'.

From Mr Paul's point of view, which is reasonable but as I say not the only one, there is a link between this book and Wilson's slightly later volume of *novelles*, *Memoirs of Hecate County*, comparable with that between *Axel's Castle* and *I Thought of Daisy*; on his view that 'to some extent everything he does – and when he takes it up – is a personal index', the relation is inevitable. In the central story, 'The Princess with the Golden Hair', Wilson certainly has rather private sources – he is thinking of Engels and Mary Burns, as well as of Casanova – and yet this is one of his most subtle and passionate comments on the evils of a society in which, as he remarked in *To the Finland Station*, 'there is very little to choose between the physical degradation of the workers and the moral degradation of the masters'. Wilson himself calls it his favourite among his works, and one can see why. Also it marked a turning point in his career; the last of the works in which commitment to public life is a central theme. The later books of travel, the bold attempt on the Dead Sea Scrolls, the works on the Iroquois, the Income Tax, the literature of the Civil War, and the culture of Canada, for all their urgent relation to his own unending self-examination and his concern with American culture, are works, by comparison, of exile. Hence the discontent of some compatriots.

But even from this very defective account of his career one can see that a stranger might very well use his privilege to call such criticism unjust. The example of Wilson – discipline, persistence, self-involvement, a willingness to acquire the means with which to practise an effective criticism – has been followed, but not adequately acknowledged, by younger Americans. To make possible an American criticism that would be strong enough for its job, to provide for it the strength, range, and subtlety of the French, was the vast undertaking. Wilson himself saw that it meant good reviewing in the periodicals. The job begins there.

It is no doubt impossible [he wrote in 1928] for an English-speaking country to hope for a literary criticism comparable to that of the French.... But when one considers the number of reviews, the immense amount of literary journalism that is now being published in New York, one asks oneself how it is possible for our reviewing to remain so puerile....

Since the death of Stuart P. Sherman, who was second-rate at best, there has not been a single American critic who regularly occupied himself in any authoritative way with contemporary literature.

He went on to list some of the evils of the situation which strong reviewing might have averted; many of them he himself was to tackle. But he also added, thinking again of himself, that first-rate criticism must come from writers: 'No such creature exists as a full-time literary critic – that is, a writer who is at once first-rate and nothing but a literary critic.' And so the task of providing America with a criticism was difficult even on the mundane level of simply finding time to do it. You had to review a lot but your reviewing would be useless unless you did other things on another level. Sometimes it wasn't possible to do both; during the years when he was reading for *To the Finland Station* Wilson, as he says, lost touch with what was going on. But by working enormously and being provident in the choice of subjects he succeeded remarkably in his attempt to do everything at once. Because he did so there *is* in America literate unacademic criticism.

One should say, then, that the size of Wilson's critical achievement, as the outsider sees it, cannot be measured by the more formal volumes, such as *Axel's Castle*, *The Triple Thinkers*, *The Wound and the Bow*, alone; one has to take account of the hundreds of shorter pieces, not merely because many of them were tributaries to these major streams, but also because they constitute in themselves that almost weekly intervention in the literary affairs of the time which probably, in the end, has the more decisive effect on taste, and on what happens next. Wilson has himself described how a career like this can be managed. In a very interesting piece called 'Thoughts on Being Bibliographed' (1943) he complains that his kind of person doesn't seem to exist any more, a writer who is a critic and a journalist, free of the oppression and patronage of academics though having of course his own problems.

To write what you are interested in writing and to succeed in getting editors to pay for it, is a feat that may require close calculation and a good deal of ingenuity. You have to learn to load solid matter into notices of ephemeral happenings; you have to develop a resourcefulness at pursuing a line of thought through pieces on miscellaneous and more or less fortuitous subjects; and you have to acquire a technique of slipping over on the routine of editors the deeper independent work which their over-anxious intentness on the fashions of the month or the week have conditioned them automatically to reject.... My [strategy] has usually been, first to get books for review ... on subjects in which I happened to be interested; then, later, to use the scattered articles for writing general studies of these subjects; then, finally, to bring out a book in which groups of these essays were revised and combined.

Using this somewhat clumsy but necessary system, he tackled the self-imposed task of carrying on the work of Mencken; one part of it, for example, was to bring home to the bourgeois intellectual world the importance of the literature of post-Symbolism and the implications of the Russian Revolution. Now, he says (in 1943), he is too old for all that; and nobody else is doing it, partly because anybody who might have qualified himself is working in a university or having his talent wrecked in a different way by *Time*, *Life*, and *Fortune*. Wilson had a perfect right to say this about people who feel he has betrayed them by refusing to bear the strain for ever. The routine outlined above takes strength, courage, discipline, none of them to be rewarded by the gift of tenure, or by long, gentle sabbaticals. One sees, sadly, why Wilson is so unkind to academics, refusing their honorary degrees, and, if he admires them, as he did Newton Arvin, Saintsbury, Gauss, Kemp Smith, Whitehead, Praz, assuming that their ability to write creatively simply takes them out of the academic category, and so does not disturb his theory.

It is the routine reviewing, somewhat disparaged by Wilson himself, that gives the best evidence of hard labour and also, often enough, of disciplined commitment. The three large volumes which collect reviews and other fugitive pieces are, what can rarely be said for such collections of periodical criticism, a great pleasure to read; the reviews frequently survive their subjects. As a great professional Wilson knows the ropes and is willing to instruct. 'The Literary Worker's Polonius', written in 1935, sets out schematically the duties of editors and contributors, the former obliged in honour to make quick decisions and quick payments, the latter needing to give the editors reasonable time to decide and consult, and to abstain from writing seductive covering letters. A whole section is given to reviewers, classified under five heads : People Who Want Work, Literary Columnists (overworked, don't expect accuracy), People Who Want to Write about Something Else (even if they let the author down, they are often interesting and should not be discouraged), Reviewer Experts (poets reviewing poets, etc., on the whole not a good thing), and Reviewer Critics. These last are extemely rare, and to earn the title an aspirant should 'be more or less familiar, or be ready to familiarise himself, with the past work of every important writer he deals with.... He should also be able to see the author in relation to the national literature as a whole and the national literature in relation to other literatures.' And so on. Only Sainte-Beuve, says Wilson, really fits into this category; but of course he does too. And when this paragon gets down to a book he must not shirk the most boring part of the job, the exposition of the contents, the summary : this is absolutely essential. Wilson does it, as a matter of fact, superbly. He really can 'establish definite identities for the books that he discusses'. It takes work, and more surprisingly brains, to do this. Yet it is only the start. In 'A Modest Self-Tribute' (1952) Wilson is again insisting on the need for critics 'to bring into one system the literatures of several cultures that have not been in close communication.... I may claim for myself, since nobody so far as I know has ever yet claimed it for me, that I have tried to contribute a little to the general cross-fertilisation....'

To do this you need more than a 'volatile curiosity', but you need that too. Some of the long essays in the latest book, which may be used to show how Wilson has wandered off in pursuit of his own private interests, are also evidence of his determination to find out what is necessary. Certainly he goes on rather about the Marquis de Sade; but he also explores *Doctor Zhivago* at great length. It strikes me as both typical and impressive that, returning for another go at T. S. Eliot in a review of 'Myra Buttle's' *The Sweeniad*, Wilson took himself off to a library to read the 'hilariously awful' epic, *Cadmus: The Poet and the World*, written earlier by Victor Purcell, the man behind the mask of 'Myra Buttle'. This later activity may not be as important as being the first to present André Malraux or Henry Miller to the American public, but it speaks of an inquisitive turn of mind and a willingness to walk to the library. Also it reminds one that one of the preservatives of Wilson's periodical criticism is that he can be rather sombrely funny. He did not much like writing for the *New Yorker*, but some of the pieces there printed have lasted wonderfully : the analysis of Ambassador Davies' prose, for instance, the attacks on detective stories (notably 'Who Cares Who Killed Roger Ackroyd?'), and the judicious distaste of the article on Lloyd C. Douglas' best-seller, *The Robe*. In fact the pieces in *Classics and Commercials* are inferior to those in *Shores of Light* only if you miss, what had to go, the special excitements of the twenties and thirties. They belong to what Wilson called 'the bleak and shrivelled forties', and they address themselves to what seemed in need of informed attention at the time : the intellectual position of Archibald MacLeish in relation to the war; the new novelists – Cain, Steinbeck, O'Hara, Saroyan; Aldous Huxley, Evelyn Waugh (two excellent essays); Sartre, Firbank, and so on, with an extended memoir of Paul Rosenfeld at the end, corresponding to the memoir of Edna St Vincent Millay at the end of *Shores of Light*. The new book, as its title suggests, wanders further from the beaten track, and has a lot about Swinburne and James Branch Cabell, but there are some comedy turns too, including Wilson getting lengthily angry about the way people abuse English.

It is, then, true but unreasonable to complain that none of this has quite the bite of earlier work, done when Wilson was in the centre of things. *The Shores of Light* contains an imaginary dialogue between Paul Rosenfeld and Matthew Josephson (one of the original *Discordant Encounters*) which is so absolutely in the centre of the first controversies on modernism as to be even now immediately relevant. It was written in 1924; forty-two years on Mr Tom Wolfe is doing well out of an *aperçu* of Josephson's in the Dialogue, which is that electric signs are nicer than art. Don't talk about art, he says—

How can you set up these trivialities as rivals to the electric sign ... a triumph of ingenuity, of colour, of imagination! – which slings its great gold–green–red symbol across the face of the heavens themselves ... ! I tell you that culture as you understand it is no longer of any value; the human race no longer believes in it. That is why I am giving my support to the campaign for Henry Ford as President. . . .

Vote for Henry Ford! The Master Dadaist of the twentieth century!

In those days Wilson, not long down from Princeton, was living in the Village and learning his job. As a critic he did most things – vaudeville, the galleries, music, theatre – but he did them as a writer, and with a growing sense of the commitments to the modern and to politics, or rather to the task of making a literature and a criticism which would not simply exclude these. His interests narrowed, perhaps, but never before each had reached fruition in a book; perhaps he foresaw a time when literature and politics would be as inextricably blended in America as in *The Triple Thinkers* he saw them to be in Russia; or a time when a new biographical criticism would profit by the thesis of *The Wound and the Bow*. But of course he changed, moved on, a stranger in a changing world. It is sometimes said that behind every criticism there is a philosophy; Wilson's is steadily pragmatic.

All our activity, in whatever field it takes place, is an attempt to give meaning to our experience – that is, to make life more practicable.

This is as true of the fictions of Sophocles as of Euclid.

Art has its origin in the need to pretend that human life is something other than it is, and, in a sense, by pretending this, it succeeds to some extent in transforming it.

This last remark belongs to 1922, and I suppose Wilson would have no reason to withdraw it now. The transformation of the world, as Wallace Stevens remarked, is the transformation of ourselves, and we do it with reason and imagination. What needs to be transformed, how transformations have historically occurred, and what is wrong with present attempts at transformation, are the legitimate and exhausting tasks of criticism. Wilson has worked at them as no other critic in his time. He dislikes my profession and my nationality, but if no American has yet claimed this for him I offer it as the most modest of tributes.

(1966)

EIGHT

CONOR CRUISE O'BRIEN

The requirement that art should edify, or at least that it shouldn't disedify, is very old; and although many assume that it is self-evidently an unreasonable requirement, others have always to concern themselves with the difficulties that arise when it is flouted. The patron of the edifying men is Plato; Aristotle is the model of the anti-authoritarians. And the issue is alive wherever you have, as in Russia or in the Catholic Church, doctrinal infallibility and the power to condemn deviations. The difference between Russia and Rome is that the church has had time to develop much more subtle and considered ways of handling the problem. Obviously you will not find Catholic aestheticians who accept I. A. Richards's account of Doctrinal Adhesion (the eighth of his 10 'chief difficulties of criticism') as 'a fertile source of confusion and erratic judgement'. On the other hand you rarely come across anybody willing to go all the way with Arthur Machen: 'Literature is the expression, through the aesthetic medium of words, of the dogmas of the Catholic Church, and that which is out of harmony with these dogmas is not literature.' In between these extremes there is a range of positions, including those of Aquinas and Maritain, the most frequently consulted of modern authorities.

'Do not separate your art from your faith,' says Maritain. 'But leave distinct what is distinct.' On the other hand art is impossible without love. Love and do as you like; but of course, if you love, what you do will be of its nature acceptable to the Christian God. In practice this means that there must be no Gidian 'collaboration with the demon', a notion condemned by Maritain as Manichean; and although the artist will be in some degree treating of base or unedifying matters, he must do so in charity, and without collusion. Thus when the artist in question is a novelist, 'the essential point is to know at what altitude he is when he makes his portrayal of evil and whether his art and his soul are pure enough ... to make it without conniving at it'.

This sounds very judicial, but is surely somewhat removed from the actual experience of reading and judging novels. So it must have seemed, anyway, to Conor Cruise O'Brien, contemplating the fury and the mire of modern fiction as well as the nature and duties of 'the Catholic imagination'. Hence *Maria Cross*,[1] in which he closely examines the work of eight Catholic writers, tackles such questions as the relation between Catholic doctrine and literature, and the extent to which his authors share the same world of imagination.

Maria Cross is a remarkable book : idiosyncratic but civilized in style, cleverly planned, learned, and witty. It contains so many good jokes (often preserved in specially built footnotes) that one begins to see how criticism could once have been a gay science. Anyone who has hitherto omitted to read it (as I had) should buy the paperback edition at once. As the main business of this review will be to question the general drift of the book, it is fair to add that the studies of individual authors, considered in isolation, are good enough to deserve comparison with Edmund Wilson at his best. The only serious lapse is the chapter on Graham Greene : only one novel is examined, and that laboriously. On Mauriac, Péguy, Claudel, and Bloy, Mr O'Brien is unfailingly perceptive and entertaining.

But it was surely perverse of him to say that this is 'not a book about Catholicism'. It is. It argues that the imagination of Christendom grasps reality only under Catholic forms; that Protestantism is the enemy not only of religion but of art; and that the mess we so often say we are in was caused by an attempt to replace what God and time have made irreplaceable for us, the faith by which alone we were enabled to understand human experience. Arguing this case, O'Brien takes on Freud and the Marxists and all the modern myth-makers, and he does so with a quite rare rhetorical power and variety, mimicking the opposition case, improving their arguments for them, damaging them with wit. Whatever the private religious beliefs of the author, this is unambiguously Catholic criticism.

The row about how far a Catholic writer may represent the human condition without a scandalous connivance at sin is, I suppose, largely a domestic matter, and O'Brien's treatment of it is important for infidels only because it earns him the necessary right to discuss works which are not merely edifying. But it is in the course of staking this claim that he goes on to argue for the uniqueness and necessity of the Catholic

1. London, Burns & Oates, 1963.

imagination, the real and only human force for creation and understanding – modern myths and symbols being only shadows of it.

Both stages of argument are sketched in the chapter on Mauriac. First, Mauriac's important novels were harshly treated by the clergy on the ground that they gave scandal in making 'perceptible, tangible ... the Catholic universe of evil'. But after *Le Noeud de Vipères* he lost his nerve, took these criticisms to heart, and henceforth wrote to illustrate an abstraction, 'the part of faith that is intellectual, not that which is emotional'. What had Mauriac lost, besides realism and intensity? The power to see in the lusts of fallen men images of the love of God, a power without which Catholic fiction is either cut off from its material, or scandalous. The book which best displays this fictional charity is *Le Désert de l'Amour*. Maria Cross is the source of pain for one man who loves her sexually, and for his son, who loves her as a sorrowing mother; the kinds of love are not in the end distinct, and her name unites the varieties of human love and suffering with the symbol by which alone they are to be understood.

Mr O'Brien finds such images of the 'tension between flesh and spirit' essential to Catholic art because 'corruption and the cross are for the Catholic the two central facts'. The Faustian failure of the modern world to hold fast to this is marked by that growth in it of evil curiosity which Bernanos records. O'Brien's writers are exiles both from the rational modern world (which forced some of them near to fascist anti-rationalism) and from their Catholic childhood. They inhabit a cemetery; but to this place of corruption the cross alone gives meaning.

To make his point O'Brien does some brilliant things with the symbolism of his writers, and notably of Péguy, Claudel, and Bloy. Rodrigue and Prouhèze in *Le Soulier de satin* spend their wedding night crucified on the same cross: '*La passion est unie à la croix*'. Bloy said 'Woman is the cross.' Man, nailed to his mother, seeks paradise in another woman and 'becomes aware of his crucifixion'. The only way we can understand the suffering of fallen man is by means of this multivalent symbol, which in its universality shares out suffering over the whole Christian community. And the pressure which gives it this human validity comes from below, not from above; all men are born to this cruciform model of passion, and its language, in so far as it is expressible, is 'the Catholic language, the *lingua franca* of suffering'. Protestantism, dead from the waist down, 'conceals the cross, refuses devotion to the mother of God', and ignores the Communion of the Saints. Hence the vast advantages of Catholic writers; hence also the special advantages of 'warped' Catholic writers, when it comes to expressing the 'tormented unconscious mind of modern ex-Christendom'.

To explain why in my view this work of criticism doesn't at once drive one into the arms of the Church, one need only look at the admittedly fine essays on Claudel and Bloy. Studying the ramifications of gold as a symbol in Claudel, O'Brien has an excursus of Empsonian splendour on the hidden French rhymes for *or* (especially *mort*). This kind of symbolic extensiveness is exceptionally pleasing to O'Brien, who for all his sharpness of mind has a strong sense of the occult. It comes out in his handling of Claudel's water-symbolism. The sea, for instance, is the centre of a complex of occult meanings : *la mère, amer, l'amour, mort*. And so on. Although Claudel is explicit enough about the sexual symbolism of water, this is, as O'Brien explains, not Freudian. It is entirely Catholic, as the scene in *Le Soulier de satin* blending sea, woman, man, sun, moon, and cross proves. The symbols in the end have fixed meanings; they all meet in the cross. But this seems contrary to what one knows of the operation of symbols in *literature* as against religion. In fact, the mistake which runs right through this book is the assumption that symbols in novels and poems are like symbols in religion, where they are, to a certain degree, fixed : the baptismal water always means the same (admittedly inexplicable) thing, as God intended it to. But every poem or novel creates a distinctive field of meanings, not all of them intended by the author, since he did not, like God, invent his medium, which is the common language.

The error might, if one wanted a label, be called a typological fallacy. It is found in an extensive form in the Catholic aesthetic of David Jones, who says, for instance, that the word 'wood' *always* recalls the cross. But the mistake isn't peculiarly Catholic; and it is also prevalent in much fashionable criticism of Yeats and the Romantics, when the attempt is to discover the exact meanings of poems by reference to the fixed meanings of symbols in a synthetic Neo-Platonic 'tradition'. It seems a hard thing to say of O'Brien, so enormously superior in intelligence and literary sense to most of the 'tradition'-mongers – but he does go some of the way with them in a process which is at once reductive and destructive.

The antiquity of the typological fallacy must be granted, and O'Brien makes much of its extraordinary revival in Bloy. He thought that an exegete should make every sentence in Scripture refer to the Trinity. He held that woman, and specifically her sexual organ, *is* the *paradisus voluptatis* of Genesis, and he shocked many people by observing that the male member was anciently thought of as an image of the cross. The man's emission of semen in the act of sex is a figure of Christ's giving up the ghost (*emisit spiritum*). Similarly, for Bloy, history has meaning only in so far as it can be seen as precisely the suffering by which we 'pay for Mary'. He extended this kind of thinking to economics (money as the blood of Christ). In a sense he is a crazed throwback to medieval typology, very different from, and also much more attractive than, a lot of sophisticated scholarly typologies we now have. He revived 'the symbolism of the Scriptures in the days of the symbolism of the *décadents*', as Mr O'Brien rightly observes. And far from being merely clinical about this curious archaistic myth-making, Mr O'Brien seems to find it superior to the analogous (but non-Catholic) inventions of Yeats. Moreover he himself employs it. Bloy illustrates for him the truth of the key saying : '*la passion est unie à la croix*'. To anybody who sees no real difference between Bloy's nonsense and the nonsense, say, of a resurrection ceremony at one of Yeats's secret societies, the real and intricate difficulty arises from one's continuing certainty that Bloy and Yeats are worth reading. And the solution has in the end to be subtler than the one which finds the value of a Yeats poem in Porphyry's Cave of the Nymphs, or of a Catholic novel in its *anamnesis* of the meanings of 'passion' and 'spirit'.

In the *Partisan Review* there appeared a story by Bernard Malamud, in which an Italian Catholic girl painter sells an American Jew a share of her studio.[2] All the time she paints abstracts based on the cross. He does abstracts based on the Star of David. She despises and lives off him, and involves him in her superstitions. Seizing a chance to make love to her, he fails, giving up the spirit too early. But one day he decides to paint himself as a priest; she sees him so dressed, pleads for absolu-

2. Published in *The Magic Barrel*. London, Eyre & Spottiswoode, 1960.

tion, and is granted it: 'Pumping slowly, he nailed her to her cross.' I wonder what Mr O'Brien would make of this rich story. It uses his symbols, but not in his way; a reading which assumed the exclusive validity of the Catholic 'community of feeling' would surely come out wrong. The fact is that like the Neo-Hermeticists of Yeats criticism, whose discipline was also founded in the age of the *décadents*, Mr O'Brien subtly re-introduces to the business of criticism an old doctrinal adhesion, a claim to exclusive inspiration which is in the end a con-spiracy against literature. What makes the Malamud story a good one isn't a community of feeling basically Catholic (or basically Jewish). Nor is it something welling up from below to take form from the fixed religious symbols employed. The symbols are no longer fixed; the business of criticism becomes difficult, inconclusive, delicate, and undogmatic in its treat-ment of symbolism.

Mr O'Brien has a good critic's perceptions of the unique order of a work of art, but, for all his disclaimers, he general-izes from them, then moves off into propaganda. Contesting Maritain, he might also have pondered Newman, who said that literature represents men as they are in themselves, 'quite in-dependent of any extraordinary aid from Heaven, or any de-finite religious belief ... it is the Life and Remains of the *natural* man'. To bring in the cross on the ground that natural lust is a type of the Passion is to use an archaism in order to bring in by the back door the pious edifying which he himself had thrown out of the front.

(1963)

NINE

ERIC BENTLEY

With one lover already under the bed, one hears the husband's knock at the door, and the second lover is crammed into the closet. Subsequently, and with the ease and speed of dreaming, the first glides to the bathroom, the second to the fire escape. Of course, it's nice to be so much better informed than the husband; but why these volleys of silvery laughter from the stalls?

This fictional situation is somewhat different from anything most of the laughers can ever have experienced. Some of the women have had lovers, and a few may have been surprised by their husbands; but few can have been disturbed under precisely these conditions. They are not laughing because they *recognise* the situation; which is why the fellow in the closet is so interesting. He is totally improbable; he is there 'for the sake of argument'. That is to say, he is just the kind of invention we habitually make for heuristic purposes, even of a trivial sort. He reminds us of other aspects of our behaviour, more familiar but equally fictive, which we have developed for our comfort, in so far as that depends on an intellectual grasp of the environment. If a wife and husband are simultaneously killed in an auto accident, the appropriate court will 'deem', that is, pretend, that the wife died first; in fact they will do so, I gather, even if she survives her husband by several days. This is an equitable dodge or fiction which prevents the double payment of estate duties. There are many such fictions, and not only in law. Vaihinger explained the degree to which intellectual activity in general is penetrated by them. Nobody confuses them with fact, and they therefore escape any critique of probability. They may be the only way to avoid the tautologies inherent in logical thinking. Bentham, who disliked legal fictions, was nevertheless willing, on certain terms, to admit 'the necessity of mixing falsehood with truth, on pain of being without ideas'. However, he excluded poetry as entirely dependent on falsehood. It was Nietzsche who pushed ahead and argued that the world, *as it concerns us*, is wholly a fiction, so that knowledge is fiction, a man-made dream which, the poet

says, must be our final belief. The test of such a fiction as the
man in the closet is not one of probability, but of human value
and human use.

There seems no reason to think that literary and dramatic
fictions are generically different from others, though it appears that even among themselves they can be in some measure differentiated by the kind of work in which they are used.
The man-in-the-closet device lacks verisimilitude; it works in
farce, but if it occurred in a novel we should be tempted to say
that this was not a novel at all, but something else. Of all living
practitioners the one who has most concerned himself with
questions of this kind, so far as I know, is Sartre; and he has
argued that words ought to give a plausible rendering of the
comfortable everyday illusion of causality, holding that because of a failure to do this *L'Etranger* was not a novel at all.
Sartre also thinks that within this context of fictive causality
human beings must be represented as indeterminate, free. 'Life,'
he notices, 'is not a novel.' He recognizes the prevalence of
comfortable fictions in it, the stale evasions of the *salauds*. The
re-imagining of reality that a novel requires is different from
these. And yet it must not depend on palpable improbabilities.
There is more to it, of course, but this, from his reviews of
Camus and Blanchot, seems roughly to be Sartre's line. I suppose it would be fairly widely acceptable.

Yet elsewhere we are able to accept as sufficient for certain
purposes degrees of probability which fall short of verisimilitude. We do so even in life; we are notionally aware of the
uniqueness or discreteness of every situation in which we find
ourselves, but presume an inherent repetitiveness in events as a
means to make ourselves easier about the future. But even this
degree of interest in probability strains the human material,
and it is a pleasant relief to find a situation from which it is
artificially, and by consent, exiled. If in life we saw a husband
about to enter the room in which we knew his wife to be in
bed with a lover, we might be concerned about a range of
possible outcomes, or we might even be amused, though it is
doubtful if we should show this, even if there were two lovers.
But in a farce the situation is pure, and the consequences determined; no great harm will come of it. The sense that there is
a real agreement to this effect, and that Shakespeare had broken
it, is behind Rymer's indignation at Othello, as we can see from
his calling the play 'a bloody farce, without salt or savour'.

Farces should not be bloody, and they should be salty. In tragedy, Rymer thought, we are entitled to ask for a plausible account of how a man came to act thus and thus; but to ask for such an account concerning the man in the closet would be to introduce questions of probability at just the wrong moment. This spoils the whole thing, since the fiction in farce does its work by excluding all such questions as perpetually bother us in life – questions of responsibility, guilt, and so forth. The characters are not free; they are types, worked like puppets and inhabiting a world in which time itself is not the time of the world. This is necessary to the operation by which this fiction discovers something of human importance. It is fiction which presumes upon probability; lest there should be a mistake about this, the extra man is in the closet.

This exercise in dramatic probability-theory is an attempt to work somewhere near the level of Eric Bentley's radical new look at the grammar of theatre. It is a very full book, founded on years of thought and experience; and it is written with a clarity which testifies to the completeness of this preparation. In short, this is a work of exceptional virtue, and readers who find more in it to disagree with than I do will still, I think, want to call it central, indispensable.

If one had to guess at the single small seed from which this burgeoning argument grows, one would guess that it was what the blurb calls 'psycho-dynamics'. Bentley, for the purposes of dramatic theory, borrows back J. L. Moreno's therapeutic psychodrama, holding that its success shows Moreno to have been right about the drama itself. The patient acts out his neurosis, the analysts play parts, and other patients, in the role of society, look on. For Bentley the idea is valuable not so much because it re-asserts the therapeutic value of the drama, though that thought is in his mind, as for the evidence it provides of an 'intimate link between theatre and life'. It supports Schopenhauer's claim that 'the drama is the most perfect reflection of human existence'. This book justifies its title by being precisely about the ways in which life manifests itself in the theatre.

Bentley is always talking about this link and this reflection, and dealing with the many difficulties they present, of which improbability is but one. It seems to me extremely creditable that he manages to do so without reducing the whole question to one of archetypes, which in turn reduce life by suppressing differences and creating resemblances. When the link, if it is to be established at all, has to be subliminal, he uses a Freudian psychology. But principally he maintains that life is, if you really look at it, dramatic; when it seems otherwise it is because we are having our conflicts in dreams.

This view precludes any generic distinction between high and low kinds; *all* theatre has this link. 'Great narrative is not the opposite of cheap narrative, it is soap opera plus.' Indeed, the higher forms are complicated by intellectual and moral activity to a degree which makes their 'life' harder to define; so Bentley gives a lot of attention to melodrama and farce. Here the problem of superficial unlifelikeness, of 'theatricality' in that pejorative sense, can be directly tackled.

First, though, there are interesting points about plot, especially on the way a plot – as in Greek drama and indeed in Shakespeare's *Hamlet* as opposed to the earlier *Hamlet* – can balance certainty and uncertainty, when the outcome is in fact known in advance. This is of course lifelike in a crude sense; one knows one will die, but not when and how. But there is more to it than that; how much more only a fictional plot which explores the issue intensively, like that of *Macbeth*, can say. The *balance* is what counts; and we can hardly achieve it except by a fiction. There is the somewhat similar matter of the plot's being unlifelike in consisting entirely of relevant action and sharp climaxes. This is one of the places in which Bentley falls back on dreams, and perhaps misses an opportunity; let me explain why I think so.

It is apparently 'natural' for us to entertain two or more different notions of time simultaneously. It is curious that Greek has three words, all with separate meanings we can recognize, to cover our notions of time. We can use them roughly to distinguish our notions. The time we are vaguely aware of as passing is *chronos*; the decisive moments (in history or in personal history) are *kairoi*. The continuum in which we achieve a kind of immortality by reproducing ourselves is *aion*. (I had better say that this is too simply put.) Now in drama all time is the time represented by *kairos*; in other words, it represents life as we habitually represent it to ourselves, as if *chronos* did not exist. And we do this consciously; in the unconscious, we are told, there is no time at all. The fiction (which is that chronic time should be ignored 'for the sake of argument') is therefore thoroughly human and involved in consciousness. When Mr Bentley writes so potently about death in tragedy and its link with the deaths of everyday life, he pauses to remind us that the *kairos* of death (the coming of our 'time') is unique in that we cannot see both sides of it. Our uncomfortable inability to do so produces characteristic fictions and the death of the tragic hero belongs to the class of apocalypses, fictions of the final *kairos*. Once more, whether we are thinking of history or of the personal life, we use, under pressure from the thought of death, the characteristic human fictions, tragedy and apocalypse; because they are so grand they produce what Goethe called *das Schaudern*, the tragic (or apocalyptic) shudder.

Though I was in that paragraph trying to develop a point of Bentley's without his recourse to dreaming, what I said confirms his view that tragedy is the most accurate representation we have of the human personality freed (by a fiction) from its normal desire 'not to go into' the matter of dying. 'We begin to live,' said Yeats, 'when we conceive of life as a tragedy.' This fiction concerning death is a maker of life; that is the use of fictions. Bentley remarks that 'the opposite of Tragedy is not Comedy but Christian Science'. Everything depends upon an induced willingness, among us guilty creatures sitting at a play, to take terror by the hand and measure the personal agony against the facts and fictions of survival. '*Wer spricht von Siegen? Uberstehn ist alles*' – Rilke. as Bentley observes, puts part of the case. The flat last lines of *Lear* put another : 'The weight of this sad time we must obey.'

In great tragedy the loss of a chronic verisimilitude is the price to be paid for a sharp rendering of life as obsessed by the idea of death. This is a point made in different ways throughout Bentley's argument. Dramatic characterization tends to produce types, because types have more general significance, more heuristic value. As every moment tends to become a *kairos*, and every character a type, so every meeting becomes an encounter, and every dialogue is preternaturally meaningful. The irrelevant, essentially inhuman fuzz is cleared off time, character, and speech; human encounters have their true rhythm, which they can only have in fiction, however much we desire it in life. And this imposition of high human fictions on the world is surely not dreamlike; it is more awake and more human than without it we can be.

The force of Bentley's argument depends, as I have said, to a

considerable degree on his answers to the questions raised by
the lower theatrical forms. He therefore gives melodrama and
farce more space than tragedy and comedy. With some air of
paradox he stresses their closeness to life : 'melodrama is more
natural than Naturalism'; and it is human, though less human
than tragedy. As to farce, it becomes the crucial case. Assuming its closeness to life, one can choose between a Platonic-
moralistic condemnation (it 'waters the growth' of undesirable
passions, which seems to be the view behind the moralistic
attack on the English Theatre of Cruelty) and an Aristotelian
cathartic theory : farce gives one a valuable emotional 'work-
out', a restorative laugh at the institution, for instance, of
marriage. Bentley's view, though it is refined and qualified, is of
the second variety.

Clearly this is right as far as it goes; but it underplays the
conscious delights of the genre. It is true that the great age of
French farce was also an age of tragedies about adultery, and a
somewhat repressive age. But one cannot give the farces to the
id and the tragedies to the super-ego; Bentley admits the large
element of intellectual interest in good farce, as in excellence
of invention and timing. Tragedy and farce, as Rymer failed to
see, are means of extracting from similar material wisdom or
comfort appropriate to different phases of human need; they
make different fictions 'for the sake of argument'. Thus in
tragedy it is assumed (as some assume in life) that you can't
have adultery off the record; that it will have consequences,
and that they will be dark and sad. Yet as a matter of experience we know there are adulteries with no public consequences
of any kind. Farce will allow this, and also assume, for the
sake of its argument, that when such consequences occur the
pain attendant upon them is not inevitable. No matter how
hopeless the situation as the husband beats on the door, and,
when he enters, locks it, he is not terrible and the end will be
happy. In the meantime, of course, there are uncertainties to
balance against this certainty, and we can admit the necessity
of the man in the closet without in the least desiring to be in
his place. In short, each form requires a restriction of probabilities and interests (though it is greater, usually, in farce)
each provides a different aspect of the *kairos*, a different help
in being human; and this is true even if you want to reduce the
psychodynamics which animate us all to a mere *bovarysme*.

On the modern anti-play, with its elastic attitude to illusion,

Bentley speaks very valuably. His strong historical sense enables him to speak with originality and understanding of Ionesco and Beckett. Having insisted throughout on the presence in all great drama of a strong intellectual, indeed ideological element, he has no difficulty in establishing its presence in professedly anti-intellectualist theatre. The drying up of the dialogue in *Waiting for Godot*, the blasting of 'illusion', the operations on the border of farce and tragedy – all these devices, in so far as they make for a considerable play, obey the general grammatical laws he lays down.

Antonin Artaud, whose views are at present having a success in the world, says in the first manifesto on the Theatre of Cruelty that the only value of theatre 'is in its excruciating, magical relation to reality and danger'. Those who are implementing his programme are paying much more attention to the occult aspect of this relation. Peter Weiss's play on Marat may have had its origin in a remark of Artaud, when he proposed 'a tale by the Marquis de Sade, in which the eroticism will be transposed, allegorically mounted, and figured, to create a violent exteriorization of cruelty, and a dissimulation of the remainder'. The result is theatrically of high interest, though it is precisely on the ideological issue that it fails; and this could be because Artaud himself never seemed quite certain of what he was talking about. I mention him only because, so far as I can see, his theory of drama is implicit in Bentley's larger and cooler thesis, and his hysteria is replaced by civil wit. For his clarity and civility Bentley pays a small price : occasionally he seems to labour the obvious. That would be hard to avoid in an enterprise of this kind; Aristotle did it, and we wish he had done it still more. If you see any crucial interest in such topics as the death of Cordelia, Godot's non-arrival, or the man in the closet, this is a book to be read and read again.

(1964)

NOVELISTS

TEN

D. H. LAWRENCE AND THE
· APOCALYPTIC TYPES

Writing novels is more like writing history than we often choose to think. The relationships between events, the selection of incident, even, in sophisticated fictions, the built-in scepticism as to the validity of procedures and assumptions, all these raise questions familiar to philosophers of history as problems relating to historical explanation. One such problem is explanation by types. They are obviously important in novels, for without them there would be no 'structure'. How do they work in history? How do we recognize a revolution? The events of a selected series cease to look random when we assimilate them to other selected series which have been identified and classified under some such term as 'revolution'. Similarly for series which can be filed under 'crisis', or under 'transitional epoch'. There is the complication that personalities involved in the events under consideration may very well have done the typing themselves, as revolutionaries generally do, and this means that historical, like fictive events, can in some measure be caused to occur in conformity with the types. Furthermore, since everybody's behaviour is indeterminately modified by the conviction that he is living through a crisis, it might be argued that history can, though with unpredictable variations, be prepared for such a conformity, even without the intervention of conscious theory. But the element of indeterminacy is so gross that we can perhaps forget this.

There are, very broadly speaking, two quite distinct and mutually hostile ways of considering 'typical' explanations. One is to assume that, with varying and acceptable degrees of 'displacement', histories and fictions cannot avoid conforming with types, so that the most useful thing that can be done is to demonstrate this conformity. However sophisticated and cautious the exponent of this doctrine may be, his thinking is likely, in the last analysis, to be sentimentally ritualistic and circular. He is nowadays much more likely to be a critic of fiction than an historian. Historians and modern theologians nowadays employ typology in a much more empirical way, a way consistent with a more linear notion of history. The historian will agree that the discovery of a motive in some action or series of fictions involves classifying it as belonging to a certain type. Unless that is done it will not appear that a motive has been discovered. Of course he will also, as a rule, agree that the material available is not always so classifiable; and so will the novelist. The distinction between these kinds of event is roughly that defined by Bultmann in respect of biblical history as a contrast between what is *historisch* and what is *geschichtlich*.[1] The novelist, as a rule, has rather more interest than the historian in the latter, that is, he more completely ignores the multitude of events that might be supposed to have occurred along with the ones he chooses to treat as specially significant. His position is neatly put by Conrad: 'Fiction is history, human history, or it is nothing. But it is also more than that; it starts on firmer ground, being based on the reality of forms.' Forms are systematized typological insights; they are, or should be, always under very critical scrutiny, because they can tempt us into unjustified archaism.

The modern theologian is forced to understand the difference between sentimental or archaistic typology and the kind which is appropriate to a belief which has had to emigrate, like the Jews, from myth into history. He professes to use the old scriptural types only as indices of the contemporaneity of the New Testament, and not as elements in a miraculous plot, devised by the Holy Ghost, to keep Old and New Testaments, and the whole of history, in a condition of miraculous concord. Of course there are atavistic theologians as well as atavistic historians, literary critics, and novelists, though it is to me an interesting reflection that modern theology got really deeply into de-mythologizing at about the time when literary critics began to go overboard for mythology.

I will not pursue that, but ask why literary people should be so liable to this atavism. One reasonably simple explanation is that our immense scepticism, our deep concern with the nature of the tools we are using, is only one of the traditions to which we are heirs. Another is a tradition of mythological primitivism which has branches of many kinds: occultism, Frazerian Cambridge anthropology, and of course Freud and Jung. In the

1. I have borrowed some notions and terms from A. C. Charity's *Events and Their After Life* (Cambridge University Press, 1966). For a fuller discussion see *Novel*, Summer 1968.

period which was formative for us there was also a fashionably circular historiography, provided by Spengler; a revival of primitive art; and, a large and seminal literature which was in various ways primitivistic and favourable to archaic typologizing. Thus, when novels are closest to history we may still ask whether their fidelity to certain types is wholly consistent with a just representation of human history.

I begin with this dogmatic introduction in order to make it clear in what relations I am considering D. H. Lawrence. Among the reasons why he continues to be thought of as a particularly important novelist is this : he believed himself to be living in a time of cosmic crisis, and partly justified this conviction by archaic typologizing. History was for him a plot devised by the Holy Ghost, and 'scientific' explanations (which would first examine and then reject this as a fiction) he found hateful. Unlike George Eliot, a predecessor in The Great Tradition, he could not separate the intuition that he lived in the great age of transition from explanations devoid of empirical interest but interesting enough to all primitivists, and indeed to historians of ideas. He knew a great deal (anti-intellectualists need to) and was exceptionally aware of the nature and history of his typologies; for example, he was a great student not only of mystery rituals but also of Apocalypse, and commentary on Apocalypse. This essay is about what he knew, and how it is expressed in various books, notably *Women in Love*.

In the 'Study of Thomas Hardy', which belongs in time to much the same period as *The Rainbow* and *Women in Love*, Lawrence observed that a man can only view the universe in the light of a theory, and since the novel is a microcosm it has to reflect a micro-theory, 'some theory of being, some metaphysic'. Of course this metaphysic mustn't obtrude and turn the novel into a tract, nor must the novelist make himself a metaphysic of self-justification, and then 'apply the world to this, instead of applying this to the world', a practice of which he found a striking instance in the ascetic Tolstoi, whom he describes as 'a child of the Law'. The fact is that Lawrence was at the moment when he wrote that passage troubled about the 'metaphysic' of the work he had in hand. That he should use so curious an expression of Tolstoi – 'a child of the Law' – gives one a strong hint as to the character of that metaphysic.[2]

2. It is worth remembering Lawrence's capacity for having things

Lawrence was obsessed with apocalypse from early youth, and he remembered the chiliastic chapel hymns of his childhood. During the war the apocalyptic coloration of his language is especially striking; sometimes it strongly recalls seventeenth-century puritanism. He considered the world to be undergoing a rapid decline which should issue in a renovation, and expected the English to have some part in this, much as Milton put the burden on God's Englishmen; Lawrence, however, dwelt more on the decadence, and seemed to think the English were rotting with especial rapidity in order to be ready first. He spoke of the coming resurrection – 'Except a seed die, it bringeth not forth,' he advises Bertrand Russell in May 1915. 'Our death must be accomplished first, then we will rise up.' 'Wait only a little while'; these were the last days, the 'last wave of time', he told Ottoline Morell. There would be a new age, and a new ethical law.

The nature of Lawrence's pronouncements on the new age and the new ethic is such that he can very well be described as a 'moral terrorist' : Kant's term for historians who think that the evident corruption of the world presages an immediate appearance, in one form or another, of anti-Christ. But he was also what Kant, in the same work (*The Disputation of the Faculties*) calls an 'abderitist', namely one who explains history in terms of culture-cycles. More specifically, and perhaps more recognizably, he was a Joachite.

Where Lawrence, who was to call himself Joachim in *The Plumed Serpent*, got his Joachitism from one can only guess. A possible source is Huysman's *Là-Bas* ('Two of the Persons of the Trinity have shown themselves. As a matter of logic, the Third must appear'). But Joachitism is a hardy plant, and as Frank E. Manuel says in *Shapes of Philosophical History*, it was particularly abundant in the literature of the French decadence and so could have formed part of that current of occultist thinking to which Lawrence was so sensitive. The doctrine varies a bit, but broadly it postulates three historical epochs, one for each per-

---

both ways. He balances his more extreme metaphysical and occult fantasies with a sophisticated pragmatism; the effect in his fiction is to have passages that jeer at Birkin's doctrines. This hedging of bets I occasionally refer to, but it gets in the way of exposition, and the reader might like to re-introduce it into his reflections if he finds something that seems unexpectedly and positively absurd in my account of Lawrence's crisis-philosophy.

son of the Trinity, with a transitional age between each. The details are argued out of texts in Revelation.

It is hardly too much to claim that the vague and powerful assumptions we all make about historical transition have their roots in Joachitism; in Lawrence, however, the relation is much more specific. The wartime Hardy study speaks of our having reached an end, or a 'pause of finality' which is not an end. It is the moment of Transition. There has been an epoch of Law, and an epoch of 'Knowledge or Love', and out of the synthesis of the two will develop the new age, which will be the age of the Holy Spirit. As in some early Joachite sects, the sexual implications of this are especially important. Lawrence holds that the principle of Law is strongest in woman, and that of Love in men (which is worth remembering when one considers Ursula and Birkin). Out of their true union in 'Consummate Marriage' will grow that ethic which is the product of Law and Love but is a third distinct thing, like the Holy Ghost. Although there is every sign that we have reached the point of transition, the art which should reflect it has not yet been invented. Obviously the big double novel he was working on was to be the first attempt at this appropriate art.

Now I daresay that some admirers of Lawrence will go a long way towards allowing one to speak of his thought, on sex and other matters, as having a strong apocalyptic colouring, yet draw the line at this very schematic and detailed application of the idea. Yet it is, I think, incontrovertible. When Lawrence spoke of 'signs' he did not mean only that everything was getting very bad, he meant that there *were* apocalyptic images and signs in the sky. The Zeppelin was one: 'there was war in heaven. . . . It seemed as if the cosmic order were gone, as if there had come a new order. . . . It seems our cosmos has burst, burst at last . . . it is the end, our world has gone. . . . But there must be a new heaven and a new earth.' This is from a letter to Lady Ottoline Morell, in September, 1915. A few days later he again calls the Zeppelin 'a new great sign in the heavens'. When he came to write the famous chapter 'Nightmare' in *Kangaroo* he again remembered the Zeppelin, 'high, high, high, tiny, pale, as one might imagine the Holy Ghost'.

In *Kangaroo* the Holy Ghost is patron of a new age which will dispense with democracy and bosses and be dominated by 'vertebrate telepathy' from a leader. As always in apocalyptic historiography, this renovation is preceded by a decadence; the 'new show' cannot happen until there has been some smashing. Lawrence's image of the transitional smasher was the terrible 'non-mental' mob, often symbolized by the troglodyte miner, one of his recurrent figures and an object of hate and love, fear and admiration. Continually reflecting on the apocalyptic types, Lawrence produced his own brand of Joachitism, as distinctive as that of Blake in *The Everlasting Gospel*, but easily identifiable, just as one can readily see the conformity between his more general apocalyptic thinking and the whole tradition. For convenience one can identify three aspects of this, in addition to the specifically Joachite notion of transition and crisis. They are : the Terrors (the appalling events of *dies illa*, the last day); decadence and renovation, twin concepts that explain one's own discontent and one's own hopes for another Kingdom, somewhere; and finally what I call clerkly scepticism, the reluctance of the literate to credit popular apocalyptism in its crude forms, with consequent historiographical sophistications.

In Lawrence there is a very personal ambiguity in these matters; he was a clerkly writer, but the popular apocalypse fascinated him just the same. He had a doctrine of symbolism which helped him to bridge this gap, and sometimes his allusions are so inexplicit that only if you are a naïve fundamentalist (in which case you probably wouldn't be reading Lawrence) or are on the lookout (in which case you are reading abnormally) will you pick them up. A good example of this is the passage in *St Mawr*, which is in general an apocalyptic story, where Mrs Witt discusses with Lewis 'a very big, soft star' that falls down the sky. Lewis is led on to talk about the superstitions of his countryside, and finally to explain what the star means to him : 'There's movement in the sky. The world is going to change again.' When Mrs Witt reminds him of the physical explanation of shooting stars, mentioning that there are always many in August, he just insists that 'stones don't come at us out of the sky for nothing'. Whatever Lewis has in mind, Lawrence is certainly thinking of Rev. vi. 13, 'And the stars of heaven fell unto the earth', which happens at the opening of the sixth seal, when 'the great day of his wrath is come'. Lawrence is explicit enough about the general apocalyptic bearing of the horse itself, and perhaps too explicit about the decadence and the possibility of a new show and Lewis's superior understanding of the situation, but in this little episode there is a set of variations on a hidden apocalyptic symbol which is in some ways even more characteristic.

What we have to see, I think, is that, explicit or inexplicit, this, the apocalyptic, is the chief mould of Lawrence's imaginative activity. In the work of the 1920s it grows increasingly explicit, for example in the Whitman essay, or in the study of Melville, where the sinking of the *Pequod* is called 'the doom of our white day'. There had always been a racial aspect to his apocalyptic thinking, as we shall see; even in his essays on Dahlberg and Huxley's *Point Counter Point* he affirms the exhaustion of the white racial psyche, the disintegration that will lead to a new show. From 1923, mostly in letters to Frederick Carter, he was offering elaborate interpretations of *Revelation*, based on a study of conventional exegesis (which he despised) and on less orthodox treatments, such as those of James Pryse, Madame Blavatsky, and Carter himself. In 1924 he wrote some articles on the subject, and in his last years worked hard on *Apocalypse*, his own commentary.

In *Apocalypse* Lawrence acknowledges that the book of Revelation, and other parts of the Bible, with which he was saturated in childhood, remained in his mind and 'affected all the processes of emotion and thought'. But in the meantime he had come to loathe it, and his long essay is an attempt to explain why, consciously and unconsciously, this 'detested' book could play so large a part in his most serious work. It has to be separated from mere vulgar credulity and subjected to a clerkly scepticism that is still not mere rationalism. Years of labour went into Lawrence's theory that the version we read in the Bible, the hateful book, 'Jewy' and 'chapel', meat for underdogs, was a horribly corrupt version of an earlier work which must have related the ritual of an authentic mystery religion. What he tries to do is to remove the 'Judeo-Roman screen' and penetrate to the fundamental rite, as it was represented in the imagery of the original pre-Christian text. This rite would be a guide to 'emotional-passional knowledge'; the editorial sophistications stood for the non-vital Christian universe. The original was quick, though the corrupt version was dead. And of course Lawrence found in Revelation his mystery ritual. There was the Great Mother, whom the Jewish and Christian editors had dissociated into one good and one bad, the Woman Clothed with the Sun and the Scarlet Woman. There was the ritual descent into hell, and the rebirth. And this *katabasis* was the type of the one the world was at present

undergoing. As in the mystery rite, the contemporary harrow-
ing of hell is to be accomplished by a sexual act. In the epoch
of the Holy Ghost we shall revert 'towards our elementals', as
Lawrence put it in that curious homage to the Paraclete, *Fantasia of the Unconscious*; to Adam reborn, love will be a new
thing; the man–woman relationship will be remade. But first
there has to be death and rebirth.

Although his commentators pay very little and then only
embarrassed attention to it, *Apocalypse* is ideologically a climax of Lawrence's work. But because he never ceased to feel
that it was not enough merely to describe the crisis, the terrors,
the death, and rebirth, he wrote over the same years a novel, a
novel which should be impregnated with this sexual eschatology. That novel was *Lady Chatterley's Lover*. As I tried to
show in an essay published four or five years ago, that book
enacts the sevenfold descent into hell and the climactic rebirth
by sex. I shan't dwell on it now, because I want to talk about
other books, and especially about one in which the apocalyptic types have a peculiar historical force, namely *Women in
Love*.

Ritual descent into hell, followed by rebirth – that is the
character of Lawrence's transitional period. The reason why
the world misunderstands what is happening is that it knows
only a corrupt Apocalypse – it sees, with Mellors, that 'there's a
bad time coming, boys', but thinks that the smashing-up will
be a way of dislodging the proud, and setting the underdogs up
instead. Actually the beneficiaries constitute an elect, isolate in
a new consciousness, synthesizing Law and Love. A mark of
this elect will naturally be the new man–woman relationship;
for the woman was law and the man love, and just as these
two epochal ethics will be transformed in the third, so will the
two Persons, Man and Woman, be, under the new dispensation,
merged in a new relationship, and yet remain distinct. The
obvious image for this sexual situation is the Trinity, of which
the Persons are distinct but not divided. And this epoch of the
Holy Ghost has no time for underdogs.

As we have seen, this programme, already implicit in the
Hardy study, requires not only a new ethics and new philos-
ophies of culture, but also its own art; so it is not surprising
that the novels Lawrence wrote during the war have much
apocalyptic figuration. *The Rainbow* came to represent the Old

Testament (Law) and *Women in Love* the New Testament (Love). The rainbow at the end of the first novel is the symbol of the old Covenant; the apocalyptic climax of the second reflects the structure of the New Testament. *Women in Love* is an end, where *The Rainbow* was a beginning; it represents the destruction of the old, and enacts the pause before the new world. It projects a kind of Utopia; but it is subjected, like the rest of the apocalyptic material, to Lawrence's own brand of scepticism.

The Rainbow is deliberately rendered as a kind of Genesis. The opening passages have a sort of Blakean gravity, like the illustrations to Job – the gravity is patriarchal. Allusions to Genesis punctuate the book. The death of old Brangwen, drunk, after a flood, makes him a sort of distorted antitype of Noah. George Ford's extremely interesting book on Lawrence (*Double Measure*) makes these and other connections with Genesis, including the references to the coming together of the sons of God and the daughters of man, which establish a typical basis for Ursula. *The Rainbow* also contains some faint but characteristic premonitions of the apocalypse to come : as when Anna sneers at the lamb-and-flag window of the church, calling it 'the biggest joke of the parish'. The lamb and flag constitute a traditional icon of apocalypse, but Anna is sneering at her husband's interest in such symbolism, as her daughter will later deride Birkin's more sophisticated apocalypse. Women are sceptics, they cling, like Anna, 'to the worship of human knowledge', they hanker after the Law. In fact Brangwen is a sort of decadent typologist, with an underdog chapel apocalypse; we are not surprised when we meet him briefly in *Women in Love* and find him grown insensitive, proletarian, obsolete.

The lamb-and-flag window is one of those glancing allusions, like the falling star in *St Mawr*, which show how these figures possessed Lawrence. The great chapter of the horses is more explicitly apocalyptic; Lawrence's discussion of the horse in *Apocalypse* establishes a direct connection with Revelation; and in the same section he once again quotes that text from Genesis, earlier used in *The Rainbow*, about the sons of God visiting the daughters of men, adding that according to Enoch these angels had 'the members of horses'. The passage is extremely complicated, as always when Lawrence's imagination is fully extended on this theme. These horses stand for the lost

potency of white civilization; (and specifically of England : this
is the gloomy patriotic element in Lawrence's eschatology);
they also stand for sexual terrors of the kind he associated with
them in *Fantasia of the Unconscious*. Of course sexual terror
and the racial decadence were closely related subjects, as one
sees most vividly in *Women in Love*.

In fact *Women in Love* exhibits all the apocalyptic types in
their Lawrentian versions – decadence and renovation in a
painful transition or crisis, elitism, patriotic fervour, sex, and
mystery. Its subject, like that of *Lady Chatterley*, is, basically,
England, and by extension the decline of 'white' racial culture
to be unimaginably redeemed in a sexual mystery. The characteristic pattern occurs with peculiar clarity in a letter of 1926 :
'they've pushed a spear through the side of my England',
means, superficially, that the country round Nottingham had
been ruined and disfigured by 'miners – and pickets – and
policemen' during the great strike; but underneath there is the
imagery of death and a new love : dancing, disciples, a new
'England to come'. There is a sort of Blakean patriotism, even
in *The Rainbow*; but Ursula in *Women in Love, is* England, for
her, as for Connie, that other sleeping beauty, there is a programme of renovation by sexual shock. We find her, after the
water-party, 'at the end of her line of life', her 'next step was
into death'. This death, she finds, is preferable to mechanical
life. But the death-flow of her mood is interrupted by the
arrival of Birkin. At once she hates him. 'He was the enemy,
fine as a diamond, and as hard and jewel-like, the quintessence
of all that was inimical. . . . She saw him as a clear stroke of
uttermost contradiction.' The life-flow of love and the death-
flow of law here clash. Birkin contradicts death, personal,
national, and cosmic. He himself often meditates on the necessary death of England; 'of race and national death' at the wedding party near the beginning; of the death of England when
he and Ursula buy the old chair; of the necessary disappearance of England in the chapter 'Continental', when Gudrun
sneers at him and calls him a patriot. But death is for him a
preparation for the new life; so he must contain and overthrow
Ursula's scepticism; and because she is England he must work
the renovation on her body.

This intermittent equation of Ursula and England gives some
indication of the means by which Lawrence matched his

apocalyptic types with history. For *Women in Love* is an historical novel. Like *Middlemarch*, to which it owes so much, *Women in Love* is a novel about a modern crisis; and it deals with it, partly, by concentrating on the condition of women question, the answer to which, as George Eliot once remarked, had been from the time of Herodotus one of the most important symptoms of the state of a society. Unlike *Middlemarch*, however, Lawrence's novel contains no positive allusion to actual history. 'I should wish the time to remain unfixed,' he wrote, 'so that the bitterness of the war may be taken for granted in the characters.' I shall postpone discussion of this radical difference of method, because the immediate need is simply to assert that *Women in Love* is nonetheless an historical novel, a book about a particular historical crisis. When Dr Leavis observes of Lawrence that 'as a recorder of essential English history he is a great successor of George Eliot', he is thinking primarily of *The Rainbow*; but he adds that '*Women in Love* has ... astonishing comprehensiveness in the presentment of contemporary England (the England of 1914)'. *The Rainbow* has 'historical depth', and studies the past in which the crisis germinated. *Women in Love* concerns itself less with evocations of a lost world than with a moment of history understood in terms of a crisis archetype. The random events of history assume the patterns of eschatological feeling and speculation.

'The book frightens me: it's so end of the world,' said Lawrence in 1916. George Ford points out that among the early titles proposed for *Women in Love* were *The Latter Days* and *Dies Irae*. And this eschatological preoccupation touches everything in the book. Consider, for example, the social aspect. Lawrence's apocalypse, as I have said, is elitist, and like the elite of the medieval Joachite sects, for instance The Brethren of the Free Spirit, his chosen ones exclude the profane from their mysteries. Birkin often remarks that people don't matter; or they matter only in so far as they may produce the terrors, the great mindless shove into the last days. The mood is reflected also in Lawrence's own letters and in *Kangaroo*. The mechanical mob has nothing to do with the true sexual mystery-religion of apocalypse; it was in their name that the Jewish and Greek bottom-dogs corrupted the text of the original Revelation. They have a false, lesser mystery, no true katabasis, but merely a parody of it. These *profani*, destructive,

even chthonic, were associated in Lawrence's mind with col-
liers, the 'blackened, slightly distorted human beings with red
mouths' who work for Gerald. To Gudrun, who has an instinctive sympathy with their debased power – Lawrence writes
several passages to make this point including the very fine one
where the workmen lust after her in her fancy stockings – to
Gudrun they are 'powerful, underworld men' in whose voices
she hears 'the voluptuous resonance of darkness'; she desires
them, related as they are to the kind of evil found in the
waterplants of 'Sketchbook', and the decadence of Halliday's
statue. If Ursula is the Magna Dea in her creative aspect, Gudrun is Hecate, a Queen of the Night. But in the renovated world
there is to be no place for her, or for her underworld men.

The real descent into hell and rebirth Lawrence can signify
only by sex. The purest expression of it is in *The Man Who
Died*, but in some ways the love-death undergone by Ursula
and Connie is a fuller image because it amalgamates heaven
and hell, life-flow and death-flow, in one act. The act is anal.
Lawrence is never explicit about it, whether in the novels or in
the essays where one might have expected some explanation of
the Holy Ghost's electing so curious an epiphany. But he has in
mind what he takes to be the basic figure of the mystery behind revelation – this is the point, for Connie and Ursula and
for England also, where life and death meet; when the shame
induced by Law is defied and burnt out. 'How good it was to be
really shameful.... She was free.' This participation in 'dreadful mysteries beyond the phallic cult', enacts death and rebirth
at once, is decadent and renovatory at once.

As the literature shows, this is not easy to discuss. One
cannot even distingush, discursively, between the sex Gudrun
desires from Loerke, which is obscene and decadent, and that
which Ursula experiences with Birkin, which is on balance
renovatory. The first comes straight out of Nordau, the second
is darkly millennialist, again like that of some medieval sects in
their Latter Days; yet in practice they presumably amount to
almost the same thing. It is an ambivalence which may have
characterized earlier apocalyptic postures, as Fraenger argues
in his book on Hieronymus Bosch. Decadence and renovation,
death and rebirth, in the last days, are hard to tell apart, being
caught up in the terrors.

Does a new world – created in the burning out of sexual
shame, in the birth from such an icy womb as in that of the

last chapters of Lawrence's novel – does such a world await the elect when the terrors of the transition are over? Do the elect rightly look forward to the epoch of the Holy Spirit? The myth in the book says yes. It says so throughout – in image after image and in a long series of antitheses: in 'Rabbit' and in 'Water-Party', in the water-weeds and butterflies, in Gerald's death journey to Gudrun's bed and in Birkin rolling naked in the pine-needles; in the flow of death and the flow of life, the imagery of *fleurs du mal* and the rose of happiness. But the book also obscures the myth. Between the flow of life and that of death there is 'no difference – and all the difference. Dissolution rolls on, just as production does … it ends in universal nothing – the end of the world. … It means a new cycle of creation after. …' Birkin is glossing his earlier remark that Aphrodite 'is the flowering mystery of the death-process'. He cannot tell Ursula quite how their Aphrodite is dissociated from that process. And here he invites her scepticism.

As Magna Dea committed to continuance, as woman the voice of Law, and as modern clerk, Ursula is repeatedly the voice of that scepticism which always, in history, attends apocalptic prophecy. When Birkin rants about the disappearance of England, she knows it cannot 'disappear so cleanly and conveniently'. It is part of the historical tension between myth and history (the long record of disappointed apocalypse) or between what Birkin thinks of as life and death. The novel fights back at myth, and where the myth says yes, the novel and Ursula often say no. The novel, as a kind, belongs to humanism, not to mystery religion; or in terms of Worringer's contemporary distinction, it cannot, because of the society that produced it, abandon empathy entirely in favour of abstraction. Thus our white decadence can never take the obscenely abstract form of Halliday's statue. And Lawrence knew this. Whereas *The Rainbow*, which looks back to a pastoral Genesis, can end with the archetypal sign of the covenant, *Women in Love* must have a modern conclusion in which nothing is concluded, a matter of disappointed love, a pattern incomplete. It allows history some ground unconquered by the types.

'Has *everything* that happens universal significance?' It is Birkin's question, and the novelist's question always. For Birkin it arises out of the repeated assertion that Gerald's type is Cain. Gerald's shooting of his brother is to Gudrun 'the purest form of accident'. But Birkin decides that he 'does not believe there was any such thing as accident. It all hung together, in the deepest sense.' Hence the subsequent death of Gerald's sister, his own visit to the depths of the lake, the region of death, and finally his death in the ice, may be seen as pre-determined. At any rate Lawrence wants us to ask questions about the truth of the types in a novel. The New Testament shows them all fulfilled, in the 'fullness of time'. Can there be such a novelistic *pleroma*, in which no event is random? If so, all the apparent randomness of the book must have significance: cats, rabbits, jewels, floods. This kind of realism finds its *figura* in random event. So the mythic type returns powerfully to its ancient struggle with history. But Lawrence never in fact allowed history to lose altogether, even in *The Plumed Serpent*, even in the narrowly schematic *Lady Chatterley's Lover*. He headed dangerously towards a typological predominance, and paid the price; the more he asserted the fulfilment of preordained types, the less he could depend on that randomness which leaves room for quickness and special grace. Mrs Morel locked out of her house, experiencing fear but burying her face in the lily – that is the kind of thing that is lost. We still have it in *Women in Love* – in a relevance altogether strange, in unique configurations. There are the naked white men round the African statue, an image not subordinated to the element of doctrine involved; or the eurhythmics and the cows in 'Water-Party'. One of Lawrence's powers was a capacity for stunning verisimilitude, a thing precious in itself – one thinks of the passage in *The Rainbow* in which Will Brangwen picks up the factory-girl at the music-hall. There are always untyped graces of this sort in Lawrence; they belong to history, and they are what all good novels ought to have. Lawrence never lost the power, but it must have seemed that its relevance to what he was doing progressively diminished.

Women in Love is the last novel in which he kept the balance. Its radical type is apocalypse, used as an explanation of the great contemporary crisis; for 'it was in 1915 the old world ended' and the great transition began. The great feat is to confront what Auerbach calls 'the disintegration of the continuity of random events' – reflected in the technique of Lawrence's novel – with the unchangingness of the types, and to do it without sinking into a verisimilar discreteness on the one hand, or into a rigid, flux-denying schema on the other. *Women in Love* studies crisis without unforgivably insulting reality. Its types do some of the work which historians also do with types.

Perhaps we can get a clearer notion of the kind of balance Lawrence had to struggle for if we look at that earlier historical novel to which he was so much indebted, *Middlemarch*. Lawrence grew discontented with George Eliot, but *Women in Love* is nevertheless his *Middlemarch*. The opening pages of the Victorian novel were in his mind when he made Ursula throw the jewels at Birkin, and again at the end when Gudrun gives the stockings to her sister – a curious dissociation of the Eliot scene, which stuck in his mind partly because of Dorothea's priggish allusion to the use of jewels by St John in Revelation. There is an important typological recall of the great passage in *Middlemarch* when Dorothea returns, desolate, from Rome: near the climax of Lawrence's book Gudrun passes a terrible night, alone with the ticking clock, in bondage to time, to the horrible mechanical Gerald, and half thinks her hair may have turned white. 'Yet there it remained, brown as ever, and there she was herself, looking a picture of health.' The slightly perfunctory nature of the prose here may be a consequence of Lawrence's feeling behind what he was doing the extraordinary strength of George Eliot's moment – Dorothea also desolate, also against a background of ice and snow, 'incongruously alive', 'glowing ... as only youthful health can glow'. It is in the same scene that Lawrence allows Gudrun to think of herself as a modern Hetty Sorrel, and of Gerald as a modern Arthur Donnithorne. It is a thought full of irony and the recognition of a change in the patterns of sexual tragedy. The very concept of the big double novel, earlier called *The Sisters*, is owed to Eliot: not only the contrasting sisters, but the deep study of two marriages at the end of a world. Ursula is his modern Dorothea, Gudrun his modern Rosamond. Ursula's mistake over Skrebensky, as George Ford says, is founded on Dorothea's mistake over Casaubon. From the start her crucial relationship was to be with Birkin, as if Lawrence had decided to shift the focus to the second union; but he knew, as he remarks in a letter, that Ursula needed this earlier barren experience also, and, with some difficulty, got Skrebensky into the story-line. Finally, he remembered that George Eliot had researched *Middlemarch*, as if to write history, and he researched *Women in Love* similarly, doing a lot of intensive reading for it in the early months of 1916.

Middlemarch is the novel of another crisis. It was begun in 1867. The sixties were thought then, and are thought now, to have been critical, a transition between two worlds. They opened with the American Civil War and ended with the Franco–Prussian War. *Essays and Reviews* come at the beginning, *Culture and Anarchy*, the First Vatican Council and the dogma of Papal Infallibility, at the end. The Education Act, which did as much as any single statute could to alter the whole character of society, became law in 1870. The source of the Nile was discovered in 1860, the Suez Canal opened in 1869. Various post-Gutenbergian techniques were taking hold : the telephone was invented, and ironclad warships, and the dynamo, and dynamite. For the first time you could telegraph to India and travel by tube. In the very year of dynamite and the telephone, Marx published the first volume of *Das Kapital*, a genuinely revolutionary event to which hardly anybody in England paid the slightest attention, and Disraeli got through his Reform Bill, an event thought by a great many people to be as fraught with revolutionary possibilities as the passage of its predecessor thirty-five years earlier. It seems not only that a world we know well was struggling to be born, but that people felt strongly, as they often do, that there was a crisis in their vicinity, even if they did not always agree with us as to where, exactly, it was.

In the year of the Reform Act, the telephone, and *Das Kapital*, George Eliot began to plan *Middlemarch*. Writing began in 1869, 'simmered' for a long time, and got properly under way in 1871. Then the story formed a union with an independently conceived story called *Miss Brooke*, and was published in eight parts between December, 1871 and December, 1872. Throughout these vicissitudes two factors remained constant. One was that this novel was to deal with 'contemporary moral history' (to steal a phrase used by the Goncourts of their own *Germinie Lacerteux*, published in 1864). The other, which seems to indicate a programme different from that of the French realists, was that from the earliest stages George Eliot set her story very firmly not in the decade that was ending but at the beginning of the thirties. Her notebook lists political and private events, which were to be cross-referenced in the narrative, and modern scholarship has illuminated this oblique historical accuracy. The author not only copied out lists of events from the *Annual*

Register but also got up medicine, hospital management, scientific research. Bible scholarship, which is equally important to
her design, she did not have to get up. She was particularly
careful about medicine, as the notebook shows; and we must
guess that this was not only because her principal male character was a doctor, but because 1832 is the date not only of the
first Reform Bill, but of a catastrophic event, the arrival in
England for the first time of the Indian cholera. It is a reasonable guess that, in the early stages of planning, she meant to
have a cholera epidemic as well as an election in *Middlemarch*.
It would be a great test not only for her doctor, but for the
well-disposed gentry with their interest in sanitary dwellings.

Cholera was a disease unknown in England before this time,
though there were of course later Victorian epidemics. This
first onslaught of the disease must have seemed a new plague
for a new age, much as syphilis had been for the period of her
previous novel *Romola*, and it coincided exactly with the
ominous political upheavals of the months preceding the passage of the Bill. She made a note to the effect that the preamble
to a bill in Parliament spoke of the disease as an infliction of
Providence, and that six members of the Commons voted for
the exclusion of this phrase. The coincidence of these events is
a sufficient explanation of her fixing upon the years preceding
the Reform Bill's passing, and her choosing an advanced young
doctor as her principal character in the 'Middlemarch' part of
the book. Other details fell into place; in the thirties but not in
the sixties she could have a serious biblical scholar who yet
remained ignorant of the advances of the New Criticism. After
all she herself had translated Strauss in the forties.

So she turned to earlier crisis-years, the years when the
civilization she knew, and which seemed in its turn to be on
the brink of radical change, was being born out of great political and scientific events. Of all English novelists she came
closest to accepting the Goncourt programme for using novels
as means of prosecuting *les études et les devoirs de la science*,
though in making one crisis the model or type of another for
the purposes of the study, she was, though with a new scientific seriousness, adopting a device not uncommon in English
fiction she knew, and which is of course a characteristic of all
narrative explanation. George Eliot was in any case not interested in radical formal innovation; her attempt is rather to
explore and modify the existing novel schemata. Thus she main-

tained, despite a conviction early on in the writing that the novel had 'too many *momenti*', the several continuous, elaborate, and interrelated plots to which readers had become accustomed.

Middlemarch has nothing in it quite like the famous intrusive chapter in *Adam Bede* ('in which the story pauses a little') but it is not without authorial interpolation, and there is one passage, uneasily facetious as George Eliot sometimes was when she felt she was being self-indulgent, which must cause pain to post-Jamesian purists. Yet it tells us something useful about the book. Mr Standish has just been reading old Featherstone's will, and we have heard how vexed the family is at Joshua Rigg's inheriting. The conclusion is that no one in the neighbourhood could be happy at this turn of events; nobody could prophesy the long-term effects of Rigg's arrival. Whereupon the novelist adds:

> And here I am naturally led to reflect on the means of elevating a low subject. Historical parallels are remarkably efficient in this way. The chief objection to them is, that the diligent narrator may lack space, or (what is often the same thing) may not be able to think of them with any degree of particularity, though he may have a philosophical confidence that if known they would be illustrative. It seems an easier and a shorter way to dignity to observe that – since there never was a true story which could not be told in parables where you might put a monkey for a margrave, and *vice versa*, – whatever has been or is to be narrated by me about low people, may be ennobled by being considered a parable.... Thus while I tell the truth about my loobies, my reader's imagination need not be entirely excluded from an occupation with lords.... As to any provincial history in which the agents are all of high moral rank, that must be of a date long posterior to the first Reform Bill, and Peter Featherstone, you perceive, was dead and buried some months before Lord Grey came into office.

That this is facetious, muddled, and evasive does not entirely destroy its value. It is one of the few places in which the novelist openly adverts to a matter which, on other evidence, she had incessantly in mind as she planned and wrote *Middlemarch*. She is merely pretending to be sarcastic on a well-worn issue, the right of novelists to concern themselves with low characters – the sort of thing she did in *Adam Bede* when she remarked correctly, though with an evil emphasis, that 'things may be lovable that are not altogether handsome, I hope'. It is the attitude controverted by Ruskin in his observations on *The Mill on the Floss* ('the sweepings of the Pentonville omnibus'). Perhaps the question had not entirely lost importance – certainly George Eliot herself had not entirely solved it, as we shall see; but it is very unlikely that she here states it with any real seriousness. For in *Middlemarch* the problem is not so much to justify one's rendering of a provincial society for its own sake as to make that society serve to illustrate a great historical crisis. The point is not that you can read lord for looby, or George IV for Featherstone, as she ironically proposes, but that if the novelist has got the detail right you can find in the book a 'parable' concerning these events in the mind and the conscience of society which, at a particular historical crisis, signal the birth of a modern age, that great theme of the modern novel.

And that is what the paragraph is trying to say. It tells us to relate the events of the novel to Lord Grey's Act and the other great changes of that time. The period of the novel is precisely the years and months before the Act. The notebook contains not only lists from the *Annual Register*, but precisely dated events for the unwritten novel. Thus the marriage of Lydgate is timed to coincide with the dissolution of July, 1830, and the height of the cholera in Paris; Mr Casaubon's death coincides with the last days of the Parliament whose dissolution in 1831 led to the General Election in May of that year, the election at which Mr Brooke failed to win his seat in what was to be the Reform Parliament. Not all these dates eventually coincided, but the book retains, as Mr Jerome Beaty has shown, a good many delicate cross-references to political events, to the vicissitudes of Peel and Wellington, the death of Huskisson, and so on. The final illness of George IV, mentioned in relation to that of Featherstone, was enough, if you coupled it with the dissolution of Parliament on the Reformism, and a general election, to make Mr Vincy ask whether all these were not signs that the world was coming to an end. But this overt though facetious allusion to the apocalyptic archetype of crisis is not repeated; the author is content with unspoken allusions and parallels. Lydgate's efforts at medical reform are specifically related to the political struggle after the dissolution of 1831; Chapter 84, of which the main business is the family's opposition to Dorothea's re-marriage, begins with an allusion to the rejection of the Bill by the Lords. And many other events are sketched in thus. The book ends a few weeks before the final enactment of the Bill. In the narrative there are a few major crises – those of the two marriages, and the attendant crises in the reformist activities of Lydgate and Dorothea; there are also minor ones, relating to religion and business, Fred Vincy's attitude to Holy Orders and Bulstrode's disgrace. But these personal crises are shadows of the historical crises, of the 'new life' struggling to be born in 1832; they are parables, to use George Eliot's word, of that crisis which is in its turn a model for the modern crisis of 1867, the leap in the dark, the end of another world. For in some ways we are all, even learned historians, Vincys. A crisis date gives history structure, and provides ways of talking about it.

This is the larger issue – crisis as a mode of historical explanation. The present point is that *Middlemarch* is a novel concerned with the end of a world. But it was expressly intended to inculcate 'a religious and moral sympathy with the *historical life of man*', and it issued from the hands of an author who was done with all manner of explanations requiring a mythology of transcendence. Such divinity as may occur in *Middlemarch* must be humanized in the manner of Feuerbach; the history must be human also, Comtian not Christian. Thus the types of Dorothea are Antigone, Theresa, even the Virgin Mary (an extravagant observation of Lydgate which the author partly endorses), but they are systematically Feuerbachized, qualified as human. Rosamund's 'confession' is another instance; it is sacramental only as to efficacy, not as to mystery. The Joachite elements in George Eliot's history belong, like those of Comte, to an age in which apocalypse has been positivized. This humanized apocalypse is what we are all familiar with, for we habitually allude to it when we consider our own historical crisis.

The type of apocalypse, however transformed, is still operative in *Middlemarch*. The word may seem very strong; it only means apocalypse of the kind Feuerbach might have contemplated had he given his attention to eschatology – a 'Copernican' apocalypse, brought down to its true level, the human crisis. It is a good many years since Mark Schorer discovered in the novel what he calls 'metaphors of . . . "muted" apocalypse', mentioning the figures of light, fire, transfiguration, epiphany, fulfilment, and the deliberate antithesis between Middlemarch and the New Jerusalem. He found prophecy and pseudo-prophecy, vision and growth. This is a muted apocalypse, certainly: the jewels of St John's Revelation are mentioned early, but the context seems to make them serve only as a way of noting Dorothea's priggish attitude to Celia. Schorer quotes a passage from Chapter 10 in which Dorothea's hopes of revelation from Casaubon's learning are given a strong though of course ironical apocalyptic tone. Above all, the historical events mentioned in the novel – again in a muted way – serve to emphasize the fulfilment of a time, and a renewal; though that, since the novel is set in the past, can be left to retrospective prophecy, the kind we, as historians, are best at. These are the last days; humanly speaking, the last days of an epoch, which is a Feuerbachian equivalent of the mythical apocalypse. The myth abandoned, this is still part of the structure of our historical thinking. And one reason why we relish *Middlemarch* still is that we understand the muted eschatology of its design.

For example, the crisis in bible criticism seemed at the time catastrophic in its implications. Casaubon, firmly planted on the wrong, mythological side of it, is typed in the same way as other characters – his name relates him ironically to the great Casaubon; he is a Milton, he is a Locke – all great men associated with major crises in the history of thought; but Casaubon's relation to them is ironically qualified, as Dorothea's is to hers, or as Lydgate's to Vesalius and the other great medical men whose names and dates George Eliot copies out so carefully into her notebook. They stand for virtues or certainties thought to be in decadence at this turn of time; though they also, by implying the meliorist scientific achievements of the succeeding age, suggest also renovation, always in apocalyptic thought the obverse side of decadence. Middlemarch itself, as Schorer says, silently proposes its antitype, The New Jerusalem.

If Casaubon's biblical methodology illuminated the historical crisis, so did Lydgate's medicine. The opposition between Lydgate and the older provincial doctors is not the whole story: the parable is incomplete if it does not include allusions to modern differentiations between typhus and typhoid, the new treatment for delirium tremens (which becomes the material of an important narrative crisis), the general theory of fever, and indeed modern developments in 'cell-theory'. Of course part of the point is that to know about all these things is not enough; that in the new dispensation as well as in any older one the virtues, under whatever demythologized form one knows them, must be preserved. A spot of commonness, a failure to apply the proper kind of attention to another person, a neglect of duty, a cheapening of love, will bring disaster. Lydgate's 'commonness', as it happens, is associated with his caste – it proceeds from an inability to treat as true persons his sexual, social, and intellectual inferiors – and so derives from a system that was beginning, with the Reform Acts (and perhaps more with the Education Act of 1870) slowly to collapse. In much the same way the dryness and sexual impotence of Casaubon reflect the sterility of a world-view that lingers on in survivors of the older ruined order.

The historical antitheses of *Middlemarch* go beyond scholarship and medicine, and are far from simple. It is not only, we see, a matter of one age, characterized by myth and ignorance, yielding to a new, of history and science, or of a supernatural giving way to a natural religion. Religious beliefs of many kinds – Fairbrother's, Fred Vincy's, Tyke's, and especially Bulstrode's – are ironically exposed at this historical crisis, but their forms survive that crisis, as fiction survives religious belief. Bulstrode's error is to suppose too exact a relationship between plot (providence) and the random actuality on which it is imposed. He takes his prosperity as a figure of his justication, as arising from divine but mechanical plotting; his God knows nothing of contingency; the logic of his plots is the logic of myth, not of everyday life. The tide of plausible human events is not in accordance with his Calvinist prediction, and his discomfiture is proof of the obsolescence of another mythology, one that was still in favour among some of the novelist's contemporaries. George Eliot has her own Feuerbachian version of predestination, worked out many times and most explicitly in Tito Melema; this and the erroneous old version play against each other in the Bulstrode crisis. That which works through Raffles is not, any longer, God; but neither is it mocked.

Many incidents are invented to strengthen the sense of an historical transition. There is the talk of new building and improvement, the tone of political dispute, Brooke's inability to command the respect of the labourer Dagley, even – great Victorian symbol of the division of time – the railway; and Garth, that wondrous necessary instrument of capital, suppressing resentment at its progress through midland meadows. This critical balance is characteristic of even the minor crises of the book. Casaubon's scholarship hangs posthumously over Dorothea in her decision to marry Ladislaw. Lydgate voting for Tyke is voting, he thinks, in the interests of progress, but they turn out to be the interests of Bulstrode; he accepts Bulstrode's saving loan, and Raffles is given medical treatment acceptable in current obsolete medical opinion, but to Lydgate's new knowledge dangerous. A good deal of the corruption, impotence, and ineffectiveness of characters in *Middlemarch* is imposed upon them by a dying but stubborn past, which is part of the price one pays for living in 'an age of transition'. This is what Dorothea means, really, when she says she will 'find out what everything costs'. She takes on the new world. Lydgate finds himself cursed by the old; he must take Bulstrode on his arm; he is not one of the elite in any new world, even in a new world of which the millennialist ideal is so severely chastened by contact with a powerful sense of reality. The scientific figures which, as has often been observed, penetrate the texture of this novel are not arbitrary reflections of the author's own interests; they establish the modernity of the problem, and they also, by indicating the tone of the future, judge the moral effectiveness of the characters who faced it then as we must now, and suggest the consequences of a failure such as Lydgate's. The eschatology is humanized, but the old judgement remains, as to type, applicable : 'I know thy works, that thou art neither cold nor hot ... so then because thou art lukewarm and neither cold nor hot, I will spew thee out of my mouth.'

Thus *Middlemarch* arranges itself as an image of crisis, and a study of the moral obligations of men in transition. Its typology relates it to the archetypes of crisis, and this is one of the ways in which we understand human history. As I said at the outset, such terms as *crisis* and *revolution* describe to our satisfaction what it is in the utter particularity, the randomness and disparateness of events, that we can recognize and understand; indeed people concerned in the making of history have often shaped it in conformity with such types, just as novelists do. Real events comply with archetypes of this kind; why should not fictional events? At the centre of this novel is a great and typical historical event. But it is only the nucleus. Round it accrete all these other images of crisis. The manner in which the basic apocalyptic figure permeates the texture is strikingly demonstrated in one of the greatest passages of the novel : the frustrated Dorothea contemplates Rome, the eternal city a wreck, a marble confusion, St Peter's and its statues disfigured by red drapery, as if seen by a diseased eye : the vision of the *urbs aeterna* blighted. 'Images are the brood of desire,' says the novelist at the opening of the fouth chapter (in which Lydgate is on the point of marrying a woman he has presented with a whip). The image of Rome is the brood of desire that fails. To balance the scene, there is the wonderful moment of Dorothea's return to Lowick and the blanched winter landscape, when the fire glows incongruously and she, seeking confirmation in the glass for her sense of deathly defeat, finds an image of health and vitality, the human and perhaps specifically female strength that comes through these crises. Lawrence – who saw so clearly that the novel must make *this* kind of sense and not fob us off with papers stuck into brandy-flasks, meticulously rendered lawsuits – Lawrence not only learned from the good and the bad in Eliot's figures, but, as we have seen, remembered and reproduced this one at the climax of *Women in Love*. He meant that Crich, like Casaubon, belonged to death, to an old order.

However the relation between story and apocalyptic type is visualized, it presupposes an imaginative feat and a large degree of intellectual control. Occasionally this fails. There are lapses : for instance in the climactic interview between Dorothea and Rosamond, by which George Eliot set so much store. This was to be a flow of Feuerbachian feeling, confession and all, and so warm and spontaneous that she claimed to have refrained from thinking about it till it happened, and then to have written it entire, without revision, a claim which the manuscripts show to be untrue. However, it has virtual truth : it suggests a deliberate letting go, a kind of moral failure (nothing in Dorothea gives her the right to be even a Feuerbachian confessor to Rosamond) and redeemed only at its end, when Lydgate, dismissed from the elect, takes up his meaner burden. This is a failure of spiritual pride, like Bulstrode's.

There are more serious faults proper to be mentioned here. One is, if one may so put it, that George Eliot runs out of love; or we could say, she too has her elite. I mean that she cannot sustain that special love by which a novelist knows and preserves the identity of characters. The indications of this are her slipping away into caricature or humour-characterization when she moves out of the sociological middle area. At the extreme edge is Mrs Dollop, in the pub, but Trumbull the auctioneer is only good for a laugh and as a handy pneumonia patient. The Garths, even, are honourable pastoral prigs about whom one wants to know no more. As one moves out from the central figures, the two married couples, towards the periphery, the figures are increasingly distorted. In a certain sense, she is interested most in the good bourgeoisie and a little above it, the Vincys to the Brookes. The others she more or less deprives of moral reality much as Lydgate deprives Rosamond, and with similar results. What happens is that an authentic relation of type to history is distorted by adherence to novel conventions which are meaningless except as reflections of a caste system. Possibly the degree of distortion is as little as could be managed in the England of the time. But one sees why Arnold Kettle can attribute the failures of *Middlemarch* – a novel about change – to a view of society and morality 'somewhat static', not incorporating 'a dialectical sense of contradiction and motion'. This is overstated, but it does locate, in this novel of crisis, a spot of commonness. Lawrence, we saw, had his own problem arising from a conscious elitism, but he contrived, partly by formal innovation, to keep it out of his novel.

Another fault of *Middlemarch* is in the plotting : or so it must seem to us. We are not, for various reasons too complicated to enter into now, so interested nowadays in what Beckett, praising Proust, called 'the vulgarities of a plausible concatenation' as our great-grandfathers, or even our grandfathers, but we cannot excuse George Eliot so simply, because in this respect she was obviously on our side, and admired narrative with a strong thematic aspect. Yet she wrote a good deal of unnecessary plot, not so much in *Middlemarch* as in *Felix Holt* and *Daniel Deronda*, but still too much. The Bulstrode affair is an instance. In its elements this is impeccable 'thinking with the story' – Lydgate's association with the banker contaminates him with an odious pre-scientific religion, and the climax turns upon an issue between old and new medical practice. The conduct of Mrs Bulstrode is a grace, one of those favours that drop upon a writer because he has worked hard for something else, and not been a slave of the types. Yet in order to get to the point of Bulstrode she invented all the perfunctory business of Rigg and Raffles, the note stuffed in the brandy-flask, the unnecessary relationship with Ladislaw. In the notebook she laboured over the elaboration of all this in such unusual detail that, as Mr Beaty very credibly suggests, it looks as if she was not interested enough to carry such essentially extraneous material in her head. And this plotting damages the modernity of the novel. It is regressive, it takes us back to a more naïve kind of novel, in which it is assumed that the mere delights of concatenation are enough, in which serious thematic or typical interest is largely a matter of luck. Such plots are anti-historical, destructive of the crisis-'set'. Of course we have many later books to be wise by; yet there is no reason why we should not say that this kind of thing diminishes the critical force of the book, given its historical theme. Once again, Lawrence knew better, but it must also be said that the comparisons are not all in his favour.

I have been re-arranging familiar elements of *Middlemarch* because I want to make it possible to think of the novel as having various aspects in common with other kinds of narrative. *Middlemarch* is, to admiring eyes, a novel explanatory of crisis, and it achieves its explanations by means which may be called historical and typological. On the whole it does this without undue violence to persons or to probabilities, remaining true not only to the aims of historical narrative, and to the typological bent of our minds, but also to our sense of fact. Looby Event serves Lord Crisis. *Middlemarch* achieves all manner of consonances between past and present, the before and after of the crisis; but its Transition, its Terrors, its decadence and renovation are thoroughly secularized; apocalypse here has emigrated out of myth into history.

I hope one can say that it is now clear how much *Middlemarch* and *Women in Love* have in common, though even when one considers the similarities the differences insist on their presence. Each deals with a topic, absolutely central to the modern novel, namely what Lawrence described as 'woman becoming individual, self-responsible, taking her own initiative'; and each associates certain bad kinds of sex with an older order, an order of death – though Lawrence did not need Casaubon's impotence, for it was clear that this had become too limiting a symbol for sexual disconnection, and Skrebensky and Crich are more than ordinarily virile. But both use marital crises as figures for vast and impersonal historical crises and revolutions; at the heart of the books there are the two couples, Casaubon and Dorothea, straddling their historical crisis, Lydgate and Rosamond not even worthy of the ordeal of initiation; Ursula and Birkin representing the mysterious struggle for a new epoch, Crich and Gudrun increasingly excluded, left to set up their own universe of death, with Loerke as its satanic priest. From this basic resemblance many others follow, which it is unnecessary to spell out.

On the major differences in the manner of representing historical crisis there is more to say. We noticed that George Eliot assumed a need for historical particularity, and therefore chose as a model of her own crisis another which she could investigate as thoroughly as she liked. Lawrence chose to write about the one that was going on all around him, and deliberately stripped it of contemporary reference. An historical novel, meaning an exploitation for the purposes of the moment of a set of events long past, is something that it is very hard to imagine Lawrence ever writing. So he 'detemporalized' his book, avoided mentioning that its events belong to the war years. The war was to be any war. Gerald had a commission, but has resigned it, as he could not do in wartime; the Pompadour is the pre-war Café Royal; and so forth.

One reason for this is simply that George Eliot was powerfully under the influence of demythologizing Germans, notably Feuerbach, whom she persistently regarded as the leaders of modern thought. Lawrence was, though uneasily, a remythologizer. 'The myths begin to hypnotize us once again, our impulse towards our own scientific way of understanding being almost spent,' as he observed in the *Fantasia*. He lived after that great literary and academic and clinical revival of mythology with which we associate such names as Frazer and Harrison, Freud and Jung; with which we associate a whole movement of modern thought which is far from exhausted now. Consequently he associated the old demythologization with an outmoded rationalism, and so far as it was consistent with his revised version of realism he gave his age of crisis the minimum of historical particularity and the maximum of mythical, or typological, or symbolic, reference. The very character of his narrative involves a recoil from mere history and from 'the vulgarities of a plausible concatenation'. He will have none of that plotting which in George Eliot soaks up so much authentic, thematic interest – no Raffles (compare Raffles as a plot agent with Loerke!), no papers wadded in brandy flasks. He will not make up stories which *explain* how one thing leads to another. There are concessions to contingency, for without them we should hardly recognize the book as a novel, but we move with the minimum of formal continuity from one crux to the next. It is true that the book starts in the traditional mode common to George Eliot and, say, Bennett in *The Old Wives' Tale* or even Tolstoi in *Anna Karenina*, but we soon see that the scene at Halliday's, for instance, exists *for* the image of the African statue and the naked men, and that 'Rabbit' is an entirely new refocusing of the novel on to a symbol of large and ultimately indeterminable significance, related by many thematic ties to the general order of the book. When the older Crich, ordinarily right outside the narrative, is needed to make a point, he is worked in, made to symbolize the dying Age of Love; actually his business is only to die, for Gerald must run from his death-bed to make love to Gudrun. Loerke is introduced and given elaborate development much too late for a major character in a more orthodox narrative. There is a good deal which receives no formal 'explanation' at all – the relations between Birkin and Crich (especially after the cancellation of the Preface), the relevance of the long discussion between Loerke and Ursula on the autonomy of forms in art. The death of Gerald's brother, and later of his sister, are related only thematically to the general design; they are certainly not tributes to contingency, but neither are they given narrative 'followability'. Lawrence does not force discontinuities on one's attention, but everybody observes them, and notes that they are much sharper here than in *The Rainbow*. The change reflects the break with the past which happens between the first and second novels of the sequence; the new manner is what Lawrence described in a famous letter to Garnett as 'futuristic', not only in narrative but in the conception of character liberated from an established set of expectations which include not only a 'certain moral scheme' but also satisfactory explanations. A new deeper concept of personality required a narrative manner more dependent, as he says, on intuition, on illogic; and it also rendered very undesirable any sharpness of historical definition, allusions to specific event of the sort found in *Middlemarch*.

If we now consider these similarities and differences in the light of what we think novels ought to be, it will, I suppose, be clear that each writer, and all writers of the same degree of seriousness, had to contend with the special pressures of their particular moments upon an essentially atavistic form; the novel tells a story. The pressure on George Eliot was of an age of scientific morality, an age too which made the first on-slaught on what used to be called the concord of the canonical scriptures, and discredited the old version of the plot of the Bible, and the plot of comparative religion; she boldly chose that as an important part of her theme. Lawrence, on the other hand, lived in a time when the scientific criticism of her German heroes had not only spread out into politics, history, and literature, but had bred a formidable counter-movement, that anti-positivism of which we still hear so much. Because it seemed important to break with pseudo-scientific categories that had lost their relevance – the traditional ideas of charac-ter, indeed of order – Lawrence abandoned plot and radically altered traditional characterization; because the truth lay in the blood and the darkness of the mind, and not in positivistic inferences from detail, he went more directly to the basic mythologies. Whereas she could assert fixed points in the his-torical flux without direct recourse to apocalyptic figures, which she would have thought, in their naked form, unin-verted by the Feuerbachian dialectic, obsolete and irrelevant, he short-circuited conventional representations of the historical course of events and drew much more nakedly on the complex imagery of apocalypse that was maturing in his own mind.

Either way there is a good deal of waste and loss, and neither book can I suppose quite match our own typologies of crisis and change. But they do touch us, and one reason why they do so is surely that under our impressions of change the explana-tory types persist. These books reflect our terrors, our contrary yet complementary types of decadence and renovation, even if they lack the peculiar quality of our own fears, and of our own ironies and reserves. We recognize that these books have ten-sions and problems essentially modern, in the sense that they grew out of an appalled sense of what it means to be modern; and this is true even though our modernism is on the surface so different from theirs, because they rest their whole weight on crisis and modernity, on modernity and history, and they seek our *kinds* of explanation for the pain of being where they are.

(1967)

ELEVEN

MUSIL

With the publication of the third instalment of the Wilkins–
Kaiser translation,[1] *The Man Without Qualities* is once more,
and this time with a certain casualness, as if the battle was
won, being referred to as one of the great novels; Musil, we are
told, is of the company of Proust and Joyce. Formerly his reputation had seemed to be, like the lights sailors call occulting,
characterized by periods of total darkness. He was famous in
Germany for a while, around 1930, when the first volume of
Der Mann ohne Eigenschaften appeared, but the second came
out just as the German-speaking world suffered a transference
of attention to Hitler, who could easily be presented, if anybody wanted to do it, as the anti-mask of Ulrich, the Man
Without Qualities, the active passivist, the perceiver of modern
consciousness as so delicately dissociated that the combination
of an inferior intellect and a fixed idea could bring us all to
barbarism. On Musil's sixtieth birthday, in 1940, no one paid
any attention; after his death in 1942 his widow with the help
of the '*Musil Gesellschaft*' (a group which contributed to a
fund for the writer's support) brought out the remainder of the
work, so far as it had gone, in a privately printed edition. In
the fifties there was a revival of interest, though still of somewhat fluctuant quality. Nobody is *ashamed*, yet, of not having
read the book. The campaign continues, and by now the whole
2,000 pages (there is no way of knowing how long the work
would have been had Musil lived) are available in German, and
four-fifths of it have appeared in English. So it ought to be
possible to make up one's mind.

I myself knew nothing of Musil except *Young Törless* (1906)
a gloomy, impressive, cerebral first novel about physical and
metaphysical misbehaviour among students at a military
academy in Bohemia, translated by Wilkins-Kaiser in 1955.

1. *The Man Without Qualities.* By Robert Musil. Translated by
Eithne Wilkins and Ernst Kaiser. Vol. I (1953); Vol. II (1954); Vol.
III (1960). London, Secker & Warburg. Vols I and II correspond to
Vol. I of the original; Vol. III to Vol. II. The unfinished part of the
work will be Vol. IV in the translation.

Consequently some of the reports on the big book surprised me, especially the publisher's claim that it was 'extremely funny', which some reviewers endorsed. Now that I have read the first three volumes I am still inclined to take issue with this and other judgements, for example Mr Toynbee's 'It is an integrated, minutely planned book.' How could he tell after one volume? Even after three it is impossible as it were to cash the story; we have seen the beginning of a change of state, of characters in the process of significant collapse, of ironical developments which will give substance to the huge gas-clouds of argument which billow round the narrator; but they haven't got far, and some of them were prevented from ever doing so by the death of the author. And he wasn't, in any case, in any ordinary sense, a *minute* planner; and, finally, the first volume taken alone gives an entirely misleading impression of the whole. So Mr Toynbee seems this time to be as far off the mark as Miss Wedgwood, who unintelligibly refers to the book as 'picaresque'; perhaps she means only that it is *not* 'minutely planned'. On the other hand Mr Toynbee is quite right, I think, in saying that Musil was often very boring, purposely, and would not, I suppose, be put out to find that his belief in the virtue of this is not universally shared.

The fact is that he started with a narrative plan that would enable him continuously to perform certain acts not very intimately related to narrative. This plan he of course modified as time went on; there was a certain cross-influence between the story and the theme as each burgeoned. But having got the main outline settled he was free to compose his vast interstitial essays, to devise his prolonged metaphysical conversations, in the confidence that he knew exactly where he was, and what was the exact nature of the relationship between these static passages and the forward-moving story. He could even, up to a point, do them in whatever order he liked; thus, the extant chapters of the last volume are not consecutive and there are large gaps between the complete sections. So you could speak of careful, indeed of elaborate, but not of minute, planning. And you might reasonably go on to infer certain qualities and defects in Musil as a novelist. One such inference would be that he is not likely to achieve much narrative tension, density of plot, or economy of structure. And this is useful information to anybody starting on Musil. Whether or no one counts the absence of these qualities as a defect depends on whether one is of Erskine's or Johnson's opinion concerning Richardson. Erskine, it will be recalled, found him 'very tedious'; but Johnson replied : 'Why, sir, if you were to read Richardson for the story, your impatience would be so much fretted that you would hang yourself. But you must read him for the sentiment, and consider the story as only giving occasion to the sentiment.' Musil looks right back to those early days; the form of his novel is, in this sense, atavistic.

Yet it is so in a most sophisticated way; and that at any rate aligns him with the contemporary *avant-garde*. It was mechanical form he disliked, though he had much too critical a mind to accept any organicist theory; he was indeed extraordinarily acute about the place of concealed metaphor in thought, and this is one such. Musil, therefore, regarded himself as free of these categories and qualities; he was the man without them, the artist, like Ulrich, on holiday from reality or what passed as reality with others. He was quite open about his contempt for narrative; at the outset – or anyway on p. 199, for Musil is a slow starter – he assures us that no 'serious attempt will be made to ... enter into competition with reality'. And he was explicit about his lack of interest in stories as such, exhibiting, when he spoke of his novel, what we at once identify as the 'oh-dear-yes' response to the question 'does it tell a story ?' In the course of the novel this reaction is given some philosophical ballast when Ulrich, the Man Without Qualities, has the following chain of thought : we live in a time when life, both as lived and as taken up into propositions about itself, has undoubtedly grown more abstract; I would not have it otherwise, since out of this abstraction grows power; with an intellectual leap I hence come upon another important abstraction, namely that:

> the law of this life, for which one yearns, over-burdened as one is and at the same time dreaming of simplicity, is none other than that of *narrative order*. This is the simple order that consists in one's being able to say : 'When that had happened, then this happened.' What puts our mind at rest is the simple sequence, the overwhelming variegation of life now represented in, as a mathematician would say, a uni-dimensional order.

And this the novel has turned to account; we do not like what is intensely here and now; the most complexity we can comfortably bear is a very little 'because' or 'in order that', such as goes to a novelist's plot. We like a straightforward sequence of facts because 'it has the look of necessity', and this gives an impression of order – as well, of course, as the sense that nothing need be done about it. But Ulrich had 'lost this elementary narrative element' and saw things more as they were; 'in public life everything has now become non-narrative, no longer following a "thread", but spreading out as an infinitely interwoven surface.'

As a matter of fact, Musil's views on how this came to be so, on what one's abstractive powers are called on to do about it, and on a series of loosely related subjects, are clearly more important to him than the rendering of the texture; and, of course, since that texture has lost its narrative character – which was after all what made novels possible – this was the only way he could see to write about it at all. Some of his characters might be stupid or ignorant enough to behave as if the old narrative way of thinking, and all the un-fluid attitudes that went with it, still worked, and this would give the oh-dear-yes story something to bite on; but for Ulrich and Musil such behaviour simply created a loose textural mesh in which their volatile opinions would be beneficently trapped, like warm air in a string vest. One of those characters, Clarisse, has a brilliant thought out of Nietzsche, and Musil's comment upon it is a good negative indication of the way both he and Ulrich do their thinking:

> The ready-for-use or 'applied' philosophy and poetry of most people who are neither creative nor, on the other hand, unsusceptible to ideas consists in just such shimmering coalescences of another man's great thought with their own small private modification of it.

Musil has no interest in great thoughts, only in what might be called the activity of consciousness; an activity paralysed in most people because of their willingness to inhabit the shelters provided by a multitude of metaphysical fictions. And these are the very things that have set up the frontier posts between mind and reality, on the dangerous ground between which Ulrich operates; and are responsible for the curious solemn apathy with which the world faces the uncategorizable catas-

trophe of the 1914 war. His business, Musil's business, is not
with truth.

I state my case, even though I know it is only part of the
truth, and I would state it just the same although I knew it
was false, because certain errors are stations on the road to
truth.

Musil had been a soldier, an engineer, a mathematician, and
a philosopher before, under the pressure of a 'ruthless impulse'
– as the English translators put it – he became an artist. If I say
this is very unlike the career of our own James Joyce it is not
simply because the comparisons between these two strike me
as absurd, but because Joyce once said, with a certain weird
accuracy, that he had the mind of a grocer's assistant, and one
can see in his works such a mind transformed by a manic
literacy. Musil's is a mathematician's mind similarly transformed. There is an interesting scene in *Törless* where the
young man is troubled by imaginary numbers like the square
root of minus one, and the mathematics master can't get outside his familiarity with them to explain, out of his own made-
up mind and body, to Törless in his adolescent indefinitiveness,
how they can be related to anything describable as truth or
order : 'we have not the time. . a little beyond you.' It was
the end of instinctive youth : 'tomorrow I shall go over everything very carefully and I shall get a clear view of things
somehow.' Somehow by rejecting the made-up mind, the great
thought, by evading the patterns that mesmerize others, Musil
tries for his clear view of everything; and a lot of his trouble is
to ensure that this includes the square root of minus one, an
imaginary, useful quantity which facilitates movement about a
whole world. When they sack Törless at the end, his peculiar
curiosity is called 'morbid' by the maths master and 'sensitive'
by the chaplain. The Head gives him his chance; is the chaplain
right, is Törless especially sensitive to 'the divine essence of
morality that transcends the limits of our intellect'? Is he, in
short, seeking religion? No, says Törless, and begins a stumbling explanation of his own consciousness that approaches the
frontier of mysticism; and that is the end of him. In so far as
he was Musil, however, it was only the beginning; and the
really curious thing about the structure of *The Man Without
Qualities* is that, in the manner of mathematics, it domesticates

the irrational and the imaginary, describes the failures and successes of a consciousness that depends in part upon both. As to reality, Ulrich can only represent it ironically, since he has dissociated himself from the usual ways of knowing it. Reality has sacked him, 'daylight mystic' as he is, and like Coriolanus he turns round and sacks reality. Musil in his turn thought the novel as a form corresponded to a failed myth of reality and so he sacked it, writing instead essays with a narrative binding. The novel fights back, and it is Musil who fails.

This he admitted, for in spite of his contempt for narrative he saw that he had provided it too sparingly in the first two volumes; and there is no doubt that the third volume, which opens with significant events occurring in reasonably rapid succession, is altogether more successful than the first two. Indeed, its first third has a persistent, surprising *novelistic* brilliance which convinces the reader that Musil was, or could have been, a novelist of quite extraordinary power. For the most part, however, *The Man Without Qualities* is written as if to illustrate one of Ulrich's theories, called 'Essayism'; just as ordinary novels reflect the myth of narrative, this one reflects the theory of the essay. Ulrich is thinking of himself, in his relation to the world, as 'a stride that could be taken in any direction, but which leads from one instant of equilibrium to the next'. These balanced moments are not hypotheses but *essays* – because an essay

in the sequence of its paragraphs, takes a thing from many sides without comprehending it wholly – for a thing wholly comprehended instantly loses its bulk and melts down into a concept.

This is using the word 'essay' metaphorically; but when the novel itself assumes this quality of Ulrich's mind, the figurative significance of the word disappears and it is transformed into ordinary-language 'essay' again. It is as if a man who argued that Sir Winston Churchill's view of life, which he endorsed, could only be called 'epic', felt obliged, on writing Sir Winston's biography, to do it in blank verse. Musil, as it happens, is extremely interested in metaphor; the mental breakdown of one of his characters, Clarisse, is heralded by a failure to dissociate certain metaphorical significations from the basic meanings of words. So one doesn't, of course, accuse him of not knowing what he was doing; nothing could be more ridiculous; but it is possible nevertheless to say that an essay is an essay. Indeed there are large tracts of the book which remind one of an Addison liberated from conventional morality and a respect for great thinkers, fitting Sir Roger and the others more subtly into his moral disquisitions, and endowed with a degree of intellectual agility he might formerly have thought unseemly.

My emphasis on the essayism of the book may sound strange to anybody who has heard only that it is a satire on the Austro-Hungary of 1914, and that it helps to explain the war.

It is easy enough to see how this got about, but it is a very partial and distorted account of the book, based on the opening thousand pages, which are merely a prologue to the real story. They do say quite a lot about 'Kakania', as Musil calls the Empire, and about its ruling class; as his main point is that they were all hopelessly out of touch with contemporary reality, it is also true that the presentation is frequently satirical. But it is precisely in this connection that he claims not to be competing with reality. He is not writing what Mary McCarthy recently called the only proper kind of novel, one with historical people and issues in it. (This is true regardless of the fact that he drew on actual persons, places, and issues.) He certainly thought that all these people, while they were being noble and clever in absurd and archaic ways, were leaving the subman to flourish unobserved : and that this was a state of affairs out of which the catastrophe of 1914 would issue quite naturally. But their antics, and indeed the war itself, interested him only as illustrations of an abstract notion that the modern mind generally was unable to grasp its environment. And that is a matter not of high comedy but of essayism. Each of the principal characters represents a version of this mental failure, and is thus related to the essayistic flow.

For all that, there is a sense of time and place, communicated with considerable and characteristic indirectness. This makes for bulk. The sheer size of the book is naturally the first thing one notices. Musil's whole method makes bulk inevitable, not because, as with Tolstoi, the population of events increases in geometrical progression, but simply because there is no event that can ever be finally dealt with. Each chapter has an old-fashioned humorous heading, and the first one is: 'Which, remarkably enough, does not get anyone anywhere'. The first useful statement of the novel, 'It was a fine August day in the year 1913', is preceded by a medieval chronography of about 150 words. The first direct speech (' "Frog-prince!" she said') is on page 51. There's nothing wrong with size, even if one disagrees that its function is to give the writer room to be boring in; but it is worth considering the contrast between this kind of thing and the brisk opening of *Anna Karenina* – on which Miss McCarthy recently commented in the same brilliant lecture – 'Everything was upset at the Oblonskys.' Indeed it is hard to think of any good, let alone great, novel, that begins so uneconomically. The loose volubility of those opening words, considered in relation to what comes of them in terms of narrative, is typical of the relation between essay and narrative in the book as a whole, and one is always struggling to see the activities of the characters as embodying rather than merely exemplifying, as doing more than providing texts for secular sermons.

The story concerns Ulrich, the Man Without Qualities, and his dealings with various groups of people in Vienna just before their spiritual and intellectual limitations met a proper requital in the war of 1914.

Ulrich, ex-engineer, mathematician, officer, having tried and failed to see the relevance of the particular myths of order enjoined upon him by these professions, is on a holiday from all such, and is undertaking a sort of reappraisal of the metaphysical problems their failure evidently raises. That is, he is temperamentally and intellectually distanced from all that goes on, and always ahead of the game, whether that is big business, thinking, diplomacy, or sex. At the instance of his father he becomes involved in the Collateral Campaign, an aristocratic but vague attempt to make plans for the celebration in 1918 of the seventieth anniversary of the Emperor's accession. Everybody concerned with this is an example of a particular kind of failure to treat closely with reality. Count Leinsdorf has hopes that there may be a fusion of the races in the Empire, and a rebirth of national energy from bourgeois culture. Arnheim, a tycoon of lofty moral tone and a bit of a spellbinder, who, as a German, should not be on the Committee at all, is working for a union of economics and the soul. General von Stumm, another who is there by mistake, and a very engaging figure, wants a bit of military common sense in the Campaign, and draws up staff college plans and lists of Great Ideas. The spiritual leader of the campaign is a cousin of Ulrich's nicknamed Diotima, wife of a high Foreign Office official, whose cast of mind is very sceptical, in a traditional way; Diotima is a noble spirit, and engaged in a profound but innocent affair with Arnheim. The Committee meets from time to time, every crank in Austria sends it some infallible and absolute remedy for all the nation's ills; at one point it almost provokes public disturbances. Ulrich abandons it for various reasons, and in the end Diotima's dream is reduced almost to ridicule before the war wipes it all out anyway.

A secondary group of characters is headed by Walter and Clarisse, friends of Ulrich, she a wild Nietzschean, he an artist *manqué*, not permitted to sleep with her and soaking himself in Wagner as a compensatory indulgence. They have on the premises a fake sage called Meingast. The other most important character is the sexual murderer Moosbrugger, in whom nearly everybody is forced to take an interest: even Ulrich's father, concerned with the legal issues of the case, the Austrian equivalent of the MacNaghten rules. Clarisse is especially concerned, and as her own madness grows, arranges through Ulrich to visit the madhouse where Moosbrugger is kept, pending a decision. There are other minor figures, doctrinaire anti-Semites, bankers, poets, all held together by Ulrich. But two more must be mentioned before one can ask more generally what Musil does with all this: the woman nicknamed Bonadea, charming but nymphomaniac wife of a legal official and Ulrich's mistress; and Ulrich's sister Agathe, whom he meets at the start of the third volume when he travels to his father's funeral, not having seen her since she was a child.

All these people are posed in a pretty static way, and the collateral campaign is naturally given satirical treatment, even if the satire is often toothless. At the end of the first volume one is inclined to ask, 'Is this all?', because as straightforward social and political satire it is simply not sharp enough. But of course the real point is slowly crystallizing out of the essay-cloud: the Campaign is a useful example of that intellectual futility, that uncritical adherence to insufficiently examined absolutes, ideas of order, panaceas, of which Ulrich's agile scepticism is the antithesis. 'Without doubt he was a man of faith, though one who believed in nothing.' This antithesis occupies Musil throughout most of the first two volumes; only with the third, after the encounter with Agathe, does he begin seriously to move forward. It is like one of those chess-games when the masters for an incomprehensibly long time make fiddling little moves at the back of the board, and then suddenly a queen leaps out. The queen is Agathe. The love between Ulrich and Agathe is what gives, or was to have given, the story sublime sense. But as it is, the reader is not, even at the end of Book Three, in possession of an extremely important fact. Ulrich we have seen in various sexual situations, but in bed only with Bonadea; before it is all over he has slept also with Diotima, Clarisse, and Agathe.

So far as the novel has got in English, these events, among others, have occurred : Diotima has developed sexological interests, greatly to her husband's concern, and is consulting Bonadea on the practical side. Clarisse has been to the asylum and seen the patients, though not Moosbrugger. Agathe has forged a codicil to her father's will, in order to cheat her husband (a lot of essayism about this). Before the end Diotima will overcome her high-minded objections to adultery; Clarisse will herself go mad and procure the escape of Moosbrugger, who will kill another woman before recapture; the Christian thinker Lindner, whom we see briefly consoling Agathe as she contemplates suicide, will take a hand in the plot; Arnheim will acquire a non-platonic mistress; the Campaign will collapse.[2] These, of course, among many other matters.

Now it is clear that the two poles upon which the whole narra-

2. Since I wrote these words Eithne Wilkins (Mrs Kaiser) has very kindly explained to me the true condition of Musil's notes and drafts, which makes these predictions and extrapolations seem overconfident. The German edition of the remains is misleading, since it incorporates obsolete draft chapters and worksheets that relate to earlier stages of the novel and not to its continuation. An account of the true state of the *Nachlass* may be found in her article 'The Musil Manuscripts' in *Modern Language Review*, July 1967; see also her article '*Der Mann ohne Eigenschaften* and Musil's "Steinbaukastenzeit" ', *Oxford German Studies*, III, 1968, in which she remarks that from the notes Musil made after 1939 it 'looks as if he has forgotten the plot'. Mrs Kaiser's collection of transcripts and letters and other material is now at the University of Reading, and Vol. IV of the Wilkins-Kaiser translation, giving a more authentic account of Musil's intentions, will happily not be long delayed.

tive turns are Moosbrugger and Ulrich. Moosbrugger – and it would be impossible to overpraise the imaginative achievement of Musil in the rendering of his mind – has the double function of pharmakos and symptom. He can be held to be a case of *victimage* – an idea taken up by Clarisse – expiating the sins of others; or his condition and his escape can signify those atavisms which we are intellectually impotent to contain, and the catastrophe of their enlargement. Around him rages the question of 'responsibility', but it is treated in the absurd jargon of academic lawyers, not as a problem demanding all the freedom and power of a mind such as Ulrich's. Moosbrugger is the subman, guiltless but fatal to society; if a whore irritates him he kills her, and supposing you make a Moosbrugger powerful he will kill all the people who irritate him, for example, by being Jewish. 'If mankind could dream collectively, it would dream Moosbrugger.' His escape coincides with the collapse of the Collateral ideals. He thinks, when he is not killing, that he is holding the world together by his own gigantic strength; he is dazzled by insights of order, calm, and beauty.

Ulrich, who saw as a schoolboy that the world's mood was the subjunctive of potentiality, calls himself a possibilitarian, being easily aware of

the well-known incoherency of ideas, with their way of spreading out without a central point, an incoherency that is characteristic of the present era and constitutes its peculiar arithmetic.

As a *person* he is as far removed from any legal or conversational category as Moosbrugger, and it is immediately after a long satirical treatment of the lawyers' argument on responsibility that he is arrested and reflects with some annoyance on police descriptions, which somehow enable him to be identified, even when he feels quite different, being sometimes tall and broad (when angry or making love) and sometimes slim and soft (when floating jellyfish-like in a great book). But what distinguishes him from Moosbrugger is the mobility of his intelligence; and what makes him different from all the others is his awareness of the disappearance of the old patterns of knowledge, the penetrability of all the old fortifications by which we keep reality out of our daily lives.

And this is the main intellectual impulse of *The Man Without Qualities*: it begins with a series of statements concerning the modern failure to contain reality, and proceeds tentatively to examine causes and deride cures: but it also gropes towards some positive therapy. This may not seem an enticing topic for a novel, and I myself, though confident that another reading would be very illuminating, have frankly finished with this book for ever; but it may be helpful anyway to abstract its programme and set it baldly down.

In the first place, knowledge itself is a disease: 'the compulsion to *know* is just like dipsomania, erotomania, and homicidal mania ... it is not at all true that the scientist goes out after truth. It is out after him. It is something he suffers from. The truth is true and the fact is real without taking any notice of him.' But we can't hope for a quietist solution; we live in a period of transition (this flat, irritating remark actually means more in Musil's context than usual) and must adjust ourselves before the horizon rushes upon us. Ulrich agrees with the passionate Hans Sepp (though deploring his Germanic mystery-religion) that we cannot afford 'character', that acting by settled conviction is the death of knowledge. He tells Agathe that 'on the frontier between what goes on inside us and what goes on outside there's some communicating link missing nowadays, and the two spheres only transform into each other with enormous losses in the process'. What with external changes and wild alterations in human conduct, 'reality is abolishing itself', says Ulrich; and he even declares a will to abolish it finally, or to settle for a life that is to reality as metaphor to truth, or literature to fact. 'You are the kind of person,' says Walter, 'who declares that the meaning of fresh vegetables is tinned vegetables.' 'I dare say you're right. You might also say I'm the sort of person who will only cook with salt,' Ulrich replies. The relative importance of different aspects of reality is determined in an entirely arbitrary way by the degree of attention given them; and in this chaos it is impossible for an intelligent man to be convinced of anything, so that – and this is one of Musil's profoundest observations –

the vigour required to believe in new movements in art and literature, and countless other things [is] wholly founded on a talent for being at certain hours convinced against one's own conviction, for splitting a part off from the whole content of one's consciousness and for spreading it out to form a new state of entire conviction.

In the domain of morality this mental condition produces a great many problems, notably that 'the distinction between Good and Bad loses all meaning when compared with the pleasure to be got from any pure, deep, and spontaneous mode of action – a pleasure that can leap like a spark, both from permissible and from prohibited actions'. Hence the sheer pleasantness of Bonadea as she moves, by a funny, inexorable law, from habitual respectability to bed; hence too the huge, subtle, ethical issues raised by Agathe's forgery and her incestuous affair with Ulrich. 'Individual cases cannot be decided morally.' 'All moral propositions refer to a sort of dream condition that's long ago taken wing and flown away out of the cage of rules in which we try to hold it fast.' In the wonderful twelfth chapter of the third volume Ulrich delivers himself of a credo, ending :

> I believe that some day before very long human beings will be – on the one hand very intelligent, on the other mystics. Perhaps our morality is even to-day splitting into these two components. I might also call it : mathematics and mysticism – practical amelioration and adventuring into the unknown.

It is hardly surprising that the General finds difficulty with these ideas.

> 'The Minister wants to know what an ethos is.'
> 'An eternal verity ... that is neither eternal nor true, but valid only for a time so that the time has a standard to diverge from.'

Stumm can make his own adjustments; Ulrich's way of 'dethroning the ideocracy', of getting away from what are satirically called 'structive conceptions of the world' (as exemplified by Expressionism), is to move out into new, exciting, dark territory, the borderland of mind and reality, where dwell high intelligence and intuition also; where metaphor and univocality, literature and life, dream and waking, march with each other on a wild frontier; where he is 'inconclusively at home in two worlds at once'.

This 'borderline' Musil had sketched as early as *Törless*; it has nothing to do with the supernatural, but a great deal to do with the power of the intelligence to understand that it always has with it as a permanent problem, of which the contours perpetually shift, the fact that there exists what it is unadapted to grasp. When Ulrich and Agathe begin to grow to their union, Musil warns off the profane: he is starting on 'a journey to the furthest limits of the possible and unnatural, even of the repulsive...' – a 'borderline case', as Ulrich was later to call it, 'one of limited and specific validity, reminiscent of the freedom with which mathematics at times resorts to the absurd in order to arrive at the truth'. And the study of this borderline involves, as a first requirement, explanations of the natural limits of modern consciousness.

Here Musil displays a qualified orthodoxy. A fruitful, unitive attitude to reality can, like Paradise, only be imagined as something once possessed and now lost. In language that reminds one of Cassirer, Ulrich explains to Agathe that the power to identify oneself with the object belongs to dream, myth, poetry, childhood; it would be in our world a step back into an old symbolic mode, and it would involve 'a reduction in reality'. If 'nothing is any longer entirely there', there is no way back except by a sacrifice of intelligence he is not prepared to consider. And the way forward is also hard. Agathe has a Yeatsian vision of unity of being, of a sainthood like water gently welling over the rim of a fountain.

But before one goes on to the subject of Musil's mystical interests, there is an important and saving qualification to be noted. From the start he will have nothing to do with that potent modern myth which goes in this country under the name of 'dissociation of sensibility'. He deals with it very early, jeering at those who 'were prophesying the collapse of European civilization on the grounds that there was no longer any faith, any love, any simplicity, or any goodness left in mankind'. 'It is significant,' he continues, 'that these people were all bad at mathematics at school.' The development of purely intellectual disciplines ('the wicked intellect') he will not allow to be a disaster; and one of the jokes about Diotima is that she talks about 'a unity of religious feeling in all human activities that has been lost since the Middle Ages'. On the contrary, Musil rejoices in the unparalleled 'precision, vigour, and sureness' of mathematical thinking, and is harsh on all kinds of wanton primitivism, all the proposals for improvement submitted to the Committee which can be classified as 'back-to' this, that, and the other.

The innocent proto-Nazi, Hans Sepp, is significantly associated with this kind of thinking, and indeed its irruptions into politics are usually the occasion for violent unpleasantness of one kind or another. No, Musil-Ulrich was not a 'back-to' man, and indeed enjoyed modern life, New Men, and especially New Women. He shows a nice sense of the curious period immediately preceding that with which he concerns himself, when, out of the established attitudes of the dying century, rose the ghosts of their antiselves. The decadence of Europe was not to be explained in these sentimental ways, but grappled with, an almost impossibly elusive fact.

Yes Musil was admittedly interested in mysticism; he kept a notebook on the subject. This was a 'daylight' mysticism, concerned with 'the becoming one of this and that' (Miss Wilkins's phrase) as it actually occurs, subject and object, intellect and imagination, male and female. This is an old theme; as Aquinas put it, *sensus est quodammodo ipsa sensibilia*. Yet the failure of modern consciousness, for Musil, is precisely a failure to give it the right treatment. Hence this notebook on medieval mysticism, headed 'Border-line Experiences'. He argues ingeniously that a great deal of the energy required for the handling of these experiences now goes into sport, 'a contemporary substitute answering to eternal needs', and calls boxing a kind of theology because it places within a cage of rules a number of reactions so complex as to defy analysis. Another usurper is art, and especially music, Walter's escape route. And what is really to be learned from the medieval mystics is that they are not in the least vague and warm, but write of the phenomena with the analytical ruthlessness of Stendhal; of the direct experience of God they can, however, say nothing except metaphorically, and the usual source of their metaphors is extreme sexual pleasure. Their example may be of assistance in the business of grasping that mysterious moment in normal perception 'before vision and feeling separate and fall into the places we are accustomed to find them in'; what is certain is that we cannot find a better metaphor. Ulrich is even willing to accept the myth of a sexual offence or change of attitude as the explanation of the fragmentary nature of our truth; he can, in a sense, accept the Fall and Original Sin.

Musil's continuous interest in various aspects of sexual play (the Major's wife, Gerda, Clarisse, Rachel, Diotima's maid, the exhibitionist outside Clarisse's house, the prostitute who accosts Ulrich, above all his sexual relations with almost every important female character) seems somehow not to have attracted much attention. Yet it is central to his whole idea. There is an early chapter called 'Explanation and interruptions of a normal state of consciousness' which describes Ulrich's reflections after he and Bonadea have made up a quarrel and gone to bed.

> The incredible swiftness of such transformations, which turn a sane man into a frothing lunatic, now became all too strikingly clear.... This erotic metamorphosis of consciousness was only a special case of something far more general; for nowadays all manifestations of our inner life, such as for instance an evening at the theatre, a concert, or a church service, are such swift appearing and disappearing islands of a second state of consciousness temporarily interpolated into the ordinary one.

And with the Major's wife he experienced, as a young officer, 'an unutterable state of being', explicitly analogous to that of the mystic. There is a notion, also, that anything like intellectual equality, and so tension, between lovers, is destructive of love; and a somewhat Shavian suggestion that man might be capable of a condition of permanently heightened consciousness exactly analogous to the sublime pleasures of the bed. But what is certain is that the dividedness of the modern mind is constantly, in this book, expressed in terms of sexuality, so that disorders of consciousness become disorders of love. And this is where Ulrich's sexual activities, with whatever degree of seriousness he takes them, become significant. With the third volume sex assumes ever-increasing importance, with Diotima's researches and the coming together of Ulrich and Agathe; and, as we have seen, before the end this element will predominate.

This is a development, therefore, from an epistemological to an amative interest; and this gives the story altogether more suggestive power. The erotic lives of Arnheim and Tuzzi, for example, the sexual limitations of Moosbrugger and the poet Feuermaul, make sense in relation to their public faces. And a topic so thoroughly mythologized as love breeds myth. Diotima, so nicknamed because of her high ideals of love, looks throughout the static part of the book like a slightly comic but charming Aphrodite Ourania; Bonadea, called after the goddess whose ritual developed into erotic orgy, is Aphrodite Pandemos. But Diotima's Campaign collapses, and she herself, having acquired a lot of equivocal information about love-making, takes Bonadea's place in Ulrich's bed, a terrestrial Venus after all. Ulrich's desire for his sister represents another kind of love, what the Platonists might call an urge to identify oneself with the beautiful as well as desirable, and there is that conformity between them, represented as a striking resemblance, which is indispensable to the union of knower and known. Clarisse, in her madness – even her language is 'borderline' – seeks union with a symbol of union, a Greek homosexual whom she thinks of as a hermaphrodite. Operating on the borderline between subject and object, Musil uses, as an illustration of this suspicious frontier-friendship, the inexhaustible metaphor of sex; great myths that are older than Plato break into the fiction.

In this aspect of Musil's art one sees yet another scrap of evidence that he was astonishingly well equipped to write a great and coherent novel; the very story that he somewhat despised begins to assume in his mind an incalculable profundity.

He has other qualifications: great gifts of metaphor (the detection of resemblances, Aristotle's criterion for genius), and these are extremely important in a novel so much concerned with the relation of metaphor to fact; the power of being unexpected, yet delightfully right; a gift of aphorism. All this could be illustrated over and over. And yet, in the end, one's reaction to the claim that his stature is comparable to that of Proust and Joyce is simple incredulity. If we were speaking of the men themselves, I suppose it would be reasonable to say that Musil had as much sheer brain as the two of them together. As a novelist, he is simply not to be thought of in their company. The reason is that they were also working on a borderline, one that Musil, in his preoccupation with others, gave too little care to: the vast, vague frontier of fiction.

The operations of Proust and Joyce caused no breach; those of Musil do so. He was a great man, and everybody should find out why; but he is also the interesting limiting case, for if ever, to change the figure, if ever we supposed that there was no limit to looseness and bagginess in the novel, this protean and apparently boundless monster, Musil proves the contrary. There *is* a point at which a novel turns into something else : a metaphysician's miscellany, interspersed with subtle *exempla*.

(1960)

Robert Musil is still the least read of the great twentieth-century novelists, at any rate in the English-speaking countries, but this neglect can hardly last much longer; and when it becomes the custom to read and value him it will seem surprising to nobody that one speaks of him as belonging to the same class as Joyce and Mann. Most of his unfinished novel, *The Man Without Qualities*, is now translated (see above); his first book, *Young Törless*, is also available in English. He wrote two important plays, and these still have to be read in German; but the most urgent need was for a version of these five stories, and that has now been most happily supplied.[3]

Musil was an Austrian, with some Czech in his ancestry. He was born in Klagenfurt in November 1880, to an engineering professor who could paint and a musically gifted mother. His school days were spent in military academies, formidable institutions of the kind described in *Young Törless*. At sixteen he abandoned the Army and studied engineering at Brno; but quite soon after graduating he gave that up, too, and went to the University of Berlin for courses in philosophy and psychology. Before he took his doctorate in 1908 he had published *Young Törless* (1906); and although he was a successful philosopher, and might equally well have been a successful engineer or indeed a successful soldier, this remarkable first novel decided the issue, and he chose a literary career. Having to combine original writing with other work – especially after his marriage in 1910 – he was first a librarian and then a newspaper editor. In 1911 he published a small book called *Unions*, containing the stories here translated as 'The Perfecting of a Love' and 'The Temptation of Quiet Veronica'. From 1914 he served in the Austrian Army, both at the front and as editor of an Army newspaper. When the war ended he worked as press

3. *Five Women*. By Robert Musil. Translated by Eithne Wilkins and Ernst Kaiser. Boston, Seymour Lawrence, 1966.

liaison officer at the Foreign Ministry and then as scientific adviser to the War Ministry. These assignments no doubt provided plenty of material for *The Man Without Qualities*, which contains, among so much else, a good deal of satire on bureaucrats. In 1922 he abandoned all other employment and became a freelance writer. This did not prove easy; in 1934 a group of friends formed a society to support him while he worked at the great, perhaps unfinishable novel. But before that he had produced, along with much journalism and two plays, the stories which came out in 1924 as *Three Women* and are the first three of the present volume. Musil fled Austria when the Nazis took over in 1938 and lived in Switzerland, working at *The Man Without Qualities*, until his death in 1942.

The Man Without Qualities is unlike the other great novels of its period in almost everything except its stature. Ironical, deeply serious, acute and extragavant, extremely personal and yet nowhere – on the surface at any rate – obscure, it is a work of fantastic intelligence, of pervasive eroticism, of completely original mysticism. It cannot be described in a paragraph, but it is an experience which no one who cares for modern literature should avoid. Even if exasperated he may recognize that this book, unfinished, extravagant, tiresome as it is, is the real thing. And the earlier stories will help him to do so.

Three Women ('Grigia', 'The Lady from Portugal', 'Tonka') was published in the middle of a great literary period and stands comparison with its contemporaries. *Unions*, thirteen years earlier, has rather more the character of the *fin de siècle*, but Musil valued it highly, perhaps because it contains, in a different blend and without irony, the same constituents – a nervous obliquity, a mystique of the erotic, a deep interest in the borders of the human mind, those uneasy frontiers with the human body and with inhuman reality – that go to the making of *The Man Without Qualities*.

Musil's is notoriously a world in political collapse, the end of a great empire; but more central to his poetic writing (at times he makes one think of a prose Rilke) is the sense of a world in metaphysical collapse, a universe of hideously heaped contingency, in which there are nonetheless transcendent human powers. These he represents always by the same complex and various image of eroticism, which reaches its fullest expression in the big novel. *The Man Without Qualities* has among its themes nymphomania, incest, and sex murder, not at all for their prurient interest but as indices of the reaches of consciousness. If one theme can be called central in *The Man Without Qualities* it is this one, and nobody could think Musil anything but overwhelmingly serious in his treatment of it. Erotic ecstasy is beyond good and evil and exemplifies the power of our consciousness to cross the borderline formerly protected by what are now the obsolete fortresses of traditional ethics and metaphysics.

Throughout his career Musil explored this borderline. He kept a notebook on medieval mysticism and labelled it 'Borderline Experiences'. It interested him that the mystic, speaking of his incommunicable experience of God, will usually do so by analogies with erotic pleasure. Ulrich, a considerable authority on love-making, decides that the transformation of a sane man into a frothing lunatic by the pleasures of the bed is only 'a special case of something far more general' – namely, our ability to undergo a quasi-erotic metamorphosis of consciousness which gives us what is in effect a second state of consciousness interpolated into the ordinary one. Like E. M. Forster, whose greatest novel, *A Passage to India*, came out in the same year as *Three Women*, Musil believed that the heightening of consciousness which makes possible the order and the perceptions of good fiction has something in common with erotic feeling; and meaningless contingency is the enemy of novels as well as of love. For Musil the two metamorphoses of consciousness – art and love – ran together, and the sheer polymorphousness of the erotic was the subject as well as the analogue of his fiction.

To some extent this was already the case in *Young Törless*, and it is altogether so in the stories here translated. All have erotic themes, and most are concerned with female eroticism and with love as a means to some kind of knowledge. Here, as in the later novel, love is extremely various and free of the considerations of parochial ethics. In 'Quiet Veronica' it is bestial, in 'The Perfecting of a Love' it is profligate. 'Grigia' and 'Tonka' are variants of the medieval *pastourelle* – the seduction, in 'Grigia', of a peasant girl by a man of higher social class, and in 'Tonka' of a shopgirl by a student; but in either case the sexual situation is a figure for what is beyond sex. To study the behaviour of people in love is, for Musil, to study the human situation at its quick. Even when there is only delighted animality, or when, as in 'Tonka', there is an avowed absence of love and of intellectual communion, in a milieu of poverty and disease, sex remains the central ground for Musil's study of the potentialities of human consciousness.

The earliest of these stories is 'The Temptation of Quiet Veronica', which appeared in an earlier and very different version as 'The Enchanted House' in 1908. One's first thought is to relate this story, in its later form, to the literature of the Decadence; but its opaque surface, and the erotic feeling which occasionally pierces it, reflect Musil's preoccupation with the penetrating of reality by consciousness under the stimulus of sex. In short, it is not a failed attempt at the literature of neurasthenia, but a perhaps overworked statement of what we have seen to be Musil's principal theme. What we remember is not the pathology but Veronica's sense of her own body as she undresses, and Johannes, on the point of suicide, sensing himself as somehow rooted in the randomness of life. 'The Perfecting of a Love' has a stronger and more visible story, and again there is a touch of romantic agonizing – 'voluptuous enervated horror . . . nameless sin'. But there is also much to distinguish it from run-of-the-mill decadence : the sharp picture of the amber twist issuing from a teapot on the first page; the detached view of Claudine dressing ('all her movements took on something of oafishly sensual affectation'); the sexuality of the stranger, which causes 'a scarcely perceptible displacement of the surrounding world'. Finally sex, represented as a defence against the 'horribly gaping contingency of all one does', achieves a low and commonplace realization in the hotel cut off by snow; and from a body disagreeably swelling with lust emerges an image of love and union. 'The Perfecting of a Love' cost Musil more nervous effort than any other work, and it is curiously central to his achievement. It is entirely lacking in the worldly irony and the 'essayism' with which, in the big novel, he tried to relate its themes to the whole surface of modern life; but it is for all that a work which, in its uncommunicative, oblique fashion, expresses an understanding of human capacity, an intelligent and modern creativeness, comparable with those displayed in the contemporary writings of Lawrence and Thomas Mann.

By the time *Three Women* was published, thirteen years later, Musil had given up this somewhat hermetic manner, though he had not, as yet, developed the ironical discursiveness of *The Man Without Qualities*. Standing between his early and late manners, this book nevertheless has the same preoccupation with the erotic metamorphosis of consciousness and might also have been called *Unions*. The difference from the earlier work could be expressed as a new willingness to find a place in his stories for straight narrative (the 'low, atavistic' element in fiction which Forster comically deplored and which troubles most experimental novelists). Not that this simpler form of satisfaction has the effect of making the stories simple, considered as a whole. They are still parables, and still, in the manner of parables, refuse to submit themselves to any single interpretation. In 'Grigia', Homo is distinguished from the peasant community by his association with urban technology as well as urban civility; there is a futile rape of the land as well as easy seduction of women. Homo rediscovers the pleasant animality of sex, and with it a love for his absent wife and perhaps even for death. The climax of the tale has an insoluble ambiguity; but it is worth noting that ambiguity is a property not only of the narrative but also of the texture of the book. There are many passages of strange resonant poetry, for instance the description of behaviour of hay when used as a love-bed. 'Grigia' has the obliquity of high intelligence and idiosyncratic creativity. So too has 'The Lady from Portugal', though its parable announces itself more clearly because its elements – love and union, spirituality and sickness – are placed at a great historical distance. And if 'Tonka' is the best of all the stories, it is so not in virtue of its more down-to-earth theme, but because one senses in it a stricter relation between the narrative and the texture.

The story of 'Tonka' seems almost commonplace beside the others, but that is only because of its superficial resemblance to the stories of Zola or the De Goncourts or George Moore. It treats of the quasi-mystical aspects of sex in the least promising of relationships. The liaison is of apparently low power; there is nothing involved that can be called love, indeed there is hardly any discernible communication between the pair. On the other hand there is a curious lack of amorous or spiritual self-aggrandizement, there is goodness and nature. Above all there is guilt, but even guilt somehow escapes the conventional categories and remains as it were unattached to real personalities. When Shakespeare's Cressida was unfaithful, Troilus could not believe his senses : 'This is and is not Cressida.' In the same situation Tonka steadfastly *is* Tonka, the 'nobly natural' shopgirl who has nevertheless quite certainly been unfaithful. These ambiguities reflect the ambiguities of human reality; Musil once wrote that he saw no reason in the world why something cannot be simultaneously true and false, and the way to express this unphilosophical view of the world is by making fictions. As Tonka's lover notices when he debates with himself the question of marrying or leaving her, the world is as a man makes it with his fictions; abolish them and it falls apart into a disgusting jumble.

All these stories have obvious autobiographical elements, roots in Musil's personal life; but much more important is their truth to his extraordinarily intelligent and creative mind. They are elaborate attempts to use fiction for its true purposes, the discovery and registration of the human world. As with all works of genius, they suggest a map of reality with an orientation at first strange and unfamiliar, but one which we may conflate with our own and so change in some measure our way of standing in the world.

(1966)

TWELVE

BECKETT

Beckett often seems to be a rather old-fashioned writer, and at one time it was permissible to think of him as a poor one as well. The justice of that can be confirmed by anybody who bothers to consult the files of *transition* and to read Beckett's contribution to the volume of 1932 ('Anamyths, Psychographs, and other Prose Texts') entitled 'Sedendo et Quiesciendo' – a performance in the manner of the Joycean monologue which makes his later novels seem by comparison lucid and refreshing.[1] About this time Beckett is said to have told Peggy Guggenheim that 'he was dead and had no feelings that were human'. He was, however, learned in a Joycean way, and was one of the few young writers said by the master to have promise. His inhumanity and his learning and his promise permitted him to subscribe to Jolas's doctrine that one needed to write 'in a spirit of integral pessimism' and to 'combat all rationalist dogmas that stand in the way of a metaphysical universe'. This task demanded a consistent and progressive deformation of language and grammar. Beckett belonged, certainly, to the primitivist and decadent *avant-garde* of 1932.

A year earlier than that he published his little essay on Proust, which I have long regarded as a model of what such books ought not to be, for it is obscure, pedantic in manner, and not, as criticism should be, in the service of the work it undertakes to elucidate. Nevertheless it is the product of a strange and well-endowed mind, and its perversity is of a kind that writers, not charlatans, occasionally display. And it has now an additional interest; for Beckett has published obviously important work, and the *Proust* not only shows his talent at a formative stage but discusses what the important work is forbidden to discuss, namely ideas. It is the best introduction to Beckett, though not to Proust.

Beckett, for example, is more passionate about Time than the occasion quite seems to require, speaking of its 'poisonous

1. *Molloy. Malone Dies. The Unnamable.* Translated by Patrick Bowles. London, John Calder, 1959.

ingenuity ... in the science of affliction', seeing men as ordinarily trapped in vulgar intellectual errors about past and future, and hiding behind 'the haze of our smug will to live, of our pernicious and incurable optimism'. The agents of this false Time are Memory (voluntary memory, of course) and Habit. But occasionally we break away from them; some shock, some involuntary memory, revives our 'atrophied faculties' and produces a 'tense and provisional lucidity in the nervous system'. These breaches of the ignoble agreement between the organism and its environment are terrible and isolating, but they are the source of all meaning, and, presumably, all pleasure. Unhappily these 'immediate, total, and delicious deflagrations' are not summoned at will. Life, for the rest, is necessarily evil; 'wisdom consists in obliterating the faculty of suffering.' In ordinary life we expiate original sin, the sin of having been born. In death, or in moments of 'inspired perception', we escape from this condition and perceive the 'only reality', 'the essence of a unique beauty', 'that damns the life of the body on earth as a pensum and reveals the meaning of the word: "defunctus" '.

This is, of course, not entirely irrelevant to Proust; but Beckett's Bergsonism has its own rapt, pessimistic quality. His intuitionist aesthetic is exactly as modern as T. E. Hulme's; but he meditates much more upon the desert in which we normally dwell than upon the delicious oases. The later Beckett is much easier to understand if one recalls these musings on Time and Habit, the inaccessibility of value, the falsity and terror of man's world, the expiatory nature of human life. We are poor almost beyond imagining, especially since we must reject the mythologies or religions which talk of eternity and redemption. Their promised revelations come to nothing; the world is a chaos, directionless (Beckett's characters never know left from right). The Beckett hero is what Wallace Stevens, another Bergsonian, called 'The prince of the proverbs of pure poverty'.

The remarkable thing about *Waiting for Godot* is the way in which these sad ideas acquire vitality. Enslavement to Time is treated in the play as the consequence of Original Sin; Vladimir and Estragon attribute their poverty to the freely-chosen Fall:

We've lost our rights?
We've waived them.
(*They remain motionless, arms dangling, heads bowed, sagging at the knees.*)

Godot is precisely the sort of tragedy Beckett spoke of in the Proust book, 'the statement of an expiation ... not the miserable expiation of a codified breach of a local arrangement, organized by the knaves for the fools ... but of the original and eternal sin'. *Godot* is 'a something something tale of things done long ago and ill-done'. And Christ did nothing to change the situation; he was merely one of the luckier poor, in a warm climate where they 'crucified quick'. 'The best thing,' says Estragon, 'would be to kill me like the other.'

The dominion of Time and Habit is illustrated by Pozzo's fussy precision in handling his watch, his pipe, his vaporizer, and the abject Lucky. Lucky, a representative slave, talks nothing but nonsense about 'a personal God ... outside time without extension who from the heights of divine apathia divine athambia divine aphasia loves us dearly with some exceptions'. Pozzo lectures on Time – the lost colours of morning, the horrors of night to come – like Swann suddenly apprehensive of the future, breaking away from that optimism which is a mere biological adaptation: 'That's how it is on this bitch of an earth.' His blindness in the second act, when he answers to the names of both Cain and Abel and is 'all men', is another way of representing the enslavement of human perception. When he falls nobody can help him up. The little cloud appears, no bigger than a man's hand – but either it means nothing or is too disturbing to be considered. The *clochards* do not want Godot; they are terrified when he seems to be coming, relieved when he doesn't. Pozzo's last speech tells the truth about Time, and Vladimir sees the point: 'Habit is a great deadener.' But his understanding fevers him, and is the prelude to an ineffective annunciation. Godot's messengers are all ineffective, and leave the poor with only Habit to confirm them in the acceptance of their due and natural misery.

What has happened to make *Godot* a major poetic play? The pessimism that was an intellectual pose in the Proust book has rotted down into images; the subman in his pure poetry has acquired the colour of myth, the banalities of Habit fall into the rhythm of poetry, the absurdities of habitual behaviour are invested with the machine-like quality of music-hall routines and get the Bergsonian laugh. Our only contact with truth is by means of the ineffectual angels, Godot's boys; and this leaves us free to feel the poetry of falling, of inertia, of the malefic vision, as when Pozzo speaks of this bitch of an earth or Mrs

Rooney in *All that Fall* exclaims 'Christ, what a planet!' Men aspire to absolute infirmity, lame, blind, crawling on the face of the earth. 'I cannot be said to be well,' says Mr Rooney, 'but I am no worse. Indeed, I am better than I was. The loss of my sight was a great fillip.' Before the messenger tells them of the cosmic disaster that made the local train run late, the Rooneys join in wild laughter at the Wayside Pulpit text: 'The Lord upholdeth all that fall and raiseth up all that be bowed down.' Beckett's decaying figures, lying on the ground, sitting in dustbins, groaning along the road to nowhere, inhabit a world in which there has certainly been a Fall, but just as certainly no Redemption.

This pessimism was part of the *transition* programme, but it is now given a visionary quality:

I listen and the voice is of a world collapsing endlessly, a frozen world, under a faint untroubled sky, enough to see by, yes, and frozen too. And I hear it murmur that all wilts and yields, as if loaded down.... For what possible end to these wastes where true light never was, nor any upright thing, nor any true foundation, but only these leaning things, forever lapsing and crumbling away, beneath a sky without memory of morning or hope of night.

So the subman Molloy. His crippled odyssey begins with his observing, in a directionless wilderness, the encounter of two men, A. and C., victim and murderer, the double type of Beckett's fallen man. With his bicycle, delusive support of lameness, emblem of falsely directed movement, he seeks his daft mother, the sole source of sustenance. Later, rejecting a form of protection that denied his humanity, he goes on alone, walking on crutches, crawling, rolling towards his probably dead mother's door, enduring 'a passion without form or stations', unable to enumerate his ills, quite unable to tell left from right. Is Molloy the ultimate subman, the modern God? 'What is needed for the definition of man is an inexhaustible faculty of negation ... as though he were no better than God.' No; Molloy is not the end. He even makes a positive recommendation: the wise response to life is ataraxy. We got where we are by 'preferring the fall to the trouble of having ... to stand fast', and now wisdom is to stay lying down. Yet Molloy's life of falling, shambling, confusing, accepting, illustrates the true nature of all human life, especially as, totally outcast, he has on occasion the power of vision, is freed from the blinkers of habit. Thus he describes the act of sex quite empirically (this is horribly funny) and is capable of intense mathematical activity. But the moral is this:

> to know nothing is nothing, not to want to know anything likewise, but to be beyond knowing anything, to know you are beyond knowing anything, that is when peace enters in, to the soul of the incurious seeker.

Then there may be a message: 'Don't fret, Molloy, we're coming.' 'Well, I suppose you have to try everything once, succour included, to get a complete picture of the resources of their planet. I lapsed down to the bottom of the ditch.' Molloy is, like everybody else, a murderer. His last image is again of the encounter between A. and C., Abel and Cain. 'One had a club.' The message came to nothing.

The moderately cheerful ataraxy of Molloy in this, the most lucid part of the trilogy, is supplemented by the story of Moran, time-bound and self-serving, whose job it is to find Molloy. His life has the cruel order of habit: he bullies his servant, torments his son, goes prudentially to Mass, masturbates systematically, and is proud of his garden. The mad barren precision of his life is one of Beckett's best things, and so is its collapse. Moran loses his son and his purpose; he lies on the ground, in love with paralysis, and acts only in order to kill a man. The messenger who comes to him is unintelligible, and seems to say that according to the Boss, a thing of beauty is a joy for ever. Could he have meant human life? Moran, less wise than Molloy, crawls homeward and speculates theologically. One problem, what was God doing before the creation? is the classic forbidden inquiry, answered by Augustine with patristic humour: devising hell for people who ask such questions. We must endure *sedendo et quiesciendo*. Moran's garden is decayed; he falls into the poverty brought on us in the first place by wicked curiosity.

Molloy is a powerful book, rich in imagery and theological wit. Yet it is an example of the harm that could come to artists devoted to what is nowadays often called 'imitative form', to rendering the delinquency of modern humanity by a deliquescence of form and language. The same may be said more forcibly of *Malone Dies*, the second novel of the trilogy. Its fullness of intellect and its poetry are occasionally Joycean, and there is a wonderful development of Molloy's words on love-making (Malone's own sexual activity is even more bizarre than Molloy's): 'Ah, how stupid I am, I see what it is, they must be loving each other, that must be how it is done.' Malone or MacMann (son of man) is bedridden and hazily situated in the world. He lives in mortal tedium. The wisest animal in the book is a learned parrot whose attempt to speak the old tag *nihil in intellectu quod non prius in sensu* always fails after the first three words, and so strikes a blow for pessimistic Bergsonism.

But *Malone Dies* reminds us that the nearer a book becomes to directionlessness, to absolute quiescence, the more trying it is to read, especially when it has no paragraphs. And the last novel, *The Unnamable*, gets even nearer to the motionless and senseless subman-god, inhabiting the darkness like a Demogorgon of impotence. He represents the hopelessness of fallen man distilled to such purity that no actual man could ever achieve it, and all are happy compared with him; so that, paradoxically, 'I alone am man and all the rest divine.' He speaks the dirty *logos* and suffers all: 'All these Murphys, Molloys, and Malones.... They never suffered my pains, their pains are nothing compared to mine' (no sorrow like unto his sorrow). He is Existence, a 'big talking ball', life without the other God; the desperate earth, for which God does nothing except to send inaudible or unintelligible messages. Even Mahood (son of God?) has died uselessly. The paragraph of 130 pages ends: 'I can't go on. I'll go on.' This is the only God we are entitled to, our own true image.

One may as well allow these books to succeed in their determined attempt to defeat comment. They are almost entirely unsuccessful; we ought to be frank about this, because literary people are usually too willing to take the will for the deed. In Beckett's plays the theatrical demand for communicable rhythms and relatively crude satisfactions has had a beneficent effect. But in the novels he yields progressively to the magnetic pull of the primitive, to the desire to achieve, by various forms of decadence and deformation, some Work that eludes the intellect, avoids the spread nets of habitual meaning. Beckett is often allegorical, but he is allegorical in carefully fitful patches, providing illusive toeholds to any reader scrambling for sense. The formal effect is almost exactly described by Winters in his comment on Joyce: 'The procedure leads to indiscriminateness at every turn. . . . He is like Whitman trying to express a loose America by writing loose poetry. This fallacy, the fallacy of expressive, or imitative form, recurs constantly in modern literature.'

(1960)

Beckett Country

How, if this novel[2] were by an unknown author, would one set about the reviewer's task of giving some notion of its contents, and throwing in an appraisal? First, perhaps, by dealing in certainties: for instance, this book was written in French under the title *Comment C'est*. The translation is by the author. It is on the whole about as literal as a comparison of the titles will suggest, though one notes a lost pun (*commencez*). And since *Comment C'est* are the last words in the book, they impart to the design a circularity which is, perhaps not too unhappily, lost in English. Where the English is obscure the French in general helps little: 'the history I knew my God the natural' comes from *l'histoire que j'avais la naturelle*. Where the English looks wrong the French looks just as wrong: 'of the four three quarters of our total life only three lend themselves to communication' sounds as if the first 'three' has got in by mistake, but the French says *quatre trois quarts* and adds to the muddle by saying *deux seuls* for 'only three'. It seems unlikely that the reader loses much in clarity by using the English version. The syntax is neither English nor French, but that of some intermediate tongue in which 'ordinary language' cannot be spoken. This language goes indifferently into French or English. It eschews marks of punctuation, although the novel is divided into paragraphs of unequal length, signifying, why not, the fluttering of some moribund intellectual pulse, rather than successive stages of meaning. At its climax the story virtually disclaims its own authenticity, and this uncertain commitment to ordinary criteria of meaningfulness is also characteristic of the language in which it is told.

The meanings present in this language are not valid outside the book, being mostly the products of intensive internal re-

2. *How It Is*. Translated by the author. London, John Calder, 1964.

ferences and repetitions. Phrases of small apparent significance occur again and again with some kind of cumulative effect: 'something wrong there', 'bits and scraps', 'quaqua', 'when the panting stops', etc. The speaker of these phrases looks forward keenly to the end of his task, frequently promising that we are near the end of the first, second, or third part, and rejoicing especially in the final paragraph, only to be thwarted by the Finnegan-begin-again trick mentioned above. In short, the whole book refuses to employ the ordinary referential qualities of language, and frustrates ordinary expectations as to the relation between a fiction and 'real life'. It is as if the old stream of consciousness were used in a situation where there is nothing but the stream to be conscious of.

Not very helpful, says the reader. What *is* the story? Well, it is spoken by a nameless man face down in mud, and apart from him its principal character is called Pim. Three sections describe how it was before, with and after this Pim, who is therefore a measure of time and history. Pim was long awaited, then he arrived and lay down in the mud beside the speaker and his sack ·full of cans; but things didn't go well, and he passed on. Where, or to whom? Before Pim, the speaker had been alone; perhaps, he thought, the 'sole elect', moving at intervals with his sack and his can opener ten or fifteen yards through the mud. His only contact with the world 'above' is the memory of a past idyllic scene with a girl and a dog; and another of a marriage that failed with the waning of desire. After Pim he sees that he is really one of a great number, all on the same impossible muddy journey. Somehow it has been arranged that its progress is circular and endless.

With Pim, the situation was at least not solitary. Pim brought a watch and one could listen to the delicious ticking away of the seconds. Furthermore, the speaker devised an elaborate signal code by which he induced Pim to speak: as by jabbing the can opener into his rectum, beating him on the kidneys, or, to make him stop, on the head. Pim, being a man, is a kind of machine, *l'homme machine* in fact, responsive to external stimuli. Nevertheless he clenches his fists in pain, and his nails grow through his palm. The close relationship of the couple is that of tormentor and victim. When Pim abandons the speaker he leaves very little, but still something, behind him, 'with Pim all lost almost all nothing left almost nothing but it's done great blessing'. This example of dream parataxis, translated into English, means, I suppose, that the residual benefits of Pim's sojourn are small but important, perhaps only because they prove that we have lived through one more stage and are nearer the last. Later we gather that as far as the speaker is concerned we can do what we like with time – reverse it, for example – so long as we always give Pim and the Primal Scene a central place in it: 'on condition that by an effort of the imagination the still central episode of the couple be duly adjusted'.

After Pim, the world is full of tormentors and their victims, an endless chain in which each man repeatedly changes his role from one to the other. Over vast stretches of time, one torments and is tormented. The speaker moves on through this suffering inflicted and received, towards reunion with Pim. But in the end the voice we are listening to rebels, denies that all he has said is quoted from some external authority, claims that it is all a fiction ('all balls'); that there was something, yes, but no 'quaqua', no *logos* or revelation from without, only himself, face in mud, making it up and mumbling. Then the last sentence, with its ambiguous denial of this disclaimer.

What kind of a story is this? Certainly there is a fiction; and there is a chain not only of torment but of rhythmical incantation. But the reader who wants more than a form commenting upon itself, an autistic stir of language, will be tempted to look aslant at the book, to seek allegory. I myself have already slipped into allegory in describing Pim's watch, and in hinting that the tormented relationship between the speaker and Pim stands for the incarnation, which, we are told, gives history such meaning as it may be said to have, and could be regarded as affording the type of human love-relations ever since (the love of the Word unable to speak a word speaks, under painful stimulus, when it is embodied in *l'homme machine*. Pim has nails through his palms, and is pierced by a kind of spear).

Perhaps, as the speaker felt when he denied the authenticity of 'quaqua', the intervention of that word was all a fiction anyway. Even so, his dreams are penetrated by it. Thus there are in the book echoes of Christian figurations of experience : hints of millennialism, of the *logos* as distorted by mud. In the first part a vague 'epiphany' suggests an involuntary memory of Eden. The sack is a figure for the body, support and burden of the soul, which the Christian centuries would have had no difficulty in recognising; in the third part we have a picture of the history of the elect parallel to Milton's in the last two books of *Paradise Lost*, except that we lack the assurance of Pim's second coming in majesty. The book offers an open invitation to such allegories, even though everybody who accepts it will soon feel lost and uncertain.

In view of all this it is, I suppose, just as well that we *do* after all know something, if only a little, about Beckett. The Speaker in this book is the latest in a long line bred from his obsession with Dante's Belacqua, who could not enter purgatory until he had relived his slothful life. Beckett's dream of life is purgatorial, or would be if salvation waited at its end; as it is, his characters are, as Mr Rooney says in *All that Fall*, 'like Dante's damned, with their faces arsy-versy'. There is a Beckett country in which we feel half at home; and we know the Beckettian *homo patiens*, sinking progressively into immobility. His role as victim and tormentor we recall from *Godot*. His relation to the past we learned from *Krapp's Last Tape*. And so on. In addition there is, to provide a physics for the Beckett world, his early book on Proust, as well as such sophisticated experiments as Mr Kenner's book. So we have some knowledge, not much, of the physical laws governing this new book; we have keys to its meanings. 'No symbol where none intended,' noted Beckett in the addenda to *Watt*; but by establishing a world of uncontrollably interrelated objects and meanings he makes this injunction impossible of fulfilment.

A few instances will serve to illustrate this. There must be a connection between Pim's watch, Pozzo's watch in *Godot*, and the passage in *Proust* on Time's 'ingenuity . . . in the science of affliction'. Time is the means by which we are punished for having been born. For Beckett as for Proust our only means of triumphing over it is the involuntary memory; in Beckett this operates infrequently and unsatisfactorily, as with Krapp's tape or the Speaker's recollection of the girl and of his marriage. We are enslaved by time; when eternity, the *nunc stans*, the *durée*, came down to save us, it apparently failed. So much for the 'succour' which, as Molloy observed, you ought to consider as a possibility before, inevitably, you reject it. Pim is one name for it. Trapped in time and space as the fallen categorize them (and what other way is there?) Beckett's figures are all, as Mr Kenner demonstrates, more or less conscious Cartesians. They are all, perhaps, Descartes himself, contemplating the world from a position prone or supine (Yeats remarked that the world changed when Descartes discovered that he could think better in bed than up).

Contemplating a world so changed, Beckett is moved to 'jettison the very matrices of fiction – narrator, setting, characters, theme, plot', and 'devote his scrutiny (under the sign of Belacqua) to the very heart of novel writing: a man in his room writing things out of his head while every breath he draws brings death nearer'. So Mr Kenner. He is also much interested by human inventions which reflect the factitious order and inter-relatedness of the objective world to which he cannot belong; his relation to this common-sense reality is exactly that of a circus clown, who can do apparently impossible things but finds easy ones incredibly complicated. The fundamental absurdity of the subject–object situation is for him figured in clowns and *clochards*; and so is our imperfect control over space, time, and death. Beckett's humour derives entirely from this. It is a stateliness of speech, a clownishness of philosophical language (dealing with the complicated things and finding the easy ones too hard); in action it is the Bergsonian pratfall. This is the humour of man as machine, whether rhetorical or locomotive.

Beckett can thus be read as a philosophical fantasist: His bicycles are Cartesian symbols, his submen Prousts who have *really* contracted out, and so forth. Sunk in a sub-social, subpsychological dream, they all merge in one's mind – Watt, Molloy, Malone, the Unnamable, the unnamed of the new book. They may sink deeper into a state of pure rejection, pure negativity – indistinguishable, as Molloy noticed, from God's. But because they are all aspects of the same figure, inhabiting similar worlds, we have relevant knowledge to bring to this new book; we can live with it, perceive something of its rhythms and stresses – in short, receive it.

That, at any rate, is a way of putting it. Yet it may tell little more than a small part of the truth about how Beckett has to be read. To emphasize the formal interest can be a fashionable way of concealing the true nature of our curiosity. Beckett is a puzzle-maker, quaint and learned. We look for clues, guess at meanings. His formal sophistication may be the meat the modern burglar brings along to quiet the *avant-garde* housedog. Under it all, he is a rather old-fashioned writer, a metaphysical allegorist. Take, for example, *Watt*. There he made his hero's name the first word of a metaphysical conundrum; and Knott, whom Watt serves, is the god defined by negatives, perhaps also time itself, inexplicably regular. Watt has only oblique religious experiences. He meets a porter whose lameness causes him 'to move rapidly, in a series of aborted genuflections', and a Mr Spiro, Catholic propagandist, who gives prizes for anagrams on the names of the Holy Family. (Out of Mr Spiro's motto, *dum spiro spero*, we get the interesting anagram *dummud*. Since *dum* is 'while', here meaning one's time on earth, it isn't hard to see why the latest hero spends his time in the mud.)

Watt, however, is not good at symbols : he had 'lived, miserably it is true, among face values all his adult life ... whatever it was Watt saw, with the first look, that was enough for Watt ... he had experienced literally nothing, since the age of fourteen, or fifteen, of which in retrospect he was not content to say, "That is what happened then." '

To enjoy Beckett, one mustn't be a Watt. When we meet, for example, the Lynch family, we must take their heroic efforts, ruined by disease, to reach a combined age of a thousand years not as merely grotesque humour, but as a hopelessly human millennialist aspiration, an absurd plot to overcome history, bring time to an end. If we know that Beckett's names and titles often contain puns, sometimes obscene, let us also look for allegorical meanings in such names as Malone and Mac-Mann, Godot, and even Pim.

This suggests that the delights offered by Beckett are of an old and tried variety. He has re-invented philosophical and theological allegory, and as surely as Spenser he needs the right to sound sub-rational, to conceal intention under an appearance of dreamlike fortuity, to obscure the literal sense. The only difference is that his predecessors were sure there was such a sense, and on this bitch of a planet he can no longer have such certainties. This difference does not affect the proposition that Beckett's flirtations with reality are carried on in a dialect which derives from the traditional language of learning and poetry. It is nevertheless true that the more accustomed we become to his formal ambiguity, the more outrageously he can test us with inexplicitness, with apparently closed systems of meaning. *How it is* differs from the earlier work not in its mode of operation but principally in that it can assume greater knowledge of the Beckett world. Such assumptions have often and legitimately been made by major artists, though we should not forget that this is not a certain indication of greatness. Prolonged attention given (from whatever motives) to a minor but complex author may allow him to make them. But who can be sure which is which? It is a perennial problem for critics of *avant-garde* art, and Beckett raises it in a very acute form.

(1964)

A Critic's View

The expression that there is nothing to express, nothing with which to express, nothing from which to express, no power to express, no desire to express, together with an obligation to express. . . .

Feeling that this is what art should be, Mr Beckett – who else? – opts, he says, for writing which deserts the plane of the feasible, 'weary of its puny exploits'. Mr Kenner[3] quotes this with some indications of agreement. More specifically, he suggests, Beckett rids himself of the problem of how to go on from Joyce by abandoning the narrative tradition with its 'idiot consistency' and fining fiction down to the point where it is clearly absurd to go on with it, except that writing is being alive and we've all been tricked into the cowardice – as Beckett called it in the Proust book – of thinking we're better suited that way.

Beckett is worth a lot of trouble, if only because of *Waiting for Godot*, and if Mr Kenner, in taking trouble, seems to absorb rather than describe the *oeuvre*, that may be said to be true of very good critics. Mr Kenner, indeed, has sent most of the great moderns spinning with the velocity of his passage, and it was not without relish that one saw he was going to give Beckett a whirl. However, the question is not whether Kenner is good at absorbing Beckett, but whether he is informative or otherwise helpful. The answer is, slowly, yes; the cost to the reader is high enough to be worth counting.

Speaking of the trilogy (*Molloy, Malone Dies, The Unnamable*), a work with 'a fastidious stench', Kenner says, among other things, that it is 'a compendious abstract of all the novels that have ever been written', 'a sardonic counterpoint to the epic tradition of the West', a progress from *sum* to *cogito*, and

3. *Samuel Beckett*. By Hugh Kenner. London, John Calder, 1962.

a happy dissolution of fiction to the point where it describes nothing but itself being written ('pure act by pure inaction', or, if you like, 'pure activity, the Ape of pure Act'). Similarly with the plays : they reduce themselves to actors acting acting before a time-bound audience being an audience – unless it walks out, it has to be. Allowing that there are historical reasons for all this, why is it good? Why is idiot randomness any better than idiot consistency? Please explain, we ask, how the trilogy sums up all the other novels, and counterpoints the epic. Well, declares Kenner, I can tell you that if Homer had been a twentieth-century Irishman living in Paris, he 'might well have written the first half of *Molloy*'.

The truth is that this critic does much more absorbing and converting than explaining. His prose is atwitch with the exertion of wit and intellect and it has a narcissistic glow. 'All Beckett's writings bring some sustained formal element to the service of some irreducible situation round which the lucid sentences defile in baffled aplomb.' This is useless. Sometimes there is a disastrous self-admiring joke : Beckett's bicycle is *maestro di color che vanno*.

However, the book does provide some information about published and unpublished work of Beckett. And Mr Beckett himself contributes a highly significant piece of information about his interest in a racing cyclist called M. Godeau, whom Kenner accordingly hails as Beckett's 'Cartesian Man in excelsis'. The book is strongest, in fact, on bicycles, the frequent occurrence of which in Beckett testifies to his interest in them as emblems of *l'homme machine*. Indeed, Beckett is obsessed with the description of movement; and the reduction of human activity to mechanical stereotypes. It is the decay of a bicycle that reduces Molloy, and the lack of one condemns the Unnamable to inert cogitation. In this Cartesian connection, Mr Kenner has usefully looked up the obscure Belgian Occasionalist Geulincx, whom Murphy quotes. This author believed that the division between mind and body was complete, rejecting the pineal gland theory, and holding that a separate act of God was required for every physical movement. The textbooks, if I remember rightly, claim that Occasionalism was knocked out by Leibniz, but according to Kenner Mr Beckett has shown it to be 'aesthetically relevant' to our time. The book is also good on the counting mania suffered by so many Beckett characters, and Mr Kenner ingeniously works out a comparison between irrational numbers and the clown or *clochard* figures – shadows behind the neat rationalist rows of bourgeois numerals.

Beckett, in the trilogy especially,

> takes stock of the Enlightenment, and reduces to essential terms the three centuries during which those ambitious processes of which Descartes is the symbol and progenitor accomplished the dehumanization of man.

This book is a rhapsody on that theme, with illustrations from Beckett. It is Kenner's own theme, though of course it isn't a novel one, and Beckett grew up with it; but I suspect that Kenner's view of it, which is the fashionable thing about our being trapped at the end of a technological epoch, is not really Beckett's. He is much more old-fashioned, having a more biological approach, and also more theological interest than this book indicates. He was also, as the Proust book shows, affected by Bergson : the bicycle is a Bergsonian laughter-maker, and the famous 'I can't go on. I'll go on' is the beastly plight of a thinker acknowledging his instinctive adaptation to life, his involuntary survival kit.

(1962)

THIRTEEN

SARTRE AND THE ANTI-NOVEL

Sartre is a very big writer, an obscure and copious writer; he has powerful and variable opinions about almost everything, and it is quite certain that so long as he is in production nobody will ever be able to grasp him firmly. Even if one tries merely to find out what he means in relation to a special and limited interest, it is by no means easy. The new work pours out, altering the picture as a whole, and, by implication at least, changing even those details which are not directly under consideration.

Thus it can be said with some assurance that Sartre is a figure of importance in the theory and practice of the modern novel; but this does not mean that we can have a clear view of his opinions, as we have, for example, of Robbe-Grillet's. In an early essay he said one ought to look behind every novel for a hidden metaphysic, and it might seem useful to have, behind *Nausea*, the immensely visible *Being and Nothingness*; indeed it has often been argued that these works are very intimately related. This is about half true, perhaps, but even if it were wholly true it would be of limited interest to most readers of the new paperback *Nausea*,[1] who might reasonably want to get to know this central work without being obliged to break into so vast and harsh a freedom-fortress as the 'essay on phenomenological ontology'. Some might choose to do so with the air of the keys, admirably simple and well-cut, provided by Mrs Warnock in what is far the most practical and humane introduction to Sartre I know.[2]

Translation lags behind, but there is a new volume of essays containing pieces from *Situations IV* and Sartre's preface to Sarraute's *Portrait of a Man Unknown*.[3] Apart from the Sarraute essay, it contains little comment on literature, but there is a good deal that ought to be taken into account whatever the angle from which one views the author. The translation (ex-

1. *Nausea*. Harmondsworth, Penguin.
2. *The Philosophy of Sartre*. London, Hutchinson, 1965.
3. *Situations*. Translated by Benita Eisler. London, Hamish Hamilton, 1965.

cept in the Sarraute piece, which was done years ago by Maria
Jolas) is slapdash, and at times worse than that, but even so the
huge and alien personality blazes through. The opening piece
on Tintoretto, too long, inappropriately rhapsodic, reminds us
that Sartre sometimes writes 'at top speed, with rage in my
heart, gaily, tactlessly'. The point is that this painter, under the
shadow of Titian, exposed or reflected the corruption of his
city : 'anxious and cursed, Venice produced a man riddled with
angst', a man whose art 'rent the age with slashes of fire' and
proved him 'a Darwinist before the fact'. It is by most standards a very bad performance; but such judgements have to be
suspended with an author like Sartre, for excess and disorder
acquire significance in the total context.

The long essay on Merleau-Ponty is in some ways a similar
problem. Although their friendship was evidently shot through
with philosophical accords and disputes, Sartre is allusive
rather than expository when he discusses their intellectual
associations. What comes through very powerfully is the
strange set of profiles their friendship and half-quarrels present : it is like something from one of the novels, or a fictional
illustration in *Being and Nothingness*. The account of how they
dealt with one another on *Les Temps Modernes* has its farcical
side; and yet what comes of this essay in the end is not
amazement at the improbable conversations of co-editors but a
fine sense of the quality of Merleau-Ponty, of a man who could
think desperately and live as one who could reasonably argue
that every life and every moment are incarnations, singularities
which deform yet illustrate the universal.

What is constantly surprising about Sartre is this charity,
this insight into others which, the early philosophical work
suggested, could not be had, but which novelists need, if only
as an 'as if'. The new book reprints his vehement attack on
Camus. At first the tone is almost comically mean.

> Your combination of dreary conceit and vulnerability al-
> ways discouraged people from telling you unvarnished
> truths. The result is that you have become the victim of a
> dismal self-importance.... Sooner or later, someone would
> have told you this. It might just as well be me.

Twenty or so pages of this, then Sartre says he has reached the
end; but he thinks of more he wants to say. He obligingly

outlines his thought for Camus, who seems to have misunderstood it, and quite gratuitously embarks upon a penetrating estimate of Camus himself in the days when he was 'alive and authentic'. There follows his obituary of Camus, this 'Cartesian of the absurd'; it is rough with sorrow and love.

Friendship and its corollary, the posturing row, are simpler in the occasional writings than they were shown to be in the third section of *Being and Nothingness*. So with the long memoir of Paul Nizan, who taught the young to be angry and refused to accept the old explanations of conditions as 'natural'; between him and Sartre, as between Camus and Sartre, the old myth of friendship, as something ultimately indestructible, intervened. Yet one would look to these essays, rapid and generous as they are, for evidence that much of the original thinking of Sartre survives the obscure Marxist 'conversion' Mrs Warnock labours to define. They are prodigiously thoughtful, and the thought has its roots in the old Existentialism.

This is also true of the essay on Giacometti, which is as impressive as the Tintoretto is tawdry; it also reads like an exemplum from *Being and Nothingness*. So, too, with the introduction to Sarraute, which calls – he may have been the first to do so – certain 'penetrating and entirely negative works' anti-novels. He admires her because her subject is inauthenticity, and because she understands, as he has understood, what he called the 'viscous'. In allowing us to face what we normally flee, she presents human reality 'in its very *existence*' and so herself, presumably, achieves a condition, or anyway a model, of authenticity. Subsequently he has attacked the formalist obsessions of the *nouveau roman*; but here he obviously admires Sarraute's tentative, exploratory rejections of all the paradigms, of what in another connection he calls 'the eidetic imagery of bad faith'.

This brilliantly concise expression, thrown away in a footnote to the piece on Merleau-Ponty, may have more value to the literary critic than anything else in the new book. Long before, Sartre had adopted the term 'eidetic reduction' from Husserl; it is part of the method of the phenomenologists. But here I take him to mean that *mauvaise foi* (a comfortable denial of the undeniable – freedom – by myths of necessity, nature, or things as they are) derives its paradigms from illusions left over from the past – as some abnormal children can 'see' the page or the object that is no longer before them. Sartre uses the phrase in a political context, as it happens, but it serves to describe in part the critical position not only of the exponents of the *nouveau roman* but also of the younger Sartre himself. He thought of some great nineteeth-century novelists as collaborators in Bad Faith, and held that it was as bad to diminish the liberty of a character by conventional devices of 'form' as to betray one's own 'project' by *mauvaise foi*. In this new *Situations* we find him asking whether music, because it has 'wrenched itself from its alienation and set about creating its essence while freely providing its own laws', cannot be a model for the working class as it tries to do the same. To do so it must ignore '*a priori* limitations', falsely said to be inherent in its nature. The artist must 'break the already crystallized habits which make us see in the *present* tense those institutions and customs which are *already out of date*'. *Passéisme* is a manifestation of bad faith.

Thus, in his own peculiar dialect, Sartre, a very inclusive thinker, makes the species 'anti-novel' a component of his system. On the proper relation of the self-created forms of the modern novel to the 'eidetic' paradigms surviving from the past – or, to put the same thing in another way, on the relations between form and freedom – there is a growing literature. Miss Murdoch calls form 'an aspect of our desire for consolation'; it interferes with the profoundest task of the novelist, which is to create irreducible and opaque persons. Every concession to form is a reduction in that 'respect for contingency' which is essential to imagination, as opposed to fantasy. In short, the eidetic imagery of novelistic forms helps to protect us from the real, is the agent of bad faith. Miss McCarthy says something like this, perhaps more superficially, when she attacks 'myth' and calls 'factuality' the one distinguishing feature of the novel. Mrs Spark has not written discursively about the problems, but her latest book is, among other things, a defence of eidetic form, and a rejection of the anti-novel.[4] Robbe-Grillet is against the retention of any paradigm which may suggest that the world means something, or even that it doesn't. 'Quite simply, it *is*.' This anti-essentialist position, logically developed, calls for a gap of the kind Camus would have called 'absurd' between the autonomous structure which is the novel and the world. The time of the novel is its own affair (as in *Marienbad*,

4. *The Mandelbaum Gate*. London, Macmillan, 1965.

there is no reference to any past or future, and the time of the film, however you look at it, is one and a half hours); and the only 'character' is the reader. The ambition of the new novel, he says, is to make something *ex nihilo* which will stand on its own without reference to anything outside it.

Sartre undoubtedly has his place in the development of this new radical formalism; that he rejects it seems to me not an indication that he is old-fashioned but a proof that his existentialism *is* a humanism. The most extraordinary claim Robbe-Grillet makes is that the new novel will appeal to ordinary people because it is truer than the old one to their own lives. This ignores the large element of the merely fictive we all use to get by – to console ourselves, as Miss Murdoch says. It's not really surprising that Robbe-Grillet should find fault with *Nausea*. He acquits Sartre of the charge of essentialism, but accuses him of escalating the characters of Roquentin and the Autodidact into a state of 'necessity', so bringing back into the novel what he should have kicked out – nature and tragedy. This is saying that Sartre uses the eidetic imagery of bad faith; that he has failed to make a novel signifying nothing, and so slipped, like any other *salaud*, into prefabricated formal attitudes. And it is true. When Sartre shows us a man in anguish, 'choosing what he will be', completely and profoundly responsible, he tries to show also that this man is 'a legislator deciding for the whole of mankind'. This man is very like the eidetic image of a tragic hero. And he is explicit that to *be* rather than to exist is to resemble the hero of a novel; the comparison recurs in *Nausea*. Whether Robbe-Grillet likes it or not, the Sartrean hero is, must be, the demythologized modern equivalent of the tragic hero; the old imagery lingers.

In the earlier volumes of *Situations* Sartre himself looked into some of the problems arising from this survival. The characters must not be predetermined by plot; they must be what a truly Christian novel would make them, 'centres of indeterminacy'. He attacks Mauriac for playing God to his characters, and also for failing to reproduce the action of time; for Sartre the temporality of a novel is satisfactory when it is closest to 'real' time. When he writes of Camus, he admires *L'Etranger* for creating its own order and expunging 'necessity' from fiction; yet he denies him the title of novelist, largely because his book lacks 'continuous duration, development, and the manifest irreversibility of time'. Curiously enough, Sartre read this book, even in some ways misread it, as if it were an anti-novel *avant la lettre*; but he is quite sure for all his admiration that *L'Etranger* is not a novel; whereas *Nausea*, for all its emphasis on absurdity and viscosity, did by implication deserve to be called one.

And so it is. It is certainly an illustration of absurdity and contingency, but also illustrates the power of fiction to free us from them. Since that is a traditional task of fiction, it is not surprising that the ghosts of old novels would not be entirely exorcised. Sartre began the book as a discontinuous and episodic work; but to write *'comme les petites filles'*, as Roquentin says, is no way to achieve a cure, which this book has to be. So it develops design and structure. *Quelque chose commence pour finir.* The novelist has to avoid the errors of Roquentin, the historian who imposes an order, and of the Autodidact, who reduces the world to an alphabet; without falsifying contingency, he has to make 'adventures' and rhythms, establish the place of the 'privileged moment' in the 'irreversible flow of time'. This is to do what has been done before. 'Beware of literature,' says Roquentin; Sartre is cautious, but remembers and echoes Proust. Roquentin comes at the end to believe that he can see the shape of his life, and that he knows how to implement the lesson he learned from the song 'Some of these days' – *il faut souffrir en mesure*. What is needed is a novel, 'beautiful and hard as steel'. *Nausea* contains the viscous and the absurd, but aspires also to this condition. Consequently it yields a little, as a fiction must, to tyrannies and consolations of inherited forms. It fakes, as good novelists fake, honestly. It is the only way for the hero-novelist to 'wash himself of the sin of existing'.

Like the *nouveau roman*, *Nausea* is a fiction that explores the forms and status of fiction; but it has a deeper tone than the new works, and this is in part because of Sartre's sense that even when nothing is beyond question 'given', everything cannot be new. Form is, under one aspect, necessarily eidetic; it persists, like friendship. A critical devotion to both will not preclude rant or betrayal; but Sartre in his way shows this devotion, and it places him not among the *passéistes* but among the heroes.

(1965)

FOURTEEN

SALINGER

What meaning, if any, can one attach to the expression 'a key book of the present decade'? It is used as a blurb in a new reprint of Mr J. D. Salinger's famous novel,[1] which was first published in 1951. Whoever remembers the book will suppose that this is a serious claim, implying perhaps that *The Catcher*, as well as being extremely successful, is a work of art existing in some more or less profound relationship with the 'spirit of the age'. It is, anyway, quite different from saying that *No Orchids for Miss Blandish* is a key book. On the other hand, there is an equally clear distinction between this book and such key novels as *Ulysses* or *A Passage to India*. For it is elementary that, although these books have been read by very large numbers of people, one may reasonably distinguish between a smaller, 'true' audience and bigger audiences which read them quite differently, and were formerly a fortuitous addition to the 'highbrow' public. But although Salinger is certainly a 'highbrow' novelist, it would be unreal to speak of his audience, large though it is, as divided in this way. What we now have is a new reader who is not only common but pretty sharp. This new reader is also a pampered consumer, so that the goods supplied him rapidly grow obsolete; which may explain why I found *The Catcher* somewhat less enchanting on a second reading.

It is, of course, a book of extraordinary accomplishment; I don't know how one reviewer came to call it 'untidy'. Nothing inept, nothing that does not look good and work well as long as it is needed, will satisfy this new public. Structural virtuosity is now taken for granted, particularly in American novels. This one is designed for readers who can see a wood, and paths in a wood, as well as sturdy, primitive trees – a large, roughly calculable audience: fit audience though many.

At the level of its untidy story, the book is about an adolescent crisis. A boy runs away from his expensive school because he is an academic failure and finds intolerable the company of

1. *Catcher in the Rye*. London, Hamish Hamilton.

226

so many phoneys. He passes a lost weekend in New York, mostly in phoney hotels, night clubs, and theatres, avoids going to bed with a prostitute and is beaten up by her ponce, meets some phoney friends, talks to taxi-drivers, wonders endearingly where the ducks from Central Park Lake go in winter, secretly visits his kid sister, indulges various fantasies of much charm and finally falls ill with exhaustion. He tells his story in a naïve sophisticated dialect, partly in the Homeric Runyon tradition, partly something more modern. Repetitive, indecent, often very funny, it is wonderfully sustained by the author, who achieves all those ancient effects to be got from a hero who is in some ways inferior, and in others superior, to the reader. (His wisdom is natural, ours artificial.) The effect is comfortably compassionate; the boy, ungifted and isolated as he thinks himself to be, is getting his last pre-adult look at the adult world, our world, into which he is being irresistibly projected. He can't stand the adolescent world either; clean, good children turn into pimply shavers with dirty minds. For sex is what alters the goodness of children. Of the girls Holden Caulfield knows, one is nice and lovable – for her he admits no sexual feeling, though her date with a crumby seducer helps to work him up to this crisis; one is a prostitute, operating in a hotel which is a comic emblem of the perverted adult world; and one is an arty phoney. Growing up is moving out of crumby phoneyness into perverted phoneyness. These phoneys, they come in at the goddam window, using words like 'grand' and 'marvellous', reading and writing stories about 'phoney lean-jawed guys named David ... and a lot of phoney girls named Marcia that are always lighting all the goddam Davids' pipes for them'. Successful people, even the Lunts, turn into phoneys because of all the phoneys who adore them. Holden, near enough to Nature to spot this, is himself knowingly infected by the false attitudes of the movies, the greatest single source of phoneyness. Only children are free of it, especially dead children.

This much you get from listening to the boy, and it sounds untidy. What Mr Salinger adds is design. Holden is betrayed at the outset by a schoolmaster (phoney-crumby) and at the end by another (phoney-perverted). The only time his parents come into the story, he has to remain motionless in the dark with his sister. The boy's slang is used to suggest patterns he cannot be aware of : whatever pleases him 'kills' him, sends him off to join his dead brother; almost everybody, even the disappointed whore, is 'old so-and-so', and 'old' suggests the past and stability. More important, the book has its big, focal passages, wonderfully contrived. Holden hears a little neglected boy singing, 'If a body catch a body, etc.' This kills him. Then he helps a little girl in Central Park to fasten her skates. Next he walks to the Museum of Natural History, which he loved as a child; it seemed 'the only nice, dry cosy place in the world'. Nothing changed there among the stuffed Indians and Eskimos; except *you*. You changed every time you went in. The thought that his little sister must also feel that whenever she went in depresses him; so he tries to help some kids on a see-saw, but they don't want him around. When he reaches the museum he won't go in. This is a beautiful little parable, and part of my point is that nobody will miss it. Another is the climactic scene when Holden is waiting for his sister to come out of school. Full of rage at the '—— yous' written on the school walls, he goes into the Egyptian Room of the museum and explains to a couple of scared children why the mummies don't rot. Of course, he likes mummies; though the kids, naturally, don't. But even in there, in the congenial atmosphere of undecaying death, somebody has written '—— you' on the wall. There is nowhere free from crumbiness and sex. As Phoebe rides the carousel, he retreats into his catcher fantasy, and then into illness.

This is only a hint of the complexity of Mr Salinger's 'highbrow' plotting. There is much more; consider the perfectly 'placed' discussion between the boy and his sister in which he tells her about the phoneys at school. She complains that he doesn't like *anything*, and challenges him to mention something he does. After a struggle, he speaks of two casually encountered nuns, a boy who threw himself out of a window, and his dead brother. He daren't grow up, for fear of turning into a phoney; but behind him Eden is shut for ever.

Why, then, with all this to admire, do I find something phoney in the book itself? Not because there is 'faking', as Mr Forster calls it. It isn't necessary that 'faking' should lead one directly to some prefabricated attitude, and this does happen in *The Catcher*. The mixed-up kid totters on the brink of a society which is corrupt in a conventional way; its evils are fashionably known to be such, and don't have to be proved, made valid in the book. Similarly, the adult view of adolescence, insinuated by skilful faking, is agreeable to a predictable public taste. Again we like to look at the book and see the Libido having a bad time while the Death Wish does well, as in the museum scenes; but I don't feel that this situation occurs in the book as it were by natural growth, any more than sub-threshold advertising grows on film. *The Catcher* has a built-in death wish; it is what the consumer needs, just as he might ask that toothpaste taste good *and* contain a smart prophylactic against pyorrhoea. The predictable consumer-reaction is a double one: how good! and how clever! The boy's attitudes to religion, authority, art, sex, and so on are what smart people would like other people to have, but cannot have themselves because of their superior understanding. They hold together in a single thought purity and mess, and feel good. The author's success springs from his having, with perfect understanding, supplied their demand for this kind of satisfaction.

It is this *rapport* between author and public, or high-class rabblement, that would have astonished Joyce. Its presence in *The Catcher* may be roughly established by comparison with Keith Waterhouse's *There is a Happy Land*, obviously in-fluenced by Salinger. It is in some ways a more genuine book; the growth of a positive evil out of the sordid innocence of a proletarian childhood is worked out in a way that prevents anybody feeling superior about it. But it isn't a 'key' book, because it is not designed for the smart-common reader. These may seem hard sayings, when *The Catcher* has given me so much pleasure. But I speak as a consumer myself, asking why the book, a few years on, seems so much less impressive. The answer seems to be that new needs are readily engendered in us, and readily supplied. Books will not last us any longer than motor-cars. Of the rabblement from which we came, we retain one characteristic, its fickleness. What pleases us will not keep, of its very nature. Joyce was right not to seek his readers in the walks of the *bestia trionfante*, Forster to stand by his aristo-cracy. Mr Salinger is not like them. Since few men will write for nobody, this fine artist writes for the sharp-common reader.

(1958)

One *Hand Clapping*

It seems impossible to review Salinger without reviewing his audience at the same time. There are other accomplished rhetoricians in the field, but no 'serious' modern novelist has quite this rapport with a large public. The two stories *Franny* and *Zooey* are seven and five years old; they appeared accessibly in the *New Yorker*, and have been widely discussed. But when they appear as *Franny and Zooey*[2] in hard covers there is a marked excitement on both sides of the Atlantic. It doesn't seem to matter that these stories are merely samples, or – to quote the author – 'early, critical entries in a narrative series I'm doing about a family of settlers in 20th-century New York, the Glasses'. It doesn't matter that other fragments of the big unrealized novel are already in print, nor that if the Glass saga ever gets written it may not contain these bits in their present form. Does it matter that *Zooey*, the longer and more ambitious of the stories, is an almost total disaster? It should, for the audience is deeply involved in it.

Salinger, if we may for a moment peer through the novelist to the *guru* underneath, is against all forms of wanting and hankering; he condemns the sort of religion that is eternity-acquisitive, and the sort of humanity that is culture-acquisitive, desiring to know, for the prestige of knowing, about Homer and Blake and Zen. And Salinger. For the really queer thing about this writer is that he very carefully writes for an audience he deplores, an audience that disposes of a certain amount of smart cultural information and reacts correctly to fairly complex literary stimuli : an audience that is familiar with Creative Writing, and has a strong stiffening of people who have turned in pretty good papers on Flaubert or Faulkner. Or Salinger. Now this audience is, under one aspect, precisely what makes the world so dreadful for Salinger's Wise Children, so they have nervous breakdowns from contact with it. But under another, it is what you have to have if you play the piano or write books or act. It doesn't know, as the Wise Children do, the difference between wisdom and knowledge; you may be acting perfectly, as a saint prays, but there will still be 'unskilled laughter coming from the fifth row'. And yet even if you're 'God's actress' you can't get along without an audience. So what you do is to work through a whimsical sorites and come out calling the audience Christ, even the lout in the fifth row. Salinger can thus exercise his art with reverence, while still despising the 'culture' which makes it possible.

2. London, Heinemann, 1962.

I do not mean to make this sound repulsive, but the truth is that the position could not be maintained if the audience were either stupid or holy: it has to be smart, and the novelist counts heavily on that. The art which has so much to say against culture-acquisitiveness really depends on it, and a lot of Salingerian legerdemain is devoted to concealing this fact. The epigraph of *For Esme with Love and Squalor* is a Zen koan: 'We know the sound of two hands clapping. But what is the sound of one hand clapping?' A brutal, occidental answer might be: Salinger without a culture-acquisitive audience. The mythical Fat Lady – the Glasses invent her as an excuse for giving good performances to stupid audiences, but really despise her ('very thick legs, very veiny.... She had cancer, *too*') – has to provide the other hand.

The Irish-Jewish Glass family consists of nice ex-vaudeville parents and seven fantastic children, two of whom, as in 'We Are Seven', are dead. These children all appeared at one time or another on a radio-show called 'It's a Wise Child' – based on the Quiz Kids of history. They all know a lot, especially about the importance of unknowing, and when they grow up they are still in this respect entitled to be called Wise Children (another reason, sympathetically suggested by Leslie Fiedler in his superb *Partisan Review* notice of this book, is that Salinger really thinks they're a lot of little bastards. This is a good example of the way Salinger attracts benevolent interpretations). Wisdom, Yeats remarked, is a property of the dead, a something incompatible with life; and the Glasses find it so. Seymour, the venerated eldest brother, committed suicide in the ravishingly written story, 'A Perfect Day for Bananafish'. Another brother is dead, another a Jesuit; a sister is married, and Buddy, the next best counsellor to Seymour, inaccessible. That leaves Franny and Zooey, with Franny in a religious crisis.

Franny has her breaking down at lunch with an oafishly cultured Ivy League date, and it is irreproachably written. *Zooey* shows her back home in the big New York apartment, an amusingly furnished womb, a cosy place for a breakdown. Mother Bessie is in attendance, and there are 'hot and cold running ghosts', especially Seymour, whose private telephone is still listed, and whose room is unchanged. But housepainters stand outside the door waiting for Franny to move out; and Zooey, in his anxiety, can only talk the author's customary desperate whimsy.

Franny's crisis is big and worrying, but pretty typical, one feels, of the Glass children; it has to do with the phoneyness of the world they grow up into, full of boyfriends discussing football, Flaubert, life. She has become obsessed with 'the Jesus prayer' – a formula by which you pray incessantly. This seems wise, but it drives her to the edge of breakdown. She wants to talk to Seymour, but Seymour is dead (Holden Caulfield had similar trouble). Buddy is away. Bessie, her mother, offers homely advice and chicken soup. It is up to Zooey to save her from the psychiatrists who might make her want to live in the world she now rejects; sweating with love, he does so, Franny accepts his advice. It is sort of religious, and also involves acting in the world as it is. The religion Salinger has to sell to his culture-acquisitive audience; the need for action he has to sell to himself. This explains the method of the book.

Signs that there *is* a method are characteristically minimized; there is a lot of carefully planned improvization. Essential information about the book is wrapped round it in a blurb or given with an air of inevitable clumsiness in a footnote (footnotes are called an 'aesthetic evil'). Buddy Glass, the narrator, takes a deal of space to explain why the book is so randomly shaped. Zooey, we hear, dislikes his brother's handling of the narrative, and, according to Buddy, further complains

> that the plot hinges on mysticism ... which ... can only expedite, move up, the day and hour of my professional undoing. People are already shaking their heads over me, and any immediate further professional use of the word 'God', except as a familiar, healthy American expletive, will be taken ... as the worst kind of name-dropping and a sure sign that I'm going straight to the dogs.

In case we don't find this sufficiently disarming, we are encouraged to believe that Zooey, in voicing these forbidden thoughts, is merely providing another example of the off-beat loving which goes on in the Glass family. The fact that it is Zooey who is voicing them is meant to prevent us from doing so. The same sort of endearing duplicity is involved in Buddy's apology for the endless talking that goes on in the book: that's the way it *was*, you can't change the Glasses. Buddy also has tricks that allow him to speak frankly of Zooey's incredible beauty, or rather the 'authentic *esprit*' of his face: a bit embarrassing, but that's the way it is. He is even capable of a parenthesis stating that 'all this data is, I think, to some degree relevant'.

The author knows the public knows he isn't clumsy; but just in case anybody thinks he's really slipped into awkward simplicity there is the television script Zooey is reading, a piece that 'stinks of courage and integrity'. 'It's down-to-earth, it's simple, it's untrue.' This is to prevent anybody using such words of Zooey; yet, all this legerdemain apart, they apply. So let us use such words; when the fog of technique and comparative religion clears away, Zooey is simple (it says, with Carlyle, 'Do the work that lies nearest to thee') and untrue.

It should in justice be said that he succeeds in all sorts of ways: with Bessie Glass, in the protracted, funny, yet economical bathroom scene that takes up half the book; with Zooey's droll, teasing ways. But not with Bessie as the priestess of the Fat Lady's altar, not with Zooey as the book of the dead. Buddy's enormous, apparently amorphous letter, which Zooey reads through as a preparation, saved Zooey years before, and provides the pattern for the saving of Franny: neat, and in some Salingerian sense, true. But the treasured wisdom of Seymour about 'unlearning the differences, the illusory differences, between boys and girls, animals and stones, day and night' had to be mediated to Buddy by a little girl in a supermarket who says her boyfriends are called Bobby and Dorothy; a similar angel passes before Zooey's eyes as he works on Franny. The missions of these girls (and of the one in 'Bananafish') may be to play tiny Iphigenia to adolescent Orestes – as Fiedler observes; but their message is death or nirvana, and for Buddy and Zooey to interpret it as a call to action in 'this goddam phenomenal world' seems false both to Salinger and the audience.

This is really the crux. Franny has got this Jesus prayer wrong: Zooey has to straighten her out. First he tries to show her she's wrong about Jesus, who was extremely tough and intelligent, a cobra not a bunny, as she seems to think. This fails; when he succeeds (under terrific emotional pressure) he does it by using Seymour's telephone; first pretending to be Buddy then not quite pretending (even Salinger couldn't quite try that) to be Seymour. What he says on the phone will keep the explicators happy for ages, since it turns on a pun: Zooey is an actor; Franny could be. Von Hügel called prayer an 'ever-increasing predominance of Action over activity', and Zooey has a similar notion in mind, perhaps (not that I understand Von Hügel's remark). Franny is well-informed on religion, and he doesn't have to spell it out. She must *act*. It seems that acting is Franny's karma; she must be God's actress, and that will be her Jesus prayer. If it seems strange to be saying a Jesus prayer to a lot of louts in a theatre, she is to remember that they're all Christ. Franny, restored, happy, and self-controlled, drops into a calm sleep.

It is to make us accept this conclusion that Salinger has worked so deviously. And, as one of his admiring audience, I find it hard to believe he could be selling anything so simple and untrue. The wise child would certainly have discounted this effort of Zooey's as a last desperate attempt to save her from the professional headshrinker. Salinger has at last over-estimated his rhetorical control over us. When Bessie's chicken soup turns out to be eucharistic, like the colonel's hash in Mary McCarthy's diatribe against Creative Writing courses, we feel let down. When Zooey's exhausting effort to save Franny's life and wisdom comes down to a trouper's advice to go out there and wow them, we know that Salinger's exhausting effort to satisfy us and himself has failed. He cannot, for all his skill, make it appear that a good performance as Pegeen Mike in *The Playboy* is an adequate substitute for being dead.

The author of *Zooey*, a work designed with extraordinary care and even a kind of passion, is certainly a master of sorts. Perhaps he's grown too fond of Seymour, perhaps he's been over-subtle about his audience. For whatever reason, he has slipped badly, and *Zooey* doesn't work. The Fat Lady, obstinately unholy, doesn't move a muscle; the artist's single hand silently beats the air.

(1962)

The Glass Menagerie

In this book[3] a couple of koans, first exhibited in the *New Yorker* in 1955 and 1959, are trapped between hard covers. The first takes the form of an anecdote about Seymour's wedding day, the second is a discursive study of Seymour's sanctity – a summary which will serve only if you underline the word

3. *Raise High the Roof Beam, Carpenters* and *Seymour: An Introduction*. London, Heinemann, 1963.

'discursive' with almost hysterical profuseness. The whole thing is dedicated to the amateur reader, to show that the author is sick of being read by people who may seem clever but are so ignorant of Zen that if they took up archery they would assume their job was to aim at the target. The second story contains several careful allusions to the peculiar and terrible relationship obtaining between this author and his readers. It is admitted that Seymour personally laid it down that the amenities of exposition ought to be respected, but argued that in this case they can't be, because of immediate needs of Buddy, the narrator. These cause certain essential modifications which unskilled readers may treat as marks of authorial self-indulgence, or as signs that Buddy is cleverly pushing St Seymour out of the limelight. Buddy suggests early on that awkward customers should cut their losses and leave right away.

'I'm told,' says Buddy, 'that I have many surface charms as a writer.' We may have been over that before, but certainly a gesture of compliment is in order for 'Raise High', a funny-sad piece with something of the period atmosphere of 'For Esmé'. Seymour fails to turn up for his wedding, abandoning Muriel, chosen for her dullness or because she was like old Charlotte, a childhood sweetheart whom Seymour once hit with a brick because he loved her. Buddy has to entertain hot and angry friends of the bride. There are cunning dips into the vast lake of Glassiana which lies beneath the Salinger surface. If I dare to say what I dislike about the story I shall give myself away at once as fatally un-hip to Seymour. For I am not moved by his soothing the 10-month-old Franny by reading her a Taoist tale, and in fact am no longer surprised that she turned out badly and fell for Zooey's bogus Zen trickery in the last book. When Seymour's journal erupts on to the page I expect and get something more than tiresome, such as the bit about his being so holy and sensitive that if he touches a thing he loves for too long – Zooey's hair or Charlotte's dress – he develops stigmata on his hands. When Buddy tells the truth about Charlotte's scars he chooses as sole audience a sympathetic funny old deaf-mute – pure Seymour this, like Zooey's bogus telephone call, and characteristic of that chic Western Zen which, Buddy assures us, the real thing will survive.

All the same, you could put this story in a book with good Salinger–Glass, such as 'A Perfect Day for Bananafish', without doing much harm. 'Seymour' is, on the other hand, close enough to mere rubbish for someone who enjoys exaggeration to call it that. Here art destroys art, or rather disorder goes through an elaborate and skilful process and comes out as disorder. Seymour is the key to Glass, and it is presumably important for us to see him plain. He is presented as a sort of American Prince Myshkin, a saintly fool whom Buddy will, in an interminable monologue, describe and expound. Because of Buddy's 'extremely pressing personal needs' the monologue eschews orderly narrative, using anecdote for purely panegyric purposes and dwelling, with a calculated air of fortuity, on the situation of Buddy himself as he writes.

Still, we do add to our knowledge of Seymour; and if you already have a fairly deep impression of his beauty, his intellect and his charity, this new onslaught of his identity may make you want, like Keats in a similar situation, to leave the room. Seymour is, frankly, 'the artist and Sick Man'. Starting life as a Wise Child on the radio, he grows up into a Seer, 'the heavenly fool ... dazzled to death by his own scruples, the blinding shapes and colours of his own sacred human conscience'. He is a top American poet; Salinger gets round the obvious creative-writing problem this creates (for poets must be harder to do than saints) by merely paraphrasing a couple of poems and describing their form: double haiku, 34 syllables, basically iambic. The poems aren't autobiographical, or don't, at any rate, refer to Seymour's most recent incarnation, but they are related to his vaudeville ancestry – 'highly literate vaudeville', a kind of Zennish balancing act. When Seymour's athletic skills are discussed it is once more the oriental aspect that is stressed, as when he wins at marbles by not aiming. His face, and his love for Buddy, are very fully described. It is part of Salinger's own technique of indirection to blur the line that divides the personality of Seymour from that of Buddy (and, incidentally, the line between Buddy and Salinger). Buddy is also something of a happy fool, as well as being very clever and inclined to treat the reader as the Fat Lady. He dwells on his resemblance to his brother and then blames himself for doing so, attributing the error to his egotism, the one thing he has that Seymour lacked.

Having found 'Seymour' very tedious at first reading I ought to add that I had a second try and found it somewhat less insufferable. If you read the book as primarily about a crisis of

Buddy's, parallel to that of Franny in the last book, and resolved in much the same way (Buddy goes off with joy to face
his audience of college girls), you might be able to stand the
rich flavour of Seymour, or even convince yourself that Seymour isn't a straight character at all because Salinger is working with irony. But in the end I don't think this will hold up.
The ironies do nothing to dispel the incense cloud round Seymour. There is a genuine sense of the sheer difficulty Buddy has
in getting what he has to say past large psychological blocks,
but the disorder that results tells us nothing about Seymour and
nothing interesting about Buddy. In short, 'Seymour' is a bigger
frost than 'Zooey'. The question as to why Salinger should devote his skill to tying himself up into knots is still intriguing,
but such topics have small staying power, and it may shortly
be superseded by the question as to what possessed so many
people to take him so seriously.

(1963)

FIFTEEN

WILLIAM GOLDING

The critical reception of Mr Golding's fourth novel, *Free Fall* (1959) was on the whole hostile; that of its predecessor (*Pincher Martin*, 1956) uncomprehending. Not since his first, *Lord of the Flies* (1954) has he enjoyed general acclaim; yet the opinion that he is the most important practising novelist in English has, over this period of five or six years, become almost commonplace. One reason for this apparent paradox is that Golding's books do not (if only because each is extremely original in construction) yield themselves at one reading: *The Inheritors* (1955) and *Pincher Martin* have been better understood with the passing of time, and the same will be true of *Free Fall*. This suggests that Golding is a difficult writer; and it would not be strange if this were true. We have become accustomed, for intelligible historical reasons, to the idea that significant works of art are necessarily obscure.

It is, however, true only in a limited sense. We may note at once that despite the roar of baffled critics Mr Golding's intentions are always simple. Of *Pincher Martin* he says 'I fell over backwards in making that novel explicit. I said to myself, "Now here is going to be a novel, it's going to be a blow on behalf of the ordinary universe, which I think on the whole likely to be the right one, and I'm going to write it so vividly and accurately and with such an exact programme that nobody can possibly mistake exactly what I mean." '[1] But he goes on to admit that his handling of the story was 'unspecific'; he did not actually *tell* the reader that Martin drowns on page 2; the evidence that he did so is oblique, and is completed only by the last sentence of the book. Golding is unlike many modern writers in his willingness to state the 'programme' of his book (and also in denying the reader much liberty of interpretation); but he does not pretend that what seems to him simple must be so explicitly and directly set down that the reader will not have to work. In short, his simplicity is a quality best under-

1. This, and several other remarks attributed to Mr Golding in this article, are derived from a transcript of a B.B.C. discussion programme.

stood as intellectual economy. His theme takes the simplest available way to full embodiment. But embodiment is not explanation; and all that can be guaranteed the reader is that there is no *unnecessary* difficulty, nothing to make the business of explaining and understanding more difficult than, in the nature of the case, it has to be.

The best course for sympathetic critics is to be a shade more explicit, to do what the novelist himself perhaps cannot do without injury to the books, which grow according to imaginative laws, and cannot be adjusted to the extravagant needs of readers. If critics have any reason for existence, this is it : to give assurances of value, and to provide somehow – perhaps anyhow – the means by which readers may be put in possession of the valuable book.

It is worth notice that Golding is to a marked degree isolated from intellectual fashion : 'I think that my novels have very little genesis outside myself. That to a large extent I've cut myself off from contemporary literary life, and gained in one sense by it, though I may have lost in another.' He is more interested in Greek than in modern literature. Thus there are in his books preoccupations one would not expect in a highbrow modern novelist – that Ballantyne was wrong about the behaviour of English boys on a desert island, or H. G. Wells about the virtue of Neanderthal men, are not opinions many would care to dispute, but few would find in them points of departure for passionate and involved fictions. In the same way Mr Golding, though he is in some degree an allegorical writer, is entirely free of Kafka's influence, which makes him very unlike Rex Warner, with whom he is sometimes implausibly compared. His technical equipment is as sophisticated as Conrad's; yet like Conrad he begins each new book as if it were his first, as if the germination of the new theme entailed the creation of its own incomparable form. (There are, however, some habitual devices – the sudden shift of viewpoint at the end of the first three novels, for instance.) Perhaps the resemblance to Conrad could be developed : an isolated indeed exiled sensibility, a preoccupation with guilt, desperate technical resource. Sometimes this last power re-invests what others have done before, old devices labelled in text-books : stream of consciousness, changing point of view, time-shifts. There was a time, according to the author himself, when he wrote novels intended to meet the requirements of the public, as far as he could guess them; but these novels failed, were never even published. Then, with *Lord of the Flies*, he saw that it was himself he had to satisfy; he planned it in very great detail, and wrote it as if tracing over words already on the page. How, in pleasing his own isolated taste, and doing it in these essentially unmodish and rather private ways, has he come to represent to so many the best in modern English writing?

The answer to this is necessarily involved, though the situation is in itself simple enough. One thinks of Mr Golding's world: he sees it swinging through its space, its wet or rocky surfaces lifting under the pull of the moon; its inhabitants, locked on to it by gravity, walking upright, containing floating brains, peristaltic entrails, secreting seed at the base of the spine, somehow free and somehow guilty. Golding once called himself 'a propagandist for Neanderthal man'; his way of looking at the world has something of the candour of Lascaux. In *The Inheritors* Neanderthal man is superseded by *homo sapiens*, who has a better brain, and weapons; but it is the innocence of the doomed predecessor that we see enacted, for, until the last pages, we see the activities of the new man, intelligent and so capable of evil, through the bewildered eyes of the old. And Golding, though he admits that we belong with the new man, supposes that we could not recapture that innocence, that natural awe for Oa, the mother-goddess, had not something of it survived in us.

I am groping for an answer to the question, how such a writer can strike us as profoundly attuned to contemporary sensibility? It seems to be that in his own way, and short-circuiting a great deal of fashionable and sophisticated mythologizing, Golding gives remarkably full expression to a profound modern need, the need for reassurance in terms of the primitive; the longing to know somehow of a possible humanity that lived equably in the whole world; the need for myths of total and satisfactory explanation. Our developed consciousness, our accumulated knowledge are marks of guilt; the fragmentary nature of our experience is the theme of our artists. To discover again the undifferentiated myth is to return to Eden or to Neanderthal man – or indeed to the primary germ-cell the splitting of which is the beginning of guilt: that is to find innocence and wisdom.

Golding has been called a writer of 'fables'; 'what I would regard as a tremendous compliment to myself,' he says, 'would be if someone would substitute the word "myth" for "fable" ... I do feel fable as being an invented thing on the surface whereas myth is something which comes out from the roots of things in the ancient sense of being the key to existence, the whole meaning of life, and experience as a whole.' And he accepts the description, 'myths of total explanation', for his works. The genesis of these myths is naturally obscure. They do not much resemble the myths of Joyce or those of Mr Eliot or Mr David Jones; yet they are related to the same Symbolist aspirations towards prelogical primitive images which animate all these authors. The differences are attributable to Mr Golding's relative isolation from any mainstream of speculation. To put it too simply : he sees a world enormously altered by new knowledge. He understands the strong reaction against this new knowledge which is characteristic of modern art, an art in love with the primitive; also the patterns of human behaviour are now very generally explained by reference to psychic residua or infantile guilt. It is a world you can blame 'science' for if you like, a world in which the myth of progress has failed; but the rival myth of necessary evil and universal guilt has come back without bringing God with it. He looks at this world understanding what it contains, as the painters at Lascaux understood theirs. He thinks of the books of his childhood – *Coral Island*, Wells's *Outline of History* – and observes that they are wrong about the world, because they thought cannibals more wicked than white men and Neanderthal man less worthy than his conqueror. These books have, in his own figure, rotted to compost in his mind; and in that compost the new myth puts down roots. When it grows it explains the ancient situation to which our anxieties recall us : loss of innocence, the guilt and ignominy of consciousness, the need for pardon. Mr Golding owns that he is a religious man. He believes that some people are saints : in *Lord of the Flies* Simon is a saint, and this is why, he says, literary people have found Simon incomprehensible; 'but he *is* comprehensible to the illiterate person ... The illiterate person believes in saints and sanctity.' (This is not the first time a modern artist has found his allies among the illiterate – Yeats and Eliot have made similar declarations.) Golding believes in human guilt and the human sense of paradise lost; he also believes in divine mercy.

The evidence for holiness lies scattered among the fragments of our world, and those fragments are represented in Golding's books; they form part of the whole. But this whole is a world of imagination, where everything is related, everything counts and truth is accessible; the world of myth. For Golding's own term is the right one; out of the single small seed grows this instrument 'for controlling ... ordering ... giving a shape and significance to the immense paradox of futility and anarchy which is contemporary history'. These are Mr Eliot's words on Joyce's myth; but they will serve for Golding. Art, says Cassirer, requires a step back into mythical thinking; perhaps this has always been so since mythical thinking became obsolete, but never has the step back been more consciously taken than in our times. And in the contrast between our consciousness of this, and the momentary forgetfulness of our Darwinian grandfathers, Golding found the theme of his first novel.

Lord of the Flies has 'a pretty big connexion' with Ballantyne. In The Coral Island Ralph, Jack, and Peterkin are cast away on a desert island, where they live active, civilized, and civilizing lives. Practical difficulties are easily surmounted; they light fires with bowstrings and spyglasses, hunt pigs for food, and kill them with much ease and a total absence of guilt — indeed of bloodshed. They are all Britons — a term they use to compliment each other — all brave, obedient, and honourable. There is much useful information conveyed concerning tropical islands, including field-workers' reporting of the conduct of cannibals : but anthropology is something nasty that clears up on the arrival of a missionary, and Jack himself prevents an act of cannibalism by telling the flatnoses not to be such blockheads and presenting them with six newly slaughtered pigs. The parallel between the island and the Earthly Paradise causes a trace of literary sophistication : 'Meat and drink on the same tree! My dear boys, we're set up for life; it must be the ancient paradise — hurrah! ... We afterwards found, however, that these lovely islands were very unlike Paradise in many things.' But these 'things' are non-Christian natives and, later, pirates; the boys themselves are cleanly (cold baths recommended) and godly — regenerate, empire-building boys, who know by instinct how to turn paradise into a British protectorate.

The Coral Island (1858) could be used as a document in the history of ideas; it belongs inseparably to the period when boys were sent out of Arnoldian schools certified free of Original

Sin. Golding takes Ralph, Jack, and Peterkin (altering this name to Simon, 'called Peter') and studies them against an altered moral landscape. He is a schoolmaster, and knows boys well enough to make their collapse into savagery plausible, to see *them* as the cannibals; the authority of the grown-ups is all there is to prevent savagery. If you dropped these boys into an Earthly Paradise 'they would not behave like God-fearing English gentlemen' but 'as like as not ... find savages who were kindly and uncomplicated ... The devil would rise out of the intellectual complications of the three white men.' Golding leaves the noble savages out of *Lord of the Flies* but this remark is worth quoting because it states the intellectual position in its basic simplicity. It is the civilized who are corrupt, out of phase with natural rhythm. Their guilt is the price of evolutionary success; and our awareness of this fact can be understood by duplicating Ballantyne's situation, borrowing his island, and letting his theme develop in this new and more substantial context. Once more every prospect pleases; but the vileness proceeds, not from cannibals, but from the boys, though Man is not so much vile as 'heroic and sick'. Unlike Ballantyne's boys, these are dirty and inefficient; they have some notion of order, symbolized by the beautiful conch which heralds formal meetings; but when uncongenial effort is required to maintain it, order disappears. The shelters are inadequate, the signal fire goes out at the very moment when Jack first succeeds in killing a pig. Intelligence fades; irrational tabus and blood-rituals make hopeless the task of the practical but partial intellect of Piggy; his glasses, the firemakers, are smashed and stolen, and in the end he himself is broken to pieces as he holds the conch. When civilized conditioning fades – how tedious Piggy's appeal to what adults might do or think! – the children are capable of neither savage nor civil gentleness. Always a little nearer to raw humanity than adults, they slip into a condition of animality depraved by mind, into the cruelty of hunters with their devil-liturgies and torture: they make an unnecessary, evil fortress, they steal, they abandon all operations aimed at restoring them to civility. Evil is the natural product of their consciousness. First the smallest boys create a beastie, a snake – 'as if it wasn't a good island'. Then a beast is created in good earnest, and defined in a wonderful narrative sequence. The emblem of this evil society is the head of a dead pig, fixed as a sacrifice on the end of a stick and animated by flies and by the imagination of the *voyant*, Simon.

Simon is Golding's first 'saint, and a most important figure'. He is 'for the illiterate a proof of the existence of God' because the illiterate (to whom we are tacitly but unmistakably expected to attribute a correct insight here) will say, 'Well, a person like this cannot exist without a good God.' For Simon 'voluntarily embraces the beast . . . and tries to get rid of him'. What he understands – and this is wisdom Golding treats with awe – is that evil is 'only us'. He climbs up to where the dead fire is dominated by the beast, a dead airman in a parachute, discovers what this terrible thing really is, and rushes off with the good news to the beach, where the maddened boys at their beast-slaying ritual mistake Simon himself for the beast and kill him. As Piggy, the dull practical intelligence, is reduced to blindness and futility, so Simon, the visionary, is murdered before he can communicate his comfortable knowledge. Finally, the whole Paradise is destroyed under the puzzled eyes of an adult observer. Boys will be boys.

The difference of this world from Ballantyne's simpler construction from similar materials is not merely a matter of incomparability of the two talents at work; our minds have, in general, darker needs and obscurer comforts. It would be absurd to suppose that the change has impoverished us; but it has seemed to divide our world into 'two cultures' – the followers of Jack and the admirers of Simon, those who build fortresses and those who want to name the beast.

Lord of the Flies was 'worked out carefully in every possible way', and its author holds that the 'programme' of the book *is* its meaning. He rejects Lawrence's doctrine, 'Never trust the artist, trust the tale' and its consequence, 'the proper function of the critic is to save the tale from the artist'. He is wrong, I think; in so far as the book differs from its programme there is, as a matter of common sense, material over which the writer has no absolute authority. This means not only that there are possible readings which he cannot veto, but even that some of his own views on the book may be in a sense wrong. The interpretation of the dead parachutist is an example. This began in the 'programme' as straight allegory; Golding says that this dead man 'is' History. 'All that we can give our children' in their trouble is this monstrous dead adult, who's 'dead, but won't lie down'; an ugly emblem of war and decay that broods over the paradise and provides the only objective equivalent for the beast the boys imagine. Now this limited allegory (I may even have expanded it in the telling) seems to me not to have got out of the 'programme' into the book; what does get in is more valuable because more like myth – capable, that is, of more various interpretation than the rigidity of Golding's scheme allows. And in writing of this kind all depends upon the author's mythopoeic power to transcend the 'programme'. Golding has this poetic power, and nowhere is it more impressively used than in his second book, *The Inheritors*.

Prefixed to *The Inheritors* is a passage from Wells's *Outline of History*, and this serves the same purpose as Ballantyne's novel in the genesis of the earlier book; it sets off an antithetical argument. 'Well's *Outline* played a great part in my life because my father was a rationalist, and the *Outline* was something he took neat. It is the rationalist gospel *in excelsis*. . . . By and by it seemed to me not to be large enough . . . too neat and too slick. And when I re-read it as an adult I came across his picture of Neanderthal man, our immediate predecessors, as being these gross, brutal creatures who were possibly the basis of the mythological bad man . . . I thought to myself that this is just absurd . . .' The difference between Golding and the Wells of the *Outline* is simple; to Wells the success of the high-fore-headed, weapon-bearing, carnivorous *homo sapiens* was progress, but to Golding it was the defeat of innocence, the sin of Adam in terms of a new kind of history.

Golding's real power, the true nature of his mythopoeic obsession, became evident only with the publication of this second book. This root-idea is, as I have suggested, a variant of the Fall, transplanted from theology. Golding is fascinated by the evidence – in the nature of the case ubiquitous – that human consciousness is a biological asset purchased at a price; the price is the knowledge of evil. This evil emanates from the human mind, a product of its action upon the environment. *The Inheritors* is about the accumulation of guilt that necessarily attended the historical success of *homo sapiens*; the intellectual superiority of Man over his simian victims is precisely measured by the cruelty and guilt which dominate his life and are relatively absent from his predecessor's. The creatures to be exterminated are almost innocent, as near it as we can imagine; they practise no deceit, have an obscure sense of life as a mystery, understand wickedness as killing, but their lives are controlled by the seasons, by inhibiting fears of water, above all by a physiological equipment excellent in its way but prohibiting intellect. They know the world with senses like an animal's; they depend much upon involuntary reflexes – keen scent, night vision, acuteness of ear; they are not men at all, and that is why they are innocent. Only after prolonged observations of the new men can Lok associate sex with cruelty, derange his senses with alcohol, offer violence to a friend, or even think of one thing or process as 'like' another. Not to know evil is, in a sense, to know nothing. The new men sail away, successful and guilty, leaving Lok with the doll-goddess which is his only image of the intelligent and creative mind. Clutching this toy, he who had known useful fear is now the prey of useless terror as well as of his animal enemies; they, the real creators, plan a bloody and intelligent future.

Technically *The Inheritors* attempts a little less than *Pincher Martin*, but has fewer flaws. The natural setting, of obvious importance, needed to be wonderfully done and is. Above all, the feat of recording observations of the activities of *homo sapiens* made with the sensory equipment of Lok is of astonishing virtuosity. We are constantly reminded of the involuntary powers that sustain him; his ears speak to him even if he will not listen, small areas of skin react with useful knowledge, the nose marvellously distinguishes and identifies. We can always see, too, that the extinction of this animal is *neccessary*, as in the passage where he observes a new man aiming at him with a bow and can no more conceive of what the man is doing than he can impute enmity to so similar a being or explain his tall face – his senses simply report a series of inexplicable events. In the heart of the book there is a remarkable passage of some fifty pages in which Lok and the female Fa observe the communal activities of the new people from a vantage-point in a tree. This is carried out with a fierce imaginative power that is not in the least inconsistent with a very minute attention to the complicated effect to be communicated. What we have to be shown is that although we are experiencing these events innocently, by way of the passive, vegetarian, inhuman senses of Lok, we *belong* down below in the clearing, corrupt and intelligent. And at the end we abruptly leave Lok; suddenly, with a loss of sympathy, observe him with our normal sight, joining the new men, our own sort. With these anxious and responsible technicians we sail away, with only a last glimpse

of superseded innocence stumbling about on the shore of a
dead world. *The Inheritors* does not, like *Lord of the Flies*,
qualify as a spanking good tale, and with its publication Golding met for the first time that uncomprehending reception with
which he is now so familiar. The book was written, presumably at white-heat, in a few weeks. It has not been surpassed.

Pincher Martin is, however, a bigger book. It is another
imaginative 'forcing' of the same seminal idea, but more
densely written, with much interweaving of image and reference – more like a poem, in fact, for undoubtedly this kind of
novel 'aspires' to the condition of poetry. It takes more reading
than the others; it lacks the adventitious accessibility of *Lord
of the Flies* and is less recognizably a story than *The Inheritors*.
For all that, its wisp of narrative is handled with great skill,
and after all the full import of the book depends upon a most
ingenious narrative device. The talent remains clearly that
which produced the earlier books, and some of the procedures,
particularly those involving the extraction of significance from
symbolic objects, are easy to recognize. And there is a continuity of theme. But it is, all the same, a book demanding
unremitting attention.

Golding has himself provided 'a mental lifeline' to readers
who find the book difficult; it appeared in *Radio Times* and it
might be useful to copy part of what he said.

> Christopher Hadley Martin had no belief in anything but the
> importance of his own life, no God. Because he was created
> in the image of God he had a freedom of choice which he
> used to centre the world on himself. He did not believe in
> purgatory and therefore when he died it was not presented
> to him in overtly theological terms. The greed for life which
> had been the mainspring of his nature forced him to refuse
> the selfless act of dying. He continued to exist separately in a
> world composed of his own murderous nature. His drowned
> body lies rolling in the Atlantic but the ravenous ego invents
> a rock for him to endure on. It is the memory of an aching
> tooth. Ostensibly and rationally he is a survivor from a tor-
> pedoed destroyer : but deep down he knows the truth. He is
> not fighting for bodily survival but for his continuing iden-
> tity in face of what will smash it and sweep it away – the
> black lightning, the compassion of God. For Christopher, the
> Christ-bearer, has become Pincher Martin who is little but

greed. Just to be Pincher is purgatory; to be Pincher for eternity is hell.

The man is called Martin so that his worldly name may be Pincher (a naval nickname for all Martins) and nobody calls him 'Christopher' until God does so at the end, out of the black lightning, as the resisting Martin shrinks to a mere pair of claws. Again the myth is worked out in fanatical detail; Martin calls his rock 'Rockall' not only because that is a real rock, but because he remembers a poor joke turning on a word which is a bad rhyme for Rockall, and which is an obscene word for 'nothing'. The geology and animal life of the rock he invents out of memories of childhood holidays. He is horribly aware of the self-deceit, the Promethean posing, the shrinking identity; he will do anything rather than accept the loss of himself, even in exchange for the mercy of God.

Martin is 'fallen man – fallen more than most'; a type of depravity. His human consciousness is an evolutionary special-ization, like a pig's snout, used to ensure handsome survival. He is hideously greedy, hence the recurrent metaphors from eat-ing. 'He takes the best part (Martin had been an actor), the best seat, the most money, the best notice, the best woman. He was born with his mouth and his flies open and both hands out to grab. He's a cosmic case of the bugger who gets his penny and someone else's bun.' But this efficiency only makes his suffering more characteristic; he declares for madness rather than ex-tinction, intellect rather than love, and makes his own most appropriate purgatory. Martin's boast is that he controls and imposes his will on the world : 'I can outwit you; you are a machine.' He is relieved to discover that the cause of appar-ently 'evil' manifestations lie entirely within himself; that his fear of the gull which makes him think of lizards originates in something he's read; that he can cure the world by curing his own disorder. There is a crucial and astonishing episode in which, with all the gestures of heroism, he undertakes to expel the poison from within him. He has eaten disgusting food, and it has made his mind sick as well as his body. 'I am in servitude to a coiled tube the length of a cricket pitch. All the terrors of hell can come down to nothing more than a stoppage. Why drag in good and evil when the serpent lies coiled in my own body?' His intelligent solution is a self-inflicted enema.

But although it is true that the evil proceeds from within

him, it will not be dispersed by intelligence. That only preserves him alive for torture, and he creates his hell with the same effort that he puts forth to preserve his identity. Of the plenitude with which this and all the related paradoxes inherent in the theme are developed I have room to say virtually nothing. But one of them requires notice, since I argue for the totality of the imaginative act. Martin's acts are willed, but also necessary; and this is beautifully translated into narrative at the point where, as officer of the watch, he gives a helm-order a moment before the torpedo strikes. The order was freely willed and murderous; it was also necessary and proper in the circumstances. All that happened was 'because of what I did', but it could not have been otherwise. Only the best in fiction has invention of this order.

This is not quite the whole story. It would seem, as a hypothesis stemming from the situation described, that another heaven might be possible, a God to whom some other question than 'If I ate them, who gave me a mouth?' might be addressed. Golding's Nathaniel, whose natural goodness Martin recognizes and resents, is there to say that only in the abandonment of the beloved self is there any way to this. Nathaniel is the second in what may be a band of Golding's elect, those who see and know. But Nathaniel is anything but a respectable saint; his religion has a seedy quality and it contributes to Martin's agony as well as shadowing it with some ecstatic alternative. It isn't a pill of doctrine but another part of the imaginative structure.

Pincher Martin is a wonderful achievement, the book of a drowned man soaked and battered by an actual sea, making substantial rock out of nightmare; it is as if one's own hands grew soft and swollen in the idiot water and bruised on the dripping stone. It is a horrible book too; because the man is shrunk so mercilessly into his minimal disgusting humanity, the fattest maggot of all; and because Golding's knowledge of human egotism and cruelty is horrible. What makes all this bearable and Golding a major novelist is the total technical control: nightmare, hysteria, every kind of beastliness and depravity are given the virtue of form. There is no distinguishing here between a compassion that might be called religious and the skill of an artist; they are the same thing. There are those who find Golding sadistic; it is a judgement that calls in question their ability to read any book whatsoever, because it betrays an insensitivity to the moral quality of form. Yeats spoke of an intellectual construct which enabled him to 'hold in a single thought reality and justice'; *Pincher Martin* is such a thought.

Of *Free Fall*, Golding's fourth and perhaps his most ambitious book, I must say that although I do not feel that I have yet got to know it well I have no expectation that it can ever possess my mind as the others have done. It should be remembered that Golding asks a lot of his critics – this is a matter, I think, of emphasis, of his not saying 'The first page and the last page are crucial.' He does not say so because it seems to him self-evident.[2] It is not in such reticences that Mr Golding fails (if he does fail); for in everything related to the shape of this myth his skill is all that it was in *Pincher Martin*. Technically *Free Fall* (which depends upon a system of 'time-shifts' devised to expose the religious significance of a man's experience) is at least as accomplished as any of the others. It is a mark of Golding's integrity that in every book he employs technical devices of remarkable ingenuity but never indulges his skill; it is never a hair's-breadth in excess of what the moral occasion demands. One's coolness towards the book has other causes.

The myth of *Free Fall* is, basically, that of all Golding's books: the Fall of Man, the expulsion from Paradise, erected wit and infected will. It is a myth which has accumulated an enormous and various theology, which does not matter until the novelist turns theologian himself. Golding's hero is examining his life (made typical life by many allegorical devices) with a view to discovering a pattern, some connection between his two worlds of experience, one deterministic, the world of empirical observation, the other a world in which the burning bush is not consumed, a world of horror and glory, heaven and hell. Sammy's conclusion (which is not the conclusion of the novel) is that 'there is no bridge'. In his brooding over different episodes in his life, Sammy Mountjoy is necessarily theologizing; in other words, there is within the book continuous comment – admittedly not directly vouched for by the author – on the myth. I do not think that this works; there is an unwonted hollowness in these passages, the shabbiness of a do-it-yourself

2. There is a perceptive study of the opening and the conclusion of *Free Fall* in an article by Ian Gregor and M. Kinkead-Weekes called 'Mr Golding and his Critics' (*Twentieth Century*, February, 1960).

theology; and the book at moments lies open to the Coleridgean charge of mental bombast – 'thoughts and images too great for the subject' – the subject being not the Fall but a *commentary* upon it. In Golding's earlier books – and this is unique in modern fiction – guilt, unconscious innocence, the taste of isolation, good and evil, are made actual, like vomit in the mouth. It is this actuality that is lacking in *Free Fall*; its absence takes the nature out of Golding's prose, it takes the plasticity out of the narrative. The crucial episode, a nightmare experience in a prison-cell, calls for, and is not provided with, the savage compassion which went into the writing of *Pincher Martin*. Yet it is in a way wonderfully composed, passionate and cunning; there is no question of a failure of power or of nerve, only – to be bold – of a flaw in the original conception.

This flaw is one to which Mr Golding's gifts render him peculiarly liable. Myths of total explanation are religious; comment upon them is theology. *Free Fall*, like *Paradise Lost*, is about *everything*; the author knows this, devises his narrative and even names his characters accordingly. Samuel Mountjoy at first misunderstands his vocation (like Samuel in the Bible) and is as a child in his slum an inhabitant of Paradise (Mountjoy). As he writes, he lives on Paradise Hill, 'thirty seconds from the shop and the local'. A central event of his life is the recognition of the beauty of a girl called Beatrice; later, by a positive act of will, he rejects the possibility of living by this vision, and subjects her to his lust. The two worlds between which his life is suspended (in a condition of 'free fall' as understood in science fiction) are represented by a religious schoolmistress and a science master called Nick. The child does not have to choose; in childhood the two worlds interlock. He chooses, as a young man, to desecrate Beatrice. The other world he finds again in a prison-camp, where he is subjected by a German officer named Halde[3] to an interrogation modelled on that of Christ in the desert. Will he reject the 'world'? Is he a son of God? He does not know enough to betray his comrades, and Halde sends him to a cell which he peoples with his own egotistical terrors; at the height of his agony he bursts out (or is let out) of the cell,

3. It has been pointed out that *Halde* means 'slope', and that this name is also allegorical, since Halde is the agent by which Sammy moves into the gravitational field of his spiritual work. Mr Golding tells me he did not think of this. It is allegorist's luck.

forgiven. He walks into the world of vision: 'The power of gravity, dimension and space, the movement of the earth and sun and unseen stars, these made what might be called music and I heard it.' Beatrice has been reduced (and this passage is as fine as anything in Golding) to an incontinent idiot in an asylum; but Sammy still finds himself called to Paradise. He cannot reconcile the two worlds but the novelist, on the last page, builds a kind of bridge between them.

That it is mythologically substantial, this bridge, I do not doubt; but I do not understand it. The novel is about delivery from the body of this death; not only about the Fall but also about regeneration. This account of it is too scanty to be fair even to my imperfect understanding of the book, but it may be enough to help me make my point: that it is not the religious but the theological element that limits the imaginative scope, and brings into the writing a kind of dry heat, a brittleness, absent before. I ought to say that Messrs Gregor and Kinkead-Weekes, in the intelligent article I have already quoted, find the theology satisfactory, and indeed orthodox. But Mr Golding is not orthodox. He has done what writers in the Romantic tradition have done before – as Mallarmé discovered Nirvana without knowing Buddhism, or as Yeats dwelt, though heretically, on the Annunciation, he has found in experience and embodied in his own myths the truths that inform all others. But to provide accounts of mystical experience is one thing – admittedly a difficult thing, if only because of the qualitative differences between St John of the Cross and a mescalin addict; to invent a mystical theology is another. The first is work for a genius, the second for a church. Not to see this is the flaw of all the Romantic and Symbolist writers who lapsed into the pseudo-theologies of occultism.

A final word on 'simplicity'. Golding's novels are simple in so far as they deal in the primordial patterns of human experience and in so far as they have skeletons of parable. On these simple bones the flesh of narrative can take extremely complex forms. This makes for difficulty, but of the most acceptable kind, the difficulty that attends the expression of what is profoundly simple. For all that I have said against *Free Fall* it is this kind of book, like the others a work of genius by a writer from whom we can hope for much more, since he is in superbly full possession of his great powers.

(1960)

William Golding's *Lord of the Flies* has sold over a million copies in the American paperback edition alone. It has, by all accounts, succeeded *The Catcher in the Rye* as the *livre de chevet* of educated American youth. I doubt if anybody is really qualified to say why this should be so : books make their way inexplicably. This one was published in 1954, and certainly it was noticed; E. M. Forster commended it and 'everybody' talked about it, but with a sense that it was caviare rather than chowder – a book to tempt an intellectual into believing he had discovered a classic at its birth, but hardly a best seller. In the years that followed Golding did much to confirm this belief, but very little towards making himself a popular novelist. *The Inheritors* is a technically uncompromising, fiercely odd, even old-fashioned book about the overthrow of Neanderthal man, very distinguished but inconceivable as a big seller; *Pincher Martin* is as difficult as it is masterly; and *Free Fall* is complex, original, and in many ways reader-repellent. Golding's fifth and latest novel,[4] coming five years after *Free Fall*, is unsurprising in one way at least : it is fire-new, written in what, despite its novelty, we can identify as a style bearing the impress of Golding's peculiar presence; but difficult, inviting only slow and submissive readers.

And yet *Lord of the Flies* has its vast readership. One can't help guessing at the reasons. For one thing, it is a comforting book; it assures us that evil is natural to men, and not something that we have recently invented. It is absolutely free of desperately 'forward' thinking – no Zen, no diagnosis of modern civilization, only of civilization. Yet it is spare and diagrammatic, and lends itself to techniques of sophisticated reading now widely taught in American colleges. Ultimately it derives from, or, as the word is, displaces, a familiar myth, that of the Earthly Paradise, which it handles ironically. And as it develops the myth with intricate passion, it alludes implicitly (as Golding, I think, could never do explicity) to Freud and to all other conceivable systematic explanations of the phenomena. One might say cautiously that the book has a kind of innocence, thinking of two things : the later novels, which are more occult; and Golding's own view, since abandoned, that there is only one true way of reading a novel, and that the author knows it best, and takes upon him the responsibility of

4. *The Spire*. London, Faber & Faber, 1965.

ensuring that a good reader can read it in that way.

This is a bad doctrine, and it does not distinguish between a novel and a riddle. It cannot be maintained in respect of *Lord of the Flies*, but Golding thought it could; and oddly enough the error had beneficial results. The novel has an extreme sharpness of outline, an exactness of invention, which come from its closeness to diagram. *Lord of the Flies* (aided, no doubt by the snowball law of popular acclaim) made its way by *not* being like Kafka, or like *Death in Venice*, by *not* being psychologically occult; the plot explains its own profundities. Furthermore, it has closed form, whereas the more brilliant contemporary American novelists have reverted to open form. You live along the lines of the book and feel, in its pattern, a total explanation. It belongs, to use a distinction of Iris Murdoch's, to the crystalline rather than to the journalistic pole of fiction. The virtuosity of (say) Philip Roth, belongs near the journalistic pole; the needs of Golding involve him in experimentation of a virtuoso order, but this is a matter of structure and hardly at all of drawing – the quick accuracy of a Roth conversation or interior. His complexities are not ways of rendering nature or society, but new shapes produced by the pressure of a theme. And there perhaps lies the principal explanation of the success of *Lord of the Flies*: it is a sharply imagined account, a new clear outline, of what one vaguely knew, and many readers are sufficiently skilled to see this outline and to be shocked by it.

And yet not everybody sees the same outlines; and Golding saw that however closed the form and limited the intention, people could not be prevented from walking round the books and validly seeing not the shape he thought he made, but others, which were there and which were good. His change of opinion was later than *Free Fall*; but even before that book there were signs that he was aware of the power of his fictions to support interpretations he himself had not foreseen. Perhaps the very contrivances of his stories persuaded him better than the remonstrances of critics; thus the best scene in *The Inheritors* – where the Neanderthal man watches his new enemies as they act out their strangeness in the clearing below him – required an imaginative feat of such intensity that its result is, self-evidently, a properly mysterious poetry and not simply a diagram of corruption as it might be observed by the different senses of such an animal.

In *Pincher Martin* there is, as it happens, something like an allegory of the situation Golding was in; for Pincher is all egotistic assertion, making plausible and familiar structures out of memories and his knowledge of his own body, indisputably, he thinks, master of his rock, defying, with growing terror, all other interpretations of his plight. But he is wrong, merely a dead man whose interpretations are fairly, for all his resistance, destroyed. In *Free Fall* there is a slightly less proprietary attitude to the theme, which consequently grows more intensely obscure. The book opens, as Golding's books always do, with an absolutely crucial thematic passage, about free will, the state preceding the free fall; but the course of Sammy Mountjoy's life is not diagrammatic, like that of the boys on the island, and the assertions of the last page (always equally crucial) are more ambiguous, less prescriptive than before. Golding has changed his attitude to his fictions. And there is also a change of manner; more than before, the force of the book is generated by the pressure of casual figures as they gain power in the turbulence of language. The later books have a linguistic density absent from *Lord of the Flies*, a quality of vision smokier, less accessible.

Although *Free Fall* disappointed me, I must say that I could not imagine a literary event more interesting to me than the publication of the next Golding novel; and here it is, a most remarkable book, as unforeseeable as one foresaw, an entire original, yet marked throughout by that peculiar presence. Golding shares with Conrad the habit of writing each new novel as if he had written no other, and certainly no book that had sold a million copies. With the other novels in our head we can of course see how it fits in the sequence: it is 'late', it is less assertive as to its possible meaning than *Lord of the Flies*; it has the later density, indeed fierceness, of language, and the power to generate meanings internally – meanings that grow out of the fiction and are not imposed from without. Consequently its themes are occult, as in *Free Fall*.

The Spire tells the story of Jocelin, Dean of some cathedral, and his efforts to realize a vision and a vow by building on to his church a 400-foot spire. That is all. And we see the entire action not so much through the eyes as over the shoulder of Jocelin; such facts as where the money came from, and what other interested parties think about the crazy dean, we gather by using the corners of our eyes. It is sometimes, for Golding's other books, both easy and useful to know his point of departure; nobody is the worse for understanding how *Lord of the Flies* is related to Ballantyne's *The Coral Island*, or for taking note of the epigraph of *The Inheritors*, which is from H. G. Wells's *Outline of History* and congratulates *homo sapiens* on his successful campaign against the Neanderthals. Here we are not told of any similar starting point; but Mr Golding must have got up the subject of how to build a spire, and the one he has in mind is Salisbury. He makes the spire 400 feet high – Salisbury is a little over that – and the highest in England, as Jocelin wants it to be. It is surmounted by a capstone and a cross, as Salisbury spire is. It is octagonal, with a skin of diminishing thickness, and has no orthodox foundation, like Salisbury, of which it has been said that the dangers and difficulties of adding the spire were enough to frighten any man in his senses from trying it. Iron bands strengthen the structure. The four columns over which the spire was raised settled or bent in Salisbury, as in the book, and the spire at once slipped out of its true perpendicular, as here. In short, this is basically the spire at Salisbury. There was even a twelfth-century bishop called Jocelin. Despite some topographical mystification, the scene is consistent with this, and especially the Hanging Stones, which must be Stonehenge. And although it is no business of ours, Mr Golding lives near Salisbury. I don't know exactly where he got the facts about the mason's craft, however.[5]

In outline the story tells how the making good of the vision entails endlessly disagreeable and unforeseeable discoveries. It seemed simple enough; yet it has sordid material causes, unsuspected sexual motives; and it can be realized only in the teeth of technical obstacles which a sane man would regard as prohibitive. The cathedral being a bible in stone, the spire will be the Apocalypse; but it is also a human body and the spire its erect phallus. It all depends upon how your attention is focussed. As Dean Jocelin himself observes, 'the mind touches all things with law, yet deceives itself as easily as a child'. The opening paragraph shows us Jocelin laughing, shaking his head so that a glory consumes and exalts Abraham, Isaac, and God; his ways of looking, the moods of his mind, make and unmake vision and sacrifice. At this point Jocelin controls a manageable glory. But there is the question of the foundations, the palpitating human substratum that must maintain this glorious erec-

5. In fact Mr Golding worked it all out himself, simply walking round the Cathedral and asking himself how *he* would have done it.

tion. And to its splendour the church is sacrificed, defiled by pagan workmen. Obscenely superstitious, they work as if taking part in some pagan rite. When they pry up the slabs at the crossways, it is clear that there are no foundations.

Against the will of the other principal Persons, against the skilled advice of the master builder, Jocelin forces the business on; whatever the foundations of the spire – whether you take them to be mud, or the corrupt money of his aunt – he will have his four hundred feet and his cross with its Holy Nail, a diagram of prayer. Rain water in the excavations finds the corpses and makes the church foul; the master builder seduces the wife of a church servant; the spire seems founded on human filth, the earth 'a huddle of noseless men grinning upward'. The workmen fool about with the model spire obscenely between their legs; but the vision persists, even in the crossways, above the pit itself: 'Here, where the pit stinks, I received what I received.' The four slender pillars are not divine but human lovers, founded precariously on filth; they sing in agony under the growing weight. The church servant disappears, and Jocelin finds pagan mistletoe in the crossways – a typical Golding narrative device, to issue in a revelation as horrible as the recognition of Beatrice in the madhouse of *Free Fall*. Jocelin fares forward: 'the folly isn't mine. It's God's Folly.... Out of some deep place comes the command to do what makes no sense at all – to build a ship on dry land; to sit among the dunghills; to marry a whore.'

Whereas Jocelin thinks of each new foot of the building as a godsent challenge to his strength personally to uphold the structure, the master builder has material problems; he devises a steel band to hold the outward thrust of the spire. Each is clear about the cost, in life and lust and increase of foulness, of this 'unruly member'. The mason's mistress dies for it – a violent death in childbirth, Golding's recurrent figure for violence and creation. 'This have I done for my true love,' thinks Jocelin with only apparent inconsequence. The workmen desert for pagan midsummer fire festivals, and Jocelin's own unruly member is tormented by the memory of the dead woman. Reporting to the Visitor from Rome, he presents himself – filthy, crazy – as 'Dean of the cathedral church of Our Lady', the church he has desecrated, deprived of services, made the scene of deadly lust. His spire is finished, the Nail driven in; it is at once half-destroyed in a storm. And yet, though built imperfectly, in folly and anguish, it is (he thinks in hubris) a spire of prayer. Then the angel strikes him.[6] He has brought ruin and loathing on himself and on the master builder and the church; he can see only the hopeless conflict between the kind of love he thought he had, and the kind that really made the vision, so that the red hair of the dead woman hangs between him and heaven, preventing prayer. On his deathbed he finds a formula for this : 'a tangle of hair, blazing among the stars; and the great club of his spire lifted towards it ... that's the explanation if I had time ... Berenice.' The antinomies of love are reconciled there; Jocelin's final gesture of assent is not to the priests around his deathbed, but to the beautiful maimed spire.

So much of the story one can tell without giving anything important away; such is the nature of Golding's power. It derives from patterns assumed by the language of the book from certain figures I haven't even mentioned : a tent, a net, a tree, as well as the mistletoe berry. Like *Lord of the Flies* it could be called a fable; but it is not a diagram. We are not to think of a prayer-spire and a phallus-spire, of Christian and pagan, devotion and lust, vision and graft. All these antinomies swirl together in the tormented mind of Jocelin, and in ours. We are even allowed to see how a deaf-mute carver understands Jocelin, and how the sacrist, a jealous, embittered, even venal man, is properly shocked by the pagan outrages on the holy vessels in his care; but Golding eschews the deliberate double vision which constitutes the plot of his first three books. Scholarly inquirers will have to look hard for a scenario here. Or, indeed, for a simple issue. Jocelin's dying thought is this : 'There is no innocent work. God only knows where God may be.' But that is not quite the point; nor is the suicide failure of the master builder (who, having gained weight by drinking, miscalculates at last the breaking strain of a rafter). Whether the vision was innocent or not, the technique sound or not, the spire is still there at the end, damaged but beautiful.

Briefly then, this is a book about vision and its cost. It has to do with the motives of art and prayer, the phallus turned spire; with the deceit, as painful to man as to God, involved in structures which are human but have to be divine, such as churches and spires. But because the whole work is a dance of figurative

6. Tuberculosis of the spine, it appears.

language such an account of it can only be misleading. It requires to be read with unremitting attention, and, first time perhaps, very little pleasure. It is second-period Golding; the voice is authoritative but under strain. The style might have been devised by some severe recluse for translating the Old Testament; it is entirely modern, without the slightest trace of god-wottery, yet it is almost unnaturally free of any hint of slang – a modern colloquial English but spoken only by one man.

Trying to characterize the dry hot urgency of this prose, I found myself unexpectedly thinking of a musician: of Vaughan Williams in the mood of *Job*. The parallel has some use, I feel. The ballet for which this music was written was based on the Blake engravings – the Old Testament in an extremely heterodox interpretation. The music is in the full voice of Vaughan Williams's already slightly archaic but fully idiomatic, mere English, pentatonic manner; it goes directly to the large statement about good and evil: Satan falling. Elihu beautiful, the sons of the morning at their sarabande. Vaughan Williams had some of the sensitive bluffness, much of the true privacy, of Golding; and he was another late starter who continually experimented but stayed out of touch with the contemporary *avant-garde*. There is a squareness, a clumsiness; but in some works – in *Job* especially, and in the later music which remembers *Job* – we hear the clear strange tones of the visionary whose idiom we can learn (a saxophone for the comforters), and who speaks as directly as may be of good and evil.

Golding writes rather like that. Look at this passage, chosen quite at random:

The evening turned green over the rim of the cup. Then the rim went black and shadows filled it silently so that before he was well aware of it, night had fallen and the faint stars come out. He saw a fire on the rim and guessed it was a haystack burning; but as he moved round the rim of the cone, he saw more and more fires round the rim of the world. Then a terrible dread fell on him, for he knew these were the fires of Midsummer Night, lighted by the devil-worshippers out on the hills. Over there, in the valley of the Hanging Stones, a vast fire shuddered brightly. All at once he cried out, not in terror but in grief. For he remembered his crew of good men, and he knew why they had knocked off work and where they were gone.

The 'cone' is the unfinished spire; we note how unashamedly the sentence passes from its rim to the easy grandeur of 'the rim of the world'. We might regret 'terrible dread', and yet it is somehow purged by the absolute plainness of reference elsewhere, by 'knocked off work', for instance. The last sentence might seem altogether too artless were it not that on this very page the whole strange plot is undergoing a subtle change of movement, modulating into violence.

It is a prose for violence. All Golding's books are violent; as I say, his basic figure for terror, violence, and bloody creation is childbirth. As such it is used in this book, and it breaks out of the language into the plot. This is part of a private vision; and one might hazardously conjecture that this novel, like some of its predecessors, is as much about Golding writing a novel as about anything else. But one need not believe that to agree that it is deeply personal. It gives one some idea of the nature of this writer's gift that he has written a book about an expressly phallic symbol to which Freudian glosses seem entirely irrelevant. It is remote from the mainstream, potent, severe, even forbidding. And in its way it is a marvel.

(1964)

SIXTEEN

IRIS MURDOCH

There are middle-aged men, fat and bald or both, content with their wives or mistresses or gentle perversities, to whom appears, disposing them in various postures of prayer and pain, the lord of terrible aspect. Perhaps love strikes them in their civilized but dirty houses looking out over Lots Road Power Station, or as they stroll in the Brompton Cemetery. In one such house lives a very old, slowly dying man, drinking champagne, reading books about spiders, handling his valuable stamp collection, or thinking of his life and meditating the possibility of forgiveness by the dead. Outside, the rain beats incessantly on the windows, the Thames threatens an Old Testament flood. In another part of the house this man's widowed son-in-law is in bed with the maid, who is named Adelaide de Crecy, and who drops only the best Wedgwood, on purpose. Observing them is a thin black mystic called Nigel, whom we in turn are to observe in the most bizarre situations – for example, tying up his sleeping twin with an ingenious machine. There is a constant interest in resemblances. There are many judgements and some slaughters, though none is either accidental or casual. The pubs of Chelsea are catalogued, the operations of a printing press described. A brief manual of arachnology is deftly divided and served to us in whispers. There is a Thames-side duel, the flood happens. People die in aeroplanes, of cancer, by drowning. They are printers, civil servants, male nurses, probation officers, and the like, just the kind of people you'd expect all this sort of thing to happen to. Of course it's all made up, and if the question should be, by whom? the foregoing fantasy is an authoritative leak.[1]

The point is simply this, that the taste of a Murdoch novel is instantly recognized, if not easily described; and despite the efficiency of her prose – very professional, very direct, though allowing for a lot to go on under the surface – this taste is somehow a bit high. Served so frequently with dishes of this kind, the diner may become fuddled or cantankerous, or he

1. *Bruno's Dream.* By Iris Murdoch. London, Chatto & Windus, 1969.

may grow, on the other hand, addicted so that Miss Murdoch's annual novel is hailed antiphonally by peevish dyspeptics who are having to give her up and gourmets who call it her best so far. To anyone trying to decide which half of the chorus to join, there is another difficulty, and it is that Miss Murdoch, seconded by Mr Bayley in his critical works, has expressed deeply pondered and very interesting views on what novels ought to be, and these views are difficult to reconcile with the novels she herself writes. As to this new novel, it may very well be her best, it may cause defections and certainly it raises all the problems very acutely.

Miss Murdoch has often said that art, in so far as it has to deal in shapes and forms, and not in the discontinuities and irrelevances of common perception and experience, can be a false consolation to us but that great art is distinguished by not being that. It is a theme of the present book. She is convinced, as she once remarked to me in an uneasy television discussion, that a writer can succumb to the pattern of his book, and so destroy the freedom of his characters for the sake of some comforting, fraudulent design. Most people (everybody except very good people) choose roles, and are in some measure diminished though comforted by them; and if a novelist reduces his people in the same way, and makes them subserve some comforting purpose of his own, he is not allowing them to be what people might and should be: baffling, impenetrable, mysterious. The power to make the necessary connections without reducing the essential mystery is, simply, love, whether in personal relations or in fiction. It is quite legitimate, here, to think of Forster; if the best self of Bloomsbury has an heir, it is Miss Murdoch.

But the preferred model is, as we all know, Tolstoy. And Miss Murdoch is extremely unlike Tolstoy. She adores patterns and plots, and there is not the slightest sign that anyone resembling Natasha or Anna, Vronsky or Pierre, will ever comply with them. She is, rather, a one-woman *commedia dell'arte*; given a *soggetto*, she will produce the most ingeniously developed performance. But here the difficulty occurs: in doing so she will have in mind many deep speculations about fiction and reality, about ethics, about language, about many other things. They will only very occasionally affect the surface of her story; some of the characteristic pleasure derives from the sense that a lot is going on down below. There, something difficult is being said, or some myth or ritual is being secretly enacted.

This isn't to say that Miss Murdoch succumbs to her pattern; in this book anyway she does not. Perhaps the *dénouement*, which is both unexpected and apt, as Aristotle wished, surprised even her. But this enhances the feeling that these amorous collisions are a sort of war-game, its moves obscured by a plausible mist of contingent detail. In this *Bruno's Dream* resembles, of course, many of her earlier books. There is, one feels, a basic game with the unstated rules of which these books in their different ways comply. Contingency is conscripted (people meet or see each other very conveniently: in the last novel the author was comically cavalier about this, and made a husband and wife die simultaneously of double pneumonia, affecting one lung apiece, perhaps). Why is the biographical detail handled with such farcical briskness? Because there is no time to be lost in getting everybody thrown into the great centrifuge of love; because there are to hand squads of significant detail, of easy, surprising, symbol-concealing dialogue. All this interests Miss Murdoch more than most people. It leads us, if we can follow down to the rite or formula which the book is half-hiding. Not that all is concealment; there is sometimes a suspicious candour. The power station and the cemetery are very large symbols of love and death. There is a purple passage about the mystical young man Nigel who thinks he is God, or a god, with puns on Omphalos, Om and phallos. There are meditations, sometimes direct, sometimes oblique, on Last Things, on the necessary and the contingent, on time as we experience it in dying and in reading novels, on ritual as a means of reversing the flow of time. If, in the end, we are consoled, rather than made to think on these things, we are, on the Murdoch view, either contingent persons, or we are dealing only with a minor work of art.

Well, she makes us say things like that; but we should also say that the pleasures she offers are unique and potent. One of them may well be that each novel contains somewhere the ghost of a major novel. This one, for example, Bruno, perhaps a Dantesque name, is at the point where the three dreams cross, past, present, future, the dreams of the dying man and the novelist have to fake into a continuum. Bruno is a Tithonus figure; he ages while the women in his life, because they are dead, do not. In his waking dream he tries to 'propriate' (propitiate?) their shades. Defeated by his father, he is a failed zoologist, a failed philatelist, a failed husband; everything he started shrank in size before he finished it, even his one love affair. Will his estranged son forgive him, enact a ritual of reconciliation? Is he repenting the right things? The omniscient, philosophic, epigrammatic author remarks that 'we regret only the frailty which the form of our life has made us own to'. For Bruno, for most, a present selects its past.

People are either necessary or contingent. Bruno's hedonist son-in-law Danby is contingent, at first anyway. Later the god strikes him into necessity for a while. The dreadful mystic Nigel, a symbol of some sort of god – peering through bedroom windows, telling tales – is, in his ecstasy, an image of the light beyond perception ('tithonic', it used to be called), a channel for such light, a 'lazar' (laser?) beam, a dancer who enacts the circular and reciprocal motions of the angels of love and death, which are finally one. (In working hours he is Bruno's nurse.) It is Bruno's desire to be reconciled with his son, Miles, who years before upset him by marrying an Indian girl called Parvati, that starts the plot. Miles is a poet, happily married to a second, more contingent wife, and giving houseroom to a plain, necessary sister-in-law, when both he and his brother-in-law (abandoning one the wife and the other the maidservant) are struck down by love for the sister-in-law Lisa, who has a First in Greats, has joined and left the Poor Clares, and is an East End schoolmistress and unpaid probation officer. Miles loses, but comes to terms with the death of Parvati and so can write good poems. Danby gets the sister-in-law; the rejected Adelaide gets Nigel's twin, who fights a duel with Danby, organized for divinge kicks by Nigel. There is a flood. Miles's wife is happy with 90-year-old Bruno. All the time it rains like hell, on the town and in the hearts, and indeed the eyes, of the characters. The valuable stamps are lost, the housefly man and the spider God are alike manipulated, and considered; Bruno fades into nontime, accompanied by love, and we reach an unexpected but still consoling end.

Hopeless love showed Miles how to face Parvati's death, and allowed his god to come. Does the novel make death poetic, as Miles's early, bad, poem did? The novel examines itself on this. If Miles is right, we learn, the power to deal with necessity, summon the god and reverse time without lying, depends upon self-abnegation, a way of seeing love as death. Nigel, indeed, says the same thing; but Miles is unlovable, Nigel phoney. Or so they seem to me, but then Miss Murdoch's necessary people often do. It is they who can find God in spiders, as well as in poems, in bed, and in death. At this level she is not writing for 'contingent persons', which most of her readers necessarily are. They seek, like Bruno, a consoling magic, a pleasing peripeteia, in life, perhaps in death; and they find it in Miss Murdoch's plots, not in her subtexts.

Nevertheless these subjects touch the nerves that great fiction assaults. The treatment of time in this book, occasionally breaking the surface in fragmentary philosophical allusion, is exceedingly rich and various, involving ritual and eschatology, but also penetrating the language: there is a casual linguistic insistence on the way in which our bodies are extended in space, our minds in time, on the ritual quality of momentary gestures, whether of men or spiders. These are the time and the space from which only the god can release us, whether as love or death. For the dying and for lovers there are no things just one after another, only last things: so death, love, and their instruments, myth and fiction, undo the work of time. But not by lying.

The reality in which they deal is a different reality from the order of ordinary poetry, as Miles (who alone of the characters lives in a clean, well-lighted place) has to learn. The contingent must be got in; it can be the smell, the spotted hands, of an aged man. Diana, the self-interested hedonist unexpectedly paired with Bruno, asks: 'Is this not the most pointless of all loves? Like loving death itself.' This reality is a difficult vocation. One can recognize that without being irresistibly drawn.

So, perhaps, with Miss Murdoch, who not only makes her sacral patterns but expresses herself, as some of her characters do, in terms of a self-interested hedonism; I mean that her rituals are hazed over by pleasure, by a love which, to the best of its ability, ostracizes death. But this book tries to get it in. What, in the end, is most beautiful about it is that we never think of these old and aging people, tortured by love and death, as absurd. The nearer they are to death, the more just and imperative their loves. Only at the point of death is the point of love fully evident; necessary persons, we gather, know that in the death of the desiring body love achieves being.

Well, that is to say too much, and say it wrongly. The book is full of delicate and unobtrusive mysteries. It is also, at all levels, arbitrarily amusing, gaily and seriously intelligent, disappointing only by the fantastically high standards it contrives to suggest. And a review which leaves most of that out should end with a simple expression of gratitude.

(1969)

SEVENTEEN

MURIEL SPARK

To 'The Girls of Slender Means'

Muriel Spark – as Derek Stanford rather quaintly observes in his new book about her[1] – is in her prime; like her own Miss Brodie she has a set, and to it should belong anybody who takes an interest in the ways fiction can body forth the shape of things unknown. This remarkable virtuoso being in her prime, new books are happily frequent, and the latest, called *The Girls of Slender Means*,[2] is, like nearly all the others, in some ways the best. They are all pretty alarming, and the reasons why they are also funny are very complicated. Some literate people dislike them, though not, so far as I know, for decent reasons. It's true that there is an unfashionable element of pure game in these books – they are about novels as well as being novels – but this is simply part of their perfectly serious way of life. It won't do to call them bagatelles. And there is another rather moral objection, quietly voiced by Mr Stanford in a footnote, to the effect that Mrs Spark lacks charity. This also misses the point, since the concept, cleared of cant, may be entertained in precisely the gratingly unsentimental way in which this pure-languaged writer understands it.

There is certainly a remoteness, a lack of ordinary compassion, in her dealings with characters, but this is part of the premise of her fiction; if we feel sorry in the wrong way, it's because our emotions are as messy and imprecise as life, part of the muddle she is sorting out. In her story 'The Portobello Road' one of the characters says of a murdered girl: 'She was at Confession only the day before she died – wasn't she lucky?' And she is described as 'speaking from that Catholic point of view which takes some getting used to'. The Spark point of

1. *Muriel Spark.* Arundel, Centaur Press. It wouldn't be true charity to call this a good book, since it is sometimes sloppily handled and, in the biographical part, a shade embarrassing. But Mr Stanford makes many profitable observations, and is interesting on the verse, which her publisher ought to reprint. (He has now done so, 1967.)

2. London, Macmillan, 1963.

view is like that, not only because she is an unremittingly Catholic novelist committed to immutable truths, but because she is uncommonly interested in the shapes assumed by these truths as perceived in the tumult of random events and felt upon insensitive fallen flesh. The question for the reader is not at all whether he accepts the truths, but whether the patterns are made good and recognized. Reading them, like writing them, is a work of the imagination, fallen or not. What establishes their validity is not the 'sharp reminders of eternity' mentioned in the blurb, but imaginative cohesion, a rightness of the shapes, a truth sensed in the fictions.

The easiest way into this kind of fiction, which shows the world as bearing obscure figurations of meaning like a novel, is by way of *The Comforters*,[3] the first of the series. Here is a novel which looks into the question of what kind of truth can be told in a novel. It creates a quite powerful sense – still not absent from later and less openly experimental stories – that to make fictions is in a way a presumptuous thing to do, because the novelist is, unlike God, free at the expense of his creatures. Of course the characters fight back : Caroline, the heroine – who as a Catholic convert knows about absolute truth and is also expert in theory of the novel – does her best to resist manipulation by the mind of the unseen novelist who is putting her into a story and trying to shape her life. So she tries to spoil the plot by an exercise of free will : 'I intend to stand aside and see if the novel has any real form apart from this artificial plot. I happen to be a Christian.' And later, when the writer tries to make her lie low in hospital and let her get on with other parts of her pretty complicated plot, Caroline forces her way back into the book by saying that she's being left out only because the writer can't cope with a description of the hospital ward. There follows a deliberately perfunctory description of the ward. The voices Caroline hears recounting or prophesying her actions are novelistic : they are one voice differentiated into many, always speaking in the past tense. (Later Mrs Spark is often, as a novelist, devious about tenses.) The novelist arbitrarily arranges fantastic and pointless coincidences. Mrs Hogg, standing for a singularly odious piety, vanishes when not in the story, having no other life.

The tone of *The Comforters* is civilized and often frivolous,

3. Harmondsworth, Penguin.

but it is naggingly about something serious, and about the difficulties of saying such things in terms of a convention so absurd
and arbitrary as a novel. The plot is deliberately complicated,
since the question asked is, how can such an organized muddle
of improbabilities, further disordered by the presumptuous
claims of the writer on space and time, say anything true or
interesting? One of the answers, if one may abstract it, is that
even among the falsities of a novel, as among the shapeless-
nesses of ordinary life, truth figures; and it does so because the
imagination, in so far as it is good, is bound by categories
which stand in a relation to absolute truth. This shows up in a
certain repeated atavism in Spark plots – the assumption must
be that the ancient patterns have a more certain relation with
the truth. Thus Caroline deals with her demon while crossing
water; but this is only an early instance of a device very important to Mrs Spark. And it doesn't detract from the frivolous
pleasures of flux.

None of the other books is so obviously an inquiry into the
way fictions work, but by now it's plain that Mrs Spark will
not relinquish the investigation. In this, as in other ways, she
remains a poet, for poets have always bothered more than
novelists about the exact nature of their chosen mode. A
Sparkian aphorism, 'There is more of everything than poetry',
is quoted with some show of disagreement by Mr Stanford, but
it seems very pregnant, and an accurate if queer account of her
novels. Of these *Memento Mori* (there is more of everything
than holy dying) seems the best known. Certainly it has a
superb morbid accuracy, a poetic concentration on a narrow
society of people and ideas. The ancient characters are all
different, united only by the common summons of death, as in
the *danses macabres*; and the most notable of them is not the
evil Mrs Pettigrew but the revitalized Charmian, a novelist
within the novel, still giving 'to those disjointed happenings a
shape', and well aware that this shape is a deception, like all
fiction. 'In life,' she says, 'everything is different. Everything is
in the providence of God.' This is the simple point; the scientist's notes perish in a fire, like the dross they are (Mrs Spark
often burns a building for parabolic purposes). He knows how
death comes, but it is Jean Taylor who knows what to do about
it, its right place among the four last things. *Memento Mori*
may be slightly overloaded with incident; at this stage Mrs
Spark wants swirling activity as well as subtle dialogue and

occult figuration.

The Ballad of Peckham Rye is nearer to fable and shorter. It has so many heavy hints about the diabolic nature of Dougal Douglas that it could be made to look like a more fictional *Screwtape Letters*, but it is really a subtle book. The typing ghost of *The Comforters* now roams arbitrarily about interfering in everybody's life. The devil as father of lies is the patron of novelists; Dougal is writing a highly fictional biography of an old woman, and he records in his notebook lists of useful if low novelist's commonplaces, useful blunters of truth and sharp perception. Like a novelist, he seduces people into wanton or even self-destructive acts : the bridegroom who says 'I won't', the head of the typing pool who is murdered. Again there is an intense concentration on a small society, again there are tell-tale atavisms (Dougal's dread of water, the cysts on his head). There is also chill Edinburgh high spirits; the novelist herself wantons with the story of the tunnel and the dead nuns.

The last of the heavily plotted books (so far) was *The Bachelors*; but the world has the same arbitrary limitation, a world of bachelors, their friends, and mistresses. Just as, in *The Comforters*, we are asked to consider the analogy between the writing of a novel and a temporary loss of sanity, we are here made to see an affinity between novel-writing and mediumship (fraudulent and authentic in indeterminable degrees, but fundamentally alien to the truth) and between mediumship and the disease of epilepsy. Mediums, like novelists, speak in a variety of voices, depend on stock responses in their audiences; yet they are no more their own masters than epileptics, who suffer (as all stories do) from atavism in the central nervous system. Yet, like writers, they are sometimes thought very wise. *The Bachelors* is a comic performance, although it is, as the hero notices, 'all demonology and to do with creatures of the air'. Its comedy arises from the corruptions it deals with; and these imply a primal innocence, which later became Mrs Spark's central topic.

Thus *The Prime of Miss Jean Brodie* treats of the loss of innocence. It may well be the best written of these cunningly written books; there is a fusion of tone and material. There is a characteristic Spark voice, slightly pedantic, produced in Scotland's good schools. In *The Comforters* she can write that Father Jerome 'had used to send the lay brother to her' – a usage probably not to be found in other living novelists. This faint pedantry suits Miss Brodie, and the book should ideally be read aloud by a lady who has preserved the Edinburgh accent in all its soft severity. The tone is now more important than the plot: ordinary expectations are flouted by skipping to and fro in time from the thirties and the schoolgirls to the present time of their maturity.

The unpredictable and often absurd acts and assertions of Miss Brodie are precisely what amuse us; but they also have unpredictable consequences (one girl burnt in the fire, being Miss Brodie's notion of dross; another, taught to transfigure the commonplace, herself uncomfortably transfigured). Miss Brodie fancies herself one of the secular elect, a modern justified sinner; and she assumes a novelist's, or God's, power over character. But her life assumes penitential patterns familiar to the instructed, and repeated with pain by the treacherous Sandy. Hindsight is liberally provided from the outset; but the dominant image is of the justified Miss Brodie presiding calmly over a lost innocence.

The new book is rather on the pattern of *Miss Brodie*; it is about a group of young ladies living in a genteel hostel near the Albert Memorial, during the months between the end of the war in Europe and the end of the whole thing. As in *Brodie*, the history of the time is touched in, neatly and with full relevance. The girls are poor though not in want, like the English generally at the time; they are beautiful in poverty, slender (some of them) in means and figure alike. They have a Schiaparelli dress, held virtually in common, and have dealings with an anarchist poet, Nicholas Farringdon, who sleeps with the most beautiful of them, Selina. We know all along about Nicholas's later martyrdom, but the focus is on the days just before the hostel is destroyed by an old bomb and a fire.

The arrangements are such that slender means and bodies become figures of beautiful poverty; but it is Selina's slenderness that enables her to destroy the image of paradise by a breach, as it were, of the rule of the order, so providing Nicholas with the vision of evil which leads him to the Church, and in the end to martyrdom. While they exist, 'the graceful attributes of poverty' are enhanced by Nicholas's anarchism, and by the poems intoned by the elocutionist Joanna. These are relevant because paradisal, or sometimes quite fortuitously, as with Drinkwater's 'Moonlit Applies' or Shelley's 'West Wind';

most relevant to the crisis is 'The Wreck of the Deutschland',
and the Anglican liturgy proper to the day of the disaster.

It may seem that the parable element bulks rather large, that
the novel is itself trying to get through the eye of a needle. But
Mrs Spark uses all her power 'to love and animate the letter'.
The commonplace may show the operation of these figures,
and others, but it is still represented with an arbitrary novelistic
richness; and if 'charity' is a word to be reserved for the future
of Nicholas, it might still be said that the society of girls is
handled with cool tenderness.

Such novels assume the reader's sympathetic participation in
muddle. they assume a reality unaware that it conceals patterns of truth. But when an imagination (*naturaliter christiana*)
makes fictions it imposes patterns, and the patterns are figures
of the truth. The relations of time and eternity are asserted by
juxtaposing poetry and mess, by solemn puns about poverty.
None of it would matter to the pagan were it not for the
admirable power with which all the elements are fused into
shapes of self-evident truth – the power one looks for in poems.
Mrs Spark, in her prime, is a poet-novelist of formidable power.

(1963)

The Novel as Jerusalem: Muriel Spark's 'Mandelbaum Gate'

People – novelists even – have been heard to say of Muriel
Spark that she is gifted and elegant, but a fantasist, a trifler.
This at any rate allows one to see why the old topic of the
death of the novel is still dusted off from time to time. Mrs
Spark is a novelist; she is not an anti-novelist or a philosophical
novelist, a realist or a neorealist, but a pure novelist. She is
evidently not of the opinion that the possibilities of the form
are exhausted, since she is continually finding new ones. Her
novels quite deliberately raise difficult questions about the
status of fiction, but she has not been driven to violence in her
attempts to answer them; she does not cut her books up or fold
them in or try to make them random. If there is to be randomness, she wants to be in charge of it. If the characters have to
be free, then their freedom will have to be consistent with
contexts not of their own devising, as in life. If the reader
thinks that the shapes and patterns, the delicate internal relationships, of a well-written novel give the lie to life and suggest impossible consolations then he must content himself with

some other thing, with whatever unconsoling fiction he can find. Mrs Spark is even somewhat arrogant about the extent of the novelist's power : knowing the end of the story, she deliberately gives it away, and in a narrative which could have regular climactic moments she fudges them, simply because the design of her world, like God's, has more interesting aspects than mere chronological progress and the satisfaction of naïve expectations in the reader. Yet all the elements of this world come from the traditional novel.

The suggestion is, in Mrs Spark's novels, that a genuine though limited relation exists between the forms of fiction and the forms of the world, between the novelist's creation and God's. *The Comforters* is quite deliberately an experiment designed to discover whether this relation does obtain, whether the novelist, pushing people and things around and giving 'disjointed happenings a shape', is in any way like Providence. This quotation is actually from *Memento Mori*; Mrs Spark's later novels are all very different from *The Comforters*, but all are in a sense novels about the novel, inquiries into the relation between fictions and truth. You may treat her last two books, *The Prime of Miss Jean Brodie* and *The Girls of Slender Means*, both very brief and exquisitely formed, as beautiful jokes; they have a constantly varying formal wit, an arbitrariness of incident under the control of the writer's presumptuous providence, that warrant the description. But like the wit of the seventeenth-century preacher, they are jokes for God's sake, fictions which have to do with the truth.

'I don't claim that my novels are truth,' she once said in an interview.[4] 'I claim that they are fiction, out of which a kind of truth emerges. And I keep in mind that what I am writing is fiction, because I am interested in truth – absolute truth.... There is a metaphorical truth and moral truth, and what they call anagogical ... and there is absolute truth, in which I believe things which are difficult to believe, but I believe them because they are absolute.' This absolute truth is, of course, the teaching of the Roman Catholic Church. The lies of fiction can partake of this truth, perhaps give it a useful, though imperfect human application. It is, perhaps, inconceivable that the creator of fiction can – in so far as he looks at what he has done and sees that it is good – make shapes and depths utterly dis-

4. Broadcast by the B.B.C. and condensed in my article 'The House of Fiction', *Partisan Review*, Spring, 1963.

similar from those of God. In a sense, this makes his work a daring kind of game. He lies like truth. He simulates the plots of God, even when he plays at being arbitrary and contingent. The tragic aspect of this is the subject of another Catholic novelist, Graham Greene, in *The End of the Affair*; Mrs Spark is more concerned with the comedy of the situation. The novelist, presumptuous, arbitrary, scheming, and faking, lying like the fiend, makes things like worlds, plots in some ways absurdly like God's.

The interest of this for nonbelievers is that even they must make worlds like plots. Even if they reject the Absolute as itself a fiction, they are by nature structure-makers and impose this human need on history, on nature, on poems, and novels. They seek and accept images of order. They need not be alienated from a novel because it represents a world designed to possess formal relationships, rhythms, and certainties under the wild muddle we see at first glance. In other words, they are as well equipped as a Catholic to understand the power and beauty of Mrs Spark's most ambitious creation game, her new novel, *The Mandelbaum Gate*.

Mrs Spark here tells a story, and a good one; she is a novelist all through, extremely inventive, at ease with complex plots. But she presents the story in discontinuous bits, blurring the climaxes, giving away the surprises. Why? Because in reality this occurs, and it occurs without making any difference to the certainties of the world and its design. She sets the story in Jerusalem because Jerusalem, as the medieval map-makers knew, is the centre of this world, the core and paradigm of God's plot. Jerusalem brings the two plot-makers together. The book is a confrontation, or rather a concord of plots. God's plot is Jerusalem itself, the ancient *données* divided by the Mandelbaum Gate. To recognize them is to know something of the ways of God to men; they lie timeless and unchanged under the extraordinary contingencies of modern Jerusalem. This is the plot the novelist confronts, with which she seeks concord. How does she set about such a task? By taking as a central figure Miss Barbara Vaughan, who is half Jewish, an English Catholic convert, and setting her down in Jerusalem on a pilgrimage to the holy places, which are divided by the Mandelbaum Gate. She is on the Jewish side of the gate; the Arabs will let her pass if convinced that she is a bona fide Christian, but they do not recognize half-Jews any more than they recognize

Israel. The story is of the adventures of Barbara on her pilgrimage, and also about her love affair and how it prospered when her lover succeeded in having his first marriage annulled at Rome. It is also about smuggling and spying and smart Arab operators and British consular officials. It is a complicated story. To explain how it is made to match Jerusalem, I shall have to speak in some detail at least about the two opening chapters.

First we meet Freddy Hamilton from the British Consulate, upper-class, talented, agreeable in his fifties, and a bit wet. He is given to composing *vers de société* in archaic verse forms, and is walking back through the Mandelbaum Gate making up a bread-and-butter letter to his weekend hostess on the Jordan side. It is to be a rondeau. He bumps into a Jewish child, then into a Jewish-looking Arab in European dress. He meets Miss Vaughan and hears her chidden by an old Jew for a dress which, though it seems modest enough in the heat of the day, offends the sensibility of two thousand years. Proceeding, he carries on with his thank-you verses as he passes a school where the children are chanting in Hebrew. He reflects on the Greek metres, 'pitting culture against culture'. At his hotel he calls for a drink, and the Israeli waiter reminds him of a line from Horace. He remembers Miss Vaughan, and the small embarrassment when she told him she was half a Jew; but in spite of that they had contrived to be comfortably English together. Miss Vaughan had complained, as the English will, of un-English activities among the natives. Her guide was interested in modern cement factories and had been reluctant to take her to the top of Mount Tabor, 'probable scene of the Transfiguration'. Then Miss Vaughan turns up, speaking of her dangerous trip to Jordan to see the other holy places, and of her archaeologist fiancé, who is seeking the annulment in Rome which she, not he, regards as indispensable to their union. Freddy does not know much about Miss Vaughan; she looks spinsterish to him. Later he learns of her sensual nature. Now he learns that her life has a different basis from his own, for he allows himself to say that he doesn't understand this fuss about an annulment. (Barbara's fiancé, being a scholar, understands it very well. Archaeologists also know that layers of irrelevance cover the original true deposits.) She quotes Apocalypse at him: 'I find thee neither cold nor hot; cold or hot, I would thou wert one or the other. Being what thou art, lukewarm, neither cold nor hot, thou wilt make me vomit thee out of my mouth.' Surely one ought not to quote Scripture in this way? Freddy departs, thinking about Greek metres.

Under the quiet of this opening, which would, I think, delight Mr Forster, chords are beginning faintly to sound. The second chapter is more decisive. Barbara is on top of Mount Tabor. In her, it seems, everything meets : Jew and Christian, the two testaments, an ability to live in the present without forgetting the historical deposit of holiness, Jewish intellect, and 'the beautiful and dangerous gift of faith'. Can all these be made one? Intelligently she studies the parts; in faith she recognizes totalities beyond criticism, whether in a person or a poem or a world. On Mount Tabor, where an earthly body was transfigured as a poem is by its totality, she thinks of the Beersheba of Genesis. It is now dominated by a Scotch-tape factory, but it is still the Beersheba of Genesis, where Jacob tricked Isaac into blessing him instead of Esau, and so earned his inheritance and his place among the fathers of Israel. God went along with this; he had not been to Eton. 'The mighty blessing, once bestowed, was irrevocable.' So, though she doesn't know it, will the College of the Rota in Rome be tricked into annulling her fiancé's marriage. Meanwhile, the Holy Land is Beersheba and Scotch-tape factories, Tabor and cement.

She remembers Jaffa, and the house of Simon the Tanner. If you recall that it was in Simon's house that St Peter had his vision of the unclean meats, the reminiscences of Barbara's childhood which follow will not need the excuse that the Jewish guide asks her why she is not of her mother's religion. Barbara remembers the double background of her childhood – the hunting Anglicans, the intellectual Jews of Golders Green, 'Passover gatherings and bell-summoned Evensongs'. She decides that she is not fragments, but a totality; she is what she is, though her parts, like the parts of Christianity after the vision of St Peter in Simon's house, are Jew and Gentile, as the Old and New Testaments are a concord, the types of one fulfilled in the other. 'She then remarked, without relevance, that the Scriptures were specially important to the half-Jew turned Catholic. The Old Testament and the New, she said, were to her – as near as she could apply to her own experience the phrase of Dante's vision – "bound by love into one volume".' Pending the true Transfiguration, which is of eternity, she decides that something of the sort is known in time, since memory, and history, bring health, and this recollection of the *données* of God's plot enables us to do as we must: 'what is to be borne is to be praised'.

The insight into a totality made up of such different parts is conveyed, in the city of Jerusalem or in a good novel, by an image. Barbara remembers an Easter vacation afternoon, spent with her English family on a tennis lawn, and as she leaves to celebrate Passover in Golders Green, 'the drawing-in of an English afternoon ... with its fugitive sorrow. "See here, Barbara," said her grandfather at Golders Green a few hours later, "these are the bitter herbs which signify our affliction in Egypt." ' The intellectual Aaronsons enacted their Passover ritual as the English rolled their pace eggs in the mild woods. Barbara, shaky on detail, is excluded from the Jewish kitchen. She is neither full Jew nor full Gentile, and so all the better for the purposes of this novel, since her double estangement mirrors the accidental deviations of the Gentile religion from its Jewish base, the New from the Old Testament. Sitting, like Deborah, on the top of Mount Tabor, she reflects on her own transfiguration in faith and sensuality, in acts of love and recognition. She will go to Jordan and finish the pilgrimage. Whatever Barbara may think of the matter, she *has* been transfigured, for the purposes of the novel, by Mrs Spark. We recall that Miss Brodie, that comic *alter ego* of the novelist, had something to say about the transfiguration of the commonplace, and so, in Sandy's case, had God.

It will be seen that these opening pages achieve certain traditional ends. They establish character, tone, background, the last very strongly since the book has to be a sort of map of Jerusalem. They found a plot: the trip to Jordan, the annulment case. If that were all, they might possibly be thought somewhat extravagant; but they have also, to use Mrs Spark's word, anagogical work on hand. This is sometimes a matter of hints in the texture (the people Freddy bumps into, his clashing Greek against Hebrew) which may be for the moment obscure, as when Miss Vaughan quotes the Book of Revelation. Such hints imitate similar hints in the texture of reality. The structural imitation begins in the second chapter, with Barbara on Mount Tabor. The fraud that serves a divine purpose is associated with Beersheba. The health-giving memory of Easter-

Passover happens at Simon's house. The old that has to be remembered underlies the meaningless variety and division of the
new : Old Jerusalem, with its shrines calling for recognition,
however perfunctory, as focuses of truth, subsisting under the
hurrying Jews, the unrecognizing Arabs, and fortuitously assembled foreigners of the new city. It is all one and capable of
transfiguration when rightly seen. Mount Tabor knew the war-
like Deborah and the shining Christ, and now sees Miss
Vaughan in love, sitting on the mountain nobody wanted to
take her to. Down in the streets wildly diverse people bump
each other in divided streets; but on some view they are one,
and the city is their happy home.

When Barbara remarks 'irrelevantly' that this reminds her
of Dante, who at the climax of his vision of Paradise saw the
scattered leaves of the world bound into one volume, *legato
con amore in un volume*, we may ask on what kind of view
she is irrelevant. Only on the impossible view that talk in
novels obeys the standards set for relevance in common talk.
We may believe, as Barbara and Mrs Spark do not, that only
in a book can the world be shown to be bound together *as* a
book. Mallarmé said something of the kind, that the world
exists to end in a book. But whether the shrines, the images, the
données exist only inside or inside and outside the book, it
remains true that in such a book people must say things that
transcend simple relevance, and so may appear irrelevant. The
use of the adverb is Mrs Spark's way of making peace with
those who think novels ought to be simple, small towns rather
than Jerusalems. Or it can be called 'faking', so that the simple
story gets told while at the same time 'a kind of truth emerges'.
The run of talk must point back to the *données*, just as the
fugitive sorrow of an English evening and the bitter herbs of
Passover have to be juxtaposed, the time between annihilated.
They are together as closely as Jewish mother and Gentile
father, in the union that produced Barbara. If the novel is to be
bound together in one volume by love, it may be necessary to
use the word 'irrelevantly' at the point of maximum relevance.
Out of the lie 'a kind of truth emerges'. Mrs Spark's comfortable expatriate English are fond of saying that the Arabs think
in symbols, by which they mean 'tell lies'. This is a good description of what novelists of Mrs Spark's stamp know they are
doing.

Virtuoso composition of Mrs Spark's kind tends to make

short novels. But *The Mandelbaum Gate* is twice as long as *Jean Brodie* and much more heavily plotted; one can't offer a clumsy commentary on the whole thing. Having established the set of her world, or her Jerusalem, in the opening chapters – the process is quite arbitrary, like God's piling layers of history and holiness on to one small region – she can make or allow the events of her story to fall within it, or even, to show her arbitrary power, outside it. What is required, as a critic once said of Milton, is that the reader should be continually on duty. It is up to him to see that the annulment plot, which turns, like a lawsuit in some vast Victorian novel, on the dubious circumstances of the fiancé's birth and the absurd intervention of a jealous woman, has to do with Beersheba and Isaac, and with human applications of absolute truth. When Scripture is quoted, it is quoted with the same 'irrelevance' I've discussed in connection with Barbara's reference to Dante. The cultivation of English wild flowers on the Israel–Jordan border, the obsessive collocation of their popular with their botanical names, and with the holy places where Freddy's friend Joanna finds them, may seem a minor and rather poetic figuration in the book, but it is firmly related to the central theme of Jerusalem, and also to the adventure story which somehow gets told. And when trefoil, lady's-finger, viper's bugloss come from Gethsemane, the Mount of Olives, Siloam, these last names are touched, as they ought to be, by the commonplace; the English names rest on the holy places, as history and the world rest on Jerusalem. In the garden where these flowers grow, Freddy writes insincere letters to his terrible mother in Harrogate, and she too will be bound, under the pressure of apocalypse, into this one volume.

In this Jerusalem, as in the real one, there must be variety, confusion, conflict, not only between Semites but between everybody. Indigenous characters soon begin to pour into the story – Orthodox Jews, Orthodox Catholics from Lebanon, Arab operators. The muezzin wakes you on the Israeli side; to touch the Wailing Wall you have to go by the gate to the Arab side. People in England, only remotely concerned, are drawn to Jerusalem, encountered in the polyglot confusion of the holy places. Barbara, Jew turned Catholic, visits the shrines disguised as an Arab. She buys from a Lebanese Christian merchant a chain with the Christian fish symbol but also with Turkish charms to counteract it.

The adventures of Barbara in Jordan, and Freddy's liberated behaviour as, in flight from his mother, he accompanies her, are narrated in discontinuous but amusing fits. The Ramdez family, all charming, all making a good living out of refugees, spying, smuggling, the peccadilloes of English and American government officials, move into the centre, as much a part of Jerusalem as the Zionists, the Scots Presbyterians, the priests, and nuns. Farce works for Mrs Spark as heavier irony for other writers; and underneath the story, with its farcical, anarchic, naturalistic incidents and encounters, are the holy places. To recognize them, even in this fugue, is what makes Barbara 'all of a piece', though a 'gentile Jewess, a private-judging Catholic'. The heart of it all is the memory, the anamnesis, of these places: Nazareth, 'where it really began'; Cana and the first miracle, for 'everything begins with that'; Capharnaum, where 'the spiritual liberation of the human race had begun'; the birthplace of Mary Magdalen. In Jerusalem, observing the 'actual Gethsemane passively laid out on the Mount of Olives', she feels the relation of this Jerusalem to that other of poetry and hymn, 'my sweete home, Hierusalem'. The pilgrimage may well be without emotion; it is essentially a simple act of recognition.

The quality of the book's imagination is suggested by the inclusion of the Eichmann trial among these objects of Christian recognition; if one had to cite a single example to show Mrs Spark's deepening power, this would serve. All Barbara hears of the trial is a dull day when Eichmann is being interrogated by his own counsel. She sees it, however, as 'the desperate heart' of the whole process: the dead mechanical tick of the discourse, words and statements divorced from all reality and all pity; and she thinks of the French anti-novel, the discourse dead, the subject living. Barbara here decides, as it were, in passing, that she has to see the holy places on the Jordan side. They are basic to *her* kind of meaning, as to Mrs Spark's. It is a meaning you may find in a novel, not in an anti-novel. The Eichmann passage is characteristic of Mrs Spark's sensibility, and of her desperate confidence in the novel. So that we may see how this confidence is based, she includes (as Camus and Iris Murdoch have included) a sermon, about the point of the holy places and their involvement with fraud and false emotion. She is telling us that her novel too gets its meaning from truths which can be misunderstood, and that it is an analogue of Jerusalem; but she is also saying that we need to see it as Jerusalem-shaped without forgetting that it contains, like the city, a good deal that may seem hard to relate to that model.

To emphasize this, the quality of observed life, she brings into play the sharp ear and the key-cold charity known from her earlier books. The dialogue is exemplary, Forsterian in its command of dialect. If she describes a cellar in Acre where the Crusader wall is still a foundation, she makes it a real cellar, not a symbol. People act credibly, are funny, make love, or fight like people in the real Jerusalem. To write such a book, one needs to be very inward with the novel as a metaphor for the world. Mrs Spark is precisely that; the book is, in an age of rather clumsy argument about fiction, a demonstration that great things can be done when a strong imagination determines to take up many aspects of the 'kind of truth' that fictions provide and bind them up into one volume.

(1965)

The Public Image

Dull grey in manner, this novella[5] imitates the mediocrity of its characters, refuses to comment upon the state of their souls, and, by the time it comes to an end, has insinuated formidably severe moral judgements. It abjures all the sprightly devices which Mrs Spark normally revels in; even the final turn of the plot is predictable. There is no Edinburgh primness and no South Kensington giggling and there are very few jokes of any kind, except the monstrous practical joke on which the story depends. In a book about role-playing the narrator adopts a poker-faced mask for herself. In the end the truth emerges as it were without prompting from her, and in this sense only the work is grimly mischievous in dealing with grimly mischievous people who, since they choose to live outside the truth, should not be taken in by practical jokes anyway.

Annabel is a mousy actress, a little slip of a thing, stupid, untalented, who becomes by luck (the attentions of a big Italian director and the fact that her eyes photograph marvellously) a big star, the English Lady Tiger. Is it better to be oneself, meagre and valid, or fiery-eyed, marvellous, and

5. London, Macmillan, 1968.

phoney? She is married to a failed actor called Frederick, who
lives off her for a while, and then becomes a scriptwriter. The
marriage is empty but somehow holds together, and is built up
by an astute Italian publicity girl as the ideal combination of
virtue and licentiousness. They live in the middle of the Rome
movie world, divided (she spending her time at the studio, he
with a mistress) but still dependent on each other. They have
an odious hanger-on called O'Brien, a Sparkian Judas figure. The
book opens at the point where they have tried to mend the
marriage with a baby and are about to set up house in a new
apartment. Then Frederick plays a tremendous joke. He invites
the most awful people he knows to a house-warming, and
while they are fouling the empty flat, and Annabel is trying to
protect the baby, he spectacularly commits suicide, leaving, for
the benefit of the Italian press, bogus letters to his dead mother,
his wife, and his girl. To save her public image Annabel has to
explain away the suicide and suppress the letters.

The second practical joke is O'Brien's: he convinces her that
he has not photocopied the letters and then uses them for
blackmail. Annabel preserves her image by exploiting knowledge acquired before the cameras, and can beat or buy
O'Brien, but at the inquest ... The final turn is predictable. The
values are unsurprising – the baby, the reliable if *rusé* Italian
director, the true choice at the end.

What makes this an authentically Sparkian piece is the re-
lentless insistence that, however smartly they may be sub-
verted, the values governing these lives are invariant; and not
only that, they are also essential to genuine colour and vitality.
These, the prose says, are lives without poetry conducted within the terms of a base and spurious competition. And into the
flat narrative furies erupt – balloons with faces floating before
the window, terrible for a moment to all but the baby, images
to corrupt, of public idiocy or worse. A trusted confidante of
Annabel's, Golly Mackintosh, hovers always in the wings and
never makes it into the book, which is full of hated, untrusted
people. Rome, a centre of truth, is also a centre of phoneys;
Mrs Spark moves from the Jerusalem of her last book to Rome,
and makes an act of presence not at St Peter's but along the Via
Veneto and in the studios. This is characteristic, too.

So is the suicide, in the Church of St John and St Paul, where
the blood of those martyrs were spilt. Annabel, hearing of her
husband's death, asks: 'But why among the martyrs? Why?'

She does not, as we may, pursue this important question; within minutes she is speaking, an instinctive protectress of her public image, of his 'falling', not 'jumping', and for a while develops an account of the death as accident which is acceptable to the press. The baby is, says the infallibly omniscient narrator, 'the only reality of her life'.

Mostly the tone is explicit, like that, with just the usual hints that what looks bizarre in a world of bizarrerie is the truth. Everywhere you have only to speak truth about people to show that they are not *dans le vrai*; but the best place to do it is Rome, where the whole scene reflects the co-existence of *bella figura* and the truth.

Finally one reflects that there is, in the relation of casual detail to an image of this truth behind it, the moral rigour which always characterizes this unsentimental author. When it is thought that the false friend has refrained from photocopying the suicide letters, Annabel's lawyer says it was very good of him. Annabel, not a clever girl but still a Sparkian, replies: 'What's good about not being bad?' A chill book, then; short, strict, very distinguished.

(1968)

EIGHTEEN

BRIEFLY NOTICED

(A) ALAN SILLITOE

'Rammel' is a word that recurs frequently in Mr Sillitoe's books. It isn't in the Concise Oxford, nor yet in the Shorter, but it makes a decent showing in the O.E.D. itself, which says that the primary meaning is branches, twigs, bits of old wood, but gives examples of its use in the Midlands and specifically Nottingham as a word for old rubbish of all sorts. One way of understanding why it is so often on the tip of Mr Sillitoe's pen is to carry out upon it the operation which Kenneth Burke calls 'joycing' : *ram* and *mel*, strength and sweetness, violence with a sexual note that the taste of honey reinforces, and the whole thing against a background of urban and industrial waste. *Rammel*, in short, means Saturday Night and Sunday Morning.

A deep and studious interest in the constituents of rammel is one of the determinants of this author's talent. True, his first book was the thing itself; but even in *The Key of the Door* it is lovingly catalogued, and the violence it promotes channelled into the peculiar tough sweetness of the sexual descriptions. Even the Forces, for all their bull, present an orderly paradigm of the industrial arrangements that excrete rammel. 'If it moves, screw it; if you can't screw it steal it; if you can't steal it set fire to it', is a rammelly ethos. Mr Sillitoe's heroes are moving out of Nottingham, but this is the mark set upon them – tough talking, drinking, screwing, stealing, insubordination. What they acquire in the world is a respect for books and thought; in this way they learn to despise rammel, to estimate the degree to which the poor who live in it are cheated and deprived. So they move out of the world that cheated them into jungle or desert, not so much in order to help the Malayan Communists or the F.L.N. as to find themselves in a world purged of rammel.

These preoccupations impose a pattern on Mr Sillitoe's novels. Their base is *Saturday Night and Sunday Morning* with its back-to-backs, factories and pubs. Their climaxes are fights with rivals and husbands, and they end in action on behalf of the militant proletariat as a means to personal salvation. This is, at any rate, the goal towards which he has been moving, and the paradigm appears in almost ideal clarity in *The Death of William Posters*.[1] The language in which it is presented has an appropriate blend of rammel and bookishness. The hero, aging a little from book to book, is potent, belligerent, a drinker (double rums with pints), victimized but independent. The difference is that he is, on the first page, on his way out of Nottingham.

Frank Dawley has sold his car, parted with his wife, and set forth. Only the flashbacks are set in Nottingham. The first section is about an affair with a district nurse in Lincolnshire – urban man in an icy pastoral environment, labouring, reading, meeting a primitive artist. The second part is set in London – an affair with an L.S.E. girl, wife of a surveyor. Each part ends with a violent encounter : Frank beats up the first husband, is knocked down by the other's car. The third and final section shows Frank on the move again, taking his girl with him, all the way to Tangier, where he leaves her, pregnant, and goes off to run guns to the F.L.N. in the desert. In *The Key of the Door* we are always being brought back to Nottingham; we have to feel it and the jungle all at the same time. Here the burden of rammel is borne by the characterization and more especially by the prose.

Sillitoe's style is one of habitual violence, a deliberate reflection of the hated, cheated prole, crossed by a certain awkward artifice, which is correlative with the hero's self-education. It is clear that the maintenance of this stylistic attitude presents him with enormous problems. There is evidence of slackness, fatigue; there is the practical difficulty of making fights violent when everything else is violent. So the language becomes loosely ecstatic, as in talk of

a hand cracking on flesh, and the purple spark-fanged floor on the sway and loose burst at Keith like a piece of ice over the eye-face, an engulfing polar cap.

Or a fist is described as 'bursting, a whale-head driving across the light, packed with flintheads and darkness'. A violent hyperbole afflicts the homely prose of the working-man hero :

1. *The Death of William Posters*. London, W. H. Allen, 1965.

'The sky eats into my brain here,' he notes. It is a thought one doubts ever got thought. Mere description blossoms with a rash of irrelevant conceits : 'The island lay like a death-mask, the tip of its black chin flashing a lighted pimple in dubious welcome to the ship.' When a man has a hangover he leaves his body and travels 'among star-sparks of half life on his way back into his eyes and brain, toes and stone-cold bollocks'. For a conceited orgasm, try : 'Flames from all her limbs leapt to the middle of her as if to greet the guest that slid so ceremoniously in.'

This is the prose of a writer dangerously stretched; and for that reason and others it occasionally reminds one of the Lawrence of *Lady Chatterley*. In one passage Sillitoe achieves the unnecessary feat of parodying a chat between Mellors and Connie. The L.S.E. graduate is in bed with Frank, and he lectures her on love and work :

> In my ideal society all advertisements would be ripped off the streets, and instead there'd be well-placed neon signs in red saying : 'Work! Work! Work!' Maybe now and again there'd be a little one going on and off saying : 'Fuck! Fuck! Fuck!'

With Frank's 'broad-shouldered nakedness looming in the half-light', Myra is healed by darkness : 'In spite of the black passion of his desires, her body seemed to belong to her again. . . .' With these blunt lectures and coitional therapy we're not far from the gamekeeper's hut and the old magic carrying out its 'desperate healing of the interrupted bloodflow'.

It seems that lust and rage, dancing attendance on a novelist's rhetoric, can have the effect of parching it. And in his concern for rhetorical effect, he can be negligent of structure. *Key of the Door* was messy, the new book is obvious and untidy. In the first part, the Lincolnshire affair, paragraphs about Frank's early life are dropped into the narrative, and especially into the dialogue, and they do a lot of harm. Sartre, who is exceptionally uneasy about fictional temporality, used to argue that novels are at their strongest in dialogue, because the time of dialogue is so closely analogous to that of the reader, so that he is in less danger of 'jumping out of the book'. There is something in this; Sillitoe's reminiscences are a great drag on the dialogue in this novel, and the reader may have some sympathy with Sartre, who would be in and out of it like the lady in bed at old fairgrounds.

It's impossible to guess how much damage all this does to a writer like Sillitoe, a writer ambitious enough to write not what Frank calls 'shit-novels' but the sort that 'prises open previously unknown regions within yourself'. He mentions Conrad, Melville, Stendhal; but Conrad stands not only for an occasional hysterical inflation but for intense concentration on form. It seems characteristic that the best writing in Sillitoe's last two novels comes at the time of his heroes' self-expression in action, and in a context of guerrilla warfare. Give him a small society of men, their ankles tied together with string, lying in ambush for the imperialist French, and he will release his hero and his style at one stroke. Even so, these advantages can be thrown away by a rhetorical over-explicitness, as in this book. 'Something in him was going to be reconstituted.... His life had to be filled from the fountains of his own desert....'

This book is certainly, by any standards the author would accept, a failure. The first – the Country – section has excellent passages registering the cold, the hero's adaptation to country ways, the fantasy of life in the cottage of the primitive painter (his masterpiece is 'Christ the Lincolnshire Poacher'). The second section – London – has a not unsubtle contrast between Frank's integrity and the endangered gift of the painter when taken up by smooth metropolitan artmen; there is also some point in making the second girl's husband nice (he loves the country and goes on three-day drunks) so that Frank doesn't have to beat him up, as he did the adman husband of the nurse. But the final – Desert – section is the best-written; the style is released with the man.

The mythical figure of Bill Posters is certainly an agreeable invention. He is the figure who at all times and everywhere 'will be prosecuted'. He represents the indestructible cunning and evasiveness by which a man survives among the rammel; admirable in some ways, his is a way of life that has to be destroyed on the way to self-fulfilment. The myth is well, if predictably, handled, and it will cause little surprise that Frank in a revery associates him with his friend's picture of Christ. Breaking free from Bill Posters, Frank attunes himself first to a Mellors-like independence (sturdily antinomian, indifferent to work as the bosses understand it, educated) and then to the sort of anguish Bill Posters, preoccupied with his incessant tricks and escapes, has no time to feel. The conversation between him and the wild and wily painter on the subject of art and pessimism, and the rejection of art in favour of action, is beneficial to the novel; but mostly Frank preaches without resistance. His hatred of the telly, the ads, the London crowd scurrying for comfort into the tube at rush hour, have imaginative vivacity; but both he and Albert the painter sink into lay figures, flatly and feebly rendered from the outside. Albert is 42 but could be seen as 'little more than a man of 30 who had already suffered the fires of life's iniquity'. Frank is labelled 'a strong character' with 'a rich mineral coal lump' of a brain. Nothing much about him really matters except the fantasy that he chucked up everything and, at the end of some nut-strewn road, killed Bill Posters.

Curious that this English dream should appear at the same moment as Mailer's *American Dream*. Mailer's is metropolitan and by comparison distinctly upper-class, but it is certainly violent, and has to do with changing the patterns of social and individual life. But that it *is* a dream is a *donnée* of Mailer's book; and for all its absurdity, its intellectual irresponsibility, its dangerously ambiguous presentation of pathological data, it shows what a difference it makes to have a richer and more relaxed rhetoric, a more natural control of the emblematic situation (in Mailer's book, the high balcony) and of the imagery necessary to writing of this kind. Avoiding the indiscriminate sensationalism of Sillitoe, Mailer, at the risk of absurdity, makes smell the king of the senses. I'd rather be found to share Sillitoe's view of the world than Mailer's magical nonsense about cancer, orgasm, and the moon; but in the unjust world of the novel it is Mailer who sounds right. They both send their violent fornicators into the violent world; what makes Mailer's much more pretentious hero work is a kind of cheating: an irony, as in the characterization of the police, which is totally absent from the English writer.

It does seem unfair. Reviewers have quoted pages of rammel from Mailer. Sillitoe feels strongly that newspapers are termites devouring civilization, and this kind of observation is made in Mailer's book only by square professors of psychology. It's just that he can write novels – look at the dialogue, proceeding as it does from situations preposterous in the last degree, but racing forward, creating its own reality. Look at the saving salute to sanity from dementia in the last paragraph. It seems the first truth about novels is still that they have to be made, and as novels, not as curtains of violent-coloured words draped over plot-props. It may be something wrong in the nature of things that allows Mailer's novel to be so much better than Sillitoe's, but it seems to be so, and there's a moral in that.

(1965)

(B) ANTHONY BURGESS

Sometimes one thinks of Mr Burgess as a swarm of language waiting for a structure to settle on. When he finds it the words descend and obscure its outline, announcing themselves as his meaning. So with, for instance, *The Clockwork Orange*. So, it now appears, with *Inside Mr Enderby*, published five years ago under the name of Joseph Kell – a book remembered very clearly, but, as it now appears, a book not remembered for all the right reasons, the meanings having been obscured by clusters of conceits as well as by amazement at the boldness of the originating notion, that of a poet who works on the lavatory.

Now Mr Burgess writes a sequel:[2] his publishers joke coyly about his success in continuing Kell's novel, rather as if he stood in the same relation to his deceased predecessor as Kingsley Amis to Ian Fleming. In a way this isn't far out: it is true that Kell and Burgess share a language, but Kell cannot at the time have contemplated anything like the present extrapolations. He wrote a good and glittering, funny and serious book. Burgess's isn't so much a chronological continuation (though it is that) as an attempt to cut deeper into the same plate – to exploit accidents of design and material – to produce and develop such meanings as lay latent in Kell and struck Burgess as patient of expansion.

The result is certainly interesting, though there's no point in denying that it suffers in some measure the ordinary fate of sequels. That which charmed and made giggle first time round tends, on repetition, to induce no more than a smile of reminiscence. Many of the whimsies we can only be asked to remember in this pleasant way, since Enderby, expelled from his habitat, the lavatory equipped with writing stool beside the

2. *Enderby Outside*. London, Heinemann, 1968.

bath filled with poems and mice, cannot return to the position
in which we shall always think of him. Already cut off from
that Eden, he must be a picaro or an exile. For much of the
time he isn't writing poetry at all, so we miss the minute record of his creative fervours. All the same, Burgess has not
changed Enderby : he still says 'For cough' to people he dislikes, though they are likely to reply in simpler orthography.
And the events and characters of the first book are immanent,
often revealed, in the sequel. In fact the new book often ex-
poses the structure of the old, upon which it is a kind of fictional commentary.

Inside Mr Enderby was a less determinedly encyclopedic,
more English *Herzog*, its hero a Herzog enjoying alienation,
committed to the trivial, impotent, abandoned, dyspeptic. He
seeks no communion with Nietzsche or General Eisenhower or
Heidegger, depending upon his own afflatus, the wind that
blows through him. Here Burgess detects Kell's hidden subject,
much as Enderby leaves the explanation of what his poems
really are about until they have got themselves down on paper.
At first it was enough to register the cherishing of the poet's
dyspepsia with all manner of indigestible food, stewed tea,
pickles ('a lone midget cauliflower swam like a doll's brain in
dense pickle'), the baroque squalor of Enderby's apartment. It
was enough to render in learned language his flatulence, and
represent onomatopoeically its manifestations : Perrrrrp, quer-
pkprrmp. His way of life must be recorded in simple terms :
cut off from women because of his disgusting stepmother, he
deals with the sexual side-effects of his creative life in the solitary manner of boyhood. Her appalling squalor determines the
filth and the chaos of his life. He feels the gulls, looks with
detachment at the world others live in. Nothing touches him
except his poetry. To him Mr Therm in the gas advertisements
is 'a smiling toy paraclete'. Crouched over his little table he
composes his wan minor poems, rumbling or defecating at the
same time. It is a Swiftian bagatelle. The joke about afflatus
and inspiration is, in fact, Swift's. The story that follows may
not have a Swiftian fidelity to the basic idea, but Enderby has
to be got moving. There is a fight, Enderby using the lavatory
seat as a weapon (his dazed opponent wears 'a lei of bottom-
polished wood'), and a disastrous trip to London, where, making a speech of thanks on the presentation of a poetry prize, he
allows his associative processes to get the better of him and

declines the 50 guineas. He falls in with other poets who plagiarize him, and is taken over by a beautiful young widow, a loathly lady in reverse, who turns in his bed from a beauty into a farting, belching, superstitious stepmother and robs him. His suicide attempt fails because death also resembles his stepmother, and he is cured by a phoney psychiatrist and given a new name: 'Enderby was the name of a prolonged adolescence.' Healthy, non-gurgling, non-masturbating Hogg now moves out of poetry into life.

Here the new book begins, with Hogg running a bar ('Piggy's Bar') in a Hilton-type hotel, quite turned off poetically, but still in essence the destructive foul-mouthed xenophobe he was before. After a party in his bar a pop-singer managed by Enderby's ex-wife Vesta is shot by a rival, who plants the gun on Enderby. He would have liked to murder this young man, who has incorporated some of his poems, stolen by Vesta, in a hugely successful volume of his own, a smart camp effort, 'like you get those good pictures with shitty Victoriana in them'. So, having a motive which would support the evidence against him, he flees. On the plane he is picked up by Miranda, a selenologist, and goes to bed with her in Seville, but in full coitus a poem comes on and he withdraws. Later he has adventures leading him to his old enemy the poet Rawcliffe, who stole his ideas and made an art-film of them in the earlier book; he decides to kill Rawcliffe, but finds him dying. He inherits Rawcliffe's pub in Tangier. A golden girl comes from nowhere and offers herself to him, discussing poetry. Enderby has to decline. We leave him solitary, minor to the end.

'The words slide into the slots ordained by syntax and glitter, as with atmospheric dust, with those impurities which we call meaning.' Certainly there is a lot of Burgessian play. A sentence, used twice, is simply an answer to the challenge: 'Write a sentence in English in which the same noun is repeated three times without intermission.' Answer: 'He has breathed on Enderby, bafflingly (for no banquet would serve, because of the known redolence of onions, onions) onions.' Yet onions also serve as a leitmotiv, are not merely atmospheric dust. There are other such devices, thematic puns (*la belle-mère, la belle mer*) parodies of pop and hipster verses; a visit to Piggy's Bar by McLuhan himself is not wholly irrelevant. The clinical bravura persists, not only in Enderby's less frequent borborygms, but in Rawcliffe's 'eroded dyspnoeal voice', and the use of 'nates' for buttocks. Enderby is the man who finds himself in the lavatory, 'calm of brerrrgh mind all aaaaafph passion gockle spent'. Yet on the whole, as I say, the surface is less amusing and surprising than that of the first book. We have to look at its inquiries into the depths of Kell's book to get a measure of its value.

The sea, the moon, death, and women are now seen to be an important subtext in these books. Enderby at one point wrote 'All women are stepmothers' on a sheet of lavatory paper and flushed it. Later he says that the muse is 'all women'. The moon draws up tides in the sea and in women, in *la belle mer* and in *la belle-mère*. The stepmother is the muse, death, the sea, even the moon or its goddess. Vesta : evening star, herald of the moon, stepmotherish glutton and burper – missing the point, Enderby recommends gin and hot water for menstrual pain. Miranda : learned in that brave new world the moon, waxing and waning, thin and fat, amorous and stepmotherish. Finally, naked and nameless, the moon-muse herself, at one with the sea and death. Rawcliffe died horribly, brave in the filth, and the muse consents to be wrapped in the robe he wore. She works on the volta of an Enderby sonnet, eats and drinks heavily, burps stepmotherly. Enderby loves her; he is almost, through Rawcliffe, ready for a life of a major poet. She gives him his chance, offers herself, having warned him that 'poetry isn't a silly little hobby to be practised in the smallest room'. But Enderby, 'not cut out for marriage', never makes it with a woman in either book, and middle-aged, withdraws from copulative majority into masturbatory minority. He can't take her 'ghastly young beauty' though his conventional worry about age is, she explains, only another instance of his cowardice and false categories. She accepts, as he must, his minor status, telling him he must just do what he can do – not, for instance, follow the Americans down the street (whom she also frequents) into 'a world of visions and no syntax'. He returns to stewed tea, borborygms, and minor poetry.

There is an almost Gravesian myth now discovered by Burgess in the Kell deposit; there are serious implications, vatic propositions about poetry, religion, sex, charity. You couldn't get Vesta right from the first book on its own : the first careless rapture, carefully repeated, displays a structure. Some of the bravura, naturally, is lost. Narrative invention grows cheaper as a novel of this kind grows longer. But Burgess is always on duty, building bits of plot to bear the meanings, prodigal of linguistic resources, be the need a Lancashire cook or an Arab sodomite. Enderby, a poet-grandson of Bloom, is surrounded by language which Bloom's maker would not have despised. Why, having persuaded the Goddess to make a brief appearance in her true form, it could not induce her to stay, is too difficult a question to open now.

(1968)

(C) JOHN UPDIKE

Any reader, coming to the end of this long novel,[3] might say – in a tone proper to himself – 'How sad!' Which reminds one that the best novel in English on the subject of couples begins with the words: 'This is the saddest story I ever heard.' But this kind of critical free association, though pleasing to reviewers, is unkind to novelists. How can one be fair to *Couples*, having in one's eye the densities, the intensities, of *The Good Soldier*? It's true that Ford is always slightly too *busy*, but he is busy about a mystery, and this mystery, in his short book, he lovingly, though not totally, exfoliates. Mr Updike has his mystery too, but he seems somehow dogged about it, elaborating it by careful assembly according to a blueprint, not, like Ford, by *progression d'effets*.

Yet the mysteries are surprisingly similar. Each of these books finds, in the behaviour and the interchanges of couples, a model of the world crisis. What we are all doing, as Ford's mad girls says at the end, is playing 'shuttlecock'. Study the religion of cock-shuttling, says Updike's novel, and you find a measure of the degree to which God has fallen out of love with America. Quantitatively, things seem to have got worse (Updike has ten couples, Ford two, though with others, shadowy, in the background). In the matter of sexual explicitness they have got better, or anyway freer. The legs one remembers in Ford's book are Maisie Maidan's, dead and sticking out from the cabin trunk she was dutifully packing when her heart, most treacherous of organs, betrayed her. The memorable Updike legs have a different character: the head of his hero, Piet Hanema, is always between them. Ford, as this suggests, is

3. *Couples*. By John Updike. London, Deutsch, 1968.

more oblique than Updike, who is serious, laborious, omniscient; his prose is sometimes – especially when recounting dreams or ecstasies – so worked, so edged, that reading it is like walking barefoot, possibly in a dream, along some interminable sharp-stoned beach. These are qualities – a packed sharpness, a flinty crowdedness – that distinguish Updike from novelists who brood intensely upon some coherent affair.

Mr Updike has, in the old word, an intendment. He announces it in an epigraph from Tillich, which mentions that we nowadays tend to regard public decisions as none of our business, simply a matter of fate, 'like Roman subjects all over the world in the period of the Roman empire; a mood favourable for the resurgence of religion, but unfavourable for the preservation of a living democracy'. So in a way *Couples* is a historical novel. The *Thresher* sinks, the principal female character hears the first news of John Kennedy's assassination at her dentist's, and so forth. As *The Good Soldier* is 'about' 4 August 1914, this is 'about' 22 November 1963, when America received the first of several signs that God was growing tired of his affair with her, leaving her pampered into decline and needing a new religion, rational, diabolic, sexy as witchcraft but without its numinousness; the first religion to leave death out.

Ten couples, then (and not all necessary, surely, a demand here if not for Origen's, then for Occam's razor). The principal matter is the love between Piet Hanema (Dutch Calvinist, church-going, but a bit of a stud – religion, he says ironically, is 'the source of my amazing virility ... a stiffening sense of sin') and Foxy Whitman (nice, but the Whore of Babylon was also foxy) who is the pregnant wife of a biochemist, and shares some of Piet's sexual interests. There are other couplings, and Piet, although he has a good wife, is in on most. The action occurs in Tarbox, an old seaside New England town, now swollen by Boston commuters, but still preserving itself as a diagram of the good old faith; its streets are labelled Charity, Prudence, Divinity, etc. and its centre is dominated by a Congregational Church with a huge weather cock, thought by the Tarbox children to be God. In the end the church burns down, but the cock is rescued by an intrepid young workman astride an enormous demolition-contractor's ball.

In the meantime Hanema, between two worlds, is a skilled restorer of Colonial architecture condemned to make a living out of jerry-building, and also an old-style Calvinist trying to make out in the 'post-pill paradise'. We find him in almost every attitude possible to an eager postulant, but he can't quite be one of the 'many blessed who believe nothing'. He is worried by the empty sky over the adulterers. As a builder he is ousted by a traditionless young man; as a lover he loses too. He enjoys sex ('the keenness of her chemistry made him whimper') but dislikes having to let his wife sleep with an evil dentist as the price of an abortion for Foxy. This dentist sickly celebrates a society where 'general courtesy replaces individual desire', in a world where life runs downhill, where the newly discovered desires of women have eaten God, and when 'there is nothing to steer by but stoicism and the stars'.

The dentist, according to the blurb, is the priest, as Piet is the scapegoat, of this new religion. But in fact they are both of them merely sad, merely victims of 'transition'. Nearly everybody is old-fashioned enough to be upset on discovering his partner's infidelity, even the dentist. Hanema is even more old-fashioned; his skills as craftsman or lover – his knack with tools – cannot save him. But somehow the faith, the cock on the church, is saved.

The reader recalls that in the sabbath the witches kiss the devil's arse. For these people, who cannot say grace before a meal but leave instead an uneasy pause to indicate tacit refusal, sex is most distinguished and serious when oral: 'we set our genitals mating down below like peasants, but when the mouth condescends, mind and body marry'. Meanwhile among the couples is one fine mind, a Korean, whose language they can't even understand, and cancer inexplicably kills him, while the sky stays empty.

Symbols, seasons, religions, ironies, Mr Updike works them all in. But there are too many couples one doesn't care about; and even in the big characters, Hanema and Thorne the dentist, for example, the muddle or vice isn't really in focus. Nevertheless, everything is seriously thought about. So strong a mythographer as Updike must always be facing a difficulty as a novelist: myth time is cyclic, history time is linear. So when Piet, or America, passes out of the sphere of influence of the love of God, we need not be too sorry; the Church has been rebuilt before. The decline of democracy, the rise of bad religions, can be reversed. If you're a linear man, Mr Updike lets you follow Piet along the pebble-strewn road to the wilderness; but the seasons, the rescued cock, are there to say you needn't. The cycle will lead you back to a pre-pill paradise: provided you can spot the myths under the stones. So 'How sad!' is somehow not sad enough: this is, for all manner of reasons, not the saddest story, though it is certainly a complicated game of shuttlecock.

(1968)

POETS

NINETEEN

PAUL VALÉRY

Modern poetry and criticism have made us all familiar with the notion that art is not so much an imitation of nature as another nature; and of this other nature criticism is perhaps the physics. Whitehead's observation that 'Nature is patient of interpretation in terms of laws that happen to interest us' seems to have some application to the second nature and its interpreters. When the interpreters are also creators, making the nature which is required to suffer interpretation by laws already adumbrated, we have something like the situation of modern poetry. 'The truth,' said Whitehead again, 'must be seasonable.' What truth seemed so to the great creator-interpreters? It is because of our anxiety to know this that so many of Mr Eliot's pronouncements have been regarded as axiomatic? But the whole of the seasonable truth is not to be found undistorted in the work of a single interpreter, or even in a single language; and that is a reason why Valéry, considered as interpreter, has high interest for English readers.

He is, as on the whole we prefer critics not to be, generally remote from texts; but this and other limitations help rather than hinder the clarity of his poetics. He gives us an unfamiliar but immediately recognizable diagram of this seasonable truth. In asserting that his value lies there, I differ, with respect, from Mr Eliot, who, thirty years after his first essay on Valéry, contributes a splendid preface to Volume VII of the *Collected Works*.[1] In it he suggests that Valéry's major achievements in poetics were to invent a new conception of the poet as a kind of literary scientist, at once dreamer and algebraist, and to provide an apology for his own poetry. But if Valéry did not also tell us something about, say, Mr Eliot himself, it would be harder to justify the translation of all his works into English. In fact this enterprise deserves great praise. These are volumes of high value; they are beautifully made, and the quality of the translation is quite remarkable. Professor Stewart's version of

1. *The Collected Works of Paul Valéry*. Edited by Jackson Mathews. Volume IV: *Dialogues*; Volume VII: *The Art of Poetry*. London, Routledge & Kegan Paul, 1957–.

Eupalinos has been famous for years, and now he has served the other dialogues with the same sinuous fidelity; Denise Folliot is a worthy coadjutor. And it was a happy chance that these volumes appeared first. They contain by no means all of Valéry's pronouncements on art, but what is to come will often repeat what is here, and these volumes provide a clear sketch of the laws of the modern poetic world.

Valéry was an intimate of Mallarmé, the Einstein of this world; but no one who thinks of the anti-intellectualism of modern verse will be surprised that he often represents himself as an ignorant man. He said he knew little of Plato, though he wrote Socratic dialogues; he professed an ignorance of Bergson which is hardly acceptable to scholarship. 'Being well read may spoil one's enjoyment of poetry,' he said. One thinks of similar statements by Eliot, by Yeats, by Stevens. Knowledge brought to the poem from Nature will be of the wrong kind; it will have little to do with the poetic Nature, 'all of whose forms and beings', says Socrates in *Eupalinos*, 'are ultimately but acts of the mind, these acts being clearly determined and preserved by their names. In this fashion they (artists) construct worlds perfect in themselves.' This discontinuity gives rise to what Valéry, commenting on his direct Symbolist ancestry, calls 'an almost inhuman state'. He touches here upon what Ortega y Gasset called 'the dehumanization of art', and on that doctrine of impersonality developed from Symbolist premises by Hulme and Mr Eliot. The human author must disappear from the poem. He must not obtrude his suffering; if to do that is human, says Valéry, 'I must declare myself essentially inhuman.' Poets must labour to make their poems as accurate as they can (Hulme's 'exact curve of the thing') and then leave them to be considered 'in complete isolation from each other and without reference to their authors'. A work has permanence in so far as it is capable of being something quite other than its author intended; this denial of the relevance of the author's intention is a basic tenet of post-Mallarméan poetry. Furthermore the work, however patient of interpretation, can never be explained. Valéry frequently expresses his contempt for explaining critics, but allows the author himself no rights in the poem. The poet is not saying but making; the poem has not meaning but being. Valéry wasn't even sure that one could properly read poems aloud without falsifying them with meaning. And this is a very clear statement of that physical (as opposed to Platonic) quality in poetry which is a central requirement of much modern criticism.

Yet Valéry is famous for his stubborn celebration of the role of Intelligence in poetry; here is another central paradox of modern poetic. In Valéry it is easier to grasp than elsewhere. First, there is the familiar distinction between *vers donnés* and *vers calculés*; the former somewhat contemptuously accepted, the latter passionately studied as the true activity of poets, the work of intelligence. Almost anyone can receive the *vers donnés*; Valéry repeatedly describes how he was visited by a musical inspiration he was unequipped to develop. Only the poet can develop this raw material, through hundreds of drafts, towards the infinitely perfectible but infinitely imperfect poem, seeking the exact curve in language never to be made absolutely precise. To offer only *vers donnés* is contemptible: *rougir d'être la Pythie!* What count are the thousands of deliberate acts of choice and calculation, the conversation of 'confused arbitrariness' into 'explicit and well-defined arbitrariness'. This is the poem, the machine for producing in others poetic states. Intelligence prevents its sliding away into mere dreaming; it also encloses the poem, makes it resistant to the wrong kinds of knowledge.

And here is another of our problems. Poems use words; the difficulty haunts poetics from Coleridge onwards. Valéry thought poetry a lucky survival anyway, the poet of today being an archaic figure using language for purposes to which it is no longer adapted. It seemed worth going on because now and then a man may still become sensitized to the value of a particular poem, and so partake of a pleasure forgotten in the modern world. But it is a daunting task, 'by means of a medium essentially practical, perpetually changing, soiled, a maid of all work, *everyday language*' to 'draw a pure, ideal Voice, capable of communicating without weakness, without apparent effort, without offence to the ear, and without breaking the ephemeral sphere of the poetic universe, an idea of some *self* miraculously superior to Myself'. The problem is to speak the speech of the poet, 'only a little of the tongue', in the language of the tribe. The poet's use of language is, says Valéry, 'nonusage – the *not saying* "it is raining".' In a famous analogy, which Mr Eliot does not like, he says that prose is to verse as walking is to dancing; prose is *instrumental*, having an end in action, but verse, like dancing, has no end outside itself. Of course the analogy is unsound; but it is very revealing.

The process of turning usage into nonusage Valéry sometimes called *musicalization*. He refines the old Romantic-Sym-
bolist yearning to have poetry as like music as possible. Musical
discourse cannot be confused with non-musical discourse;
poetic language can be confused with the *lingua franca*, but
music is not to be mistaken for natural noise. He probably contracted this deep envy of music from the Symbolist friends of
his youth, and with it the desire to make poems which were
resonant only of themselves, without external reference. Also,
of course, he envied architecture, the visible, serviceable structure almost independent of time; we like to think of poems
nowadays as having a structure in space, and possibly music
too, as Mr Eliot argues in his Preface. But, like Mallarmé before
him, Valéry found his most satisfying emblem of the desirable
poetry in the dance. He returned over and over again to the
dancer, notably in the magnificent dialogue here translated. It
contains the essence of our post-Wagnerian poetic. Dancers
had long been used for these purposes, and the formation of
modern poetic owes a lot to certain dancers in Paris, up to the
moment of Diaghilev's explosive arrival. But Valéry modified
the emblem in a characteristic way : he kept a series of photographs, taken in darkness, of dancers carrying lights. They
were a whirl of white lines, a record of the pattern of aimless
poetical acts – photographs of the second nature's lines of
force, of what happens in the universe of modern art.

What are the consequences of requiring art to be another
nature? Valéry once wrote beautifully of how, after being
shown the *Coup de Dés*, he walked with Mallarmé under a
brilliant night sky. Looking up at the stars, he seemed to see
what Mallarmé had attempted : 'he has tried at last to raise a
page to the power of the starry heavens'. Such attempts, in so
far as they succeed, will certainly be difficult, inaccessible. And
this would be a tragic story, were it not that, defying the law-
givers, we still sometimes love a poem as Phaedrus loved the
dancer – in a dream, as of enchantment by a woman; finding
too difficult the way of Socrates, who loved her because she
provided the antithesis of a dream : an absence of chance, a
world of exact forces and studied illusions.

(1959)

TWENTY

T. S. ELIOT

In the middle thirties, emerging from my remote provincial background (but we wrote poems and asked whether Browning didn't sometimes go beyond bounds), I at last discovered Yeats and Eliot; and in that bewilderment one truth seemed worth steering by, which was that these men were _remaking_ poetry. Although this recognition had very little to do with knowledge, and one waited years before being granted any real notion of the character of such poetry, it was nevertheless, as I still believe, a genuine insight. As one came to know the other great works of the wonderful years, one also came with increasing certainty to see that the imperative of modernism was 'make it new' : a difficult but in the end satisfactory formula.

These were the years of Auden, of a poetry oscillating between an inaccessible private mythology and public exhortation, an in-group apocalypse and a call for commitment to 'the struggle'. It was going to be our war; we were committed whether or not we wanted to be; and there were many poems of Auden especially which have by now disappeared from the canon, but not from the memories of men in their forties. Meanwhile, as the war approached, the indisputably great, the men of the wonderful years, were still at work. What were they doing? Their commitment they consigned, mostly, to the cooler element of prose; but we could hardly suppose they were with any part of their minds on our side. 'Making it new' seemed to be a process which had disagreeable consequences in the political sphere. I forget how we explained this to ourselves, but somehow we preserved the certainty that the older poets who behaved so strangely, seemed so harshly to absent themselves from our world – to hold in the age of the Bristol Bomber opinions which were appropriate to the penny-farthing – were nevertheless the men on whom all depended.

The death of Yeats in January, 1939, therefore seemed to us an event of catastrophic importance. The news of Eliot's death immediately brought to mind, in surprising detail, the events and feelings of that dark, cold day nearly twenty-six years earlier. These were the men who had counted most, yet had seemed to have so little in common with us. Yet on the face of it the two events seemed to have little similarity beyond what is obvious. In the months preceding Yeat's death there had been an extraordinary outpouring of poetry – how impatiently one awaited the next issue of the *London Mercury*, and, later, the publication in the spring of 1940 of *Last Poems and Plays*! And that wasn't all : there was the poet himself, masked as a wild old man or a dangerous sage; there was the samurai posturing, the learned, more than half-fascist, shouting about eugenics and war, and this at a moment when we were beginning to understand that the enemy would soon be imposing both these disciplines on Europe. But one didn't hate the poet for what he thought he knew, remembering that he had always held strange opinions without damaging his verse. 'Man can embody truth but he cannot know it,' he said in his last letter; and years before, in a line which gives modern poetry its motto, 'In dreams begin responsibilities.' He made no order, but showed that our real lives begin when we have been shown that order ends : it is for the dreams, the intuitions of irregularity and chaos, of the tragic rag-and-bone shop, that we value him, and not for his 'system' or his 'thought'. The time of his death seemed appropriate to the dream; in a few months the towns lay beaten flat.

History did not collaborate in the same way to remind us of the responsibilities begun in Eliot's dream. His farewell to poetry was taken only a couple of years after Yeats's. It was no deathbed 'Cuchulain Comforted'; it was 'Little Gidding'. Perhaps the Dantesque section of that poem grew in part from Yeat's strange poem; certainly Yeats predominates over the others who make up the 'familiar compound ghost'. The famous lines tell us what we ought to make of our great poetry and of our great poets :

> '... I am not eager to rehearse
>   My thoughts and theory which you have forgotten.
>   These things have served their purpose : let them be.
> So with your own....'

So much for the using up of a poet's thought. As a man he continues to suffer and without reward :

> 'Let me disclose the gifts reserved for age
>   To set a crown upon your lifetime's effort.

> First, the cold friction of expiring sense. . . .
> Second, the conscious impotence of rage
> At human folly. . . .
> And last, the rending pain of re-enactment
> Of all that you have done, and been. . . .'

So the ghost speaks of a Yeatsian guilt, remorse, and purgation. The man who suffers is now truly distinct from the mind that creates poems that have to be, as Picasso said of paintings, 'hordes of destructions'.

It is customary now to speak of a 'tradition of the new' in American painting, and it may even be possible to do the same of American poetry. There is no such tradition in English poetry. That our contemporaries on the whole avoid Eliot's influence is probably not important; perhaps it is the case, as Auden said in his obituary notice, that Eliot cannot be imitated, only parodied. But it *is* important, I think, that his insistence on making it new, on treating every attempt as a wholly new start, is now discounted. It may be true, as is sometimes said, that this wholly exhausting doctrine is on cultural grounds more likely to be successful in the United States than in England; certainly much of the evidence points that way. But that does not entitle us to ignore the doctrine. After such knowledge, what forgiveness? The lesson was that the craft of poetry can no longer be a matter of perpetuating dialects and imitating what was well made; it lies in an act of radical analysis, a return to the brute elements, to the matter which may have a potentiality of form; but last year's words will not find it. In consequence, the writing of major poetry seems more than ever before a ruinous and exhausting undertaking, and no poet deserves blame for modestly refusing to take it on, or even for coming to think of Eliot and his peers as Chinese walls across their literature.

This, of course, is to apply to Eliot the damaging epigram he devised for Milton. Sir Herbert Read tells me that the English poet for whom Eliot felt a conscious affinity, and upon whom he perhaps in some degree modelled himself, was Johnson. All the same it seems to me that the more we see of the hidden side of Eliot the more he seems to resemble Milton, though he thought of Milton as a polar opposite. As we look at all the contraries reconciled in Eliot – his schismatic traditionalism, his romantic classicism, his highly personal impersonality – we are prepared for the surprise (which Eliot himself seems in some measure to have experienced) of finding in the dissenting Whig regicide a hazy mirror-image of the Anglo-Catholic royalist. Each, having prepared himself carefully for poetry, saw that he must also, living in such times, explore prose, the cooler element. From a consciously archaic standpoint each must characterize the activities of the sons of Belial. Each saw that fidelity to tradition is ensured by revolutionary action. (Eliot would hardly have dissented from the proposition that 'a man may be a heretic in the truth'.) Each knew the difficulty of finding 'answerable style' in an age too late. With the Commonwealth an evident failure, Milton wrote one last book to restore it, and as the élites crumbled and reformed Eliot wrote his *Notes*. If Milton killed a king, Eliot attacked vulgar democracy and shared with the 'men of 1914' and with Yeats some extreme authoritarian opinions.

Milton had his apocalyptic delusions, but settled down in aristocratic patience to wait for the failure of the anti-Christian experiment, 'meanwhile', as Eliot said in the conclusion of 'Thoughts after Lambeth', 'redeeming the time: so that the Faith may be preserved alive through the dark ages before us'. In the end, they thought, the elect, however shorn of power, will bring down the Philistine temple; and the self-begotten bird will return. As poets, they wrote with voluptuousness of youth, and with unmatched force of the lacerations of age. And each of them lived on into a time when it seemed there was little for them to say to their compatriots, God's Englishmen. Eliot can scarcely have failed to see this left-handed image of himself in a poet who made a new language for his poetry and who transformed what he took from a venerable tradition :

> Our effort is not only to explore the frontiers of the spirit, but as much to regain, under very different conditions, what was known to men writing at remote times and in alien languages.

This is truly Miltonic; but Eliot at first moved away and pretended to find his reflection in the strong and lucid Dryden, deceiving many into supposing that he resembled that poet more than the lonely, fiercer maker of the new, of whom he said that it was 'something of a problem' to decide in what his greatness consisted.

However, a great poet need not always understand another; there may be good reasons why he should not. And Eliot certainly has the marks of a modern kind of greatness, those beneficial intuitions of irregularity and chaos, the truth of the foul rag-and-bone shop. Yet we remember him as celebrating order. Over the years he explored the implications of his attitudes to order, and it is doubtful whether many people capable of understanding him now have much sympathy with his views. His greatness will rest on the fruitful recognition of disorder, though the theories will have their interest as theories held by a great man.

Many of the doctrines are the product of a seductive thesis and its stern antithesis. The objective correlative, a term probably developed from the 'object correlative' of Santayana,[1] is an attempt to depersonalize what remains essentially the image of romantic poetry, and to purge it of any taint of simple expressiveness or rational communication. Its propriety is limited to Eliot's own earlier verse, which is deeply personal but made inexplicably so by the arbitrariness of its logical relations, its elaborate remoteness from the personal, and its position within a context which provides a sort of model of an impersonal 'tradition' – the fragments shored against our ruin. It is neither a matter of 'logic of concepts' nor something that welled up from an a-logical unconscious; in so far as it has 'meaning', it has it in order to keep the intellect happy while the poem does its work, and in so far as it has not, it has not in order to distinguish it from poems that 'make you conscious of having been written by somebody'.[2] The 'dissociation of sensibility' is an historical theory to explain the dearth of objective correlatives in a time when the artist, alienated from his environment, *l'immonde cité*, is working at the beginning of a dark age 'under conditions that seem unpropitious', in an ever-worsening climate of imagination.

1. In a letter to Mr Nimai Chatterji in 1955, Eliot says he thought he 'coined' the expression, but discovered that it had been used by Washington Allston. Eliot adds characteristically that he is not 'quite sure of what I meant 35 years ago' (Letter in *New Statesman*, 5 March, 1965, p. 361). Allston's usage is in fact quite different.

2. This is from an early essay on Pound (*Athenaeum*, 24 October, 1919) quoted by C. K. Stead in his interesting book *The New Poetic*. London, Hutchinson University Press, 1964, p. 132.

Such theories, we now see, are highly personal versions of stock themes in the history of ideas of the period. They have been subtly developed and are now increasingly subject to criticism. The most persistent and influential of them, no doubt, is the theory of tradition. In a sense it is Cubist historiography, unlearning the trick of perspective and ordering history as a system of perpetually varying spatial alignments. Tradition is always unexpected, hard to find, easily confused with worthless custom; and it is emblematic that a father of modernism should call himself Anglican, for the early Anglicans upset the whole idea of tradition in much this way.

He also called himself royalist, and this is an aspect of a larger and even more surprising traditionalism; for Eliot, in a weirdly pure sense, was an imperialist. This may seem at odds with certain aspects of his thought – his nostalgia for closed societies, his support for American agrarianism; but in the end, although he suppressed *After Strange Gods*, they grow from the same root. The essay on Dante, which is one of the true masterpieces of modern criticism, has been called a projection on to the medieval poet of Eliot's own theories of diction and imagery; but it has an undercurrent of imperialism, and can usefully be read with the studies of Virgil and Kipling.

This imperialistic Eliot is the poet of the *urbs aeterna*, of the transmitted but corrupted dignity of Rome. Hence his veneration not only for Baudelaire (where his Symbolist predecessors would have agreed) but for Virgil (where they would not). The other side of this city is the Babylon of Apocalypse, and when the *imperium* is threadbare and the end approaches of that which Virgil called endless, this is the city we see. It is the *Blick ins Chaos*.

The merchants of the earth are waxed rich through the abundance of her delicacies.... And the kings of the earth, who have committed fornication and live deliciously with her, shall bewail her, and lament for her, when they shall see the smoke of her burning.... And the merchants of the earth shall weep and mourn over her ... saying, Alas, alas the great city, that was clothed in fine linen, and purple, and scarlet, and decked with gold, and precious stones, and pearls! For in one hour so great riches is come to naught. And every shipmaster, and the company in ships, and sailors, and as many as trade by sea, stood afar off, and cried when

they saw the smoke of her burning, saying What city is like
unto this great city!

Here is the imagery of sea and imperial city, the city which is
the whore and the mother of harlots, with Mystery on her
forehead – Mme Sosostris and the bejewelled lady of the game
of chess – diminished as the sailors and merchants have dwin-
dled to Phlebas, the sea swallowing his concern for profit and
loss, and to Mr Eugenides, his pocket full of currants (base
Levantine trade) and his heart set on metropolitan whoring.
This is the London of *The Waste Land*, the City by the sea with
its remaining flashes of inexplicable imperial splendour : the
Unreal City, the *urbs aeterna* declined into *l'immonde cité*.

In another mood, complementary to this of Babylon, Eliot
still imagined the Empire as without end, and Virgil, its prophet, became the central classic, *l'altissimo poeta*, as Dante
called him. In him originated the imperial tradition. To ignore
the 'consciousness of Rome' as Virgil crystallized it is simply to
be provincial. It is to be out of the historical current which
bears the imperial dignity. In this way Eliot deepened for himself the Arnoldian meanings of the word *provincial*. The European destiny, as prophesied by Virgil, was imperial; the Empire
became the secular body of the Church. The fact that it split is
reflected in *The Waste Land*, where the hooded Eastern hordes
swarm over their plains, and the towers of the City fall. And as
the dignity of empire was split among the nations, the task of
the chosen, which is to defeat the proud and be merciful to the
subject, was increasingly identified with Babylonian motives of
profit – a situation in which Kipling's relevance is obvious.
Eliot speaks of his 'imperial imagination'; and, given a view of
history as having a kind of perspectiveless unity, Virgil, Dante,
Baudelaire, and Kipling can exist within the same plane, like
Babylon and the *urbs aeterna*, or like the inter-related motifs of
The Waste Land. Thus does the poet-historian redeem the time.
His is a period of waiting such as occurs before the apocalypse
of collapsing cities. But behind the temporal disaster of Babylon
he knows that the timeless pattern of the eternal city must
survive.

Some such imagery of disaster and continuity – 'that the
wheel may turn and still/Be forever still' – lies under *The
Waste Land* and is reflected also in Eliot's cults of continuity
and renovation 'under conditions/That seem unpropitious'. Yet

when we think of the great poem, we think of it as an image of imperial catastrophe, of the disaster and not of the pattern. For that pattern suggests a commitment, a religion; and the poet retreats to it. But the poem is a great poem because it will not force us to follow him. It makes us wiser without committing us. Here I play on the title of William Bartley's recent book, *Retreat to Commitment*; but one remembers that Eliot himself is aware of these distinctions. Art may lead one to a point where something else must take over, as Virgil led Dante; it 'may be affirmed to serve ends beyond itself', as Eliot himself remarked; but it 'is not required to be aware of these ends' – an objective correlative has enough to do existing out there without joining a church. It joins the mix of our own minds, but it dies not tell us what to believe. Whereas Mr Bartley's theologians sometimes feel uneasily that they should defend the rationality of what they are saying, the poets in their rival fictions do not. One of the really distinctive features of the literature of the modernist *anni mirabiles* was that variously and subtly committed writers blocked the retreat to commitment in their poems. Eliot ridiculed the critics who found in *The Waste Land* an image of the age's despair, but he might equally have rejected the more recent Christian interpretations. The poem resists an imposed order; it is a part of its greatness, and the greatness of its epoch, that it can do so. 'To find, not to impose,' as Wallace Stevens said with a desperate wisdom, 'It is possible, possible, possible.' We must hope so.

No one has better stated the chief characteristics of that epoch than the late R. P. Blackmur in a little book of lectures, *Anni Mirabiles 1921–1925;* though it contains some of the best of his later work, it seems to be not much read. We live, wrote Blackmur, in the first age that has been 'fully self-conscious of its fictions' – in a way, Nietzsche has sunk in at last; and in these conditions we are more than ever dependent on what he calls, perhaps not quite satisfactorily, 'bourgeois humanism' – 'the residue of reason in relation to the madness of the senses'. Without it we cannot have 'creation in honesty', only 'assertion in desperation'. But in its operation this residual humanism can only deny the validity of our frames of reference and make 'an irregular metaphysic for the control of man's irrational powers'. So this kind art is a new kind of creation, harsh, medicinal, remaking reality 'in rivalry with our own wishes', denying us the consolations of predictable form but showing us the forces of our world, which we may have to control by other means. And the great works in this new and necessary manner were the product of the 'wonderful years' – in English, two notable examples are *Ulysses* and *The Waste Land*.

The function of such a work, one has to see, is what Simone Weil called *decreation*; Stevens, whose profound contribution to the subject nobody seems to have noticed, picked the word out of *La Pesanteur et la Grâce*. Simone Weil explains the difference from destruction : decreation is not a change from the created to nothingness, but from the created to the uncreated. 'Modern reality', commented Stevens, 'is a reality of decreation, in which our revelations are not the revelations of belief'; though he adds that he can say this 'without in any way asserting that they are the sole sources'.

This seems to me a useful instrument for the discrimination of modernisms. The form in which Simone Weil expresses it is rather obscure, though she is quite clear that 'destruction' is 'a blameworthy substitute for decreation'. The latter depends upon an act of renunciation, considered as a creative act like that of God. 'God could create only by hiding himself. Otherwise there would be nothing but himself.' She means that decreation, for men, implies the deliberate repudiation (not simply the destruction) of the naturally human and so naturally false 'set' of the world : 'we participate in the creation of the world by decreating ourselves'. Now the poets of the *anni mirabiles* also desired to create a world by decreating the self in suffering; to purge what, in being merely natural and human, was also false. It is a point often made, though in different language, by Eliot. This is what Stevens called clearing the world of 'its stiff and stubborn, man-locked set'. In another way it is what attracted Hulme and Eliot to Worringer, who related societies purged of the messily human to a radical abstract art.

Decreation, as practised by poets, has its disadvantages. In this very article I myself have, without much consideration for the hazards, provided a man-locked set for *The Waste Land*. But we can see that when Eliot pushed his objective correlative out into the neutral air – 'seeming a beast disgorged, unlike,/ Warmed by a desperate milk' – he expected it, liberated from his own fictions, to be caught up in the fictions of others, those explanations we find for all the creations. In the world Blackmur is writing about, the elements of a true poem are precisely such nuclei, disgorged, unlike, purged of the suffering self; they become that around which a possible new world may accrete.

It would be too much to say that no one now practises this poetry of decreation; but much English poetry of these days is neither decreative nor destructive, expressing a modest selfishness which escapes both the purgative effort and the blame. America has, I think, its destructive poetry, which tends to be a poetry of manifesto; and in Lowell it seems to have a decreative poet. One way to tell them is by a certain ambiguity in your own response. *The Waste Land*, and also *Hugh Selwyn Mauberley*, can strike you in certain moments as emperors without clothes; discrete poems cobbled into a sequence which is always inviting the censure of pretentiousness. It is with your own proper fictive covering that you hide their nakedness and make them wise. Perhaps there is in *Life Studies* an ambivalence of the same sort. Certainly to have Eliot's great poem in one's life involves an irrevocable but repeated act of love. This is not called for by merely schismatic poetry, the poetry of destruction.

This is why our most lively sense of what it means to be alive in poetry continues to stem from the 'modern' of forty years ago. Deeply conditioned by the original experience of decreation, we may find it hard to understand that without it poetry had no future we can now seriously conceive of. It is true that the exhortations which accompanied Eliot's nuclear achievement are of only secondary interest. What survives is a habit of mind that looks for analysis, analysis by controlled unreason. This habit can be vulgarized : analysis of the most severe kind degenerates into chatter about breakdown and dissociation. *The Waste Land* has been used thus, as a myth of decadence, a facile evasion. Eliot is in his capacity as thinker partly to blame for this. Arnold complained that Carlyle 'led us out into the wilderness and left us there'. So did Eliot, despite his conviction that he knew the way; even before the 'conversion' he had a vision of a future dominated by Bradley, Frazer, and Henry James. We need not complain, so long as the response to the wilderness is authentic; but often it is a comfortable unfelt acceptance of tragedy. *The Waste Land* is in one light an imperial epic; but such comforts as it can offer are not compatible with any illusions, past, present, or future.

This is not the way the poem is usually read nowadays; but most people who know about poetry will still admit that it is a

very difficult poem, though it invites glib or simplified interpretation. As I said, one can think of it as a mere arbitrary
sequence upon which we have been persuaded to impose an
order. But the true order, I think, is there to be found, unique,
unrepeated, resistant to synthesis. The *Four Quartets* seem by
comparison isolated in their eminence, tragic, often crystalline
in the presentation of the temporal agony, but personal; and
closer sometimes to commentary than to the thing itself. When
the *Quartets* speak of a pattern of timeless moments, of the
point of intersection, they speak *about* that pattern and that
point; the true image of them is *The Waste Land*. There the
dreams cross, the dreams in which begin responsibilities.

(1965–6)

TWENTY-ONE

ALLEN TATE

It is an ancient and productive literary habit to compare things as they are with things as they used to be. 'We are scarce our fathers' shadows cast at noon.' Decisive historical events, types of the aboriginal catastrophe, acquire the character of images upon which too much cannot be said, since they sum up our separation from joy or civility. So, in Imperial Rome, men looked back to the Republic; so to this day they look back past the Reformation or the Renaissance or the Civil War, the points at which our characteristic disorders began. The practice has its dangers; the prelapsarian can become merely a moral and intellectual deep shelter, and there is some difficulty in drawing the line between the good old days of the vulgar myth and the intellectual's nostalgia for some 'organic society'. The lost paradise lies archetypally behind much worthless historical fiction, and agreeable though it may seem that the community as a whole appears to share the view that the second Temple is not like the first, the fact is that the first can be reconstructed on the South Shore, or on a Hollywood set, far more comfortably than in a work of imagination. The first requirement for such a work, on such a theme, is dry intelligence working on real information. To be obsessed by the chosen historical moment, as a theologian might meditate the Incarnation, so that one shares it with everybody yet avoids all contamination from less worthy and less austere intelligences – that is the basic qualification. Put another way, it is a power of self-criticism perhaps found only in an aristocratic, but not barbarian, sensibility. A few modern historical novelists have this quality. Mr Tate has it to an extraordinary degree, though his theme, the break-up of the Old South, is known to be unusually productive of gushing nonsense.

If, as we are told, many Americans have a confused and erroneous idea of the Old South, it is not very likely that we, founding ours on *Uncle Tom's Cabin* and *Gone with the Wind*, can avoid mistakes. Mr Tate, of course, is thoroughly informed, but it is not his business to impart information. His novel[1] is

1. *The Fathers*. London, Eyre & Spottiswoode, 1939.

Virginia-colour, steeped in the province, but if he mentions, say, Helper – a book studied by his principal character and locked away from other members of the household – he will not add that this book was called *The Impending Crisis in the South* (1857), or explain its importance. And this necessary reticence extends to matters more subtle; to the landscape and the climate, still to the European and the Yankee surprising, exotic; to the Jeffersonian politics of the old Southern aristocrat; to the archaic manners of the South and particularly to its views on personal honour, which make credible the violence of Mr Tate's climax. In fact, as presented, this climax is hardly violent at all; Mr Tate's strategy requires the maintenance of a very even tone and the preservation of the reader's distance from the events described. All the meanings are qualified by this calmness and this distance, and at certain crucial moments, narrative and symbolic, one senses the huge invisible effort the feat required. Explanation, discrimination between fact and myth, would have falsified all this, but their absence makes the work a delicate undertaking for English readers; for the tension between fact and myth is essential to the novel.

The myth of a valuable and archaic southern civilization is not without basis. Crèvecoeur could call Charleston the most brilliant of American cities. The ante-bellum South thought of itself as in a great tradition, the heir of Greece and Rome; and if its account of its aristocratic provenance was largely spurious, it was for all that essentially aristocratic in its structure. Yet it was a perversely democratic aristocracy, if only because of the slaves, whose very existence made it impossible to set difficult barriers between different classes of whites. In any case, the population was bound together by blood, by a network of cousinships that took no account of status and even included slaves. The Negro was not feared or hated in the antebellum South, and he was not – effectively at any rate – exploited (all parties, including Mr Tate's Agrarians, seem to be agreed that the slave system was extremely, perhaps, disastrously, wasteful). Any civilization is built on paradoxes, but few so curiously as this one. These backward-looking, fine-mannered men had the activity of pioneers and hunters, and their natural violence was fostered by the alternately languid and vehement climate. Civic and personal pride coexisted with a central hedonism, a passion for gaming, drinking, love-making, talking.

It was a world no outsider could improve, and one could represent the Yankee attack on slavery as directed not only against one's way of life, but against civility itself, even against God. The emphasis on personal honour is a feature of societies which feel themselves highly privileged; and South had its duelling, and was strong on the honour of women – the 'fragile membrane' as Faulkner calls it, that needs so much male blood to protect it. At the climax of Mr Tate's novel a Negro enters a girl's room and attacks her; the consequences are death, madness, sterility. But what seems a myth – the revival of some incredible tabu – is a matter of fact. Such tabus are protection from what Mr Tate calls the abyss, essential though atavistic elements of civility.

An image of civility so distinctive, and so decisively destroyed by war, can stand quite as well as that of England before its Civil War for the vanquished homogeneous culture that preceded some great dissociation, the effects of which we now suffer. It had all the gifts save art; and that, as Henry James said, is a symptom of the unhappy society. What the English Civil War meant to Mr Eliot the American means to Mr Tate; the moment when the modern chaos began, though it cast its shadow before. His book is about the antebellum South under that shadow.

The war, so considered, is also a myth with correlative facts. It is commonplace that one thing more than any other sets the Southerner apart from other Americans : he is the only American who has ever known defeat, been beaten, occupied and reconstructed, seen his society wrecked and had no power to rebuild it on the old lines. Hence, as Cash said in *The Mind of the South*, a division developed in the 'Southern psyche' – the old hedonism warred with a new puritanism, old loyalties with new destinations. A tolerant society became bigoted. The Klan attacked not only the now-hated Negroes but Jews, atheists, fornicators. And Yankee culture moved in. The link with the past, the 'traditional men', was gone. In Mr Tate's poem the Confederate graveyard stands, in his own words, for 'the cut-off-ness of the modern "intellectual man" from the world'. Could anything be saved? Mr Tate and his friends in the twenties proposed and developed an Agrarian solution for the South, and were accused of sentimental organicism, of naïvety hoping to revive the virtues of the antique world by restoring its economic forms. What they really wanted was a new society uncontaminated by the industrial capitalism of the North, a society living close to life in a manner made impossible by the great dissociation. 'I never thought of Agrarianism as a *restoration* of anything in the Old South,' Mr Tate says explicitly, 'I saw it as something to be created ... not only in the South ... but ... in the moral and religious outlook of Western man.' He sought a way of life having the kind of order that is now found only in art; an order available to all, and not only to the estranged artist. Mr Tate also proposed a theory of 'tension' in poetry (an extensive literal statement qualifies and is qualified by intensive figurative significances) which is a translation to aesthetics of this view of life. And his meditations on the South, or the image of it he has made, include these complementary literal and figurative aspects. Finally, in 1938, in this novel, he presents the image itself at its most complex, containing the maximum tension between letter and spirit, fact and myth.

Thus the calm of the book is not merely a matter of Southern dignity (though that has its place in the effect) but of intellectual control, the tightened bow. The South is matter of fact; but it is also

> a pleasant land
> Where even death could please
> Us with an ancient pun —
> All dying for the hand
> Of the mother of silences.

The 'place' of the Buchans is called 'Pleasant Hill',[2] in recognition of the basic myth; but it is not Paradise, it is merely a place where the radical human values are recognized, where the community and not the individual owns the myths which fence off the abyss. The time is just before the War. The narrator is Lacy Buchan, now old, speaking of the pleasant land as he saw it in boyhood. Memory works on a series of images: the death of Lacy's mother and the mourning of the 'connection'; a chivalric tournament; the beginning of the fighting; a Faulknerian family disaster; the burning of Pleasant Hill by Union troops. It would be difficult to exaggerate the skill and integrity of the presentation, the slow unfolding of figurative

2. Mr Tate tells me his own family home was called 'Pleasant Hill'.

significance. The principal characters are Major Buchan and his sons and daughter; George Posey, caught between the Old and the New South, who becomes Buchan's son-in-law; Yellow Jim, a Negro half-brother of Posey's. The basic fable is virtually Greek; rarely outside Greek drama is there to be found this blend of civilization and primitive ritual, the gentleman who is *euphues* but at home in actual life, and with his roots in immemorial custom.

Major Buchan's mistake – his *hamartia* – is the honourable one of backing the wrong version of history; he finds himself giving his daughter to Posey, whom he cannot understand, and adhering to the Union when his family yields to the overwhelming emotional attraction of Confederacy. All depends, in the book, upon the successful rendering of his dignity and authority, the order of his house. But the detail that shows his life and his house to be in some ways less than great – archaistic revivals of a dead past, like the splendours of the jousting – is also important. Woven into the myopically rendered texture of the book are the qualifying facts : Mr Broadacre forgetting to spit out his tobacco before making a formal oration on Southern chivalry, unsurpassed in the world; Lacy's mother conducting a household task as a little ritual 'not very old to be sure but to my mother immemorial'; the revived custom of duelling. These are the newly created traditions that Posey, the new man, dishonours. He is stronger than his opponent in the duel but will not fight it; he cannot be disarmed by the only weapon Major Buchan uses against him, a subtle withdrawal of courtesy. But his disregard for the absurd forms of his society is a symptom of his estrangement. He fears the dead, is embarrassed by the sight of a bull mounting a cow. The nature of the Buchan commitment to life he does not understand. 'They'll all starve to death,' he says. 'They do nothing but die and marry and think about the honour of Virginia.' He sells Yellow Jim, his half-brother, treating him as 'liquid capital', and so precipitates the domestic crisis of the attack on his sister. Even then Posey is half-hearted about the obligation to kill Jim, and the job is done by Semmes Buchan, Lacy's elder brother, whom Posey kills instead. He also kills his enemy Langton, a man as representative of the Old South in his corrupt activity as Semmes is in his archaic sense of honour. Posey's position in the War is ambiguous; he smuggles arms, carrying the carpet-bag which a few years later was the hated emblem of Yankee exploitation. Posey destroys the Buchans as surely as the War, and he does it out of a modern confusion, doing evil 'because he has not the will to do good'. The Old South is the Major, disowning his son for choosing Confederacy, but surrendering his house and his life rather than tell a Yankee officer that he himself is not 'seecesh'. As Lacy and Posy leave his grave, Lacy to return to the fighting, Posey to disappear on his own occasions, we learn of the last Buchan victim : Lacy. We know what to make of Posey, but there is always more to be made; as when Lacy, in his last sentence, declares his allegiance in the remarkable sentence, as rich a sentence as ever ended a novel : 'If I am killed it will be because I love him more than I love any man.' This is the reward of Mr Tate's method : his images, though always sufficient, accrete significance as the narration develops, so that the whole book grows steadily in the mind.

The dignity and power of this book depend upon the power of a central image presented with concreteness and profundity, and not upon one's acceptance of Mr Tate's history. But without his integrity of intellect and imagination the image would have been false and imperfect in ways that might have exposed it to such disagreements. By a bold device, the intervention of a ghost, Mr Tate hands on this image to us through three generations of Buchans; it is as if ratified by a time-defeating community of sentiment, and the life in it is good and transmissible as well as tragic. If we could rescue the word 'civilized' from the smart and fashionable, we could apply it, in deep admiration to this book.

(1960)

Whoever wishes to know what Allen Tate thinks his criticism is like may find out from his Prefaces, which explain that it is 'toplofty' in tone, aggressive because the only other course is to cringe. He looks back over his essays as he might over poems (for he tells us that poets can only thus discover what they think) and he abstracts certain articles of faith. There is 'a deep illness in the modern mind', it affects poetry, which, denied any 'large field of imaginative reference', tends to be complex, difficult, and important. But this must not persuade us to treat poetry as something else; it cannot explain the human predicament; rather it apprehends it 'in the mysterious limitations of form'. This is what it *does*; what it *is* is something else, and here at any rate it resembles, as Cowley noticed in *Of Wit*, that 'power divine' which 'we only can by negatives define'. R. F. Foster has recently commented on Tate's habitual negativity in this matter, but one could say that the 'tension' theory is the same kind of hard-won positive that Cowley reached at the climax of his poem : 'In a true piece of Wit all things must be, Yet all must there agree.' Much of the simple gist of Tate's criticism is in the prefaces.

He has also, in a virtually unique essay, told us what he makes of one of his poems, the 'Ode to the Confederate Dead'; and by the standards of modern poets this is a generous allowance of self-explication. So the author of a book on Tate finds some of the work done. Of course, Mr Tate qualifies carefully; in discussing the essays and the poem he is applying a doubtfully licit hindsight. There is not much point in distinguishing here between essays and poetry, for the best of the former, which come near to being the best of all modern critical essays, are in a way works of fiction, composed by the author of *The Fathers*; subtly elicited, formally constructed, ironical in a sense he and his friends taught us to recognize. Mr Foster argues, very sympathetically, that the New Criticism comes in the end to be best not as a strictly methodical kind of inquiry but as a risky, insight-conferring semi-poetry; he thinks first of Mr Blackmur in this connection, seduced, it may be, by the more intense local splendours. Yet Tate's greatest essays are finally more remarkable; they share with the poems a visionary mode, and a tough latinate vocabulary with controlled colloquial interventions – a style learnt from a despair of aristocracy.

Of course he can speak plainly, as in 'The Present Function of Criticism' and 'Literature as Knowledge'; his analyses of Morris and the early Richards are conducted with much precision. He often makes specific representations, concerning, say, graduate schools or literary quarterlies. And certainly on these occasions he is mindful of a deeper and more personal issue – his defence of the contemplative against the methodical. But neither these pieces, effective as they have been, nor others which owe their permanent interest to their radical relation with the author's practice as poet, are the really great ones. In that class one thinks of 'The Hovering Fly' with its urbane *progression d'effets*, the remote passion of its Fordian climax; and of the pieces in *The Forlorn Demon*, where contemplation is not a topic but a mode, and most of the rest of us (whether or no we would write like that if we had the talent) must feel like the political poets whom Tate consigns to childish voyages in Percy Shelley's paper boats. In this volume may be found the famous distinction between the symbolic and the angelic imaginations, the second characterizing an extreme humanist presumption, the hubris accompanying a desire to liberate poetry from its human limitations; I have wondered whether Tate here silently recalled the greatest of all Stevens' poetry, the passage on the angel in the last section of *Notes toward a Supreme Fiction*. Certainly to read the two together is to effect a sublime modern confrontation. In these beautiful and difficult essays Tate finds his full critical voice. Whether or no, as Miss Koch argued, the verse romanticises itself as it goes on, the prose surely moves triumphantly towards the idiosyncratic Thomism of these later essays, and they provide a proof of that communicability of insight asserted in the essay on Longinus.

The mode is contemplative: witness those acts of rapt attention to a few lines of Dante, or to the last scene of *The Idiot*. And Tate knows that most critics, including his own, are likely to be methodical, not contemplative. In the essay on Yeats, which so successfully relieves the poems of the burden of the System, he prophesied that 'the study of Yeats in the coming generation is likely to overdo the scholarly procedure, and the result will be the occultation of a poetry ... nearer the centre of our major traditions than the poetry of Eliot and Pound'. (It might be remarked, in passing, that critics – apart from Mr Nemerov – have strangely neglected the power of Yeats over Tate as a poet.) The prophecy has, to our cost, been fulfilled, and Yeats is now almost buried under the detritus of methodical investigation. In certain cases the poetry is valued only in so far as it can be perversely said to embody what is called 'the tradition', a nonsensical occultist jumble which is now being used to justify other poets as well, among them Keats. The practitioners of this perversion are the victims of that 'positivism' against which Tate conducted his 'toplofty' attacks; but theirs is the cringing defence, they abduct poetry, hide it in some grubby cell, and make it serve as a kind of Tarot pack. In practice, of course, these critics have just that ignorant passion for Method that Tate abhors; they savage Yeats with scholarly procedures divorced from all insight, and honour the gloss above the text.

This prelude is a way of saying that the man who sets out to write a book on Tate faces many difficulties. The extractable gist of the criticism, for instance, is already extracted in the Prefaces, and there will be a temptation to take the whole of the 'thought' methodically apart and set it up again, as if it were meccano; for who, constructing a thesis, can allow for the quasi-poetic mode and for the difference between contemplation and method? The matter is made more difficult in that the admiring critic may want to make of the 'thought' something acceptable to himself. (The best writer on Tate might be somebody who thought the 'thought' all nonsense but liked the poems.) There is another special danger in the essay 'Narcissus as Narcissus', where Tate himself (though the essay is very fine) sets his critics a bad example. He dislikes allegory and has not, I think, tried to get on terms with Spenser; but his study of the *Ode* is allegorical. The examples for his practice are distinguished though not, in this area, very successful: Dante and St John of the Cross. But the commentary on the 'Ode' virtually authorises explication by free allegory, an easy approach to the peoms which Tate's mind, in a more characteristic phase, resists, if only because the approach is methodical. Such explications invite vulgar disaster in another way, by applying the casually conceited language of the graduate school to linguistic constructs of notable precision (you might say this is caused by a professional 'hunger breeding calculation and fixed triumphs'). As to the essays, they can be torn apart, their delicate internal stresses disregarded; the parts reassembled will make theories, and contemplation will be reduced to method.

Mr Meiners[3] is an able and informed inquirer, and his book is generally intelligent and useful. He is aware of many of the difficulties mentioned above, affirming for instance that you must, in Tate's phrase, 'discuss the literary object in terms of its specific form'. Unhappily this merely tends to sharpen his preoccupation with method, and – what is much worse – his pleasure in discussing and demonstrating it. Mr Meiners is not a particularly bad case of this methodological obsession, but one notices how prevalent it is in the criticism of a new generation. (I assume, I hope not offensively, that Mr Meiners is young.) My immediate objections to it are not subtle, like Tate's, but perfectly simple. It gets in the way of the works treated;

3. *The Last Alternatives: A Study of the Works of Allen Tate.* Denver, Alan Swallow.

method in criticism is good in so far as it approximates, like the horn on an absey, to transparency. Methodological problems have a real power to excite the serious mind, which plaits the solutions into a sort of fence; then the critic contemplates the fence – all his own work – and not the field beyond. Mr Meiners begins by wondering where he should begin, quoting Alice. At the opening of Chapter 3, on Tate's poetic theories, he has some admirable remarks on the dangers and difficulties of what he is doing, remembering 'Tate's objection to the obsessive neatness of method'. But he does nothing about this, and I would agree that by such standards any book of this kind needs to be a little treacherous, since it has its own readers to consider, and must be tolerably shapely, not merely a discontinuous and repetitive commentary. A certain amount of 'faking' is inevitable. Thus one excuses Mr Meiners for this degree of betrayal. Harder to forgive are the transgressions against the simpler principle of methodological transparency, as in the passage which offers a brief history of *explication de texte* and leads up to a credo: the author believes in something like Wimsatt's 'explicative holism'. He could have let us observe him being explicatively holist and omitted this somewhat self-regarding preamble.

In fact, what follows isn't always explicative or wholesome. Mr Meiners, the holist exegete, is not immune from the familiar afflictions of the justified explicator. For example, he says of the word 'green' in the third stanza of 'Summer' in *Seasons of the Soul*, that it 'has overtones of death – witness Sir Gawain's experience. ... France is here viewed as not only dynamically alive, but, paradoxically, as barely vegetative.' Such are the ways in which explicators can demonstrate their ingenuity in the detection of meanings: 'paradoxically' admits contradictory senses without further resolution, and a familiarity with the English School syllabus does the rest. What shocks me more (perhaps unreasonably) is a mistake in this same passage, where Meiners misdates the German invasion of France. '1939' here rings so absurd to anybody who knows how '1940' *feels* that one can hardly avoid thinking the point of this poem has been lost on its explicator. I hope I am not merely exhibiting the graduate supervisor's routine insistence on accuracy in such details. The poem has to do with a particular paralysing moment; the mistake is not a year but an epoch of feeling. It seems therefore exceptionally intrusive, like the vast tact of such remarks as 'I have some recollection that Christ once said "I bring not peace but a sword,"' and 'I mention ambiguity and I do not wish to be understood,' and 'When dealing with the Goddess of Love in her Greek role we have an extremely tricky situation and I will not attempt any complete statement of it.'

What I complain of in short, is not merely egotistical intrusion, not merely 'methodological' opacity. It is a matter of tone. There should not be so great a discrepancy between text and comment without some good rhetorical reason. In Mr Meiners' book with its flashing of tools, its repeated claims to originality and dismissals of earlier critics, this discrepancy certainly exists. Perhaps this is why he does least well with the poems. They are certainly difficult to write about, but it is possible to multiply problems. The *Ode* is surely on any reasonable view an important and central poem, but Mr Meiners says very little about it; he assumes, rightly of course, that anybody who reads his book will know the *Ode* pretty well already, but by outflanking it he omits to attack the most irreducible of the problems Tate sets his readers. For it not only incarnates that contemplated past, but does so in the form of an ambiguous romantic vision which would obviously be patient of a great many different prose reductions. Meiners' assertion that *The Fathers* shares such characteristics is a good one; but the difference is that the novel finds, or improves out of Ford, a technical means clearly correlative to its intelligible purpose. The difference is between a fictional device one can be rational about, and a poetic device which is arbitrary and self-justifying. The *Ode* is the crucial instance of something that often happens in Tate's poetry – defiantly abrupt modulation into dream, and so, for interpretation, into allegory. There is a notably audacious instance at the beginning of 'Autumn' in *The Seasons of the Soul*, where the bathos is presumably intended or allowed for.

These effects Mr Meiners does little to describe, though I do not know that anyone else has done more. They are what would justify one's calling *Ash Wednesday* Eliot's most Tate-like poem, and the Tate's essay of 1931 on Eliot an important veiled pronouncement on his own poetry. He disputes Eliot's distinction of dreams into high and low, and for special purposes prefers what the other would call low ones; but he presumably agrees (or did so; these are hints of 'angelic' imagination) with Eliot's remarks in the essay on St-John Perse, when he says that the reader must be one who can feel the force of obscure relations rather than seek logical transitions, that he must sense rather than understand in any ordinary fashion the collocations of vision and wit. Incidentally, a very good example of Tate's power to give such collocations firm intellectual structure is the short poem called 'Pastoral', which Meiners mentions only to chide somebody for liking it. It seems to me a very good poem, though I see that its ironies might be called Fugitive; it presents the ancient and well-endorsed desires of the *locus amoenus* in collocation with another sanctified theme – 'love's not time's fool' – witty inverted. The potently suggested aphrodisiac ('She, her head back, waited/Barbarous the stalking tide') is in counterpoint with the 'deep hurrying mirror' of the stream, and the poem is resolved by the account of the lover at her 'wandering side' – not 'wondering', though she must in fact be wondering what has gone wrong, but 'wandering' because she cannot get anywhere she wants to be without him, and he is lost and impotent, 'plunged into the wide/Area of mental ire', and far from the conventionally sympathetic fields where lovemaking could happily occur. It isn't, of course, impossible to relate this little poem to those areas of concern towards which allegorization of Tate always points: dissociation, disintegration, considered as characteristically modern and contrasted with a better-built scheme of things. But this, if we allow it, merely strengthens the wit: 'Such meditations as beguile/Courage when love grows tall' is both a glance at *Hamlet* and a perfectly just nonce-revival of the Chaucerian sense of 'courage'. This is a very tense poem, inescapably a dream poem, inescapably witty, an invert 'Extasy'.

Donne lies behind Tate's witty dreams, though Tate is no less different from Donne than are his other modern admirers. I do not think he, any more than Eliot, has written well on Donne; but they have both, clearly, *felt* well about him; and Donne is a poet who might well be in a man's mind when he says 'in poetry all things are possible if you are man enough'. As to Tate's own work, I suppose this boldness is greatest in *Seasons of the Soul*, the poem Meiners singles out for specially full treatment. This blend of wit with dreaming wilder than Shelley's sets Mr Meiners great problems: he might well have said, as he considered it, 'anything is possible in explication of poetry if you are man enough'. With a good deal of his elaborate exposition of the poem I see no reason to agree, though it may well be that nobody else could do much better. Having called his predecessors on 'Winter' both 'wonderfully suggestive' and 'pathetically inadequate', he labours long over Venus and the Hanged God and the *aeternum volnus amoris* of Lucretius; but merely to do so creates a somewhat false impression, and whoever needs elementary help on these points is not likely to get far with the poem anyway. I should have liked more (what there is is quite good, though) on the enormously inflated sea-conceit; the occasionally dandyish diction ('sea-conceited scop'); the faintly Swinburnian deliquescence of 'living' into 'livid'; the growth in the poem of the surrealist coral with its Dantesque tree; above all on the Freudian beast who 'slicks his slithering wiles/To turn the venereal awl/In the livid wound of love'. Is there a difference between this and what Tate calls modern katachresis masquerading as metaphor? I doubt it; but the phrase is compelling enough, and has to do with the theme of the sexual wasteland discussed by Tate in the essay on Eliot I mentioned earlier. 'Venereal awl' sounds like baroque slang for the colloquial 'tool' – a calculated and sinister joke. These questions do not seem to be the kind that interest Mr Meiners. The explicator has a trade which grew up with modern poetry; yet a poem which so well illustrates Tate's prose points – a walking of the rope over an abyss of error and nonsense, learning as one goes where the next step must fall – yields very little to him. The poem-dream as 'specific' form, as the model for that knowledge which, except as analogue, is merely knowledge of itself, is essential to Tate; one may contrast the wonderful dreams of Donne, so subordinate to an external logic and rhetoric. Tate's explicator has to interpret dreams : so Mr Meiners can say 'On one level the "tossed, anonymous, shuddering sea" is a visual description; on another it is a value judgment and a behavioural description of modern life.' And it must be admitted that Mr Tate led him into this temptation, though he did not teach him this language.

Mr Meiners, one repeats, shows himself aware of the problem; one of his best observations is that Mr Tate's poetry 'depends upon a peculiarly intense vision in which objects and scenes, originally abstract, are forced to exist in a particular perception, a concrete detail, a specific sensation' – a perception none the worse for being approximately upside-down. He sees that the failures in Tate's poetry are usually related to this fact, whichever way you look at it. My only genuine complaint against Meiners is that occasionally, as in the chapter of *Seasons of the Soul*, he is swept away by his explicative fury into practices which imply neglect of this insight and others.

It is time to add that in discussions of general issues arising from the prose and the poetry Mr Meiners is thorough and often perceptive. On 'formalism', on the saving doctrine of poetry as analogy, on the problem of a poet in a society lacking 'an objective system of truth', on the myth of the ante-bellum South, and on the 'dissociation of sensibility' in all its aspects, he does a good and lively job of exposition. As an Englishman who came late to the knowledge (and love) of the man and his books, I am grateful to Mr Meiners for some expansion of my understanding of Tate, and regretful only that the demon Method has in some ways distorted the images of the great poems, the essays and the novel.

(1964)

TWENTY-TWO

AFTERTHOUGHTS ON WALLACE STEVENS

The early letters and journals[1] of Stevens show a most private man, a self-cramped man, or a man who gave everything time to mature. Long-breathed speculation preceded decisions: whether to become 'a money-making lawyer', to marry, or to write poems. He decided, he says, that fact must be met with fact; if 'life is worth living under certain conditions', these conditions involved the postponement of poetry. As it happened, business success and poetry came together, as if providence were ready to comply with such planning. There is nothing in the letters to explain how Stevens, who wrote no poetry worth preserving before he was thirty, should suddenly have written 'Peter Quince at the Clavier' and 'Sunday Morning'. One can only guess: among the things he wanted most were a home (where he could cackle in the Stevens environment, as 'toucans in the place of toucans') and 'an authentic fluent speech'. Hartford became the place of this toucan's cackling; but any other one place, if well-protected, might have done. Later, as he reasoned of these things 'with a later reason', Stevens called the 'place dependent on ourselves' Catawba. It was the mind and reality who married there, and 'they married well because the marriage-place was what they loved'. Catawba might be New Haven on an ordinary evening or Hartford in a purple light or the Tennessee in which he invested nothing but a jar; a place where the mind matches the world on equal ground. Catawba 'was neither heaven nor hell', but it was a good place to start the war or marriage between the mind and sky.

Seen from the outside, Stevens is quietly absurd. The poet of gaudiness, of pungent colour and exotic shape, was a sort of Hartford Des Esseintes. Des Esseintes' trip to London ended with a bottle of stout on a foggy night at Calais. For Stevens, Europe was a daydream about Paris, a postcard from Basel; and

1. *Letters of Wallace Stevens.* Selected and edited by Holly Stevens. London, Faber & Faber, 1967.

China a box of tea or a packet of jasmine solicited from travellers. His ephebes were exotic youths: a Korean poet, a Cuban scholar. He looked forward especially to the letters of Thomas McGreevy, with whom he could share his distaste for 'Ireland's neighbour', and of Leonard C. van Geyzel, an Englishman expatriate in Ceylon, who might not only feed one's daydreams but supply 'the very best tea procurable'. The plum survives its poems, as Stevens remarked; but whether he, as poet, could have withstood the abrasions of genuine travel without losing his bloom is a question. The world's gaudy Cockaigne for him was Florida, with Cuba and the banana-islands over the horizon. The Rome of the Santayana poem, the Florence of the dead Englishman, have the same reality as Haddam, where the thin men live, or New Haven, or Oklahoma where the firecat bristled and Bonnie and Josie danced round a stump – his sense of place has an accuracy in respect of the imagination only. While his rich friends the Churches divided their year between New York and Paris, he sat it out in Hartford, working through the summer, dictating insurance letters and philosophical poems, lunching at the Canoe Club, and walking home in the evening to whatever might be 'the combination of the moments', for example Berlioz and roses. After that, whatever books he might choose to read (he says he has time to read whatever he wants) and letters to and from, say, a Paris bookseller, or a Yale student, writing an *explication* of 'Sea Surface Full of Clouds'. It might take such a man to see that the final truth about poetry is the fictiveness of the entire world; save for a mythic core of 'reality' the world is poetry, and there to be discovered, as desperate and virginal in Hartford or New Haven as anywhere else.

Lawrence once wrote remarkably about the umbrella of fictions with which we keep out the intolerable hot diversity of chaos. For him the original artist was the one who tore holes in the umbrella, so that human life and chaos were for a moment in contact; but the rent was soon mended with another more comfortable fiction, and the need is for a succession of umbrella-tearers who will not let us dismiss all that inhuman fortuity from our lives. Stevens is the poet of that umbrella, but also of the *Blick ins Chaos*, to remember which is to be aware of poetry. (The man who so dreaded poverty in its more physical form had an acute apprehension of the more metaphysical poverty which is our lot without poetry: 'money', he once wrote, 'is a kind of poetry'.) In the thirties the 'pressure of reality' was particularly hard on the umbrella, and Stevens' attempt to meet it in the political form it then took was *Owl's Clover*, a self-confessed failure. The letters of the succeeding period, especially in the war years, silently celebrate the increase in reality's pressure by a steady concentration on the theory of poetry. 'The theory of poetry is the theory of life.' These are only apparently hermit musings, and it is not really surprising that Stevens reached his most authentic and fluent speech in poetry at such a moment; *Notes toward a Supreme Fiction* belongs to 1942. The subject is what human beings must add to the plain sense of things in order to make of the world something that suffices. The more desperate the world's poverty, the harder and the more private the poet's job. A man who does such a job well might be represented as a rabbi or a soldier, or simply as major man; but what he makes *is* a kind of poetry, and so, not necessarily but actually, the task falls to poets, and poetry is the supreme fiction, major man is a poet. Poetry is as pure and as impure as life, as reasonable and as unreasonable. Whatever is well said about poetry is well said about life. So, in his entirely solitary way, proceeding at his own slow pace towards the truth about human fiction, Stevens earned the right to regard any meditation, any half-worked out 'and yet' or 'as if', as a contribution to the great subject, the human meaning of an ordinary evening in Connecticut when beyond the mental umbrella there is chaos, the sun is meaningless except by our gift, and all the gods are dead. The subject matter of poetry is 'the aspects of the world and of men and women that have been added to them by poetry' : everything that is human or humanized.

This gives him a right to his arbitrary musing, and as rabbi (both learned and understanding poverty) he arrogates the further right to be aloofly allegorical and to go on with his thinking just so long as he chooses, without regard to the unschooled who may not follow. If you were puzzled by the Arabian in *Notes* :

> At night an Arabian in my room,
> With his damned hoobla-hoobla-hoobla-how,
> Inscribes a primitive astronomy
>
> Across the unscrawled fores the future casts
> And throws his stars around the floor —

you could write to Mr Stevens, and he would write back and tell you that the Arabian is the moon, adding that 'the reader could not possibly know this. However, I did not think it necessary for him to know.' On the other hand, he thinks that when he uses the word 'tanks' in a context suggesting Ceylon, the reader should know exactly what he means without being told. Extremely obliging in his response to letters of inquiry, he often remarks that his correspondents are mistaken not only in thinking that his poetry is plainer to him than to them but also, and habitually, in thinking that what integrates a poem is *ideas*. 'A poem must have a peculiarity, as if it were the momentarily complete idiom of that which prompts it.' Newton Stallknecht very neatly called Stevens' poetry 'a poetry of philosophical *intent.on*' – not, that is, of philosophical execution. It is useless to seek in it a simple bonding of ideas. 'One can do nothing in art by being reasonable ... it is also true that one can do nothing by being unreasonable.' Hence that range of uniquely philosophical poetry – a different thing, as Coleridge noted, from philosophy and also from poetry simply considered – in which he ranges from a kind of intense meditative mumble to a declarative candour which also, on examination, defies paraphrase. Only thus can one do the work of the dead gods, and create the 'Extraordinary Actuality'.

It is unlikely that Stevens ever really felt the criticism that all this is wildly out of touch with what most people have in mind when, 'in the metaphysical streets of the physical town', they hear 'the actual horns of baker and butcher'. He wanted to be the consort of the Queen of Fact. When Church was still thinking about founding a Chair of Poetry at Princeton, Stevens advised him that the right man to fill it would be someone who could deal with actuality without referring to poetry at all. Such a man, he said, was Hemingway – 'a poet ... and I should say offhand, the most significant of living poets, so far as the subject of Extraordinary Actuality is concerned'. A Hemingway hero must have seemed a much better image of metaphysical poverty than an Appalachian farmer or an Abyssinian 'coon'.

After the thirties Stevens gave up the attempt to compete with other theories of poverty and reality; he simply went on with his own. That is why the letters of 1942 ignore the reality that was going on in Germany, in Russia, and in the Pacific, even the warships clustered at New London a few miles from Hartford. He writes instead about 'the order of the spirit' which 'is the only music of the spheres: or rather, the only music'; about how a private press should print his book ('Light tan linen or buckram cover'); about his Dutch ancestors. Just as 'poverty' became for him a purely metaphysical concept, so did war. His was the primal war 'between the mind and sky'; his soldier was simply another figure of the youth as a virile poet. Even his 'fat girl, terrestrial, my summer, my night' is, he explains, the earth, 'what the politicians are calling the globe', and what he thinks of as the irreducible reality where all poetry (all humanity) begins. Stevens commits himself to the biggest of all as-ifs; he behaves as if poetry and the imagination are everything that is humanly important (and therefore everything that is at all important). Consequently he felt himself to be dealing incessantly with *the real*.

The philosophy of this was not for him to work out, only to brood over. Though he says that 'supreme poetry can be produced only at the highest level of the cognitive', he also holds that the kind of thinking it requires is distinct from that required by philosophizing because it is 'a creation not of meaning but of points', welcoming fortuity and logical imprecision, devoted not to clarity of expression ('what I intended is nothing') but to the blooding of abstractions. It adds to the vulgate of experience an 'and yet'. So does metaphysics; but he insists that his work has 'no serious contact with philosophy'. Stevens acknowledged an interest in Santayana, James, and Bergson, but his reading was patchy and never deep. He knew *about* Heidegger but not, apparently, even *about* Wittgenstein. When Paul Weiss asked him why he didn't take on a full-sized philosopher he replied with his usual epistolary calm, quite untouched by the criticism. Philosophy, like many other things, was his business only when it suited him to make it so. It became a part of his authentic and fluent speech, but it isn't surprising that when he sent his 'Collect of Philosophy' to a learned journal it was rejected.

Many of these letters are written as part of the para-philosophical game. The correspondents are not, as a rule, confidants; there is a certain reserve even with old friends, though the old gaudiness so personal to Stevens flashes out in letters to the young, and there is an occasional letter, like the one to Harvey Breit about the Dutch Church at Kingston which has an uncovenanted and dazzling philosophical wit. Often he is just thinking on paper, as in some poems. The long letter to a congenial correspondent, and the long poem, suited his mental style. 'Some people always know exactly what they think. I am afraid that I am not one of those people. The same thing keeps active in my mind and rarely becomes fixed.' As letters these are not obliged to be agreeable or self-consistent; but for anybody who knows the poetry they are very revealing, they do enhance one's familiarity with the drift of Stevens' meditation – its hidden structure of seasons, fictions, human fear, its bursts of gratuitous and generous happiness, as when a Norwegian girl poet calls at Hartford. They even suggest a queer kind of heroism, as if the refusal to condone poverty, to care for men in the mass, were a necessary aspect of that attempt to identify poetry and humanity, to be 'major man'.

In the long run, I think, these letters will stand as classic specimens of the preoccupations of modern poetry for such reasons as these, rather than for the direct light they throw upon actual poems. When one comes first to the book, the most obviously exciting letters are those in which Stevens, with extraordinary good humour and candour, and against the whole bent of modern practitioners, gives his own interpretations of certain poems; most remarkably there are many pages on *Notes towards a Supreme Fiction*. The interest of these is of course exceptional, and yet the comments are not, in the end, very helpful. Where the language of a poem is extraordinary, arbitrary, Stevens simply incorporates it into his paraphrases, 'practising mere repetitions', or he says he can't remember, perhaps never knew. There are certainly hints on how to read the poems, but surprisingly little help with detail.

'The object, of course,' he says of 'An Ordinary Evening', 'is to purge oneself of anything false.' He wanted to get out of the poem and himself all the left-overs of past imagining. In this sense he was tremendously modern; he was not interested in poetry as 'an aspect of history' but as a conjunction, appropriate to its moment, of the mind and its place, a world essentially indifferent. If the gods die, and statues grow rigid, what can be hoped for poems? But against this self-destructive emphasis on the ephemerality of the modern poem he built up his own world, in which there are to be found relations to some extent proof against time. Everything was implicit in *Harmonium*, and he saw it as a programme, wanting to call it *The Grand Poem: Preliminary Minutiae*. When he finally consented to a

collected edition he did so only when he felt something had
been completed, and he wanted to call it *The Whole of Harmonium*. Having felt a bit chilly towards *Harmonium* in the
years after its publication in 1923, he came to admire again in
his late years its unpredictable certainties, its strange rightnesses, the way it confirmed later poems. The *Collected Poems*
do make a 'total edifice' and an enduring meditation. There is a
lot of squiggling, marginalia, meta-metaphysical muttering,
pointlessness, wantonness, the tedium of small private sub-
jokes and sub-thoughts, and these will serve to defend Stevens'
thesis of necessary obsolescence, the inevitable decline of
imaginative objects into absurdity. But for all its fortuity and
decay *The Whole of Harmonium* looks pretty permanent, indeed 'a shining exemplum of human dignity', to borrow Allen
Tate's word for the poetry of Hart Crane – from 'Plowing on
Sunday' to 'The Rock'. An exile from most of the world, and
from most of the people about him who would have been
equal to his imaginative demands, he showed that exile, if
necessary, may be had without departures, without fuss. The
letters often show one how the polite hermit kept out the
world, hoarded the passions and the poet's scholarship that a
more orthodox life such as Crane's had to dissipate. Of course
Stevens is not the great modern poet anybody could have
predicted, but great poetry has often been surprising in its
time. To undervalue him because he seems so wantonly not to
fit the milieu or the moment is still a common error, just as it is
to overvalue him because he thinks. Rightly seen he is, in his
shy, egotistical remoteness, very central to the whole idea of
modern poetry.

How *are* we to see him rightly? The signs are, I should say,
that the vogue is ending, and the enormous effort to explain
Stevens has failed. It is a characteristic failure of our graduate
schools.

There is already a considerable number of books about
Stevens, and I have not read them all, though to make up for
this I have read some that remained unpublished, and have
written one of them myself. Although one learns something
now and again from the Stevens literature, it is on the whole
dispiriting. 'I must have been terribly wrong', one thinks, 'ever
to have supposed that Stevens was any good.' He emerges as a
tiresome doodler with a vast but not profoundly interesting

body of Thought, which he has never quite got round to articulating. The disentangling of this Thought from camp titles and periphrases is the self-appointed task of critics. Now and again there is a confluence of comment on some particularly mysterious poem, like 'The Emperor of Ice Cream', but the ordinary practice has been to ignore the fact that Stevens wrote a great many discrete poems and treat the whole *œuvre* as one poem from which one takes one's illustrations, usually with a reference to a page number in the *Collected Poems* rather than an individual work.

Here is a passage, chosen almost at random, and written by a professionally competent commentator on Stevens.

> The giant of nothingness is referred to elsewhere, most explicity in 'Aides on the Oboe,' as 'the glass man,' glass in that he is 'the transparence of the place in which/He is.' Since the place is the mind and the mind is characterised by its will to change only a substance whose nature could change with the changes of its environment – change in the light directed upon them, as glass, crystal or diamond – would be logical for the abstraction of the hero. Yet if the man of glass 'in a million diamonds sums us up,' he is also 'without external reference' – just as the mind itself is at once transparent and without external reference. 'Sea Surface Full of Clouds' is an early poem describing the response of the mind to changing light on a seascape – that is, as a transparence of the place in which it is. On the other hand, as we have seen, the mind is 'eccentric,' – a sensibility that is a thing-in-itself characterised by a will to order and a will to change, paradoxical characteristics that reflect a paradoxical reality. The glass hero in a crystal world (the poet's 'fluent mundo') is thus the first idea of mankind in the natural world – a 'human acceleration that seems inhuman,' and, one might add, an acceleration of nature that seems unnatural. (L. S. Dembo, *Concepts of Reality in Modern American Poetry*, 1966, pp. 104–5.)

Now if this is not the way to do it, and I am sure it is not, it remains true that this passage is not flagrantly inaccurate or silly. What it does is to take the meta-metaphysical mutter of Stevens and make it explicit. Nowadays the advice of Coleridge (and Eliot) to the effect that poetry can appeal strongly when imperfectly understood – advice Stevens took as a basis for his writing – is considered beneath the dignity of scholarship. What the Stevens glass man 'dewily cries' comes out as if treated by electronic recording engineers to take the dewiness out of it, and we hear such things as the man-monster never uttered, in tones remote from his. Where the harmonics of Stevens are heard they are inappropriate; as when a proof-text – 'human acceleration that seems inhuman' – is adorned by a piece of pulpit oratory (and, one might add . . .'.) which is actually an imitation of the rhetoric the poet himself went in for in the Adagia and the essays.

It is as if the Stevens *mundo* had been stripped and re-assembled, not quite in the same order. Worse still, it gives a strong impression, as I mentioned before, that here is a poet we had best not dabble with, since he is so solemnly foolish. The next paragraph is designed, almost, to confirm this rejection. 'Finally, the "auroral creature musing in the mind" is described as "the naked man" who paradoxically becomes the "plus gaudiest vir", a man constantly rejuvenated by "cataracts of facts". . . .' Who could possibly care?

Who could possibly care? It is the easy comment of our enemies. Our business is to see that people care. Yet there is, of course, some justification for this kind of commentary. Stevens didn't altogether disown the element of puzzle in his work, and he did sometimes think of his entire *œuvre* as an attempt at a Grand Poem. But we are surely in a difficult position when our attempts to make a number of discrete poems into a whole harmonium simply discredit our author, and this is what happens. What one ends up with is an argument, more or less convincing, supported by proof-texts that suggest that the original under discussion is unworthy of discussion. The effect is of the deadlier kind of tract, the brainlessly minute column of Migne. Somehow the worst of Stevens is often the most useful for illustration. Stevens' solar chariot is made up of a good quantity of junk; we shall need eventually to admit that. But some commentators reduce it all to junk.

Harmonium has little junk and is hardest to traduce. Even when a poem contains a metaphysical plot Stevens is usually content to let be the obliquity of most *trouvailles*. When there is some sort of argument in process one is never bothered to do more than keep in the right general direction. I note in Mr Nassar's recent book the most useful explanation I have yet

read of *Le Monocle de mon Oncle*, including a note by Arthur
Mizener on the lines

> Why, without pity on these studious ghosts
> Do you come dripping in your hair from sleep?

'In your hair' means 'with your hair hanging freely and
naturally' like a colonial virgin at marriage. It is good to know
this. Mr Nasser goes on to explain that the whole poem is a sort
of love-ode to the Interior Paramour. 'From a sleep of dreams
the imagination emerges with fictions that belie any absolutist's
("studious ghosts") formulation of reality, and declare true but
irrelevant Swift's satirical description that all pleasing images
are deception.' Leaving out Swift, who seems to have no business here, we can say that Mr Nasser is sort of right but that it
is not especially good to know that. I cared greatly for this
poem before I knew anything about the Interior Paramour.
What mattered was the absolutely personal assurance, the
sense of one poem as able to bear the strain of so many relations, so many *trouvailles* all in tension with each other, a
tension of wit and magniloquence, of notions made significant
only because they occurred in one spot, Catawba or Hartford,
New Haven or Tennessee or Oklahoma or Key West. Stevens' is
a poetry that makes its landscape. Elsewhere it is the poetry of
hats, of cocks, of angels, of statues; here it is a poetry of hair.
'Le Monocle' is this, and the crickets, and 'If men at forty will
be painting lakes'; it is the red bird, the damsel heightened with
eternal bloom; it is the accuracy of grotesque:

> Last night we sat beside a pool of pink,
> Clippered with lilies scudding the bright chromes,
> Keen to the point of starlight, while a frog
> Boomed from his very belly odious chords.

The gap between 'Le Monocle' and what can be said about it
in commentaries is wide; indeed this gap is always very wide in
Stevens. No commentators will say of his own efforts what
Stevens said, commenting on one of his poems: 'This is just an
explanation.' And few remember this saying: 'A poem must
have a peculiarity, as if it were the momentarily complete
idiom of that which prompts it.' He used philosophy, and any
other kind of thinking, just as it prompted him. This is equally

true of his prose. To take a short and splendid instance, his address at Bard College in 1948, in which he speaks of reality as the poet's 'inescapable and ever-present difficulty and inamorata'. He has said that the imagination is false, and then he says that it progresses by particulars, and that this makes the poet 'like a man who can see what he wants to see and touch what he wants to touch. In all his poems with all their enchantments for the poet himself, there is the final enchantment that they are true.' And after this solemn and animated play with the great abstractions that always haunted his mind, he ends by calling the poetic act 'an illumination of the surface, the movement of a self in the rock'. It might be from a poem, rather than from an address of thanks. Certainly it has a kind or argument. The thoughts and images cross, and what gives them their true relation is not argument:

> One's sense of a single spot
> Is what one knows of the universe

means less and more than Whitehead's 'every spatio-temporal standpoint mirrors the world'.

Stevens accepted Wahl's assertion that no idea is poetic, or 'that the poetic nature of any idea depends on the mind through which it passes'. On the other hand – and this is where the trouble starts – Stevens also believed, as I have said earlier, that 'supreme poetry can only be produced at the highest level of the cognitive' – or, as he puts it in the 'Collect of Philosophy', that the 'poem of poems' would have a philosophic theme. This idea is at once made richer and harder by a figure: 'That the wing of poetry should also be the rushing wing of meaning seems to be an extreme aesthetic good ... it is very easy to imagine a poetry of ideas in which the particulars of reality would be shadows among the poem's disclosures.'

Further he argues that doing philosophy has aspects analogous to doing poetry; a passage from Whitehead proceeds 'from a level where everything is poetic', and in another Samuel Alexander strains after exactness just as a poet does. 'Je tâche, en restant exact, d'être poète' – a paradox Stevens found in Jean Wahl.) But 'the probing of the philosopher is deliberate' and 'the probing of the poet is fortuitous'. He might have said that the philosopher invents and the poet discovers. 'When we want to pay final tribute to Planck we say that his thought on causality had poetic nuances.' He might have said this of Wittgenstein, had he read Wittgenstein. Two truths emerge, anyway. One is that Stevens found philosophical thinking akin to poetry, and exciting. The second is that he was not under the impression that his thinking was 'doing philosophy'. He might very well feel about his systematic critics what the poet Morris said of a reciter who read his verses for the sense alone : 'it took me a long time to get that into verse and this damned fellow takes it out again'. If the poem is finding what suffices, we should remember that the examples given are 'a woman dancing, a woman combing' – sudden rightnesses, not deliberate probing; 'a movement of self in the rock'.

The particular problem, then, for his expositors, is this element of cognitive thought. The solitariness of Stevens makes this very complicated: solitariness, literal devotion to the single spot which is oneself, is admittedly an American tradition, but it calls for great critical resource. It asks for a solitary critic. There is probably no way to talk about the 'Metaphors of a Magnifico' without being a little public, a little philosophical. But the point to remember is that when we have read it together we must read it alone : once for the plot, once for the movement of a self in a rock. And yet even this formula won't suffice. Even in *Harmonium* Stevens is at his thinking : in, say, 'The Doctor of Geneva' or 'Another Weeping Woman' or 'Explanation', in 'Valley Candle', just as much a philosophical allegory as 'The Comedian as the Letter C' :

> My candle burned alone in an immense valley.
> Beams of the huge night converged upon it,
> Until the wind blew.
> Then beams of the huge night
> Converged upon its image,
> Until the wind blew.

The kind of explanation ordinarily given simply destroys this poem's selfhood. How much harder things become when more and more comment, more and more ideas, shadow the poem's 'particulars of reality' !

After *Harmonium* the meditation becomes more continuous; there are more long poems and more trivial annotations on the commentary in the form of short ones. The flash fades, the voice mutters metaphysically : 'The theory of description mat-

ters most. . . . It is a world of words to the end of it.' All this is
rich in proof-texts. 'Chocorua to its Neighbour', its magniloquence qualified by joky nonce-words and bloodless finicking
dandyism, is a great source of proof-texts. This is Augustinian
speech as 'direct transference' not of thought but of reverie.
But we come in the end to those poems where a movement of
a self in the rock requires that, in order for the idiom to be
complete, the meditation, the metaphysical, or meta-metaphysical mutter, shall be there, in tension with the particulars,
as in 'Credences of Summer' the hayfields of Oley are the limits
of reality. The culmination of this is *Notes toward a Supreme
Fiction*, where we could not have had the passionate thinking
of the climax without many testimonies of the imagination's
truth and mercy : the chattering birds and the sexual blossoms,
the ephebe suffering at his window, the lasting visage in the
lasting bush, the true *weather* of the poem. Or, if it is not there,
the culmination is in the earned, unfaltering meditation of the
great final poems, whether long, like 'The Rock' or the poem
for Santayana, or brief, like 'The Planet on the Table' and 'As
you leave the Room'. The marriage of flesh and air in a particular poet at a particular spot is mentioned in these words about
his poems, from 'The Planet on the Table' :

> It was not important that they survive,
> What mattered was that they should bear
> Some lineament of character,
> Some affluence, if only half-perceived,
> In the poverty of their words,
> Of the planet of which they were part.

I have said little of how, as commentators on this poet, we
are to get out of our dilemma. Always, from the beginning, he
teases us into thought; and later he forces thought upon us, or,
at his best, uses it as he used colour in his early poems ('before
the colours deepened and grew small'), as among the points
which make the uniqueness of a poem. He tells us not to think
of him as philosophical, but also that if he could write anything approaching the 'poem of poems' he would *be* philosophical. The only answer I can give (and the fact that the
question is difficult doesn't make it unimportant), the only
answer is to bear down upon the particularity of the poems
themselves, the movement of a solitary self in their rock, and

its relation to the particularity of their presiding personality. It is better to grasp 'The Idea of Order at Key West' as a single unique occurrence, an invitation to one's own imagination, than to see it as part of a para-philosophical structure. It is better to feel the peculiar lines of force that dominate *Notes* than to fit it into a philosophy founded on all the other poems. But the best thing of all is to know the point where all these forces cross, the unique Catawba in which the mumblings are the local speech, the human focus of all this physical and metaphysical fortuity. That cannot be done by exploding the whole harmonium into fragments, and reassembling it into an inclusive commentary on its ideas. There are some key issues that, for pedagogical reasons, may have to be talked about discursively : but if you understand what Stevens meant by 'poverty' you know almost enough; if you can see why *Notes toward a Supreme Fiction* was to Stevens a kind of war poem you are nearly there. Then the thinking has to be muted, seen as an aspect of the ventriloquial powers of this great poet. Like all the others he celebrates the marriage of flesh and air, but in a dialect intensely local, like Bonnie's and Josey's.

We first see Stevens not in perspective, in a long tradition, but flat, like one of his early poems, arbitrary relations of colour and shape. Of course Stevens has his traditional elements, the re-incarnated blank verse for example; and the pose of the atomic isolation of his poetry, which is in a sense traditional for America. And if we complain that Stevens was given to smothering simple meanings in grave or fantastic clothing, we should reflect upon the remark : 'Poetry is like anything else, it cannot be made suddenly to drop all its rags and stand out naked, fully disclosed. Everything is complicated; if that were not so, life and poetry and everything else would be a bore.'

(1966–7)

TWENTY-THREE

W. H. AUDEN

Auden is the twentieth-century poet in something like the way Tennyson was the nineteenth-century poet. He was born ninety-eight years after Tennyson, his first book appeared one hundred and one years after Tennyson's, and anybody of about fifty or over who reads poetry must feel, as a Victorian in the same case felt a century ago, that his whole reading life coincides with one important career. It is difficult to explain how much this colours one's mind, but it certainly has an effect on the sentiments. It is a relation like a very old friendship, which may not be as active and exciting as newer ones, and which one may on occasion casually traduce, but always in the knowledge that it can never end. Just so might a man have been irritated by *The Princess* and bored by *Maud*, only to acquiesce, perhaps with a sigh, in *The Idylls of the King*.

Differences must, however, be declared, and they are many. Auden will write no *Idylls* and bore us with no Doubt; he has made himself ineligible for the Laureateship and the House of Lords, and he is unlikely to give private readings to the Queen of England. Tennyson claimed to be the greatest master of the English language since Shakespeare, but added that he had nothing to say. Auden is a great master, and there is virtually no limit to what he has to say. The parallel remains : this for some who are aging is the voice, the demeanour, of our aging century. Once taut and cold, that voice could speak to the accompaniment of a blue stare learnt from a school bully, shout in-jokes aloud, express like a surgeon in one breath our sickness and his assured jargon-protected knowledge. Now the voice is more benign, the look more tolerant, and we can share the knowledge if we want to. But there is no question that this is the same voice, or that it is a twentieth-century institution.

This gives him no Tennysonian centrality; Auden is the poet of our pluralism, a very singular person indeed. He has formed no school, is seriously eclectic ('His guardian angel/has always told him/What and Whom to read next'), and has precisely defined for himself and us – to whom he is therefore important – the unimportance of what he is doing. He agrees with

Nietzsche that 'we have Art in order that we may not perish from the Truth'. He is very private, himself polices his limits and lacks, rejoices in his immense technical resource, and takes what he wants when he wants it; from Groddeck long ago, or Lorenz now; from Graves long ago, and now, in *City Without Walls*[1] from John Hollander (because he knows a good comic verse form when he sees it). Forty years ago, in 'Paid on Both Sides', he inserted a whole chunk from a mummer's play and left us to explain to ourselves how it fitted the plot, which was about a feud. More fluent and amenable today, he still expects his 'handful of readers' to be able to 'rune'.

Readers of his criticism – notably that collected in *The Dyer's Hand* – are likely to feel that Auden's prose is more solemn than his verse, which for a long time has tended to be without much afflatus, light and conceited in tone. Though poems frequently end with a kind of bow to the Supreme Being, anything that could possibly be described as Magic is, for doctrinal reasons, excluded, and the invocations, incantations, and world-changing spells which charmed our youth are gone. Their impropriety was detected by the poet long ago, in the forties, when he worked out, with the aid of Kierkegaard and others, his religious position. One implication was that Auden could never, in the manner of some elders, confuse poetry with ethics or religion; to speak of the poet as a third order of priesthood would seem to him very wrong, and he would not, like Yeats, tell the Magical Lie, even if this were, as Yeats believed, the right way to hold justice and reality in a single thought. The Prospero of Auden's *Tempest* commentary, *The Sea and the Mirror*, is one such magician.

Renouncing magic, Auden finds in maturity good reasons to support a conviction of his youth, that there is much to be said for 'light' verse, for verse that uses the intelligence, for verse that remembers the gaiety possible to the natural man. This emphasis displeases some readers, especially some who were among his earliest admirers; for thirty years or more they have been complaining that he did not know how seriously to take himself, though in fact the course of his career is one long demonstration that he takes himself seriously enough to know exactly that. The wit and craft of his later poetry, rightly

1. London, Faber & Faber, 1970.

understood, continue this demonstration.

He at first wrote as if charged with creating mystery or uttering prophecy, and since he began in the twenties, there is nothing surprising about that; but it became clear that he was more a Dryden than a Yeats. The parallel with Dryden is indeed obvious, and is suggested in a general way by Auden's intensely professional approach to his craft and the vastness of his linguistic and conceptual resources. More specifically, he is, like Dryden, occasional poet, translator, playwright, librettist (perhaps the best in our time), songwriter, master of the styles of argument, a more important critic than his idiosyncratic prose discourse allows some people to see, and a wit. In this last capacity he has preserved longer than Dryden did the fantastic strain of his youth, and occasionally this takes one back behind Dryden to the Donne of the funeral elegies, or his imitators. The new book contains an epithalamium quite as conceited as seventeenth-century examples of the genre, and in its day quite as modern.

To enjoy it you need all your wits and at least one first-rate dictionary (Auden's own, he tells us, are 'the very best that money can buy'). Consider, for example, these stanzas, addressed to a kinswoman on her marriage.

> May Venus, to whose caprice
> all blood must buxom,
> take such a shine to you both
> that, by her gifting,
> your palpable substances
> may reify those delights
> they are purveyed for :

> cool Hymen from Jealousy's
> teratoid phantasms,
> sulks, competitive headaches,
> and Pride's monologue
> that won't listen but demands
> tautological echoes,
> ever refrain you.

Only the deities are commonplace, and the good wishes; all are forced to share the poem with some strange words and themes.

The verb 'to buxom' is obsolete, and means 'to obey'. It sits snugly beside 'take a shine to', for each is its own kind of slang, one proper to goddesses and one to ordinary lovers. The rest of the stanza means that he hopes this will enable their bodies to make actual the pleasures for which they were provided. 'Tera-toid' means monstrous, pathological, used here for its original as well as its medical sense, and instantly cut down to size by 'sulks'. As all echoes are tautological, that word here rather nicely applies to itself as well as to the echoes. In the re-mainder of the poem we are counselled to thank Mrs Nature – sometimes called Dame Kind and a member of Auden's make-shift pantheon, with Dame Philology, Dame Algebra, and occa-sionally less substantial allegorical figures – for bringing humanity to the point where the Auden clan get together for the marriage; a huge evolutionary effort, an epic of survival, must be celebrated by human beings so assembled, but as per-sons they also owe thanks to

> the One for Whom all
> enantiomorphs
> are super-posable, yet
> Who numbers each particle
> by its Proper Name.

'Enantiomorph', I see, is a term used mostly by crystallo-graphers, but in the general meaning, according to the O.E.D. *Supplement*, 'a form which is related to another as an object is related to its image in a mirror : a mirror image'. Webster, under 'enantiomorphous', seems closer to our mark : 'similar to but not superposable; related to each other as a right-handed to a left-handed glove'. The point is that for God enantio-morphs *are* superposable, though he does not fail to distinguish the individuality of each created thing. The Proper Name, thus capitalized, is an indication of one respect in which poets, in so far as they resemble Adam, are made in God's image : for 'whatsoever Adam called every living creature, that was the name thereof, which is to say, its Proper Name. Here Adam plays the role of the Proto-poet . . .' (*The Dyer's Hand*, p. 34).

The argument of the epithalamium is at once flip and seri-ous, and yet it is an argument, not just a bunch of witty, avuncular good wishes. Two 'nonesuches', two Proper Names, have decided to 'common' their lives, always a 'diffy' undertaking, and one with a long strange history; a marriage is a symbol of the superposability of enantiomorphs (if it works), and the ceremony provides a good moment to joke about the physical and also the spiritual adventures of *homo sapiens*.

The reading of such poetry is an experience about as different as possible from that of reading, say, Wallace Stevens, even though he looks more 'philosophical' and also has a very personal lexicon; the difference is that Auden's meanings are exactly defined by the unusual words : *nauntle, dindle, ramstam, noodling* are from the dialect dictionary; *depatical, olamic* are more learned. When Auden speaks of

> the *baltering* torrent
> sunk to a *soodling* thread,

or of the Three Maries *sossing* over the seamless waves, he is not, as you might suppose, inventing words. If he remarks that 'the insurrected eagre hangs/over the sleeping town' we may have to look up eagre, but once we've done that we know what he's talking about. In the poem beginning

> On and on and on
> The forthright catadoup
> Shouts at the stone-deaf stone —

I had lazily assumed that a catadoup was some sort of bird, but actually it is a Nile cataract, and this naturally makes a difference to the poem. Hence the importance of those dictionaries.

It may well occur to some old-fashioned reader that there is a price to be paid for choosing this method of celebrating 'the eachness of everything', and the price is that 'music' – Tennyson's thing – has been sacrificed. Auden's reply to this kind of criticism is that the people most likely to use it 'are the tone-deaf. The more one loves another art, the less likely it is that one will wish to trespass upon its domain.' The truth is that the 'musical' kind of poet is likely to be more concerned than Auden with the world as seen by symbolists : a blur of correspondences. If you are more interested in identity as perceived among the sorted out from creation's infinite variety, you are likely to avoid these chords and speak idiosyncratically of what you peculiarly see from where you alone stand. If you argue that humanity is given a diversity equal to that of the language-less creation precisely in language, you will want to illustrate this diversity and this language by speaking precisely. Because they cannot speak, birds (and cataracts) are unoriginal, repetitive, incapable of lying, unaware of death and time. 'Let them leave language to their lonely betters' who need it to map their worlds in time and space, and also – in the Age of Anxiety – to understand man's anxieties. This calls for large and modern lexicon.

Once, in serious mood, Auden catalogued our Anxieties. 'The basic human problem,' he said, 'is man's anxiety in time, e.g., his present anxiety over himself in relation to his past and his parents (Freud), his present anxiety over himself in relation to his future and his neighbours (Marx), his present anxiety over himself in relation to eternity and God (Kierkegaard).' This characteristically triadic formulation belongs, however, to 1941, to the period of *New Year Letter*. Since then the task of the poetry has been modified; broadly speaking, it is to celebrate what is present rather than what makes anxious, to see (with knowledge) and name (with language) whatever in the multitudinous world presents itself before you, wherever you stand. Auden always admired Hardy for 'his hawk's vision, his way of looking at life from a very great height'. This enabled him 'to see the individual life related not only to the local social life of its time, but to the whole of human history'. There are bold modern attempts to do likewise; for example, Virginia Woolf's *Between the Acts*. Auden's is different, more exact and knowing, less comprehensive and 'musical'. The most he does is to sketch the grand gestures, as in the palaeo-botanical splendour of the lines on

> that preglacial Actium when the huge
> Archaic shrubs went down before the scented flowers
> And earth was won for colour —
> > (*About the House*)

which neatly superimposes a historic upon a prehistoric battle, one time-scale on another, so that even readers who wonder whether poets need to bewilder us with 'scientific' information may have, for a second, a sharper sense of where they stand in the longer perspectives of time. Thus a lifelong love of technical language for its own sake pays off. The material isn't, as it were, orchestrated in a Woolfian way, nor is there anything like the immemorial moaning that Tennyson combines with geology. There is not even any anxiety; without music, without magic, he professes accuracy in respect of what is to stand in the Arctic Circle, in a Manhattan kitchen, or in an Austrian house.

Primarily he is a city poet. He thinks of the city in relation to geology, human evolution, and history; he remembers too that a City is emblematic of a community bound by need and love, so that the actual lower-case city is far from being the same thing. He further reflects that there are great differences between poems and cities and societies:

A society which was really like a good poem, embodying the aesthetic virtues of beauty, order, economy, and subordination of detail to the whole, would be a nightmare of horror for, given the historical reality of actual men, such a society could only come into being through selective breeding, extermination of the physically and mentally unfit, absolute obedience to its Director, and a large slave class kept out of sight in cellars.

(He saw in his youth that totalitarian aesthetics, like those of Hulme, Pound, Eliot, and Yeats, had a tendency to be reflected in totalitarian politics.) Such preoccupations not surprisingly promote a special interest in the celebrant of the city and its antecedents, in the work of seeing and making which he does under his particular roof. And so Auden, without ceasing to be reticent, writes more and more (wryly, ironically, yet charitably) about himself.

This does not shorten the historical perspective, or diminish the sense of standing on a world of rock and soil. The myth of the limestone Eden, which is recurrent but which we now associate principally with the beautiful 'In Praise of Limestone', published in 1962, has not lost its force. But in that poem the preference for limestone led to generalizations about human types with other preferences. Now the tone grows more personal, the poems more directly concerned with the curiosity that upon a particular middle-aged man, shaped thus, dressed thus, should devolve the professional task of praise. It is long enough, I admit, since he required that 'the shabby structure of indolent Flesh/Give a resonant echo to the Word' : but there is a new element of amused wonder that the spirit, no longer orgulous or bold, and established in still shabbier flesh, should 'conform to its temporal focus of praise'. In *About the House*, published in 1966, the poet meditated on the quality of the space each room represented. The study is cut off from 'life-out-there', however 'goodly, miraculous, lovable' it may be; in it poems are written, and the poet serves 'this unpopular art which cannot be turned into/background noises for study/or hung as a status trophy by rising executives'. And a poem may be, at best, 'a shadow echoing/the silent light', no more than that; but it is a great deal. And to be doing something so relatively impressive and so privileged can seem odd, especially if one happens to be doing it in the middle of an incorrigible, indifferent metropolis.

So the new book opens with a poem in alliterative five-line stanzas about the fantastic forms of Manhattan, and the inhabitants of this cliff full of folk, mechanically working nobodies whose reaction to Nothing is expressed in metres almost as old as the language :

> Small marvel, then, if many adopt
> cancer as the only offered career ...

The meditation is building up a sardonic picture of a postwar world when it is interrupted by a voice 'at three A.M./in mid-Manhattan' – which censures his *Schadenfreude*; a little psychomachy ensues, and the poet is advised to go to bed.

Teasing, moral, the meanings float down metrical streams; we should, we are told, 'look at/this world with a happy eye/ but from a sober perspective'. There is an occasional regression to old moods and styles, as in the joke-menace of 'Song of the Ogres' —

> Little fellow, you're amusing,
> Stop before you end by losing
> Your shirt ...

but by and large the new book is about the Poet at Sixty. The concluding poem is called 'Prologue at Sixty'. Characteristically it contemplates its author, first as a member of the human race :

Name-Giver, Ghost-Fearer,
maker of wars and wisecracks,
a rum creature, in a crisis always,
the anxious species to which I belong

and then as random particle and Proper Name, the descendant
of Nordic pirates, inhabitant of Austria within the limits of the
Roman Empire; member of a culture which has grasped the
relation between flesh and spirit, and which in principle
accepts the duties of acknowledging happy eachness and of
beaing witness 'to what is the case'. To the meaningful land-
scapes of his life he now adds bits of New York; a New Yorker,
sixty, turning first to the obituary columns of the *Times*, he
still has some hope of being able to share the city with the
alien young.

The little seventeen-syllable *obiter dicta* which have for a
few years past scattered themselves across his work are sometimes directly about the Poet: 'He thanks God daily/that he was
born and bred/a British Pharisee'; 'The way he dresses/reveals
an angry baby,/howling to be dressed.' And so selected
crotchets are revealed: the Poet is not vain, except about his
knowledge of metre and his friends; he wishes he were Konrad
Lorenz, and that he had written the novels of Firbank; he expects lights to turn green for him when he reaches a crossing.
He has little to complain of, living as he does, 'with obesity and
a little fame', among Americans, of whom it may be said that
they resemble omelets: 'there is no such thing as a pretty good
one'.

These little sketches contribute selectively to an image of the
Poet as benign, as saying Yea but not loudly, tamed by age,
domestic in his own kitchen, given to amusingly rueful speculations about verse, sex, God. Do we see in him any of the
lineaments, however modified, of the Poet of our youth, of
Lions and Shadows – the chill genius working all day behind
darkened windows, a gun in his desk; the technical virtuoso
who could write a double ballade on the names of toothpastes;
Stephen Spender's guru; C. Day Lewis' accompanist on the
harmonium, or Louis MacNiece's sardonic travelling companion
to Iceland, the brilliant joker of the *Letter to Lord Byron*?
Where is the public school mythopoet, the boy who cut up his
poems and stuck together only the best, terse lines, so that

sometimes they sounded like an urgent telegram received in a
nightmare —

> Coming out of me living is always thinking,
> Thinking changing and changing living,
> Am feeling as it was seeing?

Is there a trace of the louche 'Letter to a Wound', or the tone,
borrowed from cruel bullying prefects out of the world of
If . . ., that conveyed to us so valued a *frisson* in 'The Witnesses'?
Where is our deliciously minatory prophet, studding with epi-
thets he made his own a clever child's vision of disaster —

> The sinister tall-hatted botanist stoops at the spring
> With his insignificant phial, and looses
> The plague on the ignorant town.
>
> Under their shadows the pitiful subalterns are sleeping,
> The moon is usual; the necessary lovers touch?

Where is the voice, so certain of its priorities, and its audience,
that advised us of our duty in *Spain*, that battered sixpenny
pamphlet, its red now fading on our shelves, that is never re-
printed? We say nothing of the shouting, brawling Odes, the
poems spoken from behind a clinician's mask, or the *gemütlich*
apocalypse of 'Out on the lawn I lie in bed . . .' I do not know
how we can hear them in the present voice, or see them in the
present face of Auden, except by the same imaginative effort
we should need to restore our own uncrumpled faces and un-
cracked voices. But something endures, too deep for time to
eradicate; it is a rhythm of thought, convolute, indirect, persistent. One hears it in the Prologue to *Look, Stranger!* 'O love,
the interest itself in thoughtless heaven . . .' with its long-drawn
sentences, the beautiful conceit of Newton,

> who in his garden watching
> The apple falling towards England, became aware
> Between himself and her of an eternal tie;

in the last seventeen lines, of which I cannot say whether my
admiration is actual or remembered from my eighteenth year.
Certainly they represent a sort of controlled aspiration at the

end of a magniloquent poem; and now, quietened by religious certainties, lacking the long breath of youth, he ends with that still. The Love of the early poetry now speaks its Name; there is less threatening, less exaltation, but these are among the qualities that would show up in a voice print and establish the identity of the boy and the man chatting quietly in Manhattan or Kirchstetten.

Looking on that portrait and on this, we see what lies between them: a life. Living it, the Poet decided that poetry was a game, a shadow. This has, somewhat absurdly, been held against him; he suffers as much as Dryden from irrelevant censures. It is the mark of a bore, or, to use an Auden word, a juggins, to suppose that something is supremely important because you can do it well. Gardeners, scholars, atheletes often bear this mark. But, as the Poet's friend Marianne Moore decisively remarked, there are things that are important beyond all this fiddle. St Thomas Aquinas and Pascal were aware that there were things more important than their things, and Wittgenstein did not think that what cannot be said is less important than what can. All these people took their business very seriously. Games are not trivial in Wittgenstein, and Auden is not trivializing poetry when he calls it a game. Nor is he less serious because the manic threats of *The Orators* became the controlled dismissive gestures of Antonio in *The Sea and the Mirror*, the decayed city of *The Dog Beneath the Skin* merged into a benign survey of modern Manhattan. His visions of the Unjust City were made actual in the forties; we do not need those fantasies now. They belonged to their time, and it is not blindness or weakness that abandons them in favour of a wary calm. Also there is no need, when you really know, to seem knowing. The Poet will not be betrayed into a vulgar sadness; and he coexists, in the same skin, with an average sensual man. What we hear in the voice is a life; in the face we may even see an analogue of that limestone landscape, cut by intelligible streams, containing features that in themselves suggest poems, as, within the outcrops of the poet's favourite rock, goddesses lie in wait for the chisel. That is, for many of us, a landscape we grew up with. And if some slip away to sterner slopes, productive plains, or experiences more oceanic, many others will remain, and will certainly praise limestone.

(1970)